Big History:
The Big Bang, Life on Earth,
and the Rise of Humanity

David Christian, D.Phil.

THE
GREAT
COURSES

PUBLISHED BY:

THE GREAT COURSES
Corporate Headquarters
4840 Westfields Boulevard, Suite 500
Chantilly, Virginia 20151-2299
Phone: 1-800-832-2412
Fax: 703-378-3819
www.thegreatcourses.com

David Christian, D.Phil.

Professor of History
San Diego State University

Professor David Christian is Professor of History at San Diego State University, where he teaches courses on big history, world environmental history, Russian history, and the history of Inner Eurasia. From 1975 to 2000, he taught Russian history, European history, and world history at Macquarie University in Sydney.

Professor Christian was born in New York and grew up in Nigeria and Britain. He completed his B.A. in History at Oxford University, his M.A. in Russian History at The University of Western Ontario, and his D.Phil. in 19th-Century Russian History at Oxford University. As a graduate student, he spent a year in Leningrad (now St. Petersburg) during the Brezhnev era.

In the late 1980s, Professor Christian developed an interest in understanding the past on very large scales. With the help of colleagues in astronomy, geology, biology, anthropology, and prehistory, he began an experimental history course that started with the origins of the Universe and ended in the present day. Within two years, after his students persuaded him that it was a shame not to deal with the future after studying 13 billion years of history in 13 weeks, he introduced a final lecture on prospects for the future. In 1992, he wrote an article describing this approach as "big history." The label seems to have stuck, as similar courses have independently appeared elsewhere, and there are now several courses in big history at European, Russian, Australian, and North American universities.

In addition, Professor Christian has written on the social and material history of 19th-century Russian peasantry, in particular on aspects of diet and the role of alcohol. In 1990, he completed a study of the role of vodka in Russian social, political, and economic life. Professor Christian's recent publications include: *Imperial and Soviet Russia: Power, Privilege and the Challenge of*

Modernity (Macmillan/St. Martin's, 1997); *A History of Russia, Central Asia and Mongolia, Vol. 1: Inner Eurasia from Prehistory to the Mongol Empire* in *The Blackwell History of the World* (Blackwell, 1998); *Maps of Time: An Introduction to Big History* (University of California Press, 2004), which won the 2005 World History Association Book Prize and has been translated into Spanish and Chinese; and *This Fleeting World: A Short History of Humanity* (Berkshire Publishing, 2007).

Professor Christian is a member of the Australian Academy of the Humanities and the Royal Holland Society of Sciences and Humanities. He is Affiliates Chair for the World History Association and was one of the editors of the *Berkshire Encyclopedia of World History*. He also participated in the creation of the world history website World History for Us All (http://worldhistoryforusall.sdsu.edu/dev/default.htm). ■

Table of Contents

Table of Contents

Table of Contents

Big History: The Big Bang, Life on Earth, and the Rise of Humanity

Scope:

Big history surveys the past at all possible scales, from conventional history, to the much larger scales of biology and geology, to the universal scales of cosmology. It weaves a single story, stretching from the origins of the Universe to the present day and beyond, using accounts of the past developed within scholarly disciplines that are usually studied quite separately. Human history is seen as part of the history of our Earth and biosphere, and the Earth's history, in turn, is seen as part of the history of the Universe. In this way, the different disciplines that make up this large story can be used to illuminate each other. The unified account of the past assembled in this way can help us understand our own place within the Universe. Like traditional creation stories, big history provides a map of our place in space and time; but it does so using the insights and knowledge of modern science.

At first, the sheer scale of big history may seem unfamiliar—after all, historians usually focus on human societies, particularly those that had states and left documentary records. Until the mid-20th century, "history," in the sense of a chronologically structured account of the past, meant "human history" because we could only date those parts of the past for which we had written records. Since World War II, however, new dating techniques have allowed us to determine absolute dates for events before the appearance of written records or even of human beings. Radiometric dating techniques, based on the regular breakdown of radioactive materials, were at the heart of this chronometric revolution. These new chronometric techniques have transformed our ideas of the past, enabling us for the first time to construct a well-structured, scientifically rigorous history extending back to the origins of the Universe!

Telling this story is the daunting challenge taken up by big history; however, we have so much knowledge today that no single individual can be an expert on it all. Thus, you will not find in this course detailed analyses of the functioning of DNA, the causes of the French Revolution, the myths of ancient Greece, or the artistic innovations of the Renaissance—plenty of other courses offer more detailed accounts of such topics. What you *will* find is an attempt to weave stories told within many different historical disciplines into a larger story so that, instead of focusing on the details of each period or discipline, we can see the larger patterns that link all parts of the past. I am a historian, so this course inevitably reflects the expertise and biases of a historian. The same tale can also be told, with varying emphases, by astronomers and geologists. But at the heart of any such account is a core story, one that enables us to see the underlying unity of modern knowledge.

The first modern courses in big history appeared in the 1970s and 1980s. I began teaching big history in 1989; in 1991, I published an article in which (somewhat whimsically) I coined the term "big history." Though far from ideal, the name seems to have stuck, which is why we use it here in this course.

The unifying theme adopted in this course is the idea of increasing complexity. Though most of the Universe still consists of simple empty space, during almost 14 billion years new forms of complexity have appeared in pockets, including stars, all the chemical elements, planets, living organisms, and human societies. Each of these new forms of complexity has its own distinctive "emergent" properties, which is why each of them tends to be studied within a different scholarly discipline.

The introductory lectures describe the origins and aims of big history, the vast scale of the modern creation story, the central idea of complexity, and the large body of scientific evidence on which this account of big history is based. Eight major thresholds of increasing complexity provide the basic framework for this course.

The first threshold we cross is the creation of the Universe itself about 13.7 billion years ago during the big bang. This group of lectures summarizes some of the main insights of modern cosmology. We move from cosmology to astronomy in the second threshold with the creation of stars, which were the first really complex objects to appear in our Universe as well as the source of energy and raw materials for later forms of complexity. The third threshold is the creation of the chemical elements, which laid the foundations for the new forms of complexity studied within the discipline of chemistry. In the fourth threshold, where we cross from chemistry to geology, we zoom in on our own tiny corner of the Universe: the solar system and the creation of the planets, including Earth.

Earth provided an ideal environment for the fifth threshold, which takes us from geology to biology and describes the appearance of life; we survey the history of life on Earth and the evolution of our own species. The sixth threshold in this course is the appearance of human beings between 200,000 and 300,000 years ago, leading us from biology to history and marking the beginning of the first of three major eras of human history. The seventh threshold is the appearance of agriculture about 10,000 to 11,000 years ago, which supported larger and denser populations and made possible the creation of more complex human societies. Finally, the eighth threshold concerns the modern world within the last few centuries; during this period, the pace of innovation increased, creating human societies vastly more complex and integrated than those of the Agrarian era.

The final lectures of the course will peer into the future, and the course will end with a discussion of the place of human beings within the Universe.

I hope you will find the sheer scale of the course exhilarating, and I hope you will be persuaded—as I am—that each of the different time scales surveyed in this course has something important to teach us about our distinctive place within the Universe. ∎

The Origins of Agriculture
Lecture 25

Normally, tributary rulers, tribute-taking rulers, the kings and emperors of this world, were more interested in capturing wealth than in producing it. A successful war could generate wealth much more quickly and much more effectively than investment in infrastructure.

The previous lecture defined agriculture and explained why its impact was so revolutionary. This lecture discusses the evidence used to trace the origins of agriculture and asks why agriculture appeared. Why did humans in so many different parts of the world suddenly start getting the food and energy they needed in entirely new ways? Agriculture appeared at least 6,000 years before there were written records, so we must study it through archaeology. Rather than discussing the evidence abstractly, it may help to focus on a particular cluster of sites associated with the "Natufian" peoples, who lived in the Fertile Crescent (in modern Jordan and Israel) from about 14,000 to about 12,000 years ago. (The Fertile Crescent is a loop of highlands running from the Nile along the eastern shore of the Mediterranean, then west and south along the border between modern Iraq and Iran.)

Natufian sites are strikingly different from those of most foragers. Their dwellings were more substantial, often built into the ground for warmth, with well-built drystone walls. Natufians hunted gazelle, but growth bands on gazelle teeth show that they did so year-round from the same place. That and the presence of rodent bones suggest they lived in their houses year-round. Other surprises include the presence of grindstones for grains such as emmer, a type of wheat, and sickles made by setting flint blades into bone handles. Microscopic study of the blades shows they were used to harvest grains. In short, these look like agricultural villages.

However, by studying grain pollen, archaeologists can distinguish between wild and domesticated species, and it turns out that the Natufians were harvesting wild grains. They were not farmers, but sedentary or semi-sedentary foragers. Below, we will see how study of the Natufians has helped solve some of the puzzles that surround the "agricultural revolution." In Lecture Twenty-Four, we saw that agriculture appeared within a few thousand years in many different parts of the world. How can we explain this odd near-simultaneity? Let's begin by clearing away some popular misconceptions. The first is that extraterrestrials did it. In *2001*, Stanley Kubrick hinted that aliens gave humans periodical technological nudges. This idea might explain the timing (lots of monoliths?), but historians will rightly reject it until hard evidence of aliens turns up!

More influential has been the idea that agriculture appeared as a brilliant one-off invention, like the steam engine, whose benefits were so obvious that it spread rapidly from a single point of origin. This is what archaeologists call a "diffusionist" view. In the 19th century, such views were popular, at least in part because they fitted an imperialist view of civilization as something brought from advanced to less-advanced societies. Diffusionism in some form was the orthodox explanation for the origins of agriculture until recently. It is now rejected for several reasons.

- Agriculture was not one invention but a cluster of linked innovations requiring entirely new lifeways.

- Agriculture did not necessarily improve living standards, which is why many foragers who knew about farming rejected it. Archaeological evidence suggests they may have been right, for many early farmers suffered from poor health and nutrition. This idea encourages us to look for "push" rather than "pull" explanations, for factors that forced people to take up agriculture whether they wanted to or not.

- Finally, agriculture was invented not once, but many times. Diffusionist arguments cannot explain this odd timing, though they can help explain how agriculture then spread from a number of distinct centers.

Modern explanations include several interlocking factors. First, foragers already knew how to increase the productivity of favored species. Firestick farming was just one of many such techniques. The knowledge was there, so the problem is to explain why foragers in different parts of the world suddenly started using such techniques more intensively. Second, the geographical distribution of easily domesticated species may help explain the geography of early farming. As Jared Diamond has pointed out, the Fertile Crescent, where the Natufians lived, had many species like wheat, which can be domesticated with only minor changes, while other regions had species less amenable to domestication.

Third, as foragers migrated around the world, population pressure may have built up as less land was available for new migrations. Larger populations might have forced humans to use the knowledge they already had to extract more energy from a given area, to "intensify" production by introducing at least some agricultural techniques. But this argument is tricky because modern foragers often limit population growth (for example, by prolonging breast-feeding, which limits fertility, or by more violent means such as killing twins or allowing the old to die). So overpopulation should not have been a problem. Fourth, the Natufians may help us solve this last riddle, for their population began to grow fast once they settled down. This was probably because sedentary communities, which do not have to carry the old or the very young, have less need to limit population size. But why should foragers have settled down?

But for foragers sedentism can be a trap, because it may encourage population growth, making it necessary within just a few generations to start intensifying food production.

The fifth factor, climatic change, may help solve this puzzle. The last ice age reached its coldest stage about 20,000 years ago, and then climates began to get warmer. By 11,500 years ago, after a 1,500-year cold spell, they had reached temperatures similar to those of today. During the "interglacial" of the last 10,000 to 11,000 years, climates were generally warmer, wetter, and more stable than those of the ice ages. How might these changes have encouraged early forms of agriculture? Peter Richerson and Robert Boyd have argued that agriculture was simply impossible during the last ice age because climates were too unstable. If they are right, it is the stability of interglacial climates that explains the appearance of sustainable agriculture. Warmer and wetter climates may also explain why some foragers settled down, for improved climates would have stimulated plant growth, creating regions of great abundance, or "Gardens of Eden." Modern anthropological studies suggest that in such environments, foragers often become more sedentary. (Sedentary foragers are often described as "affluent foragers," because they are found in regions of exceptional abundance, such as the northwestern coast of North America.) But for foragers sedentism can be a trap, because it may encourage population growth, making it necessary within just a few generations to start intensifying food production. As populations grew, sedentary foragers would soon find it necessary to tend their crops more carefully, to water them and weed around them—in short, they would have to become farmers! In this roundabout way, pressure may have played as powerful a role in the appearance of agriculture as it did in the appearance of the first stars!

Arguments like these work well in the Fertile Crescent. Natufians almost certainly had a good understanding of natural plants and how they reproduced. They lived in a region with many promising potential domesticates such as wheat. We know from archaeological evidence that, as they became sedentary, populations grew rapidly. We know that warming climates may have encouraged them to become more sedentary by increasing the abundance of domesticable grains such as emmer. Finally, we know that farming villages appeared quite rapidly after a period of cooler climates (the "Younger Dryas," c. 13,000–11,500 BP) forced sedentary foragers to start intensifying. When climates warmed again, farming villages appeared rapidly. Elsewhere, the mix of elements was different. In Mesoamerica, nomadic foragers probably cultivated crops such as early forms of maize before they became fully sedentary. There are also tantalizing hints that root crops were farmed early in coastal regions in the tropics, but we know little of these regions because most coastal sites were flooded as sea levels rose. So, though we lack a complete explanation of agricultural origins, we know many of the factors involved, even if they may have interacted in slightly different ways in different regions. ∎

Essential Reading

Christian, *Maps of Time*, chap. 8.

Fagan, *People of the Earth,* chap. 8.

Ristvet, *In the Beginning*, chap. 2.

Supplementary Reading

Bellwood, *First Farmers.*

Diamond, *Guns, Germs, and Steel.*

Mithen, *After the Ice.*

Questions to Consider

1. How can we explain the fact that agriculture appeared within a very short time in parts of the world that had no contact with each other?

2. What can study of the Natufians tell us about the origins of agriculture?

The Origins of Agriculture
Lecture 25—Transcript

In the previous lecture, I took time out to try and define agriculture, and we saw that defining it is quite a subtle problem. So, it was worth taking a fair bit of time to explain what precisely the nature of that threshold was. Because only once we've defined it clearly and we understand the nature of the threshold can we really explain it and then understand its impact.

We also talked in general terms about why agriculture had such a revolutionary impact. We saw that the appearance of agriculture counts as one of our great thresholds of complexity, and it'll generate new emergent properties that are going to transform human history, absolutely transform it. We also saw that, like other thresholds, there are some intriguing similarities between this threshold and other thresholds, including the creation of the first stars.

Now what I want to do in this lecture is begin—or try to explain—to offer an explanation of agriculture. We begin by discussing the evidence that we can use to trace the origins of agriculture. And then I'm going to try and explain or offer an explanation for this revolutionary turning point. Why did humans in so many different parts of the world, some of them completely disconnected from each other, suddenly start getting their food and energy in entirely new ways, in a series of different parts of the world? When I say sudden, I mean sudden in comparison to the 200,000 years or so of the Paleolithic era. We'll see that agriculture pops up quite independently in several quite distinct regions.

Evidence. We have to ask the question again: How can we know about events that occurred many thousands of years ago, long before the appearance of writing? Agriculture appeared at least 6,000 years before there were written records of any kind anywhere in the world. So, this is a topic, once more, that we must study through archaeology. How? Rather than discussing the evidence abstractly, we can get a feeling for the sort of evidence that archaeologists used in handling this issue by looking at the so-called "Natufian" people and a closely related group, the Kebaran people.

And here I'm making a lot of use of the work of Steven Mithen, whose book *After the Ice* offers a sort of imaginary tour of life since the last 20,000 years by a fictional character that he calls Lubbock, after the 19th-century British archaeologist of the same name. So what happens is we follow Lubbock, who's a sort of time traveler, we follow him right around the world to a number of archaeological sites. And what he does is he visits them in real time. So we actually see, through Lubbock's eyes, what people were doing. It's a lovely way for a non-archaeologist to get a feeling for the relationship between what archaeologists actually find, which often doesn't look terribly exciting to a non-archaeologist, and the real lives that the archaeologists can construct from that evidence. So, Lubbock watches these people as they go about their daily lives. And it's a very vivid and powerful way of getting a sense of how archaeologists reconstruct the past.

The Natufian people, back to the Natufians: The Natufian people lived in the Fertile Crescent, in modern Jordan and Israel, from approximately— and all dates for this period I always have to say approximately—from approximately 14,000 to about 12,000 years ago. Let me just try and describe what I mean by the Fertile Crescent. It runs north from the Nile along the eastern edge of the Mediterranean shore through Israel, Palestine, and Lebanon to southern Turkey, and then curves east and curves down along the border between modern Iraq and Iran, and down to the Persian Gulf.

Natufian sites illustrate some of the techniques and the challenges of the sort of research archaeologists do when they're trying to study early agriculture. Now, here are some of the distinctive features of Natufian sites. First, Natufian sites are strikingly different from those of most of the sort of foraging populations you find if you're studying the Paleolithic world. Their dwellings in general were more substantial. They were often built into the ground for warmth, and they were built with well-built drystone walls. So, these are a sort of dwellings that are much more substantial than the sort of dwellings that were built by foragers throughout most of the Paleolithic era.

Secondly, they seem to have been sedentary. By "sedentary," I mean they seem to have stayed in one place most of the year, which is something that farmers conventionally do. Now, they may have left for a few weeks, but they're in one place for most of the year. How do we know this? Well,

Natufians hunted gazelle. So, you find lots of gazelle bones at these sites. And this is an illustration of some of the things that archaeologists can do with bones. You can tell from the growth bands on the gazelle teeth what age they were and what time of year they were hunted. And what this evidence shows is that they were hunting gazelle all year round from the same place. So, that's one of the pieces of evidence that they were pretty sedentary. And the other, of course, is the piece that we've already seen, that they built these very solid, durable houses. Not the sort of things you build and then leave for 11 months.

A third feature of the Natufians is that they clearly harvested grains. This is a surprise for a foraging population. You find in Natufian sites grindstones, and you can detect what they've been used on. And it turns out what they were used on was emmer, which is a form of wheat. That's spelled "e-double m-e-r." And you also find in Natufian sites, sickles. They're made by setting flint blades into bone handles, often made from the jawbones of gazelles or other hunted animals. Now, archaeologists can study the edges of these sickle blades through microscopes, and what it shows is that they have been used clearly to harvest grains. You can find the remnants of this; you can find clear evidence of this.

Now, all the evidence we've seen so far looks like an agricultural village. They're sedentary, they have solid houses, and they're harvesting grains. But some of the evidence in these villages doesn't fit in with this picture at all. And the first thing is that if you analyze the grains that they were harvesting, it turns out they were not from domesticated, but from wild, species. Now, how can archaeologists tell this? By studying grain pollen, archaeologists can distinguish, for the most part, between wild and domesticated species. This applies to plants, and also they can do the same thing, by and large, by studying animal bones. So, very often archaeologists can distinguish between wild and domesticated species. The fact that the grains were wild showed that they were not farmers—instead, they were sedentary or semi-sedentary foragers. Later we'll see how study of the Natufians has helped us to solve some of the puzzles that surround the "agricultural revolution." But we have already seen examples of sedentary or semi-sedentary foragers.

Okay, now let's try to explain the agricultural revolution. In the previous lecture, we saw that agriculture appeared within just a few thousand years in many different parts of the world. So, this is actually very odd. Why, after living apparently quite contentedly as foragers for perhaps 200,000 years, should humans suddenly start using an entirely new set of technologies? And why, when they did so, did human communities in quite separate parts of the world start doing so nearly simultaneously?

The simultaneity of this is very strange indeed. And any decent explanation of the agricultural revolution must attempt to explain it. Here's a quotation from two recent researchers on the subject of early agriculture, Price and Gebauer, in a book called *Last Hunters, First Farmers*. They write this:

> for some reason, beginning around 10,000 years ago hunters became farmers in a number of different places on the planet. The intentional cultivation of domesticated plants was an almost simultaneous yet completely independent development in Southwest Asia [by which they mean Mesopotamia, the Fertile Crescent], China and Southeast Asia, Mesoamerica, South America, and the eastern United States, transpiring within a period of approximately 5,000 years.

That's the problem we have to explain, to explain agriculture. Why this odd simultaneity?

Now, let's immediately rule out two explanations that might be tempting. Let's begin with extraterrestrials. This is one that I found I'm always gong to have to deal with when teaching this subject. The near-simultaneity of the appearance of agriculture certainly tempts many of my students to remember Stanley Kubrick's suggestion in *2001* that extraterrestrials nudged humans towards the technology of hunting. So, let's just clear this one out of the way straightaway. You remember *2001*, you remember the monoliths, that they nudge humans towards civilization of some kind by planting ideas in the minds of hominines of various kinds. Well, we're not going to even look at an idea like this, of course, until we can find some concrete evidence—so let's just get that one out of the way. We have no concrete evidence for this. We have to find a subtler way of explaining this.

Now, here's a much more serious and much more influential idea about the origins of agriculture. It probably dominated explanations of this phenomenon in the 19th century and for much of the 20th century. And it goes like this. The idea is that agriculture appeared as a brilliant one-off invention—a bit like, say, the steam engine or the Internet. And it was such a brilliant invention that once it appeared, people naturally took it up. So, what it did was it diffused from the center where it first appeared around the world. This we can describe as a "diffusionist" explanation of agriculture.

Such explanations are tempting because inventions do, indeed, spread rapidly around the world. There are many phenomena that do diffuse rapidly. And these explanations were particularly fashionable in the late 19th century because they carried some nice implications for European scholars. In an age of imperialism, they carried the implication that all the good things diffused from high civilizations to simpler civilizations. And that was very much the thinking behind 19th-century diffusionists. And the idea was that agriculture first appeared probably in somewhere like Egypt, maybe Mesopotamia, and then spread to lower civilizations.

Now, as we'll see, there are very good empirical reasons for rejecting diffusionist arguments for the initial origins of agriculture. Diffusionist arguments will be very important once we try to explain how agriculture spread from these initial points where it first appeared. But at the moment, they cannot explain why it first appeared, and above all, they cannot explain this sort of near-simultaneity that we've looked at.

So, diffusionism is now rejected broadly as a general explanation for the initial appearance of agriculture. There are several reasons for this. One is that agriculture was not a single invention like the steam engine. It's actually a cluster of linked innovations requiring entirely new lifeways. It was not the sort of thing you could have taken a patent on. Agriculture implied the domestication of crops and animals, techniques for weeding, and elementary forms of irrigation. It implied discovering the best ways of planting, protecting, and harvesting particular crops, as well as storing them. It also required new social rules, such as rules about who owned what. So, the puzzle is to explain a whole cascade of changes, not just a single intervention.

Besides, we'll see that agriculture did not necessarily improve living standards. It was not necessarily so attractive that every foraging community that learned about it was bound to take up agriculture. Modern studies of modern foraging societies have shown that many deliberately reject farming. They see farmers, they know how farmers live, and they don't want to live that way. So, we shouldn't assume without careful thought that agriculture necessarily represents an improvement in the way people lived.

Archaeological evidence suggests that those foragers who rejected the agricultural lifeway, they've had some good reasons for doing so, for many early farmers seem to have suffered from poor health and nutrition. We can tell this from archaeological evidence, such as an increase in the number of stress lines in the bones of early farmers and a decline in average height. Now, this fact, this indirect evidence that living standards may have deteriorated in some early Agrarian communities, affects how we explain agriculture. If agriculture was not such an attractive lifeway, perhaps we need to focus more on the "push" than the "pull." In other words, we need to look for factors that pushed people into agriculture rather than factors that lured them into it, as in the 19th-century diffusionist model.

And the third reason for rejecting that 19th-century model is that, as we've seen, agriculture wasn't invented once, but many times. There's not just one point from which it spreads to the rest of the world. Diffusionism can't explain this near-simultaneity we've looked at, though it will explain the later spread of agriculture.

Now, we've seen some of the difficulties of explaining agriculture. It really is quite a tricky threshold to explain. Modern explanations include several interlocking factors. And I have to admit straightaway there is as yet no completely uniform consensus on exactly what is the best way of explaining how agriculture first appeared. There's still plenty of room for debate on the issue. However, most explanations refer to the same basic factors even if they may link them in slightly different ways.

Here I'll propose a possible explanation in five main steps, five main steps just to try and clarify the logic of the argument. Unlike some models you may come across, you should note that this is a push model. It assumes that, by and large, humans were eventually pushed into agriculture rather than lured into it. Something happened that forced them to take up agricultural lifeways. It's not a pull model like the diffusionist argument we've just been talking about.

Okay, here are our five main steps in trying to explain the initial appearance of agriculture. The first of them is preexisting knowledge, by which I mean that modern studies of foraging communities have shown over and over again that they have an immense amount of knowledge about the organisms surrounding them—the plants and animals, particularly those that they use for food. They have an immense amount of knowledge. And very often that knowledge includes knowledge about how to increase the production of this particular plant or this particular animal. We've seen that firestick farming, for example, is an example of ways that foragers could increase the productivity of a particular area. The problem, therefore, is not knowledge. It's not that foragers didn't know many of the things you need to know in order to farm. They had the knowledge. So, it looks as if they simply didn't *need* to "intensify" production. So, the problem is to explain why foragers suddenly start applying this knowledge much more vigorously. The knowledge was not new; the puzzle is why they begin to apply it on a large scale. So, that's the first step: All the knowledge you need for agriculture already existed.

Now, the second step. The second step is the distribution of potential domesticates. Some animals and plants can be domesticated quite easily. Wheat is an example. Others can't be domesticated so easily. Kangaroos are an example of that. So, the exact way that animals and plants were distributed may help us explain the geographical distribution of early agriculture. In some regions there were organisms that could be turned into domesticates very, very easily indeed. In other areas, it was tougher.

Jared Diamond has pointed out in his bestseller *Guns, Germs, and Steel* that the Fertile Crescent, where the Natufians lived, had a remarkable number of species that can be domesticated with only fairly minor changes. So, this is the second point. Other regions had fewer easily domesticated species. The Americas, for example, had far fewer promising animal domesticates. Now, you may remember why. The reason may be that early humans in the Americas actually hunted them to extinction. There are very few large mammals in the Americas after the megafaunal extinctions at the end of the Paleolithic era. So, perhaps the availability or non-availability of easily domesticatable species in an area may help us explain why it appeared in some regions rather than others. It's sheerly a matter of luck, the sort of organisms around you. That's the second factor.

So, we've looked at preexisting knowledge and now the geography of domesticates. A third factor: population pressure. Now, here's where the analogies with star formation are most tempting. Population pressure is similar to the buildup of pressure that created the first stars in the earlier solar nebulae. But we'll see that growing population pressure—we can imagine how it could have driven humans into agriculture. There's more population, and you suddenly start worrying about starvation, so you start thinking, "Well, we must find ways of producing more food from a given area." So, it's a promising-looking argument, but it probably cannot explain the emergence of agriculture on its own.

It's been proposed in the work of a prehistorian, Mark Cohen, who has done very important work on the life of early farmers and on the transition to agriculture. He's shown that as foragers migrated around the world, population may have built up in a very loose sense, in the sense that humans by 13,000 years ago had entered all the large areas of the Earth that were previously unoccupied by humans. So, by about 10,000 years ago there were no new continents for humans to enter. And this may put an end to extensification, the process that I described before: the fact that to support growing populations you can simply migrate to a new area. Now, that possibility is being closed off. The Paleolithic front here, if you like, has been closed.

Now, that's a tempting argument, but there's a problem with it. And the main problem is this: Studies of modern foragers show that foragers are often very conscious of population pressure. In other words, they have a very good idea of how many people their land will support. That means that very often they systematically limit population growth. This may mean several things. It may mean prolonged breastfeeding, which limits fertility. But it may mean more violent methods, such as killing the weaker of two twins, which seems to have been a fairly common practice, or allowing the old to die: infanticide and senilicide. Now, if that's true, it means that overpopulation shouldn't have been a problem. Hunter-gatherers or foragers could adjust simply by limiting population growth.

The argument's tricky in another sense. By modern standards, the world was grossly underpopulated 10,000 years ago. But, of course, it could have still been overpopulated given the fact that foragers needed such huge areas to survive. So, that's the third argument: overpopulation. It's tempting, but before we can we use it, there are problems. So, let's see if we can overcome them.

Here's the fourth factor, and this may be a way of explaining how population growth worked: sedentism. Sedentism as a cause of population growth. Here the Natufians may help us solve the riddle. They settled down, we saw. They were foragers, but they settled down. And once they settled down their populations began to grow fast. We can see this in the rapid spread of Natufian villages in the Fertile Crescent. Why would their populations grow? Well, this was probably because once you're settled down and you have this abundant resource, this wheat and these gazelles around you, and you don't need to carry the old or the very young, there's less need to limit population size. So, once you're sedentary, perhaps population is going to start growing more rapidly. Okay, so that's the fourth factor. Sedentism may lead to rapid population growth, which may force them to start looking for new ways of getting food. But why would they settle down?

Now, that takes us to the fifth part of this argument, the fifth step. And here we introduce the one factor that we know affected the entire world and is, therefore, the best possible explanation for the simultaneity of this—and that's climate change. The last ice age reached its coldest stage about 20,000 years ago. And after that, climates began to get warmer, particularly after about 14,000 years ago. By 11,500 years ago, after a brief cold snap, they had reached temperatures similar to those of today. And during the "interglacial" of the last 10,000 to 11,000 years, climates have generally been warmer, wetter, and more stable than those of the ice ages.

Now, this fact affected the whole world, but how could this have trigged more sedentism and more population growth? Well, here's a possible argument.

One way of dealing with this is associated with the work of two Californian scholars, Peter Richardson and Robert Boyd. Now, what they argued is actually the simplest argument of all: It is that during the ice age, climate change was so erratic that sustained agriculture was simply impossible—you couldn't do it during the ice age. So their argument is: Well, once you get stable, warmer climates, foragers knew how to do agriculture—it was simply impossible before—so it's no surprise they start doing it. So, their argument implies that perhaps climate change is virtually the single key factor in the origins of agriculture. As soon as agriculture became possible, humans started doing it.

Now, any argument, as we've seen, for which climate change is crucial is attractive, because climate change is a global phenomenon. But this argument on its own isn't quite going to work, particularly if we're not persuaded that foragers are going to like the idea of farming. So, here's another approach: "Gardens of Eden" and the "trap of sedentism." Warmer, wetter climates undoubtedly led to regions where certainly plant growth but also animal populations were more abundant than they had been during the ice ages. So, this may have meant there appeared sort of pockets that archaeologists describe as "Gardens of Eden," areas of great abundance.

Now, modern studies of foragers suggest that when they find such regions, foragers will often become more sedentary. And foragers that become sedentary are often described as "affluent foragers." They're found in environments of exceptional ecological abundance. The classic example here is the northwest coast of the U.S., where many foragers settled down relying on the abundance of resources such as salmon.

So, this may explain why groups like the Natufians began to settle down, but this can be a trap. And I'll call this the "trap of sedentism." Once you're sedentary, populations start growing. And this is going to mean that within just a few generations, you're going to find that what seemed an environment of abundance is now an environment of scarcity. You have to increase food production in order to feed everyone. So, sedentary foraging communities, who've now lost probably many of their traditions as foragers, find they're going to have to increase production. There's probably not spare land around them. They're going to have to tend their crops more carefully, water them, and weed around them—in short, they're going to have to become farmers.

Now, in this rather roundabout way, pressure, population pressure, may have played as powerful a role in the appearance of agriculture as it did in the appearance of the first stars. Now, arguments like these work well in the Fertile Crescent. Natufians almost certainly had a good understanding of natural plants. They lived in a region with many promising domesticates. We know that as they became sedentary, populations grew rapidly. We know that warming climates may have encouraged them to become more sedentary. And finally, we know that farming villages appeared quite rapidly after a period of cooler climates, which put a lot of stress on local populations from about 11,000 years ago.

So, the argument works well in Mesopotamia, in the Fertile Crescent. Elsewhere, the mix of elements may be slightly different. But by and large, you should expect to find most of these factors wherever we find early agriculture. In Mesoamerica, nomadic foragers may have cultivated crops of maize before they became fully sedentary, but with these slight differences the story may hold up in most parts of the world.

Thank you.

The First Agrarian Societies
Lecture 26

The encounter between newly arrived humans and indigenous species that had no experience of humans and no understanding of how dangerous they could be may help explain the massive extent of the die-off of large mammals in Sahul in the millennia after the arrival of humans.

This lecture surveys the 5,000 years of the "early Agrarian" era, a period that is often neglected by historians because it left no written records and lacks the glamour of the great civilizations. We will see that in reality many important changes occurred during this era. We will also discuss how most people lived during the early Agrarian era. We define the "early Agrarian" era as the period beginning with the appearance of agriculture and ending with the appearance of cities and states. Globally, it lasted for 5,000 to 6,000 years, but locally, its duration varies. For example, it never began in Australia, while in neighboring Papua New Guinea, it began early and has lasted to the present day. Historians often neglect this era, but this is a mistake. It embraced at least half of the last 10,000 years and laid the foundations for the eventual appearance of Agrarian civilizations. During this era, the largest and most powerful communities were villages or small towns.

Many important changes occurred in the early Agrarian era. The most important large-scale change was the spread of agriculture in the Afro-Eurasian and American world zones. For the most part, agriculture seems to have spread by diffusion from a few initial centers.

- About 10,000 years ago, agriculture was confined to the Fertile Crescent and maybe Papua New Guinea.

- About 8,000 years ago, it could be found in China, in Southeast Asia, and along the Nile.

- About 5,000 years ago, it could be found in West Africa, Mesoamerica, the Andes, Central Asia, and parts of Europe. By then, most humans lived as small peasant farmers, and that way of life would dominate the history of the next 5,000 years.

- Within just 5,000 years, agriculture had become the dominant technology of most human societies on Earth. This was a revolutionary change in human history.

Agriculture did not necessarily spread because it was attractive to foragers. It spread, rather, because agricultural communities could generate more resources than foraging communities and could therefore support larger populations. Even the simplest farming communities could support 20–30 times as many people per square kilometer as most foraging communities. As agriculture spread, world populations rose from about 6 million to 50 million between 10,000 and 5,000 years ago. The population of Southwest Asia alone may have increased from 100,000 to 5 million between 10,000 and 6,000 years ago (Bellwood, *First Farmers*, p. 15). This meant that, though Agrarian and foraging societies often traded and lived together peacefully, when there were conflicts, Agrarian societies had more people and more resources than their foraging neighbors. This is why the Agrarian frontier slowly advanced at the expense of foragers, as farmers began to cultivate more and more regions with easily worked soils and adequate rainfall and sunlight.

Agriculture introduced a new technological dynamism into human history because it stimulated collective learning. How? With larger populations, there were more people to exchange ideas within and between communities. Population growth forced those at the margins of society to experiment with new techniques and crops. Population growth generated conflicts over land and resources, and warfare began to drive technological and social change in new ways.

For the most part, technological change took the form of micro-innovations, each adapted to particular environments. Two fundamental Agrarian techniques in this era were horticulture and swidden agriculture, each of which evolved with many local variations. "Horticulture" means farming based purely on human labor power using implements such as hoes or digging sticks, mortars, and sickles. Many horticultural communities exist even today in regions such as the Amazon basin or Papua New Guinea. In forest regions, "swidden" (or "slash-and-burn") farmers used stone axes and fire to clear trees before planting crops in the rich, ashy soil. As fertility declined within a few years, the process had to be repeated in a slow, Agrarian version of nomadism. So swidden farming initiated global deforestation.

Most early Agrarian communities can be thought of as villages, but some were large enough to be thought of as small towns. Villages and small towns were the most important and complex types of communities throughout the early Agrarian era. Jericho may be the oldest known Agrarian settlement. Lying about 20 kilometers east of Jerusalem, it has been excavated since the mid-19th century by archaeologists looking for its famous walls. Jericho's first occupants were Natufians. But by 11,000 years ago, about 1,000 people lived in 70 mud-brick dwellings, supporting themselves by farming. Few permanent communities this large had ever existed before.

> **Jericho may be the oldest known Agrarian settlement. Lying about 20 kilometers east of Jerusalem, it has been excavated since the mid-19th century by archaeologists looking for its famous walls.**

Even more densely settled was Catal Huyuk in Anatolia, which flourished 9,000 years ago. Here, mud-brick houses were built with adjoining walls, a bit like cells in a beehive, so houses were entered from the roof. Each house contained a hearth, a storage area, and exotic bull-headed statues. The inhabitants exported the tough volcanic glass known as obsidian, which was used to make fine blades. Most early Agrarian villages were smaller. Modern anthropological studies of regions such as the Papua New Guinea highlands or the Amazon basin today may give an impression of how most people lived in the early Agrarian era.

How well did the first farmers live? Did agriculture necessarily mean "progress"? We saw in Lecture Twenty-Two that, by some criteria, Paleolithic foragers lived quite well. The evidence on early farmers is mixed. The first generation or two probably lived well, enjoying improved food supplies. However, within a few generations, population growth created problems that nomadic foragers had never faced. Sedentary villages attracted vermin and rubbish, and diseases spread more easily with a larger pool of potential victims to infect, particularly after the introduction of domesticated animals, which passed many of their parasites on to humans. Studies of human bones from early Agrarian communities hint at new forms of stress, caused by the intense labor of harvest times, or by periodic crop failures, which became more common because farmers generally relied on a more limited range of foodstuffs than foragers. Periodic shortages may explain why skeletons seem to get shorter in early Agrarian villages. On the other hand, early Agrarian communities were probably fairly egalitarian. Relative equality is apparent even in large sites such as Catal Huyuk, where buildings are similar in size, though differences in burials show there were some, possibly hereditary, differences in wealth.

The early Agrarian era transformed a world of foragers into a world of peasant farmers. Within these denser communities new forms of complexity would begin to emerge. Yet by some criteria, living standards may have declined. Complexity does not necessarily mean progress! ■

Essential Reading

Brown, *Big History,* chaps. 4–5.

Christian, *Maps of Time*, chap. 8.

Fagan, *People of the Earth*, chaps. 9–13.

Supplementary Reading

Bellwood, *First Farmers.*

Coatsworth, "Welfare."

Mithen, *After the Ice.*

1. What were the most revolutionary developments during the "early Agrarian" era of human history?

2. Why have historians often neglected the "early Agrarian" era of human history?

The First Agrarian Societies
Lecture 26—Transcript

Let's begin with periodization, how we're going to slice up human history. I've already introduced the fundamental periodization of human history we're going to use in this course. We've seen it includes three main eras. The first is the Paleolithic era, which we saw lasted at least 200,000 years and possibly as much as 300,000 years. The second is the Agrarian era. It lasted about 10,000 years. And the third is the Modern era, which will last just a few years. Of course, we haven't reached the end of it yet.

Now, I need to clarify an important subordinate periodization within the 10,000 years or so of the Agrarian era. I'm going to divide the Agrarian era into two main subperiods. The first period is called the "early Agrarian" era, and the second is called the "later Agrarian" era. Obvious titles and I hope very clear. In this lecture, I'm going to focus on the first of these subperiods, the early Agrarian era.

The early Agrarian era is that part of the Agrarian era before the appearance of states and Agrarian "civilizations." That's probably the simplest way of defining it. The remarkable thing about this era is that it seems to have largely vanished from many accounts of world history, even though it lasted for at least, as we'll see, 5,000 years. Now, that is as long as the time between the appearance of the first Agrarian civilizations and today. So, it's a very long and important period of time.

One of the advantages of the wide-angle lens that we use in big history is that although sometimes you may get the sense that we lose the details, the specifics, what it can do is often see some rather large phenomena that can be easily overlooked with a small-angle lens; and one of these is the early Agrarian era.

Frankly, how can you lose 5,000 years of human history? I think I know some of the answers. One reason may be that historians are sometimes too keen to move from the introduction of agriculture to the great agrarian civilizations that this new technology eventually made possible. Another reason may be that only with the appearance of agrarian civilizations about 5,000 years ago do we start getting writing, and with writing you get written evidence. And, of course, historians are trained to use written evidence. So, this may be why historians find it very tempting to just skim over the early Agrarian era, on the assumption, presumably, that not much happened. I'm going to try and demonstrate the opposite. So, we're going to stay a bit longer in the territory of archaeologists and anthropologists, and by doing so I hope we can rediscover this lost 5,000-year era of human history.

So, the last lecture discussed the origins of agriculture, and I tried to offer a possible explanation for the independent appearance of agriculture in several different parts of the world. Now what we're doing is looking at the world in the period after the initial appearance of agriculture, and we're asking: What were early Agrarian societies like?

Okay. Now, let's be very clear about definitions. I'm going to define the early Agrarian era as the period beginning with the appearance of agriculture and ending with the appearance of cities and states. So, let's try and get the chronology clear. Globally, if we think of this on a global scale, the early Agrarian era lasted for 5,000 to 6,000 years. That's from the very first appearance of agriculture anywhere in the world to the very first appearance of agrarian civilizations, of cities and states, somewhere in the world—but locally, regionally, its duration varies. And we need to be clear about this. For example, the early Agrarian era never began in Australia. Agriculture entered Australia only in the last two or three centuries with the arrival of immigrants from Europe, "boat people" as aborigine Australians refer to them today. But the early Agrarian era did begin in neighboring Papua New Guinea. It began early, and in fact, it lasted to the present day. So, whereas in Australia there was no early Agrarian era, in Papua New Guinea, just next door, the early Agrarian era lasted probably longer than anywhere else, except perhaps for the Amazon basin.

Now, we'll see that this sort of difficulty in trying to generalize about the world as a whole is going to become more and more evident during the Agrarian era. And the reason for this is, once again, it's the dynamism of agriculture. As agriculture appeared in different parts of the world, the pace of change accelerated, and you find change occurring in different ways and at different rates in different parts of the world. And that's going to force us now to be much more careful about making generalizations about the whole world, and we're going to have to make them about particular regions.

Okay. We've seen that historians often neglect this era. I'd like to argue in this lecture that this is a mistake. It's not just that the early Agrarian era embraces such a large period. It's also that it lays the foundations for the eventual appearance of agrarian civilizations. In fact, if you don't understand the early Agrarian era, it's really hard to understand what early agrarian civilizations came out of and how they appeared.

So, let's talk about some general features of this era. Probably the most general statement we can make is this: During this era, the largest and most powerful human communities were villages or small towns. Now, I stress this because we don't normally think of villages as power centers. So, we have to make a bit of an imaginative effort to remind ourselves that for some 5,000 years of human history, villages were the most exciting, the most dynamic, the densest human communities that existed.

Now, we'll see also that a lot of change occurred during the early Agrarian era, a lot of important things happened. It was not, any more than the Paleolithic, a blank spot in human history—a period in which nothing happened. So, let me try and describe some of the important things that happened during this era.

The most important large-scale change was undoubtedly the spread of agriculture in the Afro-Eurasian and American world zones, the two largest world zones. Now, note that in the previous lecture, I critiqued what I called "diffusionist accounts" of the initial appearance of agriculture. But diffusionist accounts for the *spread* of agriculture, we'll see, make lots and lots of sense. Once it had appeared in six or seven different parts of the world, it begins to diffuse from those regions. Here's a very, very rough chronology for this process of spreading from independent centers. Ten thousand years ago, agriculture was confined to the Fertile Crescent and maybe, as we've seen, Papua New Guinea. In Papua New Guinea, very early we saw evidence of a form of agriculture based on root crops. And, in fact, we saw there may also have been a lot of agriculture practiced along coastal regions, in the tropics that are now underwater, and based on root crops. Here there may be a whole world of societies waiting to be discovered by archaeology that at the moment we know very little about.

So, 10,000 years ago, certainly in the Fertile Crescent, almost certainly some form of agriculture in Papua New Guinea, in the Australasian world zone. Note these are two completely separate world zones—no connection between them.

By 8,000 years ago you can find evidence of agriculture in China, in Southeast Asia, and also along the Nile in [northeast] Africa, in modern Egypt and Sudan. That's 8,000 years ago.

Five thousand years ago it could be found in West Africa. And also now you've got the beginnings, early signs, of agriculture in the Americas—in a third world zone, the Americas. You find early signs of agriculture both in Mesoamerica—in southern Mexico and Central America—and also in the Andes, Peru, Chile, Ecuador, parts of Bolivia. And you find it in Central Asia and parts of Europe by 5,000 years ago. Now, 5,000 years ago, remember, is an important threshold. It's when agrarian civilizations first appeared. By then—that's 5,000 years after the first appearance of agriculture—we can say, we can be very sure about this, most human beings lived as small peasant farmers. And that way of life, the life of a peasant farmer, would dominate the history of the next 5,000 years.

So, just to be clear what an important change we're talking about here, in an era that's, as I've said, often neglected: In 5,000 years, in the 5,000 years of the early Agrarian era, what had been the technology of a tiny number of communities in just two parts of the world had become the dominant technology of most of humanity. So, that's a huge and important change. This change revolutionized the lifeways of most humans. Though the lifeways of the Paleolithic era, the foraging lifeways of the Paleolithic era with their small kinship communities, persisted in many areas—indeed, they would survive in some areas well into the 20th century—they ceased for the first time in human history to be the normal lifeways of our species. They became instead the lifeways of an increasingly small minority of humans who increasingly are squeezed out of the most fertile, the most abundant, regions of the Earth. So, it's this fact that justifies the claim that the early

Agrarian era marks a profound revolution in human history, despite its near invisibility. By its end, a majority of humans found themselves within what I've described as the emerging hot spots created by agriculture.

Now, why did agriculture spread so rapidly? We'll see here that agriculture did not necessarily spread because it was attractive. In fact, we've already looked at this argument before. On the contrary, for many foragers, settling down as farmers meant taking up a harder, more monotonous, less varied, less interesting, and more precarious life. So, why should they do it? Why did so many people take up farming? The best explanation is probably this. Agriculture spread because it could generate more resources than foraging and could therefore support larger populations. Those who already habituated to the agricultural lifeways simply reproduced more than foragers. They had far more resources to support growing populations. So farming communities grew and multiplied much faster than nonfarming communities, because once established they could support larger populations. And their larger populations meant that whenever it came to a conflict between farming and foraging communities, the farming communities had many advantages, both in resources and in sheer numbers. In other words, this suggests that most people who became agriculturalists were forced into it. But the spread of agriculture and the growth of its populations were really a matter of existing agricultural populations just growing much, much faster than the populations of foragers.

Why is this true? Well, even the simplest farming communities could support perhaps 20 to 30 times as many people per square kilometer as most foraging communities. Agriculture, we've seen, is an intensive technology. Unlike foraging, which is extensive, you can support a lot more people from the same area. So, as agriculture spread, it seems that world populations also rose.

Now, let me give you some figures, but let me remind you that they are, of course, very, very tentative—but these are the best guesses we have at the moment. They are that world populations about 10,000 years ago were perhaps 5 million or 6 million. By 5,000 years ago, world populations may have risen to 50 million. Now, this is a very striking increase, indeed. The population of Southwest Asia alone may have increased from 100,000 to 5 million between 10,000 and 6,000 years ago. Remember what this really means. It means for most of human history—for 200,000 or 300,000 years—

human numbers have been perhaps a few hundred thousand, perhaps a million, rising to 5 million just very recently. And then, in the blink of an eye, in just 5,000 years, they rise to perhaps 50 million.

Now, we need to remember, of course, as I've said, just how rough these figures are—but the orders of magnitude are probably right, and they make sense. Agriculture, as we've seen, is much, much more dynamic than foraging, demographically speaking. Now, what this meant was that although agrarian and foraging societies often traded and lived together peacefully, as we've seen, if they came to conflict the agrarian societies had lots of advantages. And most important, they could generate more wealth, and they contained more people. So, these seem to be some of the reasons why the agrarian frontier slowly advanced at the expense of foragers.

As farmers spread into regions that were more suitable for farming because they had good, easily worked soils, plenty of water, and plenty of sunlight and rainfall, slowly, partly by demographic pressure, partly perhaps by actual conflict, they squeezed out local populations of foragers who may have lived there for many thousands of years.

Agriculture and change. Agriculture, we've seen, introduced a new technological dynamism into human history. And it did so because it stimulated collective learning. How? How, to introduce a modern term, did growing populations stimulate innovation? How did they accelerate what we can think of as the synergy of collective learning? This is another way of asking why agriculture generates such dynamism. Not just demographic dynamism but also intellectual and technological dynamism.

Well, I think there are several plausible general explanations for this. First, with larger populations you simply have more people who are accumulating ideas and exchanging them within and between communities. You have populations that are much larger, much, much denser than those of foraging communities. So, if collective learning, as I've argued, this distinctive ability of our species, depends above all on the exchange of ideas between individuals, we should expect that, where you have a large number of individuals, where populations are growing rapidly, the synergy of intellectual exchanges is going to grow very rapidly, indeed. That's the first explanation.

31

Now here's a second. As population grows, some people inevitably find themselves at the margins of society. So, imagine an agrarian village. It's growing, population grows, young couples may be forced to find new land at the edge on land that's perhaps less attractive than land in the middle of the village, or they may even be forced to migrate somewhere else. In order to farm this marginal land, they're going to have to tweak existing farming methods. In other words, they're going to have to experiment with new techniques, new crops, new patterns of sowing, new techniques of hoeing and weeding, and so on. So, population growth itself generated a constant series of mini-innovations in agricultural technique.

And thirdly, population growth generated conflicts over land and resources. And warfare, that is to say, large-scale organized conflicts themselves, eventually begin to drive technological change and social change in new ways.

A considerable degree of technological dynamism is already apparent in the early Agrarian era. Agriculture itself emerged in many different variations, each of them adapted to particular environments. Now, I've tended to talk of agriculture as if it was a single set of techniques, but from some points of view this is a mistake. Like foraging techniques, agriculture adapted in many small ways to different plants, landscapes, climates, and environments. So, the evolutionary spread of agriculture is a very good example of our remarkable ability to adapt, as was the spread of foraging lifeways during the Paleolithic era. Though here, things are sped up quite remarkably, as agriculture spread around the world in just a few thousand years, in contrast to the 200,000 years or so that it took foraging lifeways to make their way around the globe. That, incidentally, is a very good illustration of what I mean when I use a general phrase like the "enhanced dynamism of agriculture."

Now, so that you don't get a sense of agriculture as a homogenous uniform technology, let me describe what were probably two of the most basic agrarian techniques of the early Agrarian era. And I'm going to describe them as "horticulture" and "swidden" agriculture. Each in turn, we'll see, can be found with many regional variations, using different plants and adapting to different environments.

So first, horticulture. Anthropologists use the term "horticulture" to mean agriculture or farming that is based purely on human labor power and uses implements, such as hoes or digging sticks or mortars and sickles. So, the labor in horticulture is human. If they turn over the soil, they do it with simple hoes or sticks. And many horticultural communities exist even today. You can find many of them, for example, in the Amazon. So, if you want to think of a typical farming community in the early Agrarian era, don't think of plow agriculture. Think rather of a village in the highlands of Papua New Guinea, where people will dig the land themselves using rudimentary hoes or digging sticks, and most of the energy for this type of agriculture comes from human beings rather than from animals. That's horticulture, and it probably gives you a good general impression of what we mean by agriculture for many of the people who lived in the early Agrarian era.

But there's a second general type of technology that is really rather important and also had its own dynamism, and that is swidden agriculture, sometimes called "slash-and-burn." This is what swidden farmers do. Swidden farming, you'll find, is—what's the best way of saying it?—it's a way of farming forested lands. Swidden farmers use stone axes and fire to clear forested regions. Often they'll scar trees, let them die, and then burn them down. So, they'll burn down an area of forest. And then what they'll do, probably leaving the stumps there, is they'll plant crops in the rich, ashy soil that's left behind.

Initially, you can get very, very good yields in the ash from burned trees. But fertility will probably decline quite rapidly within a few years. So, swidden agriculture is a sort of seminomadic agriculture. Often within say 5 or 6 years, the community will have to move on. It'll have to burn a new patch of forest. And in this way, swidden families may migrate around an area of forest in perhaps migratory patterns of 50 or 60 years, waiting until the forest has regrown in an area they were in before. So, swidden farming is particularly adapted to forested regions. And the result, the impact of swidden farming is to initiate the process of global deforestation.

It's swidden farmers who really began the process of significantly reducing forest cover. Indeed, the striking recent evidence about the impact of swidden farming—the climatologist William Ruddiman has recently argued that there was a minor spike in the appearance of greenhouse gases in the early Agrarian era. And he suggests that this may have been caused in part by decline in forest cover and in part by the burning of trees. Now, if he's right, then the spread of swidden farming is an early sign of humans in the early Agrarian era beginning to have a significant impact on global climates.

While we're on the subject, Ruddiman suggests that a second spike of this kind can be observed from about 5,000 years ago. That, he argues, was probably caused by the spread of paddy rice farming in Southeast and East Asia. Paddy rice farming tends to generate significant amounts of methane, another greenhouse gas. And it's even been argued that these changes may have stopped global climates from cooling, preserving the benign conditions that are so necessary for agriculture. If so, humans, even in the early Agrarian era, are beginning to have a very significant impact on global climates— enough of an impact, in fact, to break the traditional cycle of ice ages and interglacials that had lasted for at least a million years.

Okay. Now, what I'd like to do is look at the sort of communities people lived in. I'd like to try and get some sense of how people lived in the early Agrarian era. Most early Agrarian communities can be thought of as villages. This is the typical kind of community of this era of human history. But some may have been large enough that we should think of them as small towns.

Jericho may be the oldest known agrarian settlement. It lies about 20 kilometers east of Jerusalem. It's been excavated since the mid-19th century by archaeologists looking, of course, for its famous walls. In the 1950s, Kathleen Kenyon found walls that turned out to be from almost 11,000 years old—way, way, way before Joshua. As Jericho lies 800 feet below sea level, it's probable these walls were not military defenses. On the contrary, they were intended to keep out floodwaters.

Jericho's first occupants were probably Natufians. But by 11,000 years ago, just when agriculture is beginning, about 1,000 people could be found living in 70 mud-brick dwellings and supporting themselves by farming. This is one of the earliest large communities that we know of. And again, think of this: Few permanent communities this large had ever existed. In the Paleolithic era, people had certainly gathered for brief periods (perhaps two or three weeks) in gatherings of many hundreds of people. But Paleolithic technologies simply couldn't support large numbers of people living in the same area permanently. So, such communities as Jericho 11,000 years ago represent a new phenomenon in human history—one of the many emergent properties generated by the appearance of agriculture.

Out of respect for their ancestors, the inhabitants of Jericho decorated their skulls. This is a practice we find in modern early Agrarian villages in Papua New Guinea and the Papua New Guinea Islands. And it's a very powerful reminder of the importance of kinship and of ancestors in all early human communities.

Even more densely settled was Catal Huyuk in Anatolia, southeast of the modern city of Konya. Catal Huyuk flourished 9,000 years ago. It's an astonishing site. Here, mud-brick houses were built with adjoining walls. They abutted on to each other, a bit like the cells in a beehive. So, houses were entered from the roof. Each house contained a hearth, a storage area, and exotic bull-headed statues. And the inhabitants exported the tough volcanic glass known as obsidian, which was the best way of making a hard, sharp edge before the appearance of metallurgy.

And most early Agrarian villages were undoubtedly smaller. Modern anthropological studies of regions such as the Papua New Guinean highlands or the Amazon basin today may give an impression of how most people lived in the early Agrarian era. This was, as we've seen, above all an era of villages. The village was, for most people, the most complex community they would know: the hub of power, the source of wealth, and the source of knowledge. Perhaps these weren't quite hot spots, but they were at least emerging sort of warm spots, dotted around the surface of the Earth in increasing numbers.

Now, finally, let me ask about the question of "progress," something we touched on in dealing with the Paleolithic. Is there any evidence the people lived better or worse in the early Agrarian era? This is an issue we've touched on slightly already. We saw in Lecture Twenty-Two that, by some criteria, Paleolithic foragers lived quite well.

What's the evidence on early farmers? Well, it's mixed. There's some evidence that the first generation or two probably lived well, enjoying improved food supplies. Incidentally, the evidence depends a lot on studies of the skeletal remains of early farmers. However, within a few generations, problems emerged that nomadic foragers had never faced, as sedentism generated population explosions in settlement after settlement.

Now, think about what these denser communities meant. Sedentary villages attracted vermin and rubbish. Diseases could spread more easily with a large pool of potential victims to infect. A disease bacteria can't get much purchase on a small, foraging, nomadic community. But in a village, it can keep traveling around the population, creating endemic diseases. Furthermore, living close to animals meant a lot of pathogens could pass from humans to animals, and back and forth.

So, studies of human bones from early Agrarian communities hint at new types of problems that foragers didn't have to deal with: new forms of stress, for example, caused perhaps by the intense labor of harvest times, or perhaps by periodic crop failures. This is one of the great ironies of agriculture. Farmers relied on a smaller range of foodstuffs than foragers. And that meant that if one of them didn't succeed in a given year, they were in real trouble. So, famine enters human history with the appearance of farming. Overpopulation caused periodic shortages, which may explain why skeletons in this era seem to get shorter.

And the historian John Coatsworth writes:

> Bioarchaeologists have linked the agricultural transition to a significant decline in nutrition and to increases in disease, mortality, overwork, and violence in areas where skeletal remains make it possible to compare human welfare before and after the change. These results seem to hold whether the transition occurred gradually over a long time or was forced by conquest (as in parts of the New World). Civilization, [he wrote] we now know, stunted growth, spread disease, shortened life spans, and set people to killing and maiming each other on an unprecedented scale.

Maybe he's overdoing it, but let's not assume that agriculture meant progress.

Thank you.

Power and Its Origins
Lecture 27

Power from below can exist without power from above. It doesn't work the other way around. And what that means is that to explain the slow buildup to institutionalized power over 5,000 years, we must begin by looking at forms of power from below.

I f you study the past using written records you will soon encounter states, empires, and civilizations. This is why the history of these immense, highly institutionalized power structures has been one of the central themes of historical scholarship and teaching from ancient times to the present day, in all literate traditions. States created new forms of oppression as well as new opportunities, and they would dominate the "later Agrarian" era from the moment they first appeared, about 5,000 years ago. Yet so far, we have not talked much of such things because we have been describing societies in which hierarchies were embedded in personal relationships or the rules of kinship rather than in large institutional structures such as states. Now we must try to explain the emergence of large, institutionalized power structures. We will see that their roots lay in the early Agrarian era.

To clarify the nature of the problem, we need to be clear what states are. So we will move forward to the later Agrarian era before returning to trace the roots of institutionalized power in the early Agrarian era. Following Eric Wolf, we will use the terminology of "tribute-taking" states. The word "tribute" is used here to mean resources extracted through the threat of organized force. Tribute-taking states often enjoy the genuine support of many of their subjects because, though they can coerce, they can also provide real services, just as farmers provide valuable services to their domestic crops and animals. The great world historian William McNeill has captured this ambiguous relationship well by describing tribute-taking states as "macroparasites." Like parasites, they may hurt their prey, but they must also protect their prey if they are to survive. Nevertheless, the defining quality of tribute-taking states is the ability, when necessary, to impose their will by force.

The appearance of the first tribute-taking states marks a new level of social complexity. Indeed, though I have not classified this as one of our eight major thresholds, one could make a case for doing so. States were larger, more internally varied, and more complex than the village communities of the early Agrarian era or the small, kin-based communities of the Paleolithic era. They all achieved a certain degree of stability (though eventually they all broke down). To maintain their complex structures, they mobilized the resources and energy of millions of individuals. Large projects such as the building of pyramids or the formation of armies demonstrated their power to mobilize energy, resources, and people. Tribute-taking states also generated new "emergent" properties, such as organized warfare, monumental architecture, the management of markets, and an unprecedented power to coerce.

"Power from above" depends on the capacity to make credible threats of coercion.

To understand the emergence of tribute-taking states, we need a clear definition of institutionalized (as opposed to personal) power. I will define institutionalized power as the concentration in the hands of a few people of substantial control over considerable human and material resources. Note that this definition has two components: control and the resources being controlled. The distinction matters because where there are few people and resources to control, power has limited reach. This is why power structures were less significant and less institutionalized in the Paleolithic era. As populations—as well as the goods they produced—multiplied, power began to matter more as leaders gained control over more people, more resources, and more energy.

Now we return to the early Agrarian era to trace how power structures became more significant and more institutionalized. It will help to imagine two distinct ways of mobilizing power. Though intertwined in reality, we can distinguish them analytically. "Power from below" is power conceded more or less willingly by individuals or groups who expect to benefit from subordination to skillful leaders. People expect something in return for subordination, so power from below is a "mutualistic" form of symbiosis. As societies became larger and denser, leadership became more important in order to achieve group goals, such as the building of irrigation systems or defense in war. Familiar modern examples of power from below include the election of club or team officials or captains. When we think of power as "legitimate" (e.g., the right to tax in a democratic society), we are generally thinking of it as power from below, even if it is backed by the threat of force.

"Power from above" depends on the capacity to make credible threats of coercion. That depends on the existence of disciplined groups of coercers, loyal to the leader and able to enforce the leader's will by force when necessary. In such an environment, people obey because they will be punished if they do not. This aspect of power highlights the coercive (or "parasitic") element in power relationships. The existence of jails, police, and armies is evidence that such power exists. Yet no state can depend entirely on coercion because maintaining an apparatus of coercion is costly and depends on maintaining the willing support of the coercers. No individual can single-handedly coerce millions of others. In practice, the two forms of power are intertwined in complex ways. "Protection rackets," for example, offer a service. Yet it is often the racket itself that is the likely source of danger, so does the payment of "protection money" count as a form of power from below or above? Building coercive groups is complex and costly, and the earliest forms of power emerged before such groups existed. That is why the first power elites depended mainly on power from below.

This lecture has discussed the nature of institutionalized power to help us explain how it first emerged in human history. The next lecture will ask how this analysis of power can help us understand the simple forms of power that emerged during the early Agrarian era. ■

Essential Reading

Christian, *Maps of Time*, chap. 9.

Fagan, *People of the Earth*, chap. 14.

Supplementary Reading

Harris, "The Origin of Pristine States" (in *Cannibals and Kings*).

Johnson and Earle, *The Evolution of Human Societies*.

Questions to Consider

1. What is power?

2. Is it possible to analyze power relations in today's world using the categories of "power from above" and "power from below"?

Power and Its Origins
Lecture 27—Transcript

Power in institutionalized forms—that is to say, the story of states and emperors, kings and queens, of armies and wars—has been one of the central themes of much historical scholarship and teaching. Perhaps this is, in part, because states have been traditionally great generators of records. They've generated a huge amount of written evidence. So, if you study the past using written records, what you're very likely to encounter very soon is the power of states and empires. So, the history of these immense power structures has been one of the central themes of modern historical scholarship and teaching—and in fact not just modern historical scholarship, but of historical scholarship from ancient times to the present day, and in all literate traditions. A huge amount of history writing has actually been about states, and rulers, and what they did.

And some of the earliest of all written texts, such as the great *Epic of Gilgamesh*, which we'll refer to quite soon, which describes events that occurred almost 5,000 years ago, or the earliest written records to be found in China or the Mayan regions of Mesoamerica, or the great epics such as those of Homer, are also about the doings of kings and warriors. Yet so far, we've not talked much about such things, and there is of course a very good reason for this.

In the small societies that most humans lived in for most of human history, relationships we've seen were essentially personal or familial. If you want to understand them you think about the relations within your own family—not your relations with the police, or the state, or the law. Power was certainly there in the Paleolithic, but it was personal or familial rather than institutionalized. It was embodied in customs of kinship and in the personal relations of individuals—and it was exercised within these small groups. It was not sustained and supported, as power relations are today, by large institutional structures. It was not built into large-scale institutions.

So, here's the question I want to start tackling now: When did institutionalized forms of power, these forms of power that have dominated historical thinking, when did they begin to emerge? When, to put it slightly differently, did power and hierarchy become more than a matter of family or clan politics?

Institutionalized power, we will see, is one of the most important "emergent" properties that would appear as agriculture drove human societies towards new forms of complexity. Now, tackling this question, trying to explain the origins of institutionalized power, takes us across not quite one of our major thresholds, but what we could certainly regard as a mini-threshold in this course. Its essential question we tackle in this and the next few lectures. As we'll see, institutionalized power begins to play an increasingly important role during the early Agrarian era. But to appreciate how and why these new forms of power begin to play such a central role in human history, we need to begin by thinking very clearly about the nature and role of power in human societies.

One of the first things we'll see is that there's a very close relationship between the spread and development of agricultural societies, which we looked at in the last lecture, and the emergence of institutionalized power. So, as agriculture spread during the early Agrarian era, new forms of power and hierarchy began to appear within human societies. Why and how?

Before we can get far with this question, we need to take time out to be very clear about the nature of institutionalized power. We've done this before when looking at life itself, when looking at agriculture. We've seen that to understand the origins of a phenomenon, we need to take time out to be very clear about what it is. Power, like life itself, seems obvious when you think about it. But if you try rigorous definition, it turns out to be quite as slippery as the idea of life. So, we need to define it rigorously.

Now, to clarify the nature of the problem, what I'm going to do is similar to what we did in considering the appearance of life. I'm going to move forward in time. From the appearance of agriculture, I'm going to move forward about 5,000 years to a period in which states are beginning to appear, so that we can see the results of this mini-threshold. So, I'm going to look at the beginnings and the ends of the early Agrarian period and look at the contrast between the two. Then, when we've seen what happens over that long period, we'll return to consider how we get from A—that is, the simple village societies of the early Agrarian era about 10,000 to 11,000 years ago—to B, the great agrarian civilizations that began to appear from about 5,000 years ago.

Now, the appearance of states, I've said, from about 5,000 years ago, marks a very important sub-threshold within the history of our species. It's a sub-threshold whose significance is captured rather well in the following deliberately provocative and vivid quotation from one of the great American anthropologists of the 20th century, Marvin Harris. So, this is what Marvin Harris says about the appearance of states:

> For the first time [he writes] there appeared on earth kings, dictators, high priests, emperors, prime ministers, presidents, governors, mayors, generals, admirals, police chiefs, judges, lawyers, and jailers, along with dungeons, jails, penitentiaries, and concentration camps. Under the tutelage of the state, [writes Marvin Harris] human beings learned for the first time how to bow, grovel, kneel, and kowtow. In many ways the rise of the state was the descent of the world from freedom to slavery.

This is, of course, a peculiarly bleak view of states, and it may well underestimate the extent of personal violence, personal coercion similar to domestic violence today, that undoubtedly occurred within Paleolithic societies. Nevertheless, it captures well the new scale on which power relations were constructed after the appearance of states. So, states have dominated the history of the last 5,000 years. Following Eric Wolf, who uses this terminology in a wonderful but difficult book on modern world history, *Europe and the People Without History*, I'm going to use the terminology of "tribute-taking" states. The word "tribute" is used here to mean resources extracted through the threat of organized force. This is the forcible taking of labor or resources, or even people, from one group of people by another group of people, who I'll refer to as the state.

Now, having given this definition, I don't want to give the impression we're talking ever about pure coercion. Pure coercion simply doesn't exist. Tribute-taking states often enjoy the genuine support of many of their subjects because although they can coerce, they can also, like the Mafia, provide real services—just as farmers provide valuable services to their domestic crops and animals.

My father-in-law briefly ran a business in New York. And he once told me that he contributed to the benevolent funds of the local police and he also paid another group for protection. Now, he knew exactly who he was being protected against, but he said to me: "It was still a worthwhile deal." If he hadn't paid, his business might have suffered—but because he paid, it never did. He was paying for real services.

So, we'll see in dealing with states there's always a sort of complex "symbiosis," to use a word I've earlier used, between populations who pay taxes and supply resources and the states who exact those resources partly by force and partly in return for services. The great world historian William McNeill, one of the crucial founders of modern world history in the U.S., has captured this ambiguous relationship really well. He wrote a wonderful book about the history of disease in the last 2,000 years called *Plagues and Peoples*. And in that book, and in another related book about states, he describes the state and the relationship between states and populations as a sort of unbalanced symbiosis or, in his word, as a form of "parasitism." He said it was similar to the relationship between a disease organism and its prey. If the relationship is to be stable—in other words, if the state is to survive, if the relationship is to be useful to the parasite—it's vital that the prey survive as well, which is why parasites that are too lethal never last. Most end up hurting but not killing their hosts. McNeill, accordingly, describes states as macroparasites, as opposed to the microparasites of the disease world. States, like parasites, have to offer genuine protection of some kind, and that is why many of their subjects may value the services they provide. So, this idea of macroparasitism may help us get a sense of this complex and ambiguous relationship that emerges when states appear.

And nevertheless, despite this element of mutuality, the defining quality of tribute-taking states is the ability, when necessary, to impose their will by force, to coerce. So, our question can be rephrased. Our question about institutionalized forms of power can be rephrased: How and why did such structures evolve? The ability to coerce, after all, requires quite complex structures. It depends on the construction of fairly elaborate systems of enforcement.

The appearance of the first tribute-taking states also clearly marks a new level of social complexity. Indeed, although I've not classified this as one of our eight major thresholds, one could make a case for doing so. And, in fact, I've already described this as a mini-threshold, but when preparing this course I considered seriously the possibility of describing it as one of our major thresholds. Now, I rejected that partly because I didn't want to introduce too many thresholds within human history—it would make the story too elaborate—but we still need to treat it as a very significant turning point in human history. And it's analogous in many ways to the major thresholds we've seen already in this course, and that's why I'll treat it as an important chronological marker. The appearance of the first tribute-taking states marks the end of the early Agrarian era and the beginning of what I'll call the "later Agrarian" era of human history.

We've already compared this threshold in an earlier lecture to star formation. But it's worth noting an interesting comparison also with another threshold we've seen, and that's the threshold leading to multi-cellular organisms. Remember what happened. With that threshold we saw how large numbers of individual, independent organisms find themselves slowly incorporated within larger structures within which they were much more interdependent and, in some respects, had less freedom than they had had as independent entities. Yet collectively, within these large, multi-cellular organisms— such as ourselves—cells were, of course, much more powerful than they'd been before.

So, how does the appearance of states and institutionalized forms of power make human societies more complex? Let's be clear about this. Do you remember our four key features of complexity? They were: New structures appear; new existing components are organized within a new structure. Secondly, there's a degree of stability—these new structures don't just vanish overnight, they survive for some time. Third, there are new energy flows and new emergent properties.

45

So, let's examine states with this idea of complexity in mind. They clearly had complex structures. States are larger; they have more internal differentiation. And in that sense, they're clearly much more complex than the village communities of the early Agrarian era or even more so of the small, kin-based communities of the Paleolithic era. That's the first thing— they're more complex, clearly more complex.

Secondly, they had some stability. All states that are worth talking about, all states that leave significant records, survived for a certain period of time before eventually breaking down.

Third, new energy flows. To maintain their complex internal structures, including their mechanisms of coercion, for example, they had to mobilize resources and energy on a huge scale. They controlled populations of many thousands and sometimes of many millions of people. And remember that in early human societies, human beings themselves were one of the most important sources of energy. So, it's clearer if I use the word "labor." States control people, and that means controlling energy. Large projects, such as the building of pyramids or the formation of armies, demonstrate their power to mobilize huge amounts of energy, resources, and people. So, there are large energy flows associated with states—in fact, a significant increase in the energy flows compared with those that existed with earlier human communities.

And fourth, states display many new emergent properties. And I'll be looking at these in much more detail in later lectures. Some of them include organized warfare and the building of monumental architecture. This we'll see over and over again: huge buildings, such as the pyramids of Egypt or the pyramids built by the Maya in Mesoamerica, designed as tools or for religious ceremonies that represented the awe and might of the rulers. Monumental architecture counts as a very clear sign of the appearance of tribute-taking states, and it counts also as a new emergent property. Another example is their management of markets and their unprecedented power to coerce. And we'll see more.

So, states also generate new emergent properties. In all these ways, the appearance of states counts as a significant mini-threshold, a significant increase in the level of complexity in human history and human societies.

Okay. Now, let's go back to the general idea of power. This is an idea, as I've said before, that is more slippery than it looks, and it's been debated widely within political science, in philosophy, and in sociology. We just need some very broad general definitions to help us explain the buildup to tribute-taking states, to understand how these structures were constructed over several thousand years.

Now, power, I've said, is slippery. So, what is it? How can we define it? What is institutionalized power? Here's an attempt at a reasonably clear and concise definition of institutionalized as opposed to personal power. I will define "institutionalized power" as the concentration in the hands of a few people of substantial control over considerable human and material resources.

Let me break that definition down. It's got two components, and it's important to be aware of both of them. The first component is control. Someone or some institution controls something. The second is what is being controlled, the resources being controlled. And it's important to be aware of the distinction. It matters because where there are few people and resources to control, as in Paleolithic societies, power is of limited significance. You may control one or two people, but it doesn't make a huge difference to a large number of people. It doesn't become a historical fact. So, this is why power structures are less significant in the Paleolithic era. Control may have existed, but it was exercised over very small numbers of people and resources. Individuals coerced other individuals, but the power was purely personal, exercised within family-sized groups.

Leaders or rulers didn't exist in any sense that would be recognized today. And groups took decisions rather as families do today on group outings. Here's a quotation from Richard Lee, who we've seen before—Richard Lee studied the people of the Kalahari in the late 20th century—and his description of the form that leadership took among the !Kung. You'll remember that the click is characteristic of many of the indigenous languages of South Africa.

So, this is my attempt to do the click. Okay? And this is Richard Lee on leadership in foraging communities.

> In egalitarian societies such as the !Kung's, group activities unfold, plans are made, and decisions are arrived at—all apparently without a clear focus of authority or influence. [In other words, no institutionalized forms of leadership. He goes on:] Closer examination, however, reveals that patterns of leadership do exist. When a water hole is mentioned, a group living there is often referred to by the !Kung by a single man's or woman's name. These individuals are often older people who have lived there the longest or who've married into the owner group, and who have some personal qualities worthy of note as a speaker, an arguer, a ritual specialist, or a hunter. In group discussions these people may speak out more than others, may be deferred to more than others, and one gets the feeling [he writes] that their opinions hold a bit more weight than the opinions of other discussants. [So he concludes:] Whatever their skills, !Kung leaders have no formal authority. [We could use the phrase "institutionalized authority."] They can only persuade, but never enforce their will on others.

So, this is the absence of institutionalized power. This is Paleolithic forms of leadership.

As populations multiplied, though, as well as the goods they produced, power began to matter more and more. In other words, as the resources potentially available to be controlled—think of not just people but also warehouses full of goods, grain perhaps, or precious metals—as the resources began to expand, power begins to matter a lot more, as leaders have the possibility of gaining control over more and more stuff and more energy. So, this is why the available resources are critical to the scale of different types of power.

And very roughly speaking, we can think of this as a sort of modular process. We can think of village headmen acquiring leadership roles in villages, and regional rulers gaining authority over a number of villages, then even more powerful leaders gaining authority over regional bosses. And in each case, what's happening is that individuals are finding the possibility of controlling more and more resources. This is the way that their power is slowly built up. In practice, of course, the changes are always much more complicated, and we must always remind ourselves of the dangers of an over-schematized view of historical processes.

Now, with that reminder, I return to my attempt to clarify how institutionalized power evolved. I hope now we have a slightly more subtle idea of what we mean by power, and in particular institutionalized power. And we can now go back from the first states to the early Agrarian era and start trying to explain the slow buildup of these complex institutionalized forms over several millennia.

So, we'll ask: How, after 200,000 years in which institutionalized power didn't exist, how did some individuals manage to start exerting significant power over others? Now, to understand the process, it will help to imagine two distinct ways of mobilizing power, two distinct types of power. They're really complementary. They're different faces of power. The first I'll call "power from below," and the second I'll call "power from above."

Now, let's begin with "power from below." By power from below, I mean power that is conceded to a leader by individuals or groups who expect something in return (just as domestic plants or animals expect something in return, we can imagine, from humans). They expect to benefit from subordination to skillful leaders. People expect something in return. Now, in this sense, power from below is very clearly a symbiotic relationship. As societies became larger and complex, the need for leadership increased. Leadership became more important in order to achieve group goals as groups became larger. In a group of two or three people you can do everything by consensus. In a group of several hundred you start needing leadership structures. If you want to build an irrigation system, or you want to build a wall to defend your village against a rival village, you need some organization—you need some leadership.

So, here's a very general principle. As societies get larger, they find more and more that they need leadership in order to cope with more and more complex tasks and challenges. So, this is a process driven by agriculture. Agriculture leads to larger communities. Larger communities create more possibilities for conflict, more needs for group activity, and more need for leadership.

Now, this idea of power from below is very familiar. We all experience it a lot of the time. Familiar modern examples include, for example, if you're a member of a club and you want the club to be able to function fairly efficiently in some way, perhaps to collect dues, you're probably going to elect officials. And you, as a member of the club, implicitly grant some authority to those people, and you grant them the right to take some crucial decisions. So, this is power from below. It's very, very familiar, indeed.

When we think of power as "legitimate" in the modern world as opposed to illegitimate, when we think of it as legitimate (such as the right to tax in a democratic society), we're generally thinking of it as power from below, even if it's backed by the threat of force (e.g., for not paying taxes). Now, that's power from below. It's very familiar, it's all around us, and it's a crucial component of all power systems. And we often forget about it.

Now, "power from above," the other side of power. Power from above depends on the capacity to make credible threats of coercion. Power from above, unlike power from below, which just depends on a certain amount of agreement between people on common goals, power from above depends on the preexistence of organized, disciplined groups of coercers who are loyal to a leader and able to enforce the leader's will by force when necessary.

In modern societies, the police and armies play such a role, but so do many other officials, such as tax collectors. In such an environment, people obey because they will be punished if they do not. This aspect of power highlights the coercive element in power relations—the element that I said was critical to the existence of tribute-taking states. You want to know whether there's power from above, you look for the presence of jails, police, armies, enforcers, gangs of thugs, and you know that such power exists.

Now, we also need to be clear that power from above can never exist on its own. There can be no such thing as a purely coercive state, and the reason for this is very simple. Maintaining an apparatus of coercion is costly, and it depends on maintaining the willing support of the coercers. So, the gang with which you work has to be supporting you. No individual can single-handedly coerce millions of others. There has to be some consensus at least among the coercers.

So, coercion, power from above, depends on the previous existence of complex structures of coercion. Now, it depends on the existence of complex structures. In practice, the two forms are always intertwined. "Protection rackets," for example, offer a service. It's often the racket itself that is the likely source of danger; so does the payment of "protection money" count as a form of power from below or power from above? Which was my father-in-law dealing with? He could have chosen not to pay to the police benevolent fund or to the other organization, as any member of a democratic society may decide not to pay taxes. But in both cases, there are unpleasant consequences.

Okay. This has been an elaborate attempt to clarify the nature of power. We need to understand this clearly before we can look at the details of the construction of elaborate power systems, of the structures that have dominated most of the last 5,000 years of human history.

Here's the final point I want to make. Building coercive groups is complex and costly, and the earliest forms of power emerged before such groups existed. This is why the first power elites depended mainly on power from below. Power from below *can* exist without power from above. It doesn't work the other way around. And what that means is that to explain the slow buildup to institutionalized power over 5,000 years, we must begin by looking at forms of power from below. So, now let's start asking: How, over 5,000 years, do you slowly build up from the very simple societies and structures of the early Agrarian era to the elaborate, powerful, institutionalized power structures of the later Agrarian era, to the first tribute-taking states? That's the question we tackle in the next lecture.

Thank you.

Early Power Structures
Lecture 28

> If you find infants that are buried with a lot of wealth around them, then you know not only that there were wealthy people in that society, but you know something else as well. You know that wealth could be inherited. In other words, this is not just one individual who built up their wealth during their lifetime; they could pass on their wealth to their children. And that suggests the existence of institutionalized hierarchies of wealth and power.

The previous lecture described the appearance of the first tribute-taking states and offered a simple definition of power. Now we ask: How did the first and simplest power structures evolve? The evidence we need to answer this question comes mainly from archaeology and anthropology. Archaeological research offers many indirect hints about early power relations. The relative size and wealth of houses and burials hints at inequalities of wealth and power. An example is the huge burial mount of Arzhan in the Inner Asian steppes, dating from the 8th century B.C.E. Such structures demonstrate the presence of a very significant degree of institutionalized power, enough to mobilize the resources of many hundreds of people, some of whom were required to sacrifice their own lives to honor a dead leader. Rich infant burials demonstrate the presence of inherited wealth and status. Evidence such as the terra-cotta army buried with the first ruler of a unified China, or extensive fortifications and walls, shows the presence of armies and organized coercion. The stone figures (or ahu) of Easter Island, or Britain's Stonehenge represent more modest forms of "monumental architecture." Anthropological studies of modern "early Agrarian" societies, such as those of Melanesia or the Amazon basin, suggest ways of interpreting the archaeological evidence. But we must always remember that these are modern models and we may be missing important differences between them and the first early Agrarian societies.

Why did power relations develop so rapidly in the early Agrarian era? The key was population growth. As communities became larger, more productive, and more interdependent, new problems arose, and also new

The Stonehenge in Britain is a modest example of "monumental archaeology."

forms of wealth, which created new opportunities and temptations for would-be leaders. Whenever complexity increases, new coordinating mechanisms are needed, like the nervous systems in multi-celled organisms. Like modern families, Paleolithic communities could deal with conflicts face-to-face, or simply by splitting. In early Agrarian villages, relations were often less personal and splitting was more difficult because households had invested labor and resources in crops and farmed land. Leaders were needed to resolve disputes within the community or with neighboring communities. As communities expanded, their gods generally became more magnificent and specialist priests took on the role of communicating with them. Their privileged relations with the gods gave them influence and prestige that could be parleyed into real power. In large communities, new tasks arose such as garbage collection, wall building, or the maintenance of temples and irrigation systems. These, too, required leadership. The appearance of specialists, such as warriors or artisans or scribes, made it necessary to organize exchanges of goods and services between them and the groups that produced the food and other resources they needed. The first rulers ruled because they could offer services to those they ruled. So power relations arose as a form of symbiosis.

How were leaders selected? Some acquired followers through their charismatic personalities or their skills in dispute resolution, warfare, organization, or mediating with the gods. As communities expanded in size, ideas of kinship began to be used to create hierarchies of birth. In large communities, those who traced descent to founding ancestors (real or mythical) through senior ancestral lines claimed the deference due to seniors in all kin-based systems. High birth provided a seemingly natural basis for authority. The decoration of ancestral skulls, evident even in Natufian communities, suggests how important lineage was even in the very earliest Agrarian communities.

Males dominated leadership roles in most early Agrarian communities, laying the foundation for the asymmetrical power relations known as "patriarchy." What were the sources of patriarchy? Clearly, they reflect no innate differences in political ability, for in many different societies women have shown themselves as capable as men of wielding power. The key may lie in the demographic rules of peasant societies. In peasant communities, having many children was vital to a household's success. But this demand tied women to their roles as reproducers and child rearers. Consequently, men generally found it easier to take on specialist roles, including power roles. In turn, the overrepresentation of males in public power roles encouraged the presumption that males were natural leaders, even if in most households power relations were quite variable.

The decoration of ancestral skulls, evident even in Natufian communities, suggests how important lineage was even in the very earliest Agrarian communities.

Modern anthropological studies offer helpful models of how power roles may have been constructed within small communities. One influential model is that of the "big man." In a classic 1955 study, Douglas Oliver described the "big men" or *mumi*s of the Solomon Islands, which are east of Papua New Guinea. Ambitious young men collected food from relatives and allies and then threw huge feasts of pigs, coconut pies, and sago puddings for local men. Those whose feasts were judged impressive enough could acquire enough of a following to become *mumis*. As in modern "pork-barrel" politics, gift-giving was a form of political investment because it created loyal followers. *Mumi*s could become powerful war leaders. One old man in Oliver's study remembered that, "In the olden times there were greater *mumi* than there are today. Then they were fierce and relentless war leaders.

They laid waste to the countryside and their clubhouses were lined with the skulls of people they had slain" (Harris, *Cannibals and Kings*, p. 106). As this suggests, the move from "power from below" to "power from above" could occur very swiftly.

A widely used model of authority at regional scales is that of the "chief." Chiefs normally rule over local leaders and may have little direct contact with most of their "subjects." Their power is often based on high lineage, and they may achieve god-like status. Polish anthropologist Bronislaw Malinowski once witnessed "all the people present in the village of Bwoytalu [in the Trobriand Islands] drop from their verandas as if blown down by a hurricane at the sound of a drawn-out cry announcing the arrival of an important chief" (Harris, *Cannibals and Kings*, p. 375). Archaeologists suspect the presence of chiefs when they find large structures such as pyramids or earthen mounds that required control over not just single villages but over hundreds or thousands of workers. These early forms of power rested largely (though not exclusively) on support from below, so they were too volatile to provide the basis for durable tribute-taking states. Loss of support or defeat in war led too quickly to loss of power. How was it possible to construct more durable power structures? That question leads us into the "era of Agrarian civilizations." ∎

Essential Reading

Christian, *Maps of Time*, chap. 9.

Fagan, *People of the Earth*, chaps. 14, 15.

Supplementary Reading

Harris, "The Origin of Pristine States" (in *Cannibals and Kings*).

Johnson and Earle, *The Evolution of Human Societies.*

Questions to Consider

1. What evidence do we have on the early history of power, and how reliable is it?

2. How did early leaders establish their authority without an apparatus of coercion?

Early Power Structures
Lecture 28—Transcript

We're discussing the emergence of the great power structures that have played such a dominant role in the last 5,000 years of world history. And in the previous lecture, I tried to think very carefully about the nature of power itself and to distinguish between the highly institutionalized forms of power embodied in states within the last 5,000 years of human history and the much more personal forms of power that were present in all earlier eras of human history.

Now, the strategic era for understanding how you get from A to B is, once again, the early Agrarian era. So, now we need to go back to the beginnings of that era and see if we can trace, despite the extreme paucity of the evidence, some of the main stages in the creation of these complex, institutionalized forms of power. So, we're looking at, if you like, the prehistory of the state.

The previous lecture described the appearance of the first "tribute-taking" states. I use that label and defined it as power structures that had the ability, if necessary, to impose their will through coercion. Now we ask: How did the first and simplest power structures evolve? But first, let's look at the evidence. What types of evidence do we have if we're to try and construct a good evidence-based answer to this question?

We'll see that the evidence is far from perfect. But it may be just enough to allow us to construct, in very general terms, or to reconstruct, the history of institutionalized forms of power through this critical 5,000-year era of human history. The evidence we need to answer this question comes mainly from archaeology and anthropology. This is a mix we've seen before in looking both at the Paleolithic era and the early Agrarian era.

Let's look first at archaeology. Archaeology—that is to say, the study of the remains of past communities, past societies—can offer many indirect hints about early power relations and the buildup of forms of institutionalized power. For example, the relative size and wealth of houses and burials may hint at inequalities of wealth and power. An example, just to give one example more or less at random, is the huge burial mound of Arzhan in the

Inner Asian steppes. It dates from the 8th century B.C.E.—that is to say, it was formed about 2,800 years ago. It was excavated in the early 1970s in the Russian republic of Tuva, on the border of Mongolia.

The tomb is from the early phases of the Scythian era, and it represents the burial of an important pastoral nomadic steppe leader. It included 70 distinct chambers, arranged like the spokes of a wheel. It contained about 160 saddled horses; each of these had been slaughtered for the burial. They were under a mound 120 meters wide, which probably required the labor of something like 1,500 workers according to the estimates of the archaeologists who worked on the site.

At the very center were buried a man and a woman. They wore furs and elaborate decorations. Subordinate princes, or nobles, or aristocrats were buried to their south, their west, and the north of them, which gave them the place of honor in the east. This was traditionally the place of honor in most Inner Asian pastoral nomadic societies.

Now, if you stumble across such a tomb in the arid steppe lands of Central Asia, what can you deduce about power? You could hardly avoid the conclusion that even in this not particularly productive environment, there existed very significant degrees of institutionalized power. If so many people could be mobilized to honor the death of a ruler—and quite a few of them, including these princes who are buried with the rulers, were apparently even required to honor the burial by sacrificing their own lives—you have to conclude that these people were very powerful. They ruled large numbers of people, and they had very considerable power over them, and probably very considerable coercive power. In the steppes, mobilizing coercive power in many ways is actually easier than outside of the steppes, because the pastoral nomadic lifeway is so congenial to teaching—to a training in warfare.

So, that's just one illustration of the sort of evidence we look for if we're looking for power structures. Rich infant burials demonstrate something else. If you find infants that are buried with a lot of wealth around them, then you know not only that there were wealthy people in that society, but you know something else as well. You know that wealth could be inherited. In other words, this is not just one individual who built up their wealth during their lifetime; they could pass on their wealth to their children. And that suggests the existence of institutionalized hierarchies of wealth and power.

Much more elaborate evidence can be found as well. I'm thinking of evidence such as the amazing terra-cotta army that was buried with the first ruler of the unified China, or extensive fortifications and walls. These all show the presence of armies and organized coercion. Once you find these things, you know you're dealing with powerful tribute-taking states.

Let me talk briefly about the terra-cotta army, which I was lucky enough to see a few years ago. There are 8,000 life-sized terra-cotta soldiers and their horses. They were mass-produced to some extent, but nevertheless you have quite a variety of costumes and faces. You have them wearing the precise costumes for different military ranks. They were buried to honor the first emperor of a unified China, the Qin emperor Shi Huangdi, whose dates are 260 to 210 B.C.E., and they're part of a 20-square-mile-wide mausoleum. This was discovered outside the city of Xi'an, the ancient Han capital, in 1974, by local peasants who were drilling a well. Constructing the entire mausoleum for the emperor may have required the labor of 700,000 people over many years. So, this is "monumental architecture" at its most grandiose.

We'll see that one of the most remarkable similarities between all regions where institutionalized power appears in significant forms is that you find monumental architecture. Wherever institutionalized power structures appear, rulers seem to have constructed large, grand building projects. So, they're both examples of power, because they require a lot of labor to construct them, and they show that rulers or someone had the power to mobilize a lot of labor, but they're also displays of power. So, they count, in fact, as forms of propaganda. They're designed to impress or overawe someone else with the majesty of the leaders and rulers. A smaller version of this sort of display of power is enacted in the stone figures, the ahu, these astonishing heads that you find on Easter Island. They also represent a more modest form of power as does Stonehenge in Britain.

So, archaeology can tell us a lot about these power structures. What is hard to tease out from archaeology is exactly how these power structures worked. And to get some sense of how they worked, we have to go to anthropology—

and in particular to anthropological studies of modern early Agrarian societies, such as the societies of Papua New Guinea, parts of Melanesia or the Amazon, societies that still in many ways were like the societies of the early Agrarian era.

And these modern studies can suggest ways of interpreting the archaeological evidence. As always, when we use modern anthropological evidence to interpret the past record, we must remember that these are modern models, and we may be missing important differences between them and the first early Agrarian societies.

Okay. It's no accident that we start looking at power not in the Paleolithic but within the early Agrarian era—for there's a very close relationship, as we've seen, between agriculture and the evolution of power. The emergence of institutionalized forms of power correlates very, very directly with the buildup of agriculture, the spread of agriculture, the growth of populations that we've seen as a central phenomenon in the early Agrarian era.

The key was population growth—more people and more stuff. I define power as having two elements: control and the stuff that's controlled. And the key to the buildup of larger, more institutionalized power structures is the buildup of more stuff. Larger communities with more resources, more stored resources, more warehouses full of grain and wealth, and so on.

So, as communities became larger, more productive, and more interdependent, the possibilities for building power structures developed—and something else changed, too. As they became larger, more complex, more interdependent, new problems arose that created more need for forms of leadership. So, these two things—an increased need for leadership and increased resources—help explain why the buildup of agrarian societies (their expansion in size, numbers, and resources) is the key to understanding the buildup of power structures.

Let's look at this issue of leadership. Why, as societies got larger, did the need for leadership increase? Whenever complexity increases, you have to have new coordinating mechanisms of some kind. This is certainly true once we reach the level of life and all further levels of complexity. You need something like the nervous systems in multi-celled organisms. And something like this seems to be true of human societies. Like modern families, we've seen Paleolithic communities could deal with conflict, for example, face-to-face, or simply by splitting. If two people didn't get on, one of them could simply leave and join another group. It's a very simple method of conflict resolution.

In early Agrarian villages, relations were often a lot less personal, but splitting was also more difficult, because households have invested labor and resources in crops and farmed land, and it wasn't so easy just to pick up and move. So, increasingly, to deal with conflicts within the community, leaders were needed to resolve these disputes. All leaders were needed to resolve disputes not only within the community, but also with neighboring communities as well. So, here's one function of leadership that becomes more and more important as communities get larger, more impersonal, and more complex.

A second function is religious. In the very personal world of the Paleolithic, we saw, it may have been that people thought of the world as animistic. They thought of the world as peopled with spirits of various kinds, many of them not very powerful or very large-scale—figures that might have magical powers but were probably no more powerful than you and me.

But as societies expanded, the gods seemed to have generally become more magnificent. And as that happened, worshipping them became, itself, a public task. So, specialist priests began to take on the role of communicating with these rather grand deities—and their privileged relation with the gods could give priests considerable influence and prestige that often could be parleyed into real power. For example, priests were often in a very good position to extract gifts for the gods. In Sumer, we'll see the temples of Sumer contained huge amounts of offerings from the population at large for the gods—which, of course, were not always consumed by the gods, but were sometimes controlled by the priests themselves. And in large communities other tasks arose, such as garbage collection, wall-building, or the maintenance of temples and irrigation systems. These, too, required leadership.

Another reason why leadership became increasingly important as communities become larger, denser, and more complex is the appearance of specialists and a division of labor. As you start getting small towns, early forms of cities, you start getting a number of people who are no longer peasants—they are specialists. They may be warriors, or they may be potters, or eventually they may be scribes. Now, these people, to get food and the other things they need, are going to have to swap them with other members of society. So, once you get a division of labor, you need complex systems of exchange of goods, and you need markets, and you need someone to protect the markets. Here's one more reason why leadership becomes more crucial.

So, this is one of the reasons why, as societies become more complex, they need leaders more, and power from below becomes more and more important. Populations in these large and growing communities increasingly find that they need to appoint leaders. They need to delegate power to someone. So, this is one of the mechanisms by which new forms of leadership emerge.

Who became the leaders? How did you get to be one? Well, in the sort of environment I've been describing so far, the crucial quality may be skill. The people who step into leadership positions are often people who have particular skills. So, someone who is widely respected for their honesty, their understanding of tradition, their understanding of traditional ethical rules, may well be widely accepted as a mediator. And they'll be conceded a position that today we might describe as a position of judge. Or someone, for example, who is regarded as profoundly religious, someone who communicates very naturally and easily with the gods, may very easily acquire a leadership position in relations with the gods (or someone with particular skill in warfare or organization). So, there are people who step into leadership roles because they have skills. Now that's one of the ways early forms of leadership undoubtedly emerged.

But the other form is birth. In Paleolithic communities, it was generally not too hard to figure out who was related to whom within kinship systems. You're dealing with communities of very small numbers of people who have relations with neighboring communities as well. But once you have a community of several hundred or a thousand people, figuring out relationships becomes much more complex, so that kinship systems have to adapt to the growing size of communities.

And as communities expand in size, increasingly what tends to happen is they begin to construct what we can think of as mythological genealogies. These are genealogies that often take the following form. They'll trace everyone in the community, or most people in the community, to some mythical or semi-mythical ancestor who may have lived several generations in the past. But once you do this, you start being forced to classify people in different ways, because the question that naturally arises within any kinship system is: "Okay, so you're related to this distant founding ancestor, but precisely how? Are you descended perhaps from the youngest daughter of that ancient ancestor, or are you descended from the eldest son of that ancient ancestor?"

These sorts of questions can become very important in a world that thinks of all social relations in terms of kinship. And so what very often happens is that in such an environment, you start developing aristocracies. These are people whose lineage is higher. They are descended from the senior lines, of the senior lines, of the senior lines, and can trace their way all the way back to the senior lines of the founding father. So, this is one of the mechanisms that can create a sense of aristocracy. And very often, in large communities, those who can trace their descent directly to these founding ancestors through senior lines will claim the deference due in a small family to seniority.

So, high birth can begin to provide a seemingly natural basis for authority. One of the archaeological pieces of evidence for this, or for the importance of ancestry, may be something we've seen already, and that's the decoration of ancestral skulls, which was done so carefully even in Natufian communities. And it suggests how important lineage was even in the very earliest agrarian communities.

There is one more question about who becomes a leader: the question of power and gender. Why, in leadership systems over and over again, do males appear disproportionately, in disproportionate numbers, in these institutionalized power structures? Males dominated leadership roles in most early Agrarian communities, laying the foundations for the asymmetrical power relations that are often described as "patriarchy."

What are the sources of patriarchy? Clearly it's not because women are incapable of exercising power. I say this as someone who grew up in a country with a queen who's been in office now for over 50 years, which was revolutionized in the 1980s under a female prime minister, Margaret Thatcher, probably one of the most powerful ruling figures in modern British history. So, clearly we must look for other reasons.

A lot of research has been conducted into this issue in the last few decades, and as yet there's not a perfect consensus, but here are some possible explanations. One takes us back to the demographic rules of agrarian societies and the fact that they were very different from those of foraging societies. This is something we've seen already. In foraging societies there often seem to have been systematic attempts to limit populations—and there's a very good reason for this. You, in a nomadic community, you simply cannot carry people who can't carry themselves. And also foraging communities, certainly modern foraging communities, are very often very sensitive to the carrying capacity of their environment. So, we've seen that foraging communities seem often to have deliberately limited populations. But once they settle down, once they become farmers, the rules change—and they change radically.

In most of the agrarian societies we know of—so it's a reasonable bet that this applied also to earlier agrarian societies—one of the crucial rules for the success of an individual household was: Have as many children as you possibly can. Now, one of the reasons for this is that one of the few factors of production (to use an economist's term) that most households could control was labor. They often couldn't control exactly how much land they had, or cash they had, or capital; labor was the one they could control. And maximizing the amount of labor available on your farm may enhance your wealth, but it may also provide protection in old age. So, having lots of children seems to have been a crucial rule in most peasant societies.

But what did this mean for women? What it meant for women is that throughout their reproductive years they were tied largely to their roles as reproducers and as child rearers. Consequently, men, who weren't tied nearly as closely to these roles, found it much easier to take on specialist roles as societies became more complex, as the division of labor emerged— and, particularly, as power roles began to emerge.

So, this may explain the initial imbalance in power roles, but then something else takes over, the symbolism and mythology of power. Once power roles emerge, and you find that most of the people who occupy them are male, this can very easily generate the presumption that males were natural leaders. So, I think that this may be the source of the sort of mythology of patriarchy, the idea that males are natural leaders. Even if in most households power relations in practice were probably quite variable.

Okay. Now, let's try and look at some small-scale forms of power, the kind of embryonic forms of power that probably emerged in the early Agrarian era. And here we rely largely on modern anthropological studies. They offer some very helpful models of how simple forms of power may have emerged. And I'm going to focus on two of these models. Let me say immediately that these models *are* models. They are sort of tools to thinking rather than necessarily terribly precise descriptions of what actually happened. Because, the truth is, we don't really know. So, we have to use these models.

The first is the "big man," and the second is the "chief." So, let's look at the idea of the big man. And the big man was, as far as we know, invariably a man. In a classic 1955 study, Douglas Oliver described the "big men," or the *mumis*, m-u-m-i-s, of the Solomon Islands east of Papua New Guinea. Ambitious young men would go around to their relatives and friends collecting food. Then they would throw a huge feast. Now, the feast might include pigs, it might include coconut pies, it might include sago puddings for local men. So, they throw this huge feast. At the end of the feast they're broke; I mean, everything they've collected has gone. So, at first sight it's hard to see what they gain out of this.

Those whose feasts were judged impressive enough, however, could acquire enough of a following to become *mumis*. So, what they gain out of this is prestige, and they also gain debts, as it were, that they can cash in later on. So, though they may end up impoverished as a result of collecting all of this stuff and then giving it away again—a widely used term for this process, incidentally, is "potlatch," from similar practices on the northwest coast of North America—the result of giving away this stuff is that you create potential followers; they owe you something. And you can cash in these debts sometime in the future. This is very like modern so-called "pork-barrel" politics. Gift-giving is a form of political investment.

So, here's a very early form of power that we can describe as a form of power from below. You've bought powerful allies by giving them gifts. Now, this form of power could be turned quite rapidly into a rather coercive form of power. *Mumis* could become powerful war leaders. One old man in Oliver's study remembered that, and I quote:

> In the olden times there were greater *mumis* than there are today. Then they were fierce and relentless war leaders. They laid waste to the countryside and their clubhouses were lined with the skulls of people they had slain.

So, this business of giving away stuff to recruit followers was very, very serious politics, and it could lead quite quickly to quite coercive politics. So, the move from power from below to coercive power could be very swift indeed. Still, in this sort of world, the power to coerce rested mainly on the ability to line up loyal followers.

As Marvin Harris writes, in the passage from which I have taken these quotations: "Without warfare, the potential for control inherent in the egg of redistribution would never have hatched." And, of course, the leader—to retain their power—has to keep finding goods and handing them out. So, this is a fairly precarious form of power.

Now let's look at the second model of power, the chief. And again, let me just stress that this is a model. In fact, it's so schematic in some ways that these are labels that many anthropologists are uncomfortable about using. So, I just need to remind you that these are sort of tools for thinking about how power may have worked, rather than anything more specific.

The concept of "chiefs" is often used to refer to leaders that normally rule over other leaders. So, here we have two or three levels of power. They may have little direct contact with most of their "subjects." Their power is often based on high lineage and birth. Very often, chiefs acquire a leadership role because of aristocratic birth. The Polish anthropologist Bronislaw Malinowski, who did very important work in the early 20th century in Melanesia, once describes witnessing how, and I quote:

> [How] all the people present in the village of Bwoytalu [in the Trobriand Islands] drop from their verandas as if blown down by a hurricane at the sound of a long, drawn-out cry announcing the arrival of an important chief.

Unlike the *mumis*, whose relationship with their followers is quite personal, the chief is a more remote figure—in fact, much more god-like. Chiefs in the Trobriand Islands ruled many thousands of people, they wore special shell ornaments to show their status, and others were forbidden to even stand so that their heads were higher than that of the chief. So, these are figures that are almost god-like.

Archaeologists suspect the presence of chiefs when they find large structures such as pyramids or earthen mounds, which required control over not just single villages, but over hundreds or thousands of workers. And at their most powerful, chiefs can wield very considerable power, indeed.

A French explorer, Le Page du Pratz, lived briefly among the Natchez tribes of the Mississippi in 1720. And in the words of the prehistorian Brian Fagan:

> He found himself in a rigidly stratified society—divided into nobles and commoners and headed by a chieftain known as the Great Sun—whose members lived in a village of nine houses and a temple built on the summit of an earthen mound.

Pratz witnessed the funeral of the Great Sun. His wives, relatives, and servants were drugged and then clubbed to accompany him in death. So, as Fagan points out, this is a unique description, because very soon these societies would be destroyed by the arrival of European diseases.

Okay, in summary: We've seen that institutionalized power must begin with power from below. We've seen how significant forms of power could be built largely on support from below. But how is it possible to take the next step—to build forms of power that are much more institutionalized, much more bureaucratized, much less dependent on sort of constant personal negotiation between the ruler and their followers? How do you get, in short, to the level of tribute-taking states, which will introduce the next mini-threshold, the "era of agrarian civilizations"?

Thank you.

From Villages to Cities
Lecture 29

The appearance of Agrarian civilizations, from about 5,000 years ago, marks an important subordinate threshold in this course.

With Agrarian civilizations we get, for the first time, cities, states, and ... writing! This means that for the first time we have written evidence, precise dates, and even some names. In short, we enter the realm of what many historians might regard as "real history." Suddenly, we have a mass of information and ideas. This creates new problems. Whereas in discussing biology or geology there was a broad consensus about the main ideas, historians debate endlessly about the main lines of historical development, so there is more room for controversy here than in any earlier part of this course. From now on, our main challenge will be to avoid getting too caught up in the details or the controversies of historians and try to keep our eye on the overall shape of human historical development.

Lectures Twenty-Nine through Thirty-Seven survey the 5,000 years or so during which "Agrarian civilizations" dominated the history of most people on Earth. This is the largest single group of lectures in this course. This lecture defines Agrarian civilizations and offers a brief chronology of their initial appearance. Then we turn to Mesopotamia, located in modern Iraq, to describe how increasing productivity created the foundations for some of the earliest Agrarian civilizations.

The term "civilization" can be used in many different ways, so I need to explain that I use it neutrally, as a label for a particular type of human community. I do not use it to imply any value judgments about these communities. However, I will argue that Agrarian civilizations were more complex than all earlier human societies. Agrarian civilizations had distinctive characteristics.

- They had large, networked communities of many millions of people.

- These communities contained cities and tribute-taking states with bureaucracies and armies.

- Most of their resources came from agriculture, and most of their inhabitants (often as many as 90%) were small-holding peasants living in villages.

Like agriculture, Agrarian civilizations evolved independently in different parts of the world. But because they depended so much on agriculture, they appeared in regions where agriculture was well established.

- Just over 5,000 years ago, the first Agrarian civilizations appeared in Mesopotamia and Northeast Africa/Egypt.

- About 4,500 years ago, the first Agrarian civilizations appeared in North India/Pakistan.

- Just over 4,000 years ago, the first Agrarian civilizations appeared in northern China.

- About 2,500 years ago, the first Agrarian civilizations appeared in Southeast Asia, sub-Saharan Africa, around the Mediterranean, and also in a new world zone, the Americas.

- During the last 1,500 years, states appeared by diffusion in one or two islands of the Pacific zone, but none were large enough to count as fully developed Agrarian civilizations.

The emergence of Agrarian civilizations was driven mainly by increasingly productive technologies that generated more resources and larger populations. Two clusters of innovation were particularly important in Afro-Eurasia: the "secondary products revolution" and irrigation. Archaeologist Andrew Sherratt (1946–2006) identified a cluster of innovations he called the "secondary products revolution." When first domesticated, animals were used mainly for their meat and hides, which meant you had to slaughter them to make use of them. From about 5,000 years ago, new methods of exploitation evolved over a wide area reaching from Northwest Africa to the

Eurasian steppes. These made it possible to exploit animals throughout their lifetime by using their "secondary products," or resources they generated while alive. These techniques included the use of milk for food and wool for cloth-making. They also included exploitation of the draft power of large animals for riding and transportation or for pulling plows. Oxen or horses can deliver up to four times as much power as human beings, so this change counted as an energy revolution. Animal power allowed farmers to plow soils more deeply and to farm soils with tougher surfaces. It also revolutionized transportation in both commerce and warfare. In arid steppe regions, these innovations laid the foundations for pastoralist communities, which were largely nomadic, relying primarily on the exploitation of domestic animals that they grazed by traveling to different sites through the year. Pastoral nomadism would create new types of communities, which because of their mobility and military skills would play a vital role in the history of Afro-Eurasia.

As we have seen, some of the earliest farming communities appeared in the Fertile Crescent, around the edges of Mesopotamia.

A second group of innovations was linked to irrigation. Irrigation means artificially introducing water to regions with limited natural rainfall but fertile soils and plenty of sunlight. Such regions can often be found in arid lands with alluvial plains (regions that are regularly flooded by large rivers). Mesopotamia, the land within the loop of the Fertile Crescent, was such a region. Literally, "Mesopotamia" means "land between the rivers," the rivers being the Tigris and Euphrates. Most of it is within modern Iraq.

Archaeologists have lavished much attention on Mesopotamia, so here better than anywhere else, we can see how increasingly productive technologies prepared the way for the first Agrarian civilizations. As we have seen, some of the earliest farming communities appeared in the Fertile Crescent, around the edges of Mesopotamia.

By 9,000 years ago, some farming communities were starting to settle the arid plains of Mesopotamia itself, but only in better-watered regions. As they pushed into the arid lowlands, they developed simple forms of irrigation.

By 8,000 years ago, there were many villages of irrigation farmers settled along the major rivers north of modern Baghdad. Some were beginning to build substantial canal systems.

By 7,000 years ago, villages were multiplying, particularly along the Euphrates to the south of modern Baghdad, in the lands of what would later be known as "Sumer." Villages of the Ubaid culture often appear in small clusters near small towns with up to 4,000 people. They dug canals sometimes several kilometers long, grew barley and dates, and kept cattle and sheep. They also fished and caught water birds.

Rising productivity encouraged population growth and the emergence of larger towns that provided markets and other services to surrounding villages. Some, such as Eridu, contained large temples from perhaps as early as 6,000 years ago.

As populations increased, trading systems began to link entire regions into networks of trade. Catal Huyuk, in Turkey (see Lecture Twenty-Six), owed its wealth to the trade in obsidian, a volcanic glass that is extremely hard and can be used to make sharp and durable blades. Obsidian from Catal Huyuk and other sites was traded over many hundreds of miles. Other trade goods in early Agrarian Mesopotamia included shells, precious stones such as turquoise, and eventually pottery. By 8,000 years ago, the spread of distinctive forms of pottery such as Halafian ware and the presence of other goods such as obsidian, traded over hundreds of miles, shows that significant exchange networks were evolving between the multiplying villages of Mesopotamia.

The multiplication of villages, the appearance of an increasing number of larger towns, and the development of extensive trade networks had created the largest concentrations of people and resources and the most active systems of regional exchanges ever known. Now we're ready to describe the appearance of the first Agrarian civilizations in ancient Sumer. ■

Essential Reading

Bentley and Ziegler, *Traditions and Encounters*, chap. 2.

Brown, *Big History*, chap. 6.

Christian, *Maps of Time*, chap. 9.

Supplementary Reading

Nissen, *The Early History of the Ancient Near East*.

Ristvet, *In the Beginning*, chap. 4.

Trigger, *Early Civilizations*.

Questions to Consider

1. What features distinguish "Agrarian civilizations" from the communities of the early Agrarian era?

2. Why did the size of the largest human communities grow significantly in the early Agrarian era?

From Villages to Cities
Lecture 29—Transcript

We've traveled a long distance in this course, and we've accomplished a lot. Let me just remind you of some of the things we've done. In just 28 lectures, we've created a Universe. We've created stars. We've allowed the stars to create chemical elements. Using those chemical elements, we've created entire solar systems, including our Earth. We've created life. We've created human beings, and we've allowed those human beings to develop agriculture, a much more productive technology than the earlier technologies they used.

So now what we're going to do is to set up the appearance of the large exotic communities known as "agrarian civilizations." These have been one of the central subjects investigated by historians, and we'll find that a lot of things change once we cross this mini-threshold with the appearance of agrarian civilizations.

The previous group of lectures described the origins of agriculture, some features of the earliest agrarian societies, and we looked at the emergence of simple forms of power and hierarchy. We looked at how power slowly built up as populations built up and as agriculture spread. And we've seen how during the early Agrarian era—as populations rose—larger, denser, and eventually more complex communities began to appear. And as they got more complex they began to need power structures, and at the same time the resources for leaders began to build up—so the possibilities for larger forms of power began to expand.

And eventually, this buildup in types of power and in the scale of power led to the crossing of what I've called a new "mini-threshold," and that's associated with the appearance of the first tribute-taking states and the first agrarian civilizations. And that mini-threshold, we saw, was crossed about 5,000 years ago. Crossing this threshold takes us into the second major subdivision of the Agrarian era. And I'm going to call that the "era of agrarian civilizations," or sometimes I'll call it the "later Agrarian" era; those two terms are more or less interchangeable.

What we'll see in the era of agrarian civilizations are remarkable new forms of social, technological, and cultural complexity. These, if you like, are the new emergent properties associated with this new level of complexity, associated with agrarian civilizations. But there's one more distinctive feature of this threshold. This is the era in which writing and written documents appear for the first time in human history—so that for the first time in this course, we can look at the past using written documents. At last, we enter what many historians may be tempted to call the domain of "real history."

And a lot does indeed change, as we enter the last 5,000 years of human history. This is the era of human history on which professional historians have lavished by far the most attention, precisely because written records are available. So at last, for this period, we have masses of scholarship, and we have masses of information. In fact, suddenly you'll have been aware of this, that for a long time we've asked questions for which there was very, very slender data. We had to work really hard to scrabble around and find data to answer some of the big questions. Now, suddenly, the situation is very different. We're drowning in information. So for earlier periods, we had to really work hard for our data. Now, increasingly, the problem is going to be rather different. We're going to have to find a way—if we're going to maintain the big history perspective—we're going to have to find a way to navigate through a sort of blizzard of information.

In this course, I want to alert you to the strategies we're going to adopt to do that. We're going to try to capture the main lines of development of human society throughout the world. And that will mean letting go of many of the details of that history—and trying to see human history at large scales, trying to see the very large shapes. This is like the ant trying to see the whole elephant rather than just the wrinkles. So we're trying to see the very large patterns, without getting too bogged down in the details. Now, that is not always easy.

And I want to alert you to one more change that occurs at this point. You'll understand that there is a huge amount of room for debate over the interpretation of some of the large trends in human history. And this is particularly because, for the most part, historians have tended not to look at the past on very large scales.

So before we go any further, I must alert you to the fact that here, more than in most earlier parts of this course, I've often had to try to distill a clear story from scholarship that allows plenty of wriggle room for debate. In the parts of the course dealing with the sciences, I could often summarize a consensus position. There was almost universal agreement among the scientists, and I could just summarize that position. Within the discipline of history, by and large, there is—for the most part—much less consensus, particularly about the very large patterns. So, much of the rest of this course counts as a slightly more tentative attempt to identify, among the massive information, the very large patterns and the main lines of development. So, there's more room for controversy here than in any earlier part of this course.

Okay. That's a way of introducing some of the changes we're going to encounter as we cross this divide into the era of agrarian civilizations, about 5,000 years ago.

Lectures Twenty-Nine to Thirty-Seven, the next group of lectures, survey the 5,000 years or so during which agrarian civilizations dominated the history of most people on Earth. This is the largest single group of lectures in this course—and it has to be admitted that we lavish so much attention on it, in part, simply because we do have more information than for earlier eras.

Now, let me be clear about definitions, particularly about this phrase I've used, "agrarian civilizations." I've already defined tribute-taking states, which are one of the central components of agrarian civilizations. But I need to be clear how I'm using this phrase "agrarian civilizations." What were agrarian civilizations?

In this lecture, I'll offer a careful definition of agrarian civilizations. Then, I'm going to offer a brief chronology of the appearance of the first agrarian civilizations. And we'll see that, like agriculture, agrarian civilizations appeared quite independently in several different parts of the world. It's an odd phenomenon, but it's not quite as odd as the independent appearance of agriculture—because, as we've seen, there is clearly a close link between the appearance of agriculture and the eventual appearance of agrarian civilizations. So if we've solved the problem of agriculture to some extent, we've solved the problem of the independent appearance of agrarian civilizations. Agriculture, as it were, lit a fuse that ignited agrarian civilizations several millennia later.

Now, after a brief chronology, I want to turn to one particular region, to Mesopotamia, in modern Iraq. This is the region in which the first agrarian civilizations appeared, and we'll describe how increasing productivity in the lands of modern Iraq created the foundations for the first agrarian civilizations, which emerged about 5,000 years ago.

Okay. Definitions. Let's clarify what we mean by "agrarian civilizations." "Agrarian civilization" is a label that can be used in distinct ways, so I need to be very clear about how we're using the phrase in this course. I'll use the term "agrarian civilization" to refer to the large communities that emerged around the first tribute-taking states. "Agrarian civilization" is, therefore, a broader term than "state," or even "tribute-taking state." Tribute-taking states are merely one component of agrarian civilizations.

Now, the word "civilization" itself is slippery. In the 19th century, it was often taken for granted that when you said "civilization" you were referring to a type of society that was distinctly superior to most of the smaller-scale societies that existed at their edges. So I need to be clear straightaway that I'm not using the word "civilization" in a judgmental sense. It does not imply superiority or inferiority. I'm simply using it to refer to a very specific type of human community. I imply no value judgments. However, I will make some judgments about degrees of complexity. Though, as we've seen already, there's nothing intrinsically good about complexity, or bad. Complexity is just complexity.

So, by "agrarian civilizations," I mean, first, large human communities of many hundreds of thousands and maybe many millions of people. That's the first distinguishing feature. They were huge. They were huge compared with the two other main types of human communities that we've looked at so far—the first being the kinship groups of the Paleolithic, the small family-sized nomadic groups that dominated in the Paleolithic era, and the second being the village communities, several hundred people, maybe a thousand or two, living together more or less permanently, that dominated the early Agrarian era. So, agrarian civilizations are a new type of community, and they are vast. They include millions of people.

The second feature, main feature: Most of their resources came from agriculture, and that meant that most of their inhabitants were small farmers or peasants. Agrarian civilizations were founded firmly on the technological breakthroughs associated with agriculture and on the ability of agriculture to extract more resources from the environment and, therefore, to support larger and denser communities. So what this means is that most of the people in agrarian civilizations were peasants, and most of the resources that sustained agrarian civilizations were generated by peasant households.

So we need to remind ourselves—if you do a sort of quick association test, and you think of civilization, I'm betting you'll start thinking of grand monuments, of pyramids, of palaces, and so on. We need to remind ourselves that despite these great monuments, this was really a world of peasants. In fact, there's a sort of very rough rule of thumb when thinking about agrarian civilizations, and it's this. Given the levels of productivity of most pre-modern forms of agriculture, it normally took, roughly speaking—and this is just a rule of thumb—nine peasants to support one city dweller. So what this implies, I hope, is obvious. In most regions of agrarian civilizations, we're talking about a world in which perhaps 90% of the population were peasants or small farmers.

So that's the second crucial ingredient of agrarian civilizations. First, they're huge; secondly, they're based on agriculture, and that means most of their population were peasants. And that means that throughout this era, most people lived as peasants. If you and I were to be transported randomly into the era of agrarian civilizations, randomly put somewhere in that society, the odds are that we'd be peasants.

Third, agrarian civilizations also contained cities and tribute-taking states. They're all shaped by the presence of institutionalized power on large scales, in the form of tribute-taking states. And they were also shaped by the presence within them of these demographic hot spots that we call "cities."

Okay. So those are three very general features. Later on, we're going to look at some other important emergent properties that arise once agrarian civilization appears.

Now, world history courses often focus on the differences between different agrarian civilizations. Eventually, we're going to do the same thing. We're going to look at some of these critical differences that are shaped by geography, by cultural traditions, and so on. But initially we're going to focus on some of the remarkable similarities between them. Indeed, the notion of agrarian civilizations is useful precisely because all agrarian civilizations shared a remarkable amount of common features. They seem to contain the same basic components. So from the wider perspective of big history, what stands out about this era is not so much the variations between distinct civilizations—the variations, say, between Chinese civilization and Muslim civilization—as the idea of agrarian civilization as a distinctive type of community, a distinctive phenomenon within human history.

Okay. We've seen that their major components are peasants and peasant farms, whose work supports cities, states, and the various institutions associated with them—from organized armies to literate bureaucracies and organized markets. It's the fact that all these components seem to appear together that encourages us to think of these as a single type of human community.

Now, let's talk in very general terms about chronology. When did the first agrarian civilizations appear? Here's a very broad, global chronology of the appearance of the first agrarian civilizations. Like agriculture, as we've seen, agrarian civilizations evolved differently in different parts of the world, but because they depended so much on agriculture, you could more or less predict where they were going to appear. They appeared precisely in those regions where agriculture was well established.

Let's begin 5,000 years ago—roughly speaking, 5,000 years ago. The first agrarian civilizations appeared about 5,000 years ago in Mesopotamia, in the southern part of modern Iraq. The largest city today is probably Basra in this area. But also, they appeared along the Nile. Agrarian civilizations appear in both these two zones at about the same time.

About 500 years later—that's to say about 4,500 years ago—the first agrarian civilizations appeared in the northern parts of the Indian subcontinent, along the Indus River, in what is today Pakistan. That's the second area. And in that area, almost certainly, there were some contacts with Mesopotamia— so there may have been an element of diffusion here. How independent the appearance of civilization was in the Indus Valley region is still not absolutely certain.

We move forward another 500 years. About 4,000 years ago, we get the first evidence of agrarian civilizations appearing in northern China, along the Yellow River. Then about 2,500 years ago, the first agrarian civilizations appeared in Southeast Asia, sub-Saharan Africa, around the Mediterranean, and also for the first time in a second world zone, the Americas. And they appear in Mesoamerica and also in the Andes region during the 1st millennium B.C.E.—that is to say, about 2,500 years ago.

And here's a final date: During the last 1,500 years, states appeared in one or two regions of the Pacific Zone—in regions such as Hawaii. This, you'll remember, is the third of our four world zones. But the communities that appeared in these regions were probably too small to count as fully developed agrarian civilizations. So you can decide whether you want to call them "agrarian civilizations" or not.

Now, if you follow this chronology on a map and you can remember the chronology of the spread of agriculture, you'll see straightaway that the map of early state formation matches the map of agrarian origins, because it was agriculture that generated the raw materials for civilizations, just as clouds— solar nebulae—generated the raw material for stars.

Now what I want to do is turn to one particular region and try and see if we can pan in on this process of agrarian civilization appearing—and that region is Mesopotamia. I want to see if we can trace some of the processes that led to the appearance of agrarian civilization in that one region. Now here, as elsewhere, the emergence of agrarian civilizations depends on this buildup of agrarian resources. In other words, it depends on the process by which agriculture generates larger and larger populations, denser populations, more communities, and it depends on improvements in the technology and productivity of agriculture.

In Mesopotamia, and also in several other parts of Afro-Eurasia in which agrarian civilizations would emerge, two large clusters of innovations would play a particularly important role. They would stimulate agriculture, and they would boost this process of increasing populations and increasing the resources available in society. And these processes are, these innovations are, the "secondary products revolution" and irrigation. So I'm going to talk about each of these innovations.

We saw earlier that agriculture began with fairly simple technologies, but slowly, slowly, those technologies were tweaked and improved as people moved to different areas. And these two innovations can count as large-scale examples of this process of slow, continuous improvement in the technology of agriculture.

Let's begin with the secondary products revolution. The idea is associated with the work of an archaeologist, Andrew Sherratt, who died in 2006. Andrew Sherratt identified a cluster of innovations that he called the "secondary products revolution." Let me explain what he meant by this. Sherratt pointed out that when they were first domesticated, animals were used mainly for their meat and hides. What this meant was you had to slaughter them in order to exploit them. And that meant that early farmers who had domesticated animals were keeping these animals, more or less, simply keeping them in reserve until they were slaughtered. So they were protecting them, they were putting work into protecting them, they were feeding them, and they were looking after them—sometimes for many years until they slaughtered them—without getting much benefit from them. Now, that may be great for the animal, but from a modern economist's point of view, this is just not very efficient.

What Sherratt points out is that from about 5,000 or 6,000 years ago, throughout quite an area—from Mesopotamia into parts of the Eurasian steppes, the borderlands between modern Russia and Europe, for example—a whole series of new technologies appear. And they have this common feature that they all allow you to exploit animals while they're still alive. They allow you to exploit the animals' "secondary products"—those are products that you can use without killing the animal.

Now, here are some of the secondary products that could be used by these techniques. They include the use of milk for food. Milking is, we take it for granted, but it's actually a reasonably sophisticated technology, and humans couldn't really use milk until they developed ways of digesting it. Sometimes this involved genetic changes. It's clear that some communities that use milk a lot, they use dairy products a lot, have undergone minor genetic changes that allow them to process milk throughout their life rather than just in childhood, which is normal. But milking itself as a technology is quite complicated. So this emerges, the earliest evidence is it's about 5,000 or 6,000 years old.

And a second secondary product is wool for cloth-making—using the fibers of sheep, camels, and other large domestic mammals for cloth-making— for making clothes, for making shoes, and eventually for making tents, for making carpets.

So, milk and wool. But a third whole group of secondary products includes energy. Remember, we're talking about large mammals here. We're talking about horses, camels, oxen, and slightly smaller organisms such as goats, but it's the large ones that are crucial here. People learned to use their energy. This is very important. It's immensely important because it constitutes, in effect, a sort of energy revolution that took place towards the end of the early Agrarian era. An ox or a horse can deliver up to four times as much power as a human being, so if you can harness that power you suddenly have access to a lot more energy than before.

What did they use this energy for? Well, animal power allowed farmers to plow soils more deeply. If you have an ox or a horse pulling a plow, you can cut much deeper into soils, and you can cut your way through really tough soils. And what this meant is that you can turn over the soils more deeply and, also, you can bring into cultivation areas that simply couldn't be cultivated using traditional hoes or digging sticks of some kind. So plow agriculture greatly expanded the area that could be brought into cultivation and generally probably increased the productivity of agriculture. Using horses, camels, and oxen for their traction power also revolutionized transportation in both commerce and warfare.

In arid steppe regions, these innovations were of really revolutionary importance because they laid the foundations for pastoral nomadism. These are communities that rely almost entirely on domesticated animals, rather than domesticated plants. And they tend to be nomadic, because one of the most efficient ways of using these domesticated animals is to let them graze over a wide area, and to do that you have to travel with them.

It's often been supposed that pastoral nomadism developed in parallel with agriculture and at the same time. But evidence that has accumulated in recent decades makes it very clear that this is not true. Pastoral nomadism evolved later, as farmers in regions well-adapted to grazing but less well-adapted to crop growing began to introduce the new technologies of the secondary products revolution. It became possible to extract more resources, more energy, to get more value out of domesticated livestock. And eventually, this made it possible to build an entire lifeway around the exploitation of domesticated livestock. And it seems that what happened is livestock farmers in sort of marginal farming lands—perhaps on the border between modern Russia and Kazakhstan—began grazing their animals over large areas, developing larger herds, and eventually becoming more or less nomadic. And think what this means: Humans can't digest grass, but these domesticated animals can. So suddenly, you have a technology that allows you to extract the energy in the grass, in the great steppe lands of Eurasia and all the way down into the savannah lands of East Africa.

So pastoral nomadism opens up vast new terrain for exploitation—and we can detect the presence of pastoral nomads in the Eurasian steppes in part by the appearance of burial mounds (or kurgans). You don't find villages; what you find is burial mounds. And the earliest clear evidence of pastoral nomadism comes from the steppes on the border between Russia and Kazakhstan and dates to about 5,000 to 6,000 years ago.

Okay. This innovation would lay the basics, eventually, for the great pastoral nomadic empires, such as those of Genghis Khan. Now, I've spent too much time on pastoral nomadism because it fascinates me so much. So, let's talk briefly about irrigation. It's simpler to understand. This is the second great group of innovations.

Irrigation means artificially introducing water to regions with limited natural rainfall but fertile soils and plenty of sunlight. You find such regions particularly in hot climates, arid climates with alluvial plains—that is to say, regions that are regularly flooded by large rivers that bring fertile silts down with them—and Mesopotamia is such a region. In fact, literally, "Mesopotamia" means the "land between the rivers," the rivers being the Tigris and Euphrates.

So irrigation, once it's introduced, can have a huge impact on populations. Suddenly—you have these fertile soils, but no water to farm with—now, if you introduce irrigation, suddenly you can farm them, and you can get huge yields and sudden increases in population. And that's why irrigation has been crucial to the emergence of agrarian civilizations.

Now, how did these innovations prepare the way for the evolution of agrarian civilization in Mesopotamia? Archaeologists have lavished a lot of attention on Mesopotamia—so here we can track this process, probably more clearly than anywhere else. We saw that the first farming communities appeared in the Fertile Crescent, a ring of highland around Mesopotamia, around the edges of Mesopotamia. And here, they could use rainfall. There was enough rainfall for simple forms of farming—but eventually some of them began to migrate down into the arid lowlands.

By 9,000 years ago, you have some farming communities already beginning to descend through the highlands of the Zagros Mountains, east of modern Iraq, and settling the arid plains—but as yet, only in regions where there's enough water for crops. Then they begin to push further into the arid lands, and some begin to develop very simple forms of irrigation.

By 8,000 years ago, there were many villages of irrigation farmers settled along the major rivers and tributaries north of modern Baghdad. Some of them are already beginning to build substantial canal systems, but they still rely largely on seminatural forms of irrigation.

The site of Choga Mami, to the east of modern Baghdad, is a good illustration of this. The village lies between two tributaries, so that you could divert water to flood the fields and then drain it away again. And the village may have had 1,000 people living in it.

And then things began to speed up. By 7,000 years ago, villages are multiplying, particularly along the Euphrates and even in the lands to the south of Baghdad, in the lands of what would later be known as "Sumer." Villages of the so-called Ubaid culture appear, sometimes in small clusters near larger settlements, some of which have as many as 4,000 people, and we can think of as small towns.

They dug canals, sometimes several kilometers long. They grew barley and dates, and they kept cattle and sheep. They also fished and caught water birds. As the archaeologist Brian Fagan points out, these settlements must have depended on organized, communal efforts. There must have been quite a lot of politics going on and quite a lot of leadership. You needed to get raw materials to build houses from the plentiful supplies of sand, clay, palm trees, and reeds between the rivers. But digging even tiny canals required a lot of effort. The backbreaking task of clearing silk from clogged rivers was hard work and took a lot of organization.

We see larger communities appearing, more elaborate irrigation, more organization. And eventually, rising productivity is going to encourage population growth and the emergence of more and more of these medium-sized towns. As population increases throughout Mesopotamia, particularly in the arid lands watered by the Tigris and Euphrates, you start finding more integration between these towns and communities. We find trade goods being moved over large areas. Obsidian from Çatal Hüyük in southern Turkey appears throughout much of Mesopotamia. You also find that clay pottery types of particular kinds, such as Halafian ware, appear over very large areas, traded over 600 miles or more.

All of these processes mesh together. Populations are growing, they're becoming more interdependent. The technologies are becoming more productive. It's all of these processes together that will eventually lay the foundation for the quite rapid appearance in Sumer towards the end of the 4th millennium B.C.E., just over 5,000 years ago, of the first agrarian civilizations. We'll discuss that in the next lecture.

Thank you.

Sumer—The First Agrarian Civilization
Lecture 30

And one more detail that actually strikes a very modern ring. Around the edge of these cities, archaeologists have found evidence of sort of shantytowns—as immigrants from the countryside tried to make a living, often without great success, in the big cities.

How did the buildup of human and material resources described in the last lecture generate the first tribute-taking states, the first Agrarian civilizations, and the first real cities? All these developments occurred, with surprising suddenness, just before 3000 B.C.E., in Sumer, at the southern edge of Mesopotamia. As with earlier thresholds, many different components were suddenly arranged into something new. Before we go further, we need to clarify dating systems. For several lectures, I have given dates as archaeologists do, in years "BP" or "before present." However, historical scholarship is dominated by a different convention, derived ultimately from the Christian calendar, and from now on we will shift conventions, giving dates in years "B.C.E." (before the Common Era) or "C.E." (Common Era). This system is essentially identical to the older convention of dates "B.C." (before Christ) and "A.D." (*anno domini*) but reflects a (not entirely successful) attempt to be less culturally specific. For better or worse, the convention now dominates scholarship in world history. To get from dates "BP" to dates "B.C.E." or "C.E.," you deduct 2,000 years. So 4000 B.C.E. is the same as 6000 BP. That's where we start, somewhere near modern Basra.

In 4000 B.C.E., Sumer was a swampy backwater. However, lively trade networks traversed the region, and its rich soils attracted increasing numbers of immigrants. Between 4000 and 3000 B.C.E., climates became drier. This made it easier to farm the land as swamps began to dry out, but eventually it forced more and more people to settle in the region's rapidly growing towns. These towns controlled increasingly scarce water supplies through large irrigation systems. In the centuries before 3000 B.C.E., 10–20 powerful cities appeared quite suddenly. They included Ur (Abraham's home city, according to biblical tradition), Uruk, Nippur, Lagash, and Eridu. By 3000 B.C.E., Uruk may have had 20,000 to 50,000 inhabitants. They lived in whitewashed mud-brick houses along narrow streets. At the center, on an artificial mound 12 meters high, stood the "White Temple," dedicated to the goddess Inanna, a goddess of both love and war. Around the main part of the city was a massive wall, more than 7 meters tall in some places. The *Epic of Gilgamesh*, the world's oldest recorded epic, includes a description of Uruk, which though written down only around 1200 B.C.E., may capture something of the city's appearance in the reign of King Gilgamesh, at about 2750 B.C.E. Modern archaeology also allows us to imagine what life in ancient Uruk may have been like. We have an ancient map of nearby Nippur dating from about 1500 B.C.E. The map shows the city's walls, gardens, and canals, as well as a large temple complex.

Indeed, in Sumer, the earliest rulers may have been priests of some kind, as many of the earliest large buildings seem to have been temples rather than palaces.

Sumer's first cities were the densest and most complex communities that had ever existed. Uruk's 20,000 to 50,000 people lived in just 2.5 square kilometers, an area that would barely have supported a single individual using the foraging technologies of the Paleolithic era. Unlike foraging communities or the villages of the early Agrarian era, cities were not self-sufficient, as many of their inhabitants were not farmers. So cities had to control nearby "hinterlands" of peasant villages. They also traded along Mesopotamia's great rivers and across the seas.

Now we discuss some of the distinctive "emergent" properties of the earliest Agrarian civilizations. Many city dwellers were specialists, dependent on markets for essential supplies. A document from about 2500 B.C.E., the "Standard Professions List," mentions many different professions, including soldiers, farmers, priests, gardeners, cooks, scribes, bakers, coppersmiths, jewelers, snake charmers, and even the profession of king! Markets were also vital because southern Sumer lacked basic materials such as wood. So rulers supported merchants who traded within a "world system" reaching to Egypt, North India, Central Asia, and Anatolia. (A world system is a large region unified by extensive trade networks.)

Cities needed defensive walls and irrigation systems. These could be built and maintained only by powerful rulers capable of organizing huge labor levies. Rulers controlled labor through slavery or "corvée" (forced labor). Forced labor was important because in societies without modern energy supplies human beings were the most easily exploitable stores of energy. (From the point of view of rulers, humans were living, intelligent, "batteries," a perspective that helps explain the pervasiveness of forced labor and slave labor in all Agrarian civilizations.) The discovery of crude, mass-produced beveled-rim bowls in Sumerian cities is evidence that the government provided rations for workers or slaves. To maintain the favor of the gods, it was necessary to build and supply temples. Indeed, in Sumer, the earliest rulers may have been priests of some kind, as many of the earliest large buildings seem to have been temples rather than palaces.

Rulers ruled through literate bureaucracies, powerful taxation systems, and paid armies, features that would reappear in all tribute-taking states. Just as farmers extracted ecological "rents" from their domesticated crops and animals, the rulers of Sumer's city-states collected resources from their subjects. We call these "tributes" because, like modern taxes, they were raised in part through the threat of coercion. New, institutionalized hierarchies emerged, with the wealthy and powerful at the top and slaves and war captives at the bottom.

To keep track of their growing wealth, rulers needed new methods of accounting. These eventually evolved into the first writing systems. At first, accounts were kept using tokens representing objects. Then, marks were cut into clay using wedge-shaped papyrus stalks to represent objects such as sheep or units of grain. The step from accounting to a writing system that can imitate spoken language is associated with the "rebus" principle. The Sumerian symbol for an arrow looked like an arrow. But the word for "life" happened to sound like the word for "arrow" ("*ti*"), so the symbol for arrow could be used for the more abstract idea of "life." By early in the 3rd millennium, such changes meant that writing could record chronicles and even poetry, some of which can still be read today. With such huge resources, rulers could hire paid enforcers or armies. This is the crucial step from "power from below" to "power from above." Much early Sumerian writing describes wars fought by well-organized armies, and a Sumerian mosaic of

2600 B.C.E., known as the *Standard of Ur*, depicts the army of Ur, with its donkey-drawn chariots and large convoys of captives.

Inspiring awe by lavish displays of power was one of the keys to statehood. The royal tombs of Ur, from the late 4th millennium B.C.E., show the spectacular riches rulers could accumulate and the extraordinary expense lavished on tombs, temples, and palaces. As in the royal burials of many early Agrarian civilizations, servants of the ruler were often killed and buried to serve in the afterlife. From late in the 3rd millennium B.C.E., the typical form of monumental architecture in Mesopotamia would become the ziggurat, a stepped pyramid-like temple dedicated to the gods, of which the best preserved today is that of Ur.

Two more significant changes occurred about 1,000 years after the appearance of the first states. Sumer's city-states were united under a single ruler, Sargon, who ruled from c. 2370 to 2316 B.C.E. from a city called Akkad in northern Sumer. This pattern of imperial expansion would recur many times in later Agrarian civilizations. In the centuries after Sargon, Sumer's population crashed, apparently as a result of over-irrigation, which led to salination and undermined the region's fertility. This pattern, too, would recur many times in the history of Agrarian civilizations.

Voilà! A whole series of linked features came together to establish the first tribute-taking city-states in ancient Sumer. In the next lecture we ask: How similar was the process of state formation in other early Agrarian civilizations? ■

Essential Reading

Christian, *Maps of Time*, chap. 9.

Fagan, *People of the Earth*, chap. 15.

Ristvet, *In the Beginning*, chap. 4.

Supplementary Reading

Fernandez-Armesto, *The World*, chap. 3.

Nissen, *The Early History of the Ancient Near East*.

Trigger, *Early Civilizations*.

Questions to Consider

1. What were the most important "emergent properties" of the earliest Agrarian civilizations?

2. What were the crucial preconditions for the appearance of the first tribute-taking states about 5,000 years ago?

Sumer—The First Agrarian Civilization
Lecture 30—Transcript

One of the curious features of big history is that agrarian civilizations seem to arrive so late. I've had colleagues who've been shocked at how late they arrive in my big history course. We're now up to Lecture Thirty, and finally we get to agrarian civilizations. But I do hope that you're getting a sense of how the much wider perspective of big history can help put very familiar subjects in new context. What we're really seeing is how the familiar topics of history, and particularly of world history, are not just givens. The big history perspective forces us to see that very clearly. They, too, have a history—and the history had a history, and the history had a history, and so on. So what we're really doing is setting them in a context consisting of all these multiple scales that we deal with in big history.

In a sense, in a minor way, that's what we've been doing in the last few lectures. Now we look at the appearance of the first agrarian civilizations. And we focus on southern Mesopotamia, where the process has been studied with peculiar thoroughness, which means that we can see the process probably more clearly than anywhere else in the world.

So, how did the buildup of human and material resources that I described in the last lecture generate the first tribute-taking states, the first agrarian civilizations, and the first real cities? All of these developments occurred with surprising suddenness, just before 3000 B.C.E., in the last few centuries before the turn of the millennium, in Sumer, at the southern edge of Mesopotamia. Now, I'm afraid that here we have one more threshold. Many components are suddenly arranged into something new. This is something that happens each time we get a new level of complexity: the first cities, the first tribute-taking states, and the first agrarian civilizations.

We're going to focus on Sumer for the present, but we'll look at other areas in the next lecture. So back to Sumer, although there's just one more bit of business I must deal with before we actually go to Sumer—and that concerns chronology and the labels we use for chronology.

So far it has usually been enough if I give a date to describe dates as before the present, and I've used the archaeologists' terminology of "BP"—"before present." We saw that this is how radiometric dates are conventionally given. Technically it means "before 1950," but that's not going to worry us most of the time. There's a sort of intuitive logic to such dates.

But once we get into an era where we have documents, it makes much more sense to start using a more familiar way of dating events, and that is the convention that used to use the terminology of B.C. and A.D. Now of course, that comes ultimately from the Christian calendar: "B.C." means "before Christ"; "A.D." means "*anno domini*," or "the year of the Lord." And what I'm going to use is a slightly modified terminology: "B.C.E." or "C.E." B.C.E. means "before the Common Era." C.E. means "in the Common Era." The system is essentially identical, of course, to the older system. The only reason for using it—and I'm not making a very strong argument for this—is that it has become the convention in writing on world history, and it is just slightly less tightly tied to the traditions of a particular culture, European Christian culture.

So that's the terminology I'm going to use from now on, dates B.C.E. and C.E. And just remember the simple rule: To convert from dates BP into the system we'll use from now on, you deduct 2,000 years. So 4000 B.C.E. is 6000 BP. Okay? That's more or less where we're going to start.

So let's now imagine ourselves transported to Sumer—southern Mesopotamia, near the Persian Gulf—about 6,000 years ago. So we're in Sumer 6,000 years ago, in 4000 B.C.E., remember. Sumer before this period was a swampy region; it was a delta region. It was the delta of the Tigress and Euphrates. Andrew Sherratt described it as a backwater, as just an area of mud. "People," he writes, "did live there, in grass huts and using clay sickles, but it was not the most lively spot on earth."

However, that would begin to change from about 4000 B.C.E.—and the fact that trade networks passed through the region may have been a crucial part of it. As Andrew Sherratt has argued, the fact that there were abundant trades far to the north and probably in lands to the south meant that this was a region that traders passed through. That may have encouraged the growth of communities in this region—and so did another thing: the fact that beneath those swamps there were very rich soils and eventually the region started to dry out. So climate change plays a crucial role in the story, and as the swamplands of Sumer begin to dry out, this turns into a region that can potentially support large numbers of people—and it begins to attract immigrants.

So during the next 1,000 years—from 4000 to 3000 B.C.E., and again, that's from 6,000 to 5,000 years ago—climates became drier. This made it easier to farm the land as swamplands began to dry out. But eventually, when the drying process went too far, it began to force more and more people to settle in the region's rapidly growing towns—as region after region became not just dry, but positively arid. And so gradually you find that people are forced into towns, into towns that control scarce water supplies and irrigation systems. Now, the other thing that may have forced them into towns may have been conflict over resources as the land dried. So, what the drying did was first attract a lot of immigrants to the south and then force more and more of them into towns that controlled water supplies.

So what the archaeologists see in Sumer between 4000 B.C.E. and 3000 B.C.E. is a very rapid buildup of population—and then, quite suddenly, these populations seem to move out of villages and into a series of towns. Then, 10 to 20 powerful cities appear quite quickly late in the 4th millennium, in the centuries before 3000 B.C.E. They include Ur, Abraham's home city according to biblical tradition—they include Uruk, Nippur, Lagash, and Eridu. Most of these towns, we can still identify them. There are still some remains that can be excavated today.

By 3000 B.C.E., the city of Uruk may have had 20,000 to 50,000 inhabitants. Now, by modern standards, 20,000 to 50,000 inhabitants is not a particularly impressive town. It's a sort of a medium-sized, small to medium-sized town, but remember the context. In 3000 B.C.E., a town of 20,000 to 50,000 inhabitants had to count as one of the densest, largest communities that had ever existed in human history. And probably Uruk or maybe one of its rival cities were almost certainly the largest communities on Earth at the time.

How did people live in Uruk? They lived in whitewashed, mud-brick houses along narrow streets. At the center of Uruk—on a huge, artificial mound 12 meters high, which must have taken a lot of labor to build—stood the so-called "White Temple." This was dedicated to the goddess Inanna, a goddess of both love and war. She has some interesting similarities to the Egyptian goddess Isis and the Hindu goddess Kali. And it's always tempting in these situations to think there may have been some cultural diffusion between these different regions. Inanna is also associated with the planet Venus. Around the main part of the city there was a massive wall, sometimes more than 7 meters tall.

The *Epic of Gilgamesh* is probably the world's oldest recorded epic. And what it describes is the epic adventures of a King of Uruk who probably, if he really existed, reigned from about 2750 B.C.E. The versions we have today were written down only in 1200 B.C.E., but it still may capture something of the city's appearance in the reign of King Gilgamesh. This is early in the 3rd millennium B.C.E. Actually, I have to take a moment just to say, in this course, we've had to work from indirect evidence so long that it's really fun to be able to use documentary descriptions at last.

So, here we go. Now, at last, written sources give us the sort of sharp focus that historians are used to. And we can begin to actually name people and name places, and we can actually begin to sort of think our way into an entire world. Well, here's the description from *Gilgamesh* of the city:

> [Gilgamesh] had restored the holy Eanna Temple and the massive wall of Uruk, which no city on earth can equal. See how its ramparts gleam like copper in the sun. Climb the stone staircase, more ancient than the mind can imagine, approach the Temple of Eanna, sacred to Ishtar [that's another name for Inanna], a temple that no king has equaled in size or beauty, walk on the wall of Uruk [says the poem], follow its course around the city, inspect its mighty foundations, examine its brickwork, how masterfully it is built, observe the land it encloses: the palm trees, the gardens, the orchards, the glorious palaces and temples, the shops and marketplaces, the houses, the public squares.

It's one of the oldest literary texts we have, and I hope you'll agree it at least creates the illusion of quite a vivid picture of a place. The modern description is a description in general of a number of Sumerian cities, and it comes from the writing of an archaeologist—Susan Pollock. Now, she has a long description of these cities, and I'm going to just cherry-pick some of the nicer parts. She writes:

> The area inside a city's walls was densely built up but not in a uniform manner. [She gives a wonderful sense of the sort of chaos of some of these early cities.] There is only occasional evidence [in Sumer] for systematic city planning, and most areas of cities probably grew organically. [In other words, ad hoc, higgledy-piggledy.] Streets varied from narrow lanes to broader routes 2–3 meters wide and served not only as passageways but also as convenient places in which to dump garbage. Abandoned buildings were used as receptacles for garbage disposal, along with cleared areas where no buildings stood.

In general, we're going to see this over and over again. In early cities, the problem with waste disposable was very rarely handled well. She writes that:

> Large quantities of waste material were discarded at the edge of the city, perhaps in an attempt to organize refuse disposal. ... Open spaces, occupied houses as well as abandoned ones, and garbage dumps were also used [sometimes, and this actually to a modern era is quite shocking] as places to dispose of the dead, sometimes casually and sometimes in formal burials.

Her description goes on to describe how these cities, to some extent, had a slightly rural feel in them. For example, you could find small livestock—you could find some pigs—and you could find gardens. She also gives a nice description of the sort of vibrant, noisy quality of these cities:

> The dense architecture, narrow lanes, wide range of activities, and diverse population must have made [these] Mesopotamian cities vibrant, noisy, smelly, sometimes bewildering and dangerous, but also exciting places.

> Houses [now she goes on to describe the architecture] were usually constructed abutting one another. Over time, as the composition

and fortunes of a family changed, walls might be knocked down or erected, doors blocked or created, additions constructed, or portions sold.

In many ways, the houses she describes also could be recognized today. She writes, many of them:

had flat roofs, with access to them by staircase or ladder. Just as today in the Near East, inhabitants of ancient Mesopotamian communities may have used roofs for a variety of activities, including sleeping in summer, drying items, and other tasks that required a large layout space.

And one more detail that actually strikes a very modern ring. Around the edge of these cities, archaeologists have found evidence of sort of shantytowns—as immigrants from the countryside tried to make a living, often without great success, in the big cities.

So I hope that gives you some sort of feeling for the quality of life in these early cities. We even have a map, by the way, of one of these cities: Nippur. The map dates from about 1500 B.C.E., but it is the first street map we have in world history. It shows the city's walls, its gardens, and its canals as well as a large temple complex.

Now, these early cities that appear quite suddenly in Sumer were the densest and most complex communities that had ever existed. Uruk's 20,000 to 50,000 people lived in just 2.5 square kilometers. That's an area that could barely have supported a single individual using the foraging technologies of the Paleolithic era. So this is an astonishingly dense congregation of people.

Unlike the foraging communities or the villages of the early Agrarian era, these dense communities are not self-sufficient. Cities have never been self-sufficient. They couldn't support themselves. Many of their inhabitants were simply not farmers; they depended (for getting food and other resources) on relations of control and exchange with nearby peasants. Though some of the population could have been farmers traveling outside of the city during the day to farm their lands, for the most part, these cities had to control nearby "hinterlands."

So a city almost by definition is a seat of power, and what this meant was forcing the peasants of nearby villages to supply them with goods—sometimes in return for a degree of protection or help with the maintenance of irrigation systems, often simply by force. These cities also traded along Mesopotamia's great rivers and across the seas, partly because this was indeed an arid land by now and many resources—including stone and wood—were in quite short supply.

Now, I've talked a lot about complexity and emergent properties. So let's try and look at some of the emergent properties that appeared quite quickly as the first agrarian civilizations evolved.

First: cities and institutionalized power. The inhabitants of the first cities had many needs that could only be met by appointing powerful rulers. So these places were seats of power, and that's why I've argued they include some of the first tribute-taking states ever to appear. They're also sites of specialization and a division of labor. Now, specialization and division of labor—these count as emergent properties of agrarian civilizations. What I mean by this is that in the village communities of the early Agrarian era, basically everyone did the same thing. Everyone, more or less, with very minor exceptions, was a farmer. And probably in the villages of Mesopotamia this continued to be true. In cities it's no longer true. Many city dwellers are specialists. They don't grow food. They're dependent on markets for essential supplies—and, therefore, they need to be in an environment where states can police and organize markets.

There's a document from Sumer from about 2500 B.C.E. called the "Standard Professions List." It mentions many different professions, including, and I'll list just some of them: soldiers, farmers, priests, gardeners, cooks, scribes, bakers, coppersmiths, jewelers, even snake charmers, and even the profession of king!

Now, markets were vital also because Sumer—as we've seen—lacked basic materials, such as wood. So, rulers supported merchants who traded within what we'll call a "world system." This is a terminology we'll use more later on. That is a large area of several interlinked agrarian civilizations between which there was a lot of trade. And this world system reached to Egypt, to

North India, to Central Asia, and to Anatolia. We can tell this because we find in the archaeology of all of these regions goods that come from Sumer.

Another emergent property: warfare linked with power. Cities needed defensive walls and irrigation systems. These could be built and maintained only by powerful rulers who could organize huge labor levies. Rulers controlled labor, to some extent, probably through slavery, fairly coercive forms of control (or "corvée" in other words), obligations imposed on free people to occasionally supply labor instead of resources as tributes. Forced labor was important in all early Agrarian civilizations for a very simple, ecological reason. In societies without modern energy supplies, human beings themselves are the most exploitable sources of energy, apart from domesticated cattle. Humans were, from the point of view of rulers, living "batteries." That, incidentally, explains why throughout the era of agrarian civilizations, slavery was such a powerful institution. If you keep slaves you have supplies of living energy, and they also happen to be reasonably intelligent as well.

So, humans were stores of useable energy for warfare, excavation, building, ditch digging, and so on. In several of the cities of Sumer, archaeologists have found mass-produced, very basic, beveled-rim bowls—and these were interpreted as evidence that the government was providing rations for huge levees of workers (or slaves).

Now, in these cities, another emergent property we can describe it as—we find more organized forms of religion very closely linked to institutionalized forms of power. To maintain the favor of the gods—particularly if you want to maintain the favor of very powerful gods that can look after not just an individual person or household but an entire city—it was necessary to build and supply temples, such as the Eanna Temple at Uruk, which was dedicated to Inanna. Indeed, in many of these Sumerian cities, there are powerful hints that the first real rulers late in the 4th millennium may actually have been priests of some kind. It's certainly striking that the first very large buildings we find in them tend to be temples rather than palaces.

One more emergent property: bureaucracies, tributes, hierarchies, writing, and armies. Actually, these all sort of tend to go together. Rulers ruled through literate bureaucracies, powerful taxation systems, and paid armies. These are features that would reappear in all tribute-taking states.

Tributes. Let's look at tributes first. Just as farmers extracted what we can think of as ecological "rents" from their domesticated crops and animals—by which I mean that in return for protection, they take a part of each crop or each herd in return for helping the crop or herd to reproduce next year. In the same way, rulers of Sumer's city-states collected resources from their subjects—and we call these "tributes" because, like modern taxes, they were raised at least in part through the threat of coercion.

And we find hierarchies and classes. New hierarchies emerged, with the wealthy and powerful at the top and slaves and war captives at the bottom. Here is William McNeill's description of Sumer's class system. We've met William McNeill before. He's one of the doyens of modern world history. And in a recent world history that he wrote with his son, John McNeill, he writes:

> Sumerian cities comprised three distinct elements. A group of privileged citizens farmed irrigated land nearby, and headed substantial households comprising relatives, a staff of dependent field workers, and a few imported slaves. Outside the walls, on the riverbank, a harbor community accommodated merchants, caravan personnel, traders, and sailors who came and went, bringing necessary imports to the city like timber, metals, and other precious materials, while exporting woolen textiles, date wine, and other manufactures in exchange. The most distinctive element of Sumerian cities, however, was the presence of one or more divine households, or temples. These households were much larger than private ones, but the distribution of duties and income among members conformed in essentials to the way tasks and rewards were arranged within private households.

And in Uruk he'd have been referring to the Eanna Temple of Inanna.

Another crucial emergent property is bureaucracies and writing, the writing on which they were founded. How did writing emerge? We'll see this in all agrarian civilizations; it seems to have emerged out of accounting. So this is what seems to be the logic for the emergence of writing. And this seems to be the explanation for the odd fact that writing appears with agrarian civilizations. We've seen a sudden buildup of populations and a sudden buildup of resources. So suddenly we have rulers who control large amounts of resources, large amounts of people, but also large warehouses full of stuff—full of grain, full of precious metals that are being traded, full of stored tributes of various kinds.

Now, if they've got these large amounts of stuff—we can call them "treasuries" in a later terminology—they clearly needed some method of keeping track of this stuff. If you have only a small amount of stuff you don't need to keep track of it, but if you're really building up large amounts you need to keep track of it. So suddenly rulers need accounting, and it's these accounting methods that eventually evolve into the first writing systems. Now, how it did so varied from civilization to civilization, but this is what happened in Sumer.

At first, it seems, accounts were kept using tokens that sort of represented objects. Now this could be a bit cumbersome. You could actually accumulate a lot of these tokens to represent a lot of objects. Then, it became common to cut marks in clay using wedge-shaped papyrus stalks to represent objects, such as sheep or units of grain. And very often you can do sort of little cartoon-like drawings to do this. Now, that's accounting, and it's quite easy to see how you can develop quite a useful accounting system in this way. But how do you move from accounting systems to a written language that can convey, say, the *Epic of Gilgamesh*?

The crucial step here seems to be what is known as the "rebus" principle. Here's an illustration of how it worked. The Sumerian symbol for an arrow, the cuneiform—cuneiform, incidentally, means "wedge-shaped"; if you look at cuneiform writing, you'll find that these sliced papyri produce wedge-shaped marks in clay—so the Sumerian symbol for an arrow in cuneiform looked, of course, like an arrow. This is easy enough to imagine. But as it happened, the word for "life," which is an abstract concept, which is hard to know how you could represent it in cuneiform or in a diagram, the word for "life" happened to sound almost exactly like the word for "arrow," and the word sounded something like "*ti*." Now what this meant was that the symbol for an arrow could be used for the more abstract idea of "life." And this seems to be the crucial move to take you from what begins as an accounting system to a written language that can be used as richly, or almost as richly, as spoken language.

By early in the 3rd millennium, such changes meant that writing could record chronicles and even poetry. And because now, finally, for the first time in human history we have poetry, I can't resist citing an example of an early Sumerian lullaby. These sorts of documents suddenly allow us to feel that we're really getting into the world and psyche of humans who lived many millennia ago. Now, don't correct my Sumerian pronunciation. I'm just going to try and give you some feeling of how this goes:

> *Usa nganu usa nganu*
> *Usa nganu ki dumungashe*
> *Usa kulu ki dumungashe*
> *Igi badbadani u kunib*

Now, that's just the first four lines. And it means something like this:

> Come sleep, come sleep,
> Come to my son,
> Hurry sleep to my son,
> Put to sleep his restless eyes

I think it's wonderful the way that writing and documents can take us into a world in a way we've not been able to do before.

Okay. Let's move on. More emergent properties: armies. With such huge resources, rulers could hire paid enforcers or armies. This is the crucial step from "power from below" to "power from above." Much early Sumerian writing describes wars fought by well-organized armies, and a wonderful Sumerian mosaic of 2600 B.C.E., which is known as the *Standard of Ur*, depicts the army of Ur, with its donkey-drawn chariots and large convoys of captives. It's really worth looking at.

And another crucial emergent property is monumental architecture: huge buildings or structures that are designed to impress your enemies, but also to impress your subjects. They're one of the keys to statehood. The royal tombs of Ur, from the late 4th millennium, show the spectacular riches that rulers could accumulate and the extraordinary expense lavished on the creation of awe-inspiring tombs. As in the royal burials of many agrarian civilizations, servants and relatives of the king were often killed and buried to serve the king in afterlife. And from late in the 3rd millennium B.C.E., the typical form of monumental architecture in Mesopotamia would become the ziggurat—a stepped, pyramid-like temple dedicated to the gods, of which the best preserved today is that of Ur. The Tower of Babel has often been interpreted as a reference to the ziggurat of Babylon, which was dedicated to the god Marduk. The Babylonian word *bab-ili* meant "gate of god."

Now, two more significant things occur about 1,000 years after the appearance of the first states, and I'll describe these just very briefly. The first is the appearance late in the 3rd millennium, under a ruler called Sargon, of the first multi-city state—the first imperial state in the region. And it's based on a city called Akkad in northern Sumeria. We actually have busts of Sargon. This is one of the first great rulers whose names we know.

And finally, there is another crucial development that would recur in many agrarian civilizations. I'll call this "ecological overreach." The cities of Sumer frequently experience catastrophic floods. These are the basis of the stories of biblical floods. But there was an even greater danger: In around 2000 B.C.E. there is a massive crash of populations in Sumer, and eventually it destroys Sumerian civilization. Civilization will drift north in Mesopotamia. The fundamental cause seems to have been over-irrigation that led to an increase in salts of various kinds in the soils and reduced fertility of the soils, sharply reducing productivity of agriculture, leading to a sharp decline in production, and, eventually, undermining Sumerian civilization.

This was a sign that these wonderful complex structures that appeared were also extremely fragile, and we see this is true of most agrarian civilizations. So, voilà! A whole series of linked features have come together to establish the first agrarian civilizations with all their complexity, and also their fragility.

Thank you.

Agrarian Civilizations in Other Regions
Lecture 31

> The Nile was a wonderful river along which to trade. Trade winds heading south and river currents heading north made sailing up and down the river relatively easy. And we know that Egyptian rulers sent expeditions for ivory and gold, for example, to Nubia and Punt, in modern Ethiopia, and also to Lebanon for its famous cedars. We still have fine illustrations of a fleet that was sent by Hatshepsut—one of the few female pharaohs, who ruled soon after 1500 B.C.E.

How typical was Sumer of Agrarian civilizations in general? Agrarian civilizations were constructed using the huge human and material resources generated in regions of flourishing agriculture, so each civilization was shaped to some degree by the cultural traditions and ecology of the regions in which it emerged. This lecture briefly surveys six different areas in which Agrarian civilizations appeared early. The main exception to the general rule that agriculture generated civilizations is in tropical areas such as Papua New Guinea (and perhaps the Amazon basin). Here, agriculture may have appeared early, but it was based on root crops that could not be stored for long periods. As William McNeill argues, the lack of storable wealth may explain why these regions never supported Agrarian civilizations.

Within the Afro-Eurasian world zone, Agrarian civilizations emerged along fertile river systems in four different regions. We have seen how Sumerian civilization arose in the Euphrates-Tigris basin, in the form of a cluster of competing city-states all dependent on irrigation. Nearby, in modern Sudan and Egypt, an Agrarian civilization appeared at about the same time, based on the remarkable natural irrigation system of the Nile River. The annual floods of the Nile, the world's longest river, brought nutritious silts from the south. After about 5000 B.C.E., the Sahara desert became drier, and more people settled in the Nile Valley. As in Sumer, populations grew rapidly, but here most settled in a long ribbon of villages along the Nile. Wheat and barley, introduced from Mesopotamia around 5000 B.C.E., flourished.

So did watermelons and other crops from Sudan. By 4000 B.C.E., village communities stretched from the Nile Delta to Nubia, in modern Sudan.

Small kingdoms appeared and were rapidly united within a single large state. Around 3100 B.C.E., a southern ruler called Menes (or Narmer) unified the region north of Aswan into a single empire. The *Narmer Palette*, probably engraved by a contemporary, shows the pharaoh smiting his enemies. Cities were less important than in Mesopotamia, though Menes established a capital at Memphis, south of modern Cairo. Unlike the rulers of Sumer, who were either priests or kings, Egypt's "pharaohs" were treated as gods.

Their tombs, the pyramids, reflect their high status. The largest, the pyramid of Cheops, was built between 2500 and 2600 B.C.E., using 2.3 million limestone blocks.

Despite occasional periods of political breakdown, Egyptian dynasties ruled the Nile region for almost 2,600 years. The regularity of the Nile floods may explain

The annual floods of the Nile, the world's longest river, brought nutritious silts from the south.

why Egyptian civilization avoided the sort of ecological collapse experienced in many other early Agrarian civilizations. A hieroglyphic writing system developed early here, possibly under indirect Mesopotamian influence. Trade winds heading south and river currents heading north encouraged trade along the Nile. Egyptian rulers sent expeditions for ivory and gold to Nubia and Punt and for timber to Lebanon. We still have fine illustrations of a fleet sent by Hatshepsut.

Early in the 3rd millennium, cities and states appeared in the north of modern Pakistan and India. The Indus river brought rich Himalayan silts but flooded less predictably than the Nile. By 2500 B.C.E., there were many small towns and at least two huge cities, now known as Harappa and Mohenjo Daro. Each had about 40,000 inhabitants. Houses and streets were built along a carefully planned grid system using prefabricated bricks. There were water and sewage systems, uniform systems of weights and measures, specialized crafts, markets, and extensive trade with Mesopotamia and Central Asia. Here, too, a writing system evolved. Unfortunately, it has not yet been deciphered, so our knowledge of this civilization depends entirely on archaeology. The absence of obvious palaces or royal tombs limits our understanding of the political system. The Indus Valley civilization collapsed early in the 2nd millennium. Overpopulation may have caused ecological collapse through deforestation, erosion, flooding, and desertification.

The earliest Agrarian civilizations in China emerged along the Yellow River, whose fertile "loess" soils formed from dust blown in from Inner Asia. Agriculture was productive, but flooding was a perennial problem. Chinese traditions describe two ancient dynasties, the Xia and Shang. Cities and states appeared along the eastern Yellow River late in the 3rd millennium. The Xia dynasty was probably one of several regional kingdoms. Its capital, at Erlitou, has been recently excavated. The Shang dynasty ruled for much of the 2nd millennium B.C.E. Bronze metallurgy and horse-drawn chariots, as well as wheat and barley, may have arrived from the West. The Shang controlled many cities. They had large armies equipped with mass-produced weapons and armor, and they built massive royal tombs and palaces. There may have been other similar kingdoms in other regions of China. Shang writing, using symbols carved on tortoise shells or other bones, can still be read today. Here, writing was linked to divination, a skill highly valued in rulers. Rituals were important, but deities and priests played a smaller role than in Mesopotamia or Egypt.

Agrarian civilizations appeared later, but quite independently, in two regions in the Americas. We will survey these civilizations in more detail in Lecture Thirty-Seven. "Mesoamerica" includes southern Mexico and parts of Central America. The first incipient civilizations appeared among the "Olmec" during the 2nd millennium B.C.E. In the 1st millennium, cities and states also appeared in the Oaxaca valley, in modern Mexico. By the 1st millennium C.E., there were cities and states throughout Mesoamerica. Here, great river valleys played a lesser role than in Afro-Eurasia, though techniques for increasing agricultural productivity included forest clearance and the creation of large artificial swamplands. In the Andes, state systems emerged in the 1st millennium B.C.E. along the arid coasts of Peru (where they relied largely on fishing) and in the Andean uplands around Lake Titicaca (which relied on maize, potato, and quinoa). Exchanges of crops and other goods between lowland and upland regions laid the foundations for the first large empires.

The Inka Empire, which flourished in the 15th and early 16th centuries C.E., was the first to link these centers into a single political system.

This brief tour of some of the earliest Agrarian civilizations hints at their variety. But there were also some remarkable similarities, which we return to in the next lecture. ∎

Essential Reading

Bentley and Ziegler, *Traditions and Encounters*, chaps. 3–6.

Christian, *Maps of Time*, chap. 9.

Fagan, *People of the Earth*, chaps. 15–18, 21, 22.

Supplementary Reading

Brown, *Big History*, chap. 6.

Fernandez-Armesto, *The World,* chap. 4.

Mann, *1491.*

Questions to Consider

1. What were the most important differences between the earliest regions of Agrarian civilization?

2. How important was religion in the appearance of Agrarian civilizations?

Agrarian Civilizations in Other Regions
Lecture 31—Transcript

Lecture Thirty described the appearance of the first agrarian civilizations in Sumer. What I'd like to ask now is how typical that process was and how typical Sumer was of agrarian civilizations. If we're going to deal with the idea of agrarian civilizations as a larger category of human societies, we need to try and get a quite precise idea of the degree of difference between them and the degree of similarity between them. So we can't just assume that Sumer was typical, though I will argue that in many ways it was. Indeed, in a remarkable number of ways, it was. And I'll argue that these similarities are easier to see through the wide-angle lens of big history than through the narrower lens that's normally used in historical scholarship. Nevertheless, having said that, it's also important not to overlook the many significant differences that existed between particular civilizations. And what I want to do in this lecture is note some of the more significant differences between civilizations and the slightly different ways in which they appeared in region after region.

The nature of historical scholarship has tended to ensure that describing these differences, the specific features of particular regions of agrarian civilization, has been one of the dominant preoccupations of historians. Partly, this sort of scholarship has been driven by forms of nationalism. The history profession has been shaped profoundly by nationalism as it became more professional in the 19th century. And what states did, of course, what states expected of historians was that they would write nationalist histories—they would write about "our" people. And so this is one of the powerful things that steered historians towards the idea of describing particular civilizations in their own terms.

But there's another factor as well that's driven historians in this direction—the typical structure of the history profession, since history became a professional, scholarly discipline, late in the 19th century. Historians tend to train as specialists in particular areas, either their own country or some other country. And there are a lot of skills and techniques to be acquired in order to become a specialist. You have to learn the language, and you have to get familiar with the archives in a particular region. So if you're a Chinese historian—or, say, a Russian historian—you've already invested a lot in that civilization, that culture. And this tends to steer historians towards questions about the distinctive nature of the particular civilization they're looking at.

So in this course, we're going to be trying to resist the sort of gravitational pull of these questions and stand back and look at the general features. But meanwhile, let's try and get a sense of the important differences that did exist, drawing on this extraordinarily rich body of scholarship that has been built up in the last century or so. So here, we'll touch on some of the more striking differences between civilizations.

Agrarian civilizations, we've seen, were constructed using the huge human and material resources generated in regions of flourishing agriculture. So one of the factors that undoubtedly led to differences between different civilizations was the precise geography of the regions in which they developed and the precise nature of the types of agriculture on which they were founded. We've seen that regions of flourishing agriculture, in general, were a bit like the hot spots created by stars—but as with stars, the precise nature of the end product could depend on the size, and nature, and the precise nature of the raw materials from which they were created. Each region of agrarian civilization, therefore, was shaped by the particular type of agriculture that emerged and the geography of the region in which it emerged.

Now, there's one important exception to the types of rules we've seen, and I'd like to describe that first, before looking at some of the main areas of agrarian civilization. And this is tropical areas, such as Papua New Guinea, and perhaps the Amazon basin—areas where agriculture may have emerged (sometimes quite early, as in Papua New Guinea) but was based on root crops. That is to say, on crops that couldn't be stored as easily as you could store grains such as rice, or wheat, or maize. The result in these regions was that the transition from flourishing agricultural systems to regions of agricultural civilization seemed, at some stage, to get blocked.

Here is W. H. McNeill's description of how this blockage occurred. And this helps us understand why so few agrarian civilizations appeared in tropical regions or in regions such as Papua New Guinea. And why in Papua New Guinea, despite 10,000 years of agriculture, you don't get an agrarian civilization. This is from the book he wrote with his son, John McNeill, called *The Human Web*. This is what McNeill writes, on agriculture in tropical regions:

> Even if tropical gardening [that is, the growing of root crops using techniques of horticulture] antedated grainfields by thousands of years [and it certainly did in some regions], ... it remained comparatively insignificant for human history as a whole. That is because tropical gardeners leave roots and fruits where they grow until ready for consumption. Grains that ripen all at once must be harvested and stored; and the consequent availability of concentrated supplies of food in farmers' storage bins and jars made the rise of states and cities possible. Priests and soldiers could demand and get part of the grain harvest from those who had raised it as a price for protection from supernatural and human harm. But without storage, massive and regular transfer of food from farmers to city folk was impracticable, inhibiting social and occupational differentiation. Consequently [he concludes], the specialized skills of urban life could not arise on the basis of tropical gardening, however productive it might be.

So this is the one great exception to the rule that where agriculture developed, it tended to accumulate—to build up large populations and provide the basis for the eventual appearance of agrarian civilizations.

Now, I want to go on and look at six different areas where agrarian civilizations appeared fairly early. These are areas where agrarian civilizations seem to have appeared either completely independently of influences elsewhere or, perhaps, under very limited influence from other regions.

I'll begin with the Afro-Eurasian world zone. Here what is striking is that agrarian civilizations emerged along fertile river systems in four different regions. We've already seen this happening in Mesopotamia. We've seen why fertile river systems were so strategic. When irrigated, such regions could support the rapid development of very large populations. They could generate population explosions as soon as you introduce viable systems of irrigation.

Let's begin with Sumer, where we were in the last lecture. We've seen how Sumerian civilization arose in the Euphrates-Tigris basin in the form of a cluster of competing city-states, all dependent on irrigation. Now, what's striking is that it doesn't actually arise in those areas where rainfall agriculture is possible. Here you see a very slow, gentle buildup of population. It arises in the south, where you get a very sudden population explosion, caused by the fact that irrigation is introduced into a fairly arid region. So it's the sudden population explosion that seems to have been crucial here. And these rivers are also crucial because, as we've seen, they tend to bring silts down and generate very fertile soils. So with irrigation, you can suddenly get very highly productive agriculture.

Here, priests and temples seem to have played an important role in the emergence of tribute-taking states, and states emerged primarily in the form of small city-states in the 3rd millennium. Though by the late 3rd millennium, secular rulers—such as Gilgamesh—have become more and more important, and eventually, by about just before 2000 B.C.E., we find an overall ruler, Sargon, ruling several of these cities—in fact, ruling the whole of Sumer.

So that's the broad pattern we've seen in Sumer. Now let's look at Sudan and Egypt. In modern Sudan and Egypt, an agrarian civilization appears at about the same time, based on the remarkable natural irrigation system of the Nile River. The annual floods of the Nile, which is probably the world's longest river—I say probably, incidentally, because there's competition with the Amazon for this title; but it's certainly one of the world's longest rivers—the annual floods brought nutritious silts from the south, and sort of spread them over the lands to either side of the river. After about 5000 B.C.E., the Sahara Desert—which before that had been a lot wetter than it is today and had supported quite a large number of small farming populations—began to get drier, and people are squeezed out of the Sahara and into the Nile Valley. So as in southern Sumer, populations appear to have built up quite rapidly, and at least one of the factors involved was climate change.

But in this case (unlike Sumer) populations grew not in tiny, concentrated cities, but in a long ribbon of villages along the Nile. Wheat and barley is introduced probably from Mesopotamia about 5000 B.C.E. They both flourished, as did watermelons and other crops from Sudan (from the south).

And by 4000 B.C.E., we have village communities stretching from the Nile Delta (in the north) to Nubia (in modern Sudan). Then, small kingdoms begin to appear. These were then quite rapidly united, late in the 4th millennium, into a single large state. This is a process that happened much quicker here than in Sumer.

Just before 3000 B.C.E., in perhaps 3100 B.C.E., a southern ruler called Menes—or in some sources Narmer—unifies the region north of Aswan into a single empire. If you go to the Egyptian Museum in the center of Cairo—and I had the chance to visit that just two years ago, this is the great museum that also contains the remains of the Pharaoh Tutankhamen—you can see the *Narmer Palette*. It's a beautiful engraved slab of stone with images and hieroglyphic writing—and it was probably engraved at the time of Narmer. It shows the pharaoh, very typically for this sort of royal propaganda, smiting his enemies.

Cities were less important in Egypt than in Mesopotamia, though Menes did establish a capital at Memphis. There were cities south of modern Cairo. So here, power was based on a long, almost continuous ribbon of irrigated villages extending along the Nile. This was not strictly a city, but it was a large area of almost continuous settlement—a sort of almost-city, a colossal assemblage of many closely linked villages.

Unlike the rulers of Sumer, who seem to have been either priests or kings, Egypt's "pharaohs"—from very early on—seem to have been treated as gods. Their tombs, the pyramids, reflect their high status. When I went to Egypt for the first time, I had the chance to see the Pyramids of Giza, and I have to say that they were far more impressive seen directly than any picture I had seen, and they really are awe-inspiring. If you want to inspire awe in your population, it's a wonderful way of doing it. So if they can awe a modern visitor, they must have been astonishing to contemporaries. The largest, the Pyramid of Cheops, was built between 2600 and 2500 B.C.E. It used about 2.3 million limestone blocks, each weighing about 2.5 tons. So think of the labor involved in building this thing. It's staggering.

Despite occasional periods of political breakdown, Egyptian dynasties would rule the region for almost 2,600 years. They show remarkable stability, much more than in Sumer or Mesopotamia, and the geography of Egypt may help explain some of its more distinctive features. And perhaps the crucial thing here is the regularity of the Nile floods. They may explain why Egyptian civilization avoided the sort of ecological collapse experienced in Sumer towards the end of the 3rd millennium B.C.E., just around 2000 B.C.E., and (as we'll see) in many other early Agrarian civilizations.

Here, a hieroglyphic writing system developed early—possibly under Mesopotamian influence, but it's so different that that influence can't have been overwhelming. Here, writing took the rather different form of hieroglyphics, rather than the cuneiform writing of Sumer.

There were developed trading systems. The Nile was a wonderful river along which to trade. Trade winds heading south and river currents heading north made sailing up and down the river relatively easy. And we know that Egyptian rulers sent expeditions for ivory and gold, for example, to Nubia and Punt, in modern Ethiopia, and also to Lebanon for its famous cedars. We still have fine illustrations of a fleet that was sent by Hatshepsut—one of the few female pharaohs, who ruled soon after 1500 B.C.E. The expedition to Punt returned with many exotic goods—including gold, ebony, baboons, and myrrh.

So I hope that gives a very general impression of some of the distinctive features of Egyptian agrarian civilizations. Now, let's cross to the east, to the Indian subcontinent.

Early in the 3rd millennium, cities and states appear in the north of modern Pakistan and India, in what has come to be known as Harappan civilization. Here, too, there was a distinctive geography—but once again, a large, fertile river system plays a crucial role. This region was dominated by the presence of the Indus River. The Indus River brought very rich silts down from the Himalayas, but its flooding was much less predictable than the Nile, so the Indus is a more dangerous river, quite frankly, than the Nile—as the Tigris and Euphrates, incidentally, were also more dangerous than the Nile.

In this region, too, population seems to have built up quite rapidly, and the appearance of the first agrarian civilization seems to have been the result of some sort of population explosion. By 2500 B.C.E., in an area where there hadn't been huge populations before, you quite rapidly find a lot of small towns and at least two huge cities. These are now known as Harappa and Mohenjo-Daro. They are the best-known archaeological sites in this region, but there are many, many other sites. Each of these cities had probably, and you'll understand that there's some guesswork involved here, but it has been estimated about 40,000 inhabitants, making them about the same size as Uruk. And as we've seen, for the time, these are colossal megalopolises.

Houses and streets were built along a grid system using prefabricated bricks. Now here, we get much more of a sense of urban planning than we do in the higgledy-piggledy streets of a place like Uruk. The cities seemed to be more spacious and more carefully planned. We know there were water and sewerage systems. There were apparently uniform systems of weights and measures. There were also all the other things we see: highly specialized crafts and markets and quite significant evidence of international trade. We know that Harappan civilization traded with Central Asia. In fact, evidence has been found of communities of Harappan merchants in Central Asia late in the 3rd millennium. And they also traded with Mesopotamia. And again, we know this because we find trade goods from these regions. So that's one powerful reminder that none of these civilizations was entirely self-contained.

In Harappan civilization, too, a writing system evolved; however, the Indus writing system has never been deciphered. So our knowledge of Harappan civilization, at the moment, is rather rudimentary. It depends on archaeology. We cannot read the inscriptions that survive from this region, which is very frustrating. And it limits our ability to understand how the political system worked. The fact that there seem not to have been large palaces also makes it really hard to get a handle on how the politics of these systems worked. So here the inability to use the written records really is extremely frustrating. It greatly limits our understanding of aspects of this world, such as its religious traditions and also its political traditions. One of the questions we'd love to ask of Harappan civilization, for example, is: To what extent did its traditions survive in later Indian subcontinent traditions? For example, some of the surviving sculptures from Harappan civilization seem to show figures in yoga positions; what does this mean?

The Indus Valley civilization collapsed early in the 2nd millennium, and it collapsed very rapidly indeed. We're not absolutely certain why. It used to be thought that invasions from the north were an important part of this, but now the tendency is to stress ecological factors. Overpopulation may have caused ecological collapse through deforestation, erosion, flooding, and desertification. So here we have a second spectacular example of ecological overreach, leading to an almost total decline of agrarian civilization in the region for many centuries—a very powerful reminder that the complexity of agrarian civilizations, like all forms of complexity, may be associated with fragility.

Now let's move further east. This is the fourth region, East Asia and China. The earliest evidence of agrarian civilizations in China emerges along the Yellow River, whose fertile "loess" soils—that's l-o-e-double s—were formed from dust blown in from Inner Asia. If you go to Beijing today, you'll see haze, which has a lot to do with cars, but the other thing it has to do with is the Gobi Desert kind of blowing in and settling in Beijing. Agriculture along the Yellow River, in northern China, was highly productive, but flooding was always a problem. And as a result, finding ways of controlling water flow seems to have been one of the earliest problems tackled by Chinese rulers.

Chinese traditions—and written traditions go back a long way, or they allude to very ancient periods—they describe two ancient dynasties, the Xia and the Shang. A possibly mythic King Yu was the legendary founder of the Xia dynasty, and it's symptomatic that he spent a lot of his time finding ways of preventing flooding. Cities and states, mini-states, begin to appear along the eastern Yellow River late in the 3rd millennium. This is about the time when Sargon unified much of Sumer.

The Xia dynasty was probably one of several regional kingdoms, but the only one to which we have written references. Its capital, a city called Erlitou, has been recently excavated. The Shang dynasty ruled for much of the 2nd millennium. Bronze metallurgy becomes important, and horse-drawn chariots are used in warfare. The chariots probably arrived from the west, from the steppe lands, maybe even further west, as well as wheat and barley. One of the great unresolved issues in Chinese archaeology is the extent of diffusion from the far west, from Mesopotamia or perhaps even from India.

The Shang rulers controlled many cities. They had large armies equipped with mass-produced weapons and armor, and they built massive royal tombs and palaces, so we're clearly dealing with very substantial states. And there may have been other similar kingdoms, kingdoms of similar scale, in other regions of 2nd-millennium China.

Writing emerged here, too, but here it seems to have emerged by a slightly different path from in Sumer. It's not clear how crucial a role accountancy played. It probably did play some role, but attempts to divine the future, attempts of divination, seem to have been a crucial role here. Shang writing appears using symbols carved on tortoise shells or other bones, and some of these symbols can still be read today. Here we have remarkable continuity in the writing systems. And writing, as I said, was closely linked to divination. One of the forms of divination involved taking a shell, heating it up, looking at the cracks, and using the cracks to forecast the future. Rituals clearly played a very important role both in family life and in political life, but deities and priests seemed to have played a somewhat smaller role than in Mesopotamia or Egypt.

Now, this brief survey may give some sense both of the similarities and some of the more important differences between the great civilizations of Afro-Eurasia. Of course, I'm not even pretending it can do justice to the many detailed nuances that distinguish cultural or religious life in these different regions.

Now I want to move onto the Americas—and let me remind you that now we're crossing to an entirely separate world zone. So the appearance of agrarian civilizations in the Americas is quite distinct. There's no evidence at all, at the moment, of any form of diffusion from Afro-Eurasia. In the Americas, agrarian civilization appears independently in two distinct regions. We'll survey these civilizations in much more detail in Lecture Thirty-Seven, so here I'll just mention some of the crucial features.

The first of these two regions is "Mesoamerica." Mesoamerica includes southern Mexico and parts of Central America. The first, let's call them incipient, civilizations, because there's plenty of room for debate about whether we should call these agrarian civilizations yet or not, but they're certainly well on the way to being agrarian civilizations—appear among a people that archaeologists call the "Olmec," during the 2nd millennium B.C.E. In the 1st millennium B.C.E., we get very clear evidence of cities and states, and the first ones appear in the Oaxaca valley, where Monte Albán is widely regarded as the first major city to appear in the Americas. Incidentally, I'll come back and talk about the Olmec in a later lecture. They are absolutely fascinating, and they produce these wonderful basalt heads that you will have seen.

Okay, back to the 1st millennium B.C.E. This is when the first clear evidence appears of agrarian civilizations in the Oaxaca valley. By the 1st millennium C.E.—that is to say, we're about between 2,000 and 1,500 years ago—there were cities and states throughout much of Mesoamerica. Now, in this region, great river valleys appear to have played a less important role than in the great civilizations of Afro-Eurasia—though here, too, in each region, you can identify techniques that allowed agricultural productivity to rise. These included the clearing of forestlands, particularly in the regions that would become the heartlands of Mayan civilization in the Yucatán later on, and they also included the planting of crops in artificial swamplands. This is a quite distinctive American form of irrigation, and this would provide the basis for the rapid population growth around what later became the Aztec capital of Tenochtitlán within the last millennium. So that's Mesoamerica, and we're going to look at Mesoamerican civilization in much more detail later on.

Finally, in the Andes, state systems emerged in the 1st millennium B.C.E. along the arid coasts of Peru and up into the highlands. Along the Andes, in this region, the crucial thing seems to have been the linking by trade and through political systems of different ecological regions. Along the arid coasts of Peru, there were abundant fisheries. In the Andean uplands around Lake Titicaca, for example, you could grow maize, potato, and quinoa. And here anthropologists argue that it's the flows of wealth and trade between these regions that generated the commercial flows and the energy flows on which the first agrarian civilizations were formed. Exchanges of crops and other goods between lowland and upland regions, therefore, laid the foundations for the first large empires. And the first really large empire in this region is probably the Inka Empire, which flourished in the 15th and 16th centuries C.E.

Now finally, let's note the negative. In other words, let's note where agrarian civilizations didn't appear—above all, the fact that they don't appear in the Australasian zone. Papua New Guinea had agriculture. It might have supported flourishing populations, except, as we've seen, its agriculture was based on root crops. And in Australia, you never get agriculture until it's brought there by European migrants in the 18th century—though we'll see, in a later lecture, that forms of intensification certainly occurred here. The trajectory, even in Australia, is towards intensification—but you don't get agriculture, you don't get agrarian civilizations.

Okay, this brief tour, I hope, of the earliest agrarian civilizations has hinted at some of their variety, but we've seen there were also striking similarities. And I'm going to explore those more carefully in the next lecture.

Thank you.

The World That Agrarian Civilizations Made
Lecture 32

So, the many striking similarities between Agrarian civilizations, even where there were no significant contacts, count as one of the most interesting and important factors about human history because they provide powerful reasons for thinking that human history is in some sense directional—that it was shaped by large, general factors that you could only see if you look at human history on a large scale.

Why were all Agrarian civilizations so similar despite the limited contact between them? Why did human societies in different parts of the world not evolve in utterly different ways? The fact that they did not suggests that there are large forces, perhaps related to our astonishing adaptability as a species, that drive human history in particular directions despite local differences in geography and cultural traditions. It is tempting to think that, ultimately, those similarities derive from the human capacity for collective learning, which ensured that, over time, human societies—wherever they might appear—would acquire increasing resources that would allow the appearance of larger and more complex societies. In short, it may be collective learning, the defining feature of our species, that helps explain the apparent directionality of human history. This lecture concentrates on general features of the 4,000-year era dominated by Agrarian civilizations. Instead of discussing each civilization in turn, we will discuss Agrarian civilization in general. As Robert Wright puts it, "if we relax our vision, and let these details go fuzzy, then a larger picture comes into focus: As the centuries fly by, civilizations may come and go, but civilization flourishes, growing in scope and complexity" (Christian, *Maps of Time*, p. 283).

Though labels for eras and types of societies are artificial, we need them because to understand the past we have to break it into manageable chunks. Chronologically, we will use two interchangeable labels for the epoch from 3000 B.C.E. to about 1000 C.E.: the "later Agrarian" era and the "era of Agrarian civilizations." This epoch was dominated by Agrarian civilizations.

Spatially, it is helpful to divide the world before modern times into four separate world zones. The Afro-Eurasian world zone includes the African and Eurasian continents and offshore islands such as Britain and Japan. It was the most ancient zone because this is where humans evolved. It was also the largest and most varied world zone, which may explain its dominant role in world history. It was where agriculture and Agrarian civilizations first appeared. The American world zone was the second-largest world zone, though it was settled late, probably within the last 13,000 to 15,000 years. This was the second zone in which Agrarian civilizations evolved independently. The Australasian world zone includes modern Australia and Papua New Guinea, as well as offshore islands such as Tasmania. Though agriculture did appear in Papua New Guinea, Agrarian civilizations did not evolve independently in this world zone. The Pacific zone was settled within the last 4,000 years by seafaring communities from Southeast Asia, who brought agriculture with them. Here, some elements of Agrarian civilizations did appear by diffusion on some of the larger islands such as Hawaii. But no island was large enough to support large Agrarian civilizations.

At the core of all Agrarian civilizations were tribute-taking states. States exacted resources in labor, goods, or cash.

Not everyone lived within Agrarian civilizations even in the era of Agrarian civilizations. Beyond their borders were regions inhabited by peoples regarded, at least by the rulers of Agrarian civilizations, as "barbarians." In some regions, such as Australia, most people continued to live in foraging communities like those of the Paleolithic era, and many lived in such communities until the 20th century. Many people lived in small farming communities with rudimentary political structures like the villages of the early Agrarian era. In arid regions of Afro-Eurasia, there were communities of pastoral nomads, some of which, like the Mongols, posed serious threats to neighboring Agrarian civilizations. Finally, there appeared the Agrarian civilizations that are the main subject of this lecture. This list provides a rudimentary, four-part typology of pre-modern human societies that reminds us of the great variety of adaptations developed by our species.

Now we focus on some of the shared features of the largest and newest of these communities: Agrarian civilizations. Agrarian civilizations were huge and complex, with hundreds of thousands, or millions, of inhabitants linked by religion, trade, economics, and politics. They were supported by the surplus labor and produce of peasant farmers, who made up most of the population. (As a rule of thumb, in most Agrarian civilizations, it took about nine peasants to support one city dweller.) Peasant life was tough. Egyptian documents from late in the 2nd millennium B.C.E. provide a vivid description of peasant life and the many trials caused both by natural disasters and the demands of tribute-takers. Elite groups, particularly in towns and cities, supported themselves by exchanging specialist skills as artisans, traders, warriors, priests, and rulers.

At the core of all Agrarian civilizations were tribute-taking states. States exacted resources in labor, goods, or cash. Tributary rulers claimed the right to exact resources but backed up their claims with the threat of force. We call such exactions "tributes." Their coercive power depended on organized armies that could defend against external attacks and suppress internal resistance. Administrative tasks, such as the collection and storage of tributes, or the administration of justice and law, were handled by organized groups of literate officials. The documents we have used earlier in this lecture provide a vivid account of the attractions of being a scribe and official. Writing appears in all Agrarian civilizations, though in some cases (e.g., the Inka), it assumed rudimentary forms. Tributary rulers built "monumental architecture": tombs, palaces, and temples designed to display their majesty and power. At lower levels, rulers depended on local nobles or officials, who duplicated their power on smaller scales.

Within Agrarian civilizations there were steep, and relatively rigid, hierarchies of wealth and power. Class hierarchies ranked groups by their lineage and social status. Aristocracies were distinguished by their lineage, power, lifestyle, and wealth. Members of the ruling elites generally despised the peasants who generated most of society's wealth. They also tended to regard those outside Agrarian civilizations as inferior or subhuman. And they normally despised merchants, whose wealth came not from tributes but from entrepreneurial activity. Power hierarchies shaped gender hierarchies. As most rulers were men, women rulers were generally regarded as exceptional (which is why the Pharaoh Hatshepsut is often represented wearing a fake beard). However, women often ruled indirectly, through husbands, lovers, or fathers. And women rarely lacked rights entirely. The oldest surviving legal code, compiled by Mesopotamian emperor Hammurabi (who reigned circa 1792–1750 B.C.E.), recognizes their right to divorce abusive husbands.

This lecture has surveyed some general features of Agrarian civilizations. In the next lecture, we ask: How did Agrarian civilizations change during the 4,000 years after their first appearance? ■

Essential Reading

Christian, *Maps of Time*, chap. 10.

Ristvet, *In the Beginning*, chap. 4.

Supplementary Reading

Ehrenberg, *Women in Prehistory.*

Trigger, *Early Civilizations.*

Questions to Consider

1. Did Agrarian civilizations share enough features to justify treating them as a major "type" of human community?

2. Of all the features shared by Agrarian civilizations, which do you regard as the most important?

The World That Agrarian Civilizations Made
Lecture 32—Transcript

The previous two lectures described the emergence of agrarian civilizations in several different regions, and we saw that they had some distinctive features. Now what we're going to do is focus once more on their similarities. We want to understand agrarian civilizations as a distinctive phenomenon in human history—one of the emergent phenomena, if you like, generated in the course of human history. Such phenomena can tell us a lot about our nature as a species, which is why it's important to stand back and try to see them clearly, and not get too tangled up in the specific details of specific civilizations.

Why were all agrarian civilizations so similar despite the limited contacts between them, particularly early on in the era of agrarian civilizations? It's very important to appreciate that the similarities between them—and there are a lot, as we'll see—are, in fact, odd. Why should humans not have developed, for example, utterly different types of communities as each region went its own merry way, so that we'd have seen absolutely no similarities between human history in different parts of the world?

What pressures might have steered human history in different regions along loosely similar paths? Of course, the question is particularly striking if you contrast the Afro-Eurasian and American zones, because at present we have no evidence of any significant contact between these regions. So, as with the history of agriculture, this odd simultaneity suggests very powerfully that though our gifts as a species did not rigidly determine the course of human history, what they did do was they tended to nudge it in distinctive directions. And, very loosely, we can even define the nature of that direction. Collective learning ensured that, over time, humans would control more and more resources. That would allow populations to grow. That would allow for denser and inevitably more complex types of communities. And once these more complex, denser communities have emerged, people in quite different parts of the world were likely to find themselves facing many of the same challenges: how to organize large groups so as to achieve collective goals, goals they all shared; how to prevent excessive conflict within and between groups; how to defend themselves when conflict was unavoidable; how to deal with garbage; how to deal with disease; and so on.

All these problems were bound to emerge once denser, more complex communities appeared. And the fact that the challenges were rather similar may explain why there are so many interesting similarities in the solutions that humans came up with—quite independently—in different regions. So, the many striking similarities between agrarian civilizations, even where there were no significant contacts, count as one of the most interesting and important factors about human history because they provide powerful reasons for thinking that human history is in some sense directional—that it was shaped by large general factors that you could only see if you look at human history on a large scale.

So, here and in the next few lectures, we'll be looking at some of these similar features and trends. This lecture concentrates on some of the general structural features of the 4,000-year era that was dominated by the presence of agrarian civilizations. Instead of discussing each civilization in turn, we'll discuss these large features that they all seemed to have shared. As Robert Wright puts it:

> If we relax our vision, and let [the] details go fuzzy, then a larger picture comes into focus: As the centuries fly by, civilizations may come and go, but civilization flourishes, growing in scope and complexity.

Now, let me take a little time out to be clear about some definitions and labels. Though labels for eras and types of societies are inevitably artificial, we need them, because to understand the past, and particularly to see the large patterns that we look for in big history, we have to break the past into manageable chunks. Now, remember that we are using two linked labels for the epoch from 3000 B.C.E. to about 1000 C.E. Essentially, they're synonyms. One is the "later Agrarian" era and the other is the "era of agrarian civilizations." So if I use one of these labels, I'm implying the other. They mean the same thing. The later Agrarian era or era of agrarian civilizations was dominated—it was the era dominated by agrarian civilizations. And agrarian civilizations, we've seen, are large, networked regions with cities—

it's the word "cities," incidentally, that explains the word "civilizations"; "civilizations" is related to the Latin word for citizen—and tribute-taking states. And all of this is sustained by the labor of millions of peasants or small farmers.

Now, there's a second piece of terminology we need to clarify, although we've used it already, and that's the idea of "world zones." Before the Modern era, human history played out in four separate world zones. These had virtually no contact with each other, though within the zones there was at least some degree of contact right across them. So, it was as if human history took place on four separate planets. Now this, we've seen, is a direct result of the fact that geologically speaking we live in an era of the planet's history when the continental plates are scattered, scattered over the surface of the Earth. So, that's what generates this parallel history in different world zones. And it's the parallels between the different histories of different world zones that raise some of the deepest questions about the driving forces of human history.

Now, let me just briefly summarize some of the main features of each of these zones. The zones, incidentally, existed of course in the Paleolithic era, but they become really, really significant and helpful as a conceptual device in the Agrarian era, and particularly in understanding the later Agrarian era. So, let's look at them.

First, the Afro-Eurasian zone, the zone that includes Africa and Eurasia—these two huge landmasses. The Afro-Eurasian world zone includes not only Africa and Eurasia, but also offshore islands, such as Britain and Japan. It was the most ancient of the world zones because this is where humans evolved, in Africa. It was also the largest and the most varied of the world zones. It reaches from the tropics to the Arctic, and it reaches almost around at least a third of the world. And this may explain—this combination of age, diversity, and size—may explain its dominant role in world history. This, we've seen, is where agriculture first appeared, as well as the earliest agrarian civilizations. So, in some sense, the pace of history has also sped up at least in some parts of this world zone.

The Americas are the second world zone. Since the two American continents touched each other a few million years ago, this is counted as one world zone. In a slightly different geological environment they might have counted as two. So, the American world zone, North America and South America, was the second largest, though it was settled quite late, probably within the last 13,000 to 15,000 years—although it's conceivable, as we've seen, that some settlement was earlier. Now, this was the second world zone in which agrarian civilizations appeared quite independently—though they appeared, as we've seen, significantly later than in Afro-Eurasia.

The third world zone I've called "Australasia." The Australasian world zone includes modern Australia and Papua New Guinea, as well as offshore islands such as Tasmania. And one justification for linking those three areas is that, as we saw, during the last ice age they were indeed a single landmass, when world sea levels were lower than they are today. Now, this was the second of the world zones to be occupied by humans. Humans arrived here probably as early as 50,000 years ago. But in this world zone, the striking and interesting thing is that, though agriculture did appear in Papua New Guinea, it was based there on root crops, which could not be stored easily and did not, therefore, provide the foundation for flourishing agrarian civilization. And in the main part of this zone, in the Australian continent, agriculture itself did not appear. So here, no agrarian civilizations emerged. That's the third world zone, the Australasian zone.

The fourth often gets omitted in surveys of this era. It's the Pacific zone. It was settled within the last 4,000 years by seafaring communities from Southeast Asia who brought the elements of agriculture with them. So here in this zone, some elements of agrarian civilization, or probably we should say sort of embryonic signs of agrarian civilization, did appear, and they appeared on some of the larger islands, such as Hawaii. But in general, the islands of the Pacific were too small to support communities large enough to count as major agrarian civilizations.

So in summary, we can say that agrarian civilizations appeared in only two of our world zones, the Afro-Eurasian and American zones, though humans had appeared in all four zones—and in some sense, agriculture had appeared in all four zones.

Now, before we return to agrarian civilizations, we need to remember one more thing about them, and that is that they never included all human societies. Do you remember the bar scenes in *Star Wars*? Here you find odd, somewhat dangerous-looking people who are clearly from the edges, from the margins. They are "barbarians." All agrarian regions, all agrarian civilizations, were surrounded by regions that their elites tended to look down upon and regard as "barbarians." For the Greeks, incidentally, the word "barbarian" may have been a way of conveying the sort of stammering noise that they heard when listening to foreigners. So, not everyone lived within agrarian civilizations, even in the era of agrarian civilizations.

What other types of communities were there? Well, getting a clear list of this will help, because it'll help us get a sense of the major types of human communities that coexisted in this era. This era, we'll see, is one of the most varied eras in human history.

Okay. One of the major groups that continued to exist on the borders, usually on the borders or sometimes well beyond the borders, of agrarian civilizations were communities of independent farmers. Many people continued to live in small farming communities with rudimentary political structures. Now, these are survivals, if you like, of the villages of the early Agrarian era. So, these communities represent survival of the world of the early Agrarian era. Much of northern Europe, incidentally, consisted of communities like this in the time of the Roman Empire. This was the barbarian frontier that the Romans fought in northern Europe.

Now, the second type of community is pastoral nomads. In arid regions of Inner Asia, parts of North Africa, parts of East Africa, and in the Middle East, there were communities of pastoral nomads. Some of them, like the Mongols in the 13th century, would pose very serious threats to neighboring agrarian civilizations. And the reason for this is that the lifeway of pastoral nomads inculcated military skills—the capacity to move through the landscapes, the ability to hunt, the ability to manage large animals, endurance—so that pastoral nomads were ferocious and dangerous enemies. You could simply mobilize most of the men, and you've got an army. I've done a fair bit of reading about pastoral nomads, and they absolutely fascinate me, and I wish I could justify devoting more time to them in this course. But the only thing

I'll say is that these pastoral nomadic communities, particularly the ones in Asia, would form very, very powerful rivals to great agrarian civilizations. On the north Chinese border, for example, conflict with pastoral nomads was probably the dominant issue in foreign policy for some 2,000 years. So, pastoral nomads are immensely interesting and immensely important, but reluctantly I'm going to have to move on.

The third major type of human community that we need to remember about throughout the era of agrarian civilizations is foraging communities—that is to say, communities that lived with the sort of technologies that we saw in the Paleolithic era. In some regions, such as Australia, everyone continued to live in foraging communities. Foraging remained the dominant technology, the dominant lifeway in Australia until modern times. And foraging communities could be found in Australia and many other parts of the world, indeed, right into the 20th century.

So, when we talk about agrarian civilizations, we must never forget that there are also these other communities. And though they were less numerous than the populations of agrarian civilizations, they occupied very large areas of the world.

So, now the typology of different types of human communities that were slowly building up has four main members: kin-based foraging communities typical of the Paleolithic; the communities of farmers living in villages or very small towns that was typical of the early Agrarian era; third, the pastoral nomadic communities of the steppes and of arid zones; and finally, the large, complex communities of agrarian civilizations. This typology gives us a good idea of the range of different types of community that our species could live in. And it's striking to contrast this range, by the way, with the much more limited range we find in our close relatives, the great apes. This is one more reminder of the astonishing variety of ways in which our species has lived in the course of its history.

Now let's turn finally to agrarian civilizations. And I want to summarize some of the crucial structural similarities between them. Wherever they appeared, whether there was contact between them or not, agrarian civilizations showed some similar features.

The first is size. Agrarian civilizations are very large communities. Compared to all earlier human communities, they were huge and complex, with hundreds of thousands or millions of inhabitants—linked by religion, trade, economics, and politics. So, the appearance of agrarian civilization marks a sort of quantum leap in the size and interconnectedness of human communities. That's the first feature: size.

Secondly, what supported them? What sustained them? They were supported by the surplus labor and produce, above all, of peasants—of peasant farmers—who made up most of the population. Peasant life was tough in agrarian civilizations, and to illustrate this I want to use some wonderful vivid passages from an Egyptian document written about 3,200 years ago, at the end of the 2nd millennium B.C.E. This document consists of advice to a young man about the types of careers to take up, and the first piece of advice you'll see is: Do not be a peasant. It's a reminder that within agrarian civilizations, peasants didn't just feed themselves. That alone was tough enough. But, like domestic animals, they also had to support others, and forcing peasants to support others could be a brutal process.

So, let's look at this document. The document begins by describing the trials of being a peasant:

> By day [it goes], he cuts his farming tools; by night he twists rope. Even his midday hour he spends on farm labor. [In other words, being a peasant is endless. There's always something to be done. It goes on:] He equips himself to go to the field as if he were a warrior. The dried field lies before him; he goes out to get his team. [His team of draft animals.] When he has been after the herdsman for many days, he gets his team and comes back with it.

So first, he has to go and locate his team, which has gotten lost. Then, the document goes on to describe how the team of oxen may have drowned in a swamp. He has lost his oxen, one of his most crucial capital assets. So, he has to borrow a team from someone else. He scatters seeds, and they are immediately eaten by snakes, according to this document—and because his seeds are eaten he has to borrow seed as well as a team of draft animals. Now finally, he gets in trouble with an official, the all-powerful scribe. And at this point we see how the state, the tribute-taking system, also causes headaches for the peasant. So, here's how this section goes:

> Now the scribe lands on the shore. He surveys the harvest. Attendants are behind him with staffs, Nubians with clubs. One of them says [to the peasant]: "Give grain." [That conveys very nicely, actually, the fundamentally arbitrary and brutal way in which tribute-taking states often demanded resources: "Give grain."] "There is none," [says the peasant. The document continues:] He is beaten savagely. He is bound, thrown in the well, submerged head down. His wife is bound in his presence. His children are in fetters. His neighbors abandon them and flee. When it's over, there's no grain.

Now, this is a vivid, literary, and heightened account of the role of the peasantry, but as someone who spent a fair bit of time studying the life of 19th-century Russian peasants, I have to say, I don't really think it's overdrawn. Being a peasant in the era of agrarian civilizations really was tough.

Now, another general feature of agrarian civilizations is specialization and a division of labor. This is a world in which, unlike the world of the early Agrarian villages where most people lived roughly the same, you get in agrarian civilizations a vast range of different specializations, different "professions." Minorities, particularly in towns and cities, supported themselves by exchanging specialist skills.

Now, the Egyptian document I've just used describes several of these professions. So, let me quote it again. And once again this, remember, is a warning to a young man not to attempt these professions. "The potter," it goes on, "is smeared with earth, like a person one of whose folk has died. His hands and feet are full of clay; he is like one who is in the mire." Then it goes on to describe another profession, the sandal-maker, someone who works with leather: "The sandal-maker mixes tan; his odor is conspicuous; his hands are red with madder like one who is smeared with his [own] blood." So, it's a whole range of professions, a great diversity of professions.

Now here's a fourth critical feature of agrarian civilizations, and that's the existence of tribute-taking states. At the core, these are the organizing centers of agrarian civilizations. At their core, we find tribute-taking states. I've defined why I've used this term already. States exacted resources in labor, goods, or cash. Tributary rulers and their servants claimed that they had the right to exact resources. They often claimed that that right was based on religious sanctions, that they had the blessing of the gods. But they could always back up those claims with a threat of force. And we call such exactions "tributes." Their coercive power depended always on the existence of organized armies—or, at minimum, retinues of some kind that could defend against external attacks and could also suppress internal resistance. Or, as in the case of the scribe we've just seen, could impose their will on resistant taxpayers.

Administrative tasks within tribute-taking states—such as the collection and storage of tributes, or the administration of justice and law—were handled by organized groups of literate officials. Now, the document we've been quoting portrays the life of a scribe, and now its author gets to the point. Because what the author is going to recommend to the young man it has been written for is: Be a scribe. This is a much more attractive life than that of the tribute-paying classes, because now you're entering the elite world of tribute-takers. So, here's the description of being a scribe:

> You call to one and a thousand answer to you. You stride freely upon the road and do not become like an ox to be handed over. … attired in fine raiment, with horses, whilst your bark is on the Nile, … you are provided with [attendants], moving freely and inspecting. A villa has been built in your city, and you hold a powerful office, by the king's gift to you. Male and female slaves are in your neighborhood, and those who are in the fields in holdings of your own making will grasp your hand.

This gives you some feeling for being a lord in this world, a member of the elite classes.

Writing, of course, is crucial to the work of the scribe. And writing in some form appears in all agrarian civilizations—though in some cases, as in the case of the Inka, it assumed fairly rudimentary forms. In most cases, it seems to have begun as a form of accounting or record keeping, and then eventually it turned into quite a literary form.

Tributary rulers in all tributary states built "monumental architecture": tombs, palaces, and temples designed to show their majesty and power. These were sort of a form of pre-modern propaganda. They were designed to impress enemies and to impress their own subjects. But they were also a demonstration of their power, because it took a lot of organization to build these things. And at lower levels, rulers depended on local nobles or officials, who duplicated their power on smaller scales, such as the scribe we've been describing.

Now, a fifth general feature of agrarian civilizations is the existence of hierarchies, and often quite rigid hierarchies. It's tempting to think of the word "caste" when we describe them. Hierarchies are very often based on birth, but not exclusively. There were steep hierarchies of wealth and power. Class hierarchies ranked groups by their lineage and social status. Aristocracies were distinguished by their lineage, power, lifestyle, and wealth. And this was a world that was acutely conscious of rank and status. Members of ruling elites generally despised the peasants who generated most of society's wealth. And again, you can pick that up from the passages I've just been reading.

They also tended to regard those outside agrarian civilizations as inferior or subhuman, uncivilized in fact, as in the following document from an 18th-century Qing dynasty emperor, Yongzheng. Emperor Yongzheng writes in 1730:

> What makes humans different from animals are the principles of morality. The Five Relationships are the basis of human morality; if you defy one of them, you are not human. The primary relationship of these is that of ruler and subject. [In other words, if you don't exist within an agrarian civilization, you're not really a human being.] How can we call people human if they have no rulers! Those who want to get rid of rulers are just like animals. … Those who are given rulers by Heaven's mandate, but try to defy Heaven [in other words, rebels], cannot avoid being exterminated by Heaven.

Now, this was his polite way, or not so polite, of saying that the pastoral nomads on China's northern frontier, with whom he had engaged in a major war, barely counted as humans because they were beyond the pale, outside of agrarian civilizations.

Another group that the elites of tribute-taking societies often despised were merchants. Though merchants were sometimes very wealthy and powerful, they were often deeply despised by aristocrats. Now here's a document that illustrates this, and it again comes from China, but this time from China in the Han era, the 2nd century B.C.E. And this writer clearly sees merchants as standing below peasants because they didn't seem to do anything very useful. This was a conventional, Confucian idea of the nature of social hierarchies. "Well-to-do merchants," writes our source, Ch'ao Ts'o:

> Well-to-do merchants accumulate goods and redouble their profits, while the less well-to-do sit in their shops and sell. They control the markets and daily enjoy their ease in the cities. They take advantage of the pressing needs of the government to sell at twice the normal price. Their sons do not plough or hoe. [In other words, they don't do anything very productive or useful.] Their daughters do not raise silkworms or weave. They have fancy clothing and [they] stuff themselves on millet and meat.

This conveys quite well the sort of derisional scorn of merchants that is characteristic of tribute-taking elites.

Power hierarchies also shaped gender hierarchies. As most rulers were men, women rulers were generally regarded as exceptional—which is why, incidentally, the Pharaoh Hatshepsut is often represented wearing a fake beard. However, women often ruled indirectly—through husbands, lovers, or fathers. We shouldn't think that women were absent from these power structures at all.

The Byzantine historian Anna Comnena, whose dates are 1083 to 1153, describes very vividly the immense power wielded by her [grandmother]. And here is a description from her history that conveys well the power of her [grandmother]. It was composed—her history of the reign of her father,

Alexius Comnenus, incidentally, was composed—in a monastery where she had been exiled after an unsuccessful plot. And she modeled her work on the great Greek historians. She writes:

> One might be amazed that my father accorded his mother such high honor ... and that he deferred to her in all respects, as if he were turning over the reins of the empire to her and running alongside her while she drove the imperial chariot, contenting himself simply with the title of emperor. ... He took upon himself the wars against the barbarians and whatever battles and combats pertained to them, while he entrusted to his mother the complete management of [civil] affairs; the selection of civil magistrates, the collection of incoming revenues and the expenses of the government.

She was, argues Anna Comnena, one of the most expert politicians of the time. And I think that account suggests that we should always look for powerful women in the background when we're thinking of tribute-taking states. Though women formally were subordinate, very often they were crucial in traditional power structures.

Okay. Now, let's summarize some of this. In this lecture, I've tried to survey some of the general structural features of agrarian civilizations. In the next lecture, we start looking at how agrarian civilizations evolved over the 4,000 years since their first appearance.

Thank you.

Long Trends—Expansion and State Power
Lecture 33

By 5,000 years ago, by 3000 B.C.E., there were probably about 50 million people on Earth. Now, what this means is that in the early Agrarian era, human populations had multiplied by about 10 times. Then by 1,000 years ago, at the end of the later Agrarian era, there may have been about 250 million people on Earth.

The previous lecture described some general features of Agrarian civilizations. The next three lectures ask: How did Agrarian civilizations change during the 4,000 years of the later Agrarian era? They focus on Afro-Eurasia, the largest and most influential of the four world zones. This lecture describes two ways in which Agrarian civilizations in Afro-Eurasia expanded during almost 4,000 years. First, Agrarian civilizations occupied larger areas and incorporated more people. Second, as rulers got more skillful at their craft, and knowledge of "governance" accumulated within elite groups, the power and reach of states increased.

In the course of 4,000 years, Agrarian civilizations spread to incorporate most of the population of the Afro-Eurasian world zone. Five thousand years ago (in 3000 B.C.E.), Agrarian civilization existed only in Sumer and Egypt. Four thousand years ago (in 2000 B.C.E.), Agrarian civilizations also existed in the north of the Indian subcontinent and along the Yellow River in northern China. By 2,000 years ago, Agrarian civilizations were also flourishing around the Mediterranean basin, in southern China, and in parts of Southeast Asia. By 1,000 years ago, Agrarian civilizations had spread to sub-Saharan Africa, and to both western and eastern Europe.

Estonian American scholar Rein Taagepera has tried to quantify these changes by estimating the areas included within states in "megameters." A megameter is approximately the size of modern Egypt. Though very approximate, these calculations do seem to indicate some clear trends. In 3000 B.C.E., states controlled just 0.2 megameters, which is almost 0.2% of the area of Afro-Eurasia that is controlled by modern states. (Today, of course, states control virtually the entire landmass of Afro-Eurasia, so this is a reminder of how exotic and unusual the first Agrarian civilizations were when they appeared.) In 1000 B.C.E., Agrarian civilizations controlled almost 2.5 megameters (about 2% of the area of Afro-Eurasia that is controlled by modern states). By 1 C.E., with the appearance of huge empires in Persia, China, and the Mediterranean, Agrarian civilizations covered 8 megameters (about 6% of the area under modern states, and about 40 times the area controlled by the very first states). By 1000 C.E., Agrarian civilizations covered about 16 megameters, which is still only about 13% of the area controlled by modern states.

What do these figures suggest? First, they imply population growth. Agrarian civilizations included the most flourishing and productive regions on Earth, so they were the regions in which populations grew most rapidly, and their growth is therefore a key ingredient in the growth of world populations. Ten thousand years ago there were 5–6 million people on Earth. By 5,000 years ago, there were about 50 million people, so the population had multiplied by about 10 times in the 5,000 years of the early Agrarian era. By 1,000 years ago, there were about 250 million people on Earth, so the population had multiplied by about 5 times in the 4,000 years of the later Agrarian era. These figures suggest that, though populations continued to grow in the later Agrarian era, they grew no faster than in the early Agrarian era. Taagepera's figures also remind us that even quite recently many people in Afro-Eurasia still lived outside Agrarian civilizations, in small communities of pastoralists, foragers, or independent peasants. However, Taagepera's figures also chart a fundamental transformation in human history because they suggest that within just 4,000 years most humans on Earth lived within Agrarian civilizations. Agrarian civilizations had become the normal type of community for human beings in Afro-Eurasia (and probably throughout the world).

The area under Agrarian civilizations expanded, in part, because tributary rulers learned to control larger areas. In 3000 B.C.E., states were novelties, and their rulers were unsure of the best ways of managing such vast and complex communities. Over 4,000 years, their political, military, and economic skills improved, and so did their reach and power. The basic challenge was to maximize the resources rulers extracted from populations consisting mainly of small-holding peasants. We call resources extracted in this way "tributes," to contrast them with "gifts" (which are given freely) and "profits" (which are generated through exchanges in competitive markets). The trick was to maximize resource extraction without exhausting the capacity of peasants to keep paying.

Roughly speaking, we can track increasing power by charting the increasing size of states. Rein Taagepera has estimated changes in the areas controlled by particular states. His calculations highlight four main eras in the expansion of state power. The first city-states covered tiny areas. Uruk covered about 2.5 square kilometers (a tiny fraction of 1 megameter), though its rulers also controlled nearby villages. The first Mesopotamian state to include several city-states, that of Sargon of Akkad (2371–2316 B.C.E.), may have controlled 0.6 megameters. In the 2nd millennium B.C.E., the largest states—those of Egypt at its height and Shang China—controlled about 1 megameter of territory, and most controlled much less. So 1 megameter seems to have been a rough upper limit for empires formed before the 1st millennium B.C.E. The Persian Achaemenid Empire, founded by Cyrus II in 560 B.C.E., marks a sudden increase in the size of large states. It covered about 5.5 megameters. For the next 1,500 years, the largest states ranged from about 4 megameters (the Roman Empire) to about 10 megameters (the earliest Islamic empires). In the last 1,500 years, much bigger empires have appeared, starting with the Mongol Empire, which briefly controlled about 24 megameters. These estimates hide eras of collapse and decline, such as the decline of Mesopotamian states early in the 2nd millennium through ecological collapse. Nevertheless, with the benefit of hindsight the long trend toward increasing state power is unmistakable.

How did states expand their power and reach? Rulers increased their military authority partly by recruiting larger armies and equipping them with increasingly sophisticated weapons, such as chariots and siege weapons. Some of the more important innovations, particularly in cavalry warfare, came from the pastoral nomads of the Eurasian steppes. Road building and the establishment of courier or post-horse systems allowed rulers to send armies, supplies, and messages over large distances. We have a wonderful description by Herodotus of the Persian "Royal Road" built between 550 and 486 B.C.E. between southern Persia and modern Turkey. As bureaucracies expanded, they became more effective at managing tax collection over large areas by supervising the activities of local power brokers. The Achaemenid Empire, for example, set quotas in silver for each of its main provinces, and police spies checked up on tax collection. States also developed subtler ways of mobilizing resources. As their reach increased, states created large zones of relative stability within which peasants and merchants flourished, so both populations and available resources increased. In such times, the interests of rulers, peasants, and merchants came closest together, and the most farsighted rulers understood that protecting the interests of those they ruled was often the most effective way of generating taxable wealth. Rulers became increasingly adept at using tributes: first, to bind the ruling elites together through the sharing of privilege; and second, to overawe their subjects by displays of power such as military triumphs or the building of religious monuments that displayed their closeness to the gods.

Rulers increased their military authority partly by recruiting larger armies and equipping them with increasingly sophisticated weapons, such as chariots and siege weapons.

This lecture has surveyed the spread of Agrarian civilizations and their increasing power over almost 4,000 years. The next lectures will ask about rates of innovation in the later Agrarian era. Did Agrarian civilizations encourage or discourage the capacity for innovation that is such a distinctive feature of our species? ∎

Essential Reading

Brown, *Big History*, chaps. 6, 7.

Christian, *Maps of Time*, chap. 10.

Supplementary Reading

Taagepera, "Size and Duration of Empires."

For details on particular civilizations, see Bentley and Ziegler, *Traditions and Encounters;* and Fernandez-Armesto, *The World.*

1. What evidence is there that, broadly speaking, the power of tribute-taking states increased in the 4,000 years after the appearance of the first states?

2. What new techniques and methods enhanced the power and reach of Agrarian states?

Long Trends—Expansion and State Power
Lecture 33—Transcript

For the next group of lectures it might help if we imagine ourselves in a sort of combination time machine and space machine, orbiting the Earth somewhere and looking down during the era of agrarian civilizations over 4,000 years. And what we're going to be looking for is a sort of pattern of spread, and rise and fall, over those 4,000 years. So, that's what we're going to do. We're going to accelerate the pace of history very much, and we're going to look at it from outside the Earth, take the view from space.

The previous lecture described some general features of agrarian civilizations as if agrarian civilizations were static. Now what we do is we start looking for long-term changes over 4,000 years. What were the main changes in this era that was dominated by these huge, complex societies we've called "agrarian civilizations"? Can we stand back from the details and focus on the major changes? Can we see them as if from space? That's the question we tackle in this and the next few lectures.

So we ask: How did agrarian civilizations change during the 4,000 years of the later Agrarian era? In this and the next two lectures, I'm going to focus on the Afro-Eurasian world zone. It's by far the largest, it's by far the oldest, and by almost any criteria, it's the most influential of the four world zones. And then after these three lectures I'm going to look at the rest of the world, and that will allow us to try to get a sense of how typical the experience of Afro-Eurasia was, how great the variety was of historical trajectories in different parts of the world during this era.

And beneath this comparison of different world zones there lurks this deeper question that we've touched on already: Do civilizations, or do human societies more generally, change perhaps in somewhat similar ways? Do they evolve in roughly similar directions? Or do they, for the most part, go their own ways? This question has a bearing on the even deeper issue of whether or not there are long-term tendencies in human history that have shown up wherever conditions were somewhat similar.

And by now you'll not be surprised to find that I will be arguing that there were, indeed, some striking similarities. Human history is not just the story of random change, so that every society could go entirely in its own direction. There are these long-term steering factors that seem to have driven human history, even in very different regions, along roughly similar trajectories. So, we want to get a sense of both the similarities and the differences between different agrarian civilizations and different world zones in this period.

And we'll see that one of the reasons for some similarities is diffusion—the fact that over time, agrarian civilizations in some regions began to touch on each other. They began to exchange goods, ideas, and people. And eventually they began to affect each other.

So, that's one of the reasons for the similarities. But when we look across world zones, we'll be comparing regions that had virtually no contact at all with each other. So, that is the real test of the long-term similarities and the trajectories of history in different regions.

Okay. So, what we're going to see is that there are, indeed, a lot of differences, but underneath them we're going to find some striking and, I think, deeply interesting similarities that can tell us a lot about the nature of human history and, indeed, about the nature of being human.

Now, on to Afro-Eurasia and the Afro-Eurasian world zone. What I want to do in this lecture is to describe two distinct ways in which agrarian civilizations in Afro-Eurasia expanded during almost 4,000 years. Now, this is very much the view from our combination "space and time" capsule—over 4,000 years, but we're focusing on Afro-Eurasia.

The first is expansion. I want to look at the way agrarian civilization, this new type of human community, spread around Afro-Eurasia, how it occupied larger areas and incorporated more and more people—so, the expansion of agrarian civilizations. Secondly, I want to look at the increasing power and reach of tribute-taking states. States are at the core of all agrarian civilizations. And we'll see that over 4,000 years their power expands—their capacity to control resources, their capacity to control people—as rulers became more skillful at their trade and more knowledgeable about how to rule. That knowledge, political knowledge if you like, accumulated over 4,000 years. So, there's an emerging political technology.

As knowledge and understanding of "governance" and the nature of power began to accumulate within the elite groups that ran tribute-taking states, we'll see, their reach increased and so did the power of these states. So, these states got larger, and they seem to have gotten better at the task of organizing and ruling these large and complex societies.

Okay, so first, expansion. I want to look at the way agrarian civilization as a type of community expanded in the Afro-Eurasian world zone over 4,000 years. During this period, agrarian civilizations of some kind spread to incorporate most of the population of the Afro-Eurasian world zone.

We begin 5,000 years ago, in 3000 B.C.E. Five thousand years ago, agrarian civilization existed in Sumer, in southern Mesopotamia, and also in Egypt, and that's it. Four thousand years ago, in about 2000 B.C.E., we can add one or two new areas. Agrarian civilizations, we can say, also seem to have existed in the north of the Indian subcontinent and along the Yellow River in northern China. Now, I need to qualify that, of course, by saying that there is no absolutely rigid marker of the appearance of agrarian civilization. So, once again, these are rough sketch-map dates I'm giving. But agrarian civilizations light up in the Harappan region, along the Indus valley in the north of the Indian subcontinent and in northern China, along the Yellow River.

By 2,000 years ago, agrarian civilizations were also flourishing around the Mediterranean basin—this is the era of the Roman Empire, remember—in South China, the Chinese Han Empire is now dominating not only the north of China, but also the south, and also in parts of Southeast Asia. And then by 1,000 years ago, agrarian civilizations had spread to Africa south of the Sahara, and to both western and eastern Europe.

We can get a slightly better sense of what this really means if we try, roughly speaking, to measure the expansion of agrarian civilization. And here we're talking not just about the states but the areas they controlled as well. None of them had rigid borders. So, again, there's a fair amount of guesswork here. But there's an Estonian scholar who has attempted to make some very rough calculations about the area incorporated within agrarian civilizations over this 4,000-year period. And this is the Estonian American scholar Rein Taagepera. And here are some of his figures.

He estimates the area included within states in square "megameters." To get a sense of what we mean by a square megameter, a square megameter is probably roughly the size of modern Egypt. So, now we need to upload a sort of mental map of Egypt to get a feeling for what a megameter is. These are very rough calculations, of course, like Eric Chaisson's calculations of energy flows. But what we'll see is that they do help us to get a sense of a larger pattern, even if there is plenty of wiggle room on the details. And here are the results of his calculations.

In 3000 B.C.E., states controlled just 0.2 square megameters. Now, Taagepera calculates that this represents about 0.2% of the area of Afro-Eurasia controlled by modern states today. And, of course, that essentially means the whole of Afro-Eurasia. This is a tiny area. Today, states control virtually the entire region. So, what these figures show, what this first set of figures shows, is that when agrarian civilizations first appeared in Sumer and Egypt, they were quite remarkable. They were exotic; they were very rare. They affected a tiny number of people initially. The vast majority of people 5,000 years ago—and we need to remember this, because agrarian civilizations are so exotic they'll tempt us to think about them and to forget everything else—we need to remember that most people still lived in the types of village communities that had become the dominant type of human community during the early Agrarian era.

In 1000 B.C.E.—we've now moved on 2,000 years—agrarian civilizations controlled almost 10 times that area, almost 2.5 square megameters. But even that's only about 2% of the total area of Afro-Eurasia that's controlled by modern states. Now, this is a very significant expansion, but it's still a reminder that most of Afro-Eurasia remained outside agrarian civilizations.

Then, 2,000 years ago, with the appearance of huge empires in Persia, China, and the Mediterranean, agrarian civilizations covered about 8 square megameters. This is about 6% of the area under modern states. This is about 40 times the area controlled when states first appeared. So, this gives us a pretty good feeling for the expansion of agrarian civilizations, even if it also reminds us of how much of Afro-Eurasia remained beyond their borders.

And by 1000 C.E., agrarian civilizations, according to Rein Taagepera's calculations, covered about 16 square megameters. Now, that's still only about 13% of the area controlled by modern states, but it's about 80 times the area controlled by the very first states just 4,000 years before. So, that gives us a very rough way of measuring this process of expansion, measuring the area controlled by agrarian civilizations.

Now, on the assumption that these figures are not too widely inaccurate, what do they mean? Let's try and summarize what they're telling us. One thing they clearly mean is population growth. Agrarian civilizations included the most flourishing and the most productive regions of agriculture on Earth. So, these were the regions in which we should expect populations to be growing most rapidly. And the growth of the populations is, therefore, a key ingredient in the growth of agrarian civilizations. Now, unfortunately, we can't measure precisely the growth of populations within agrarian civilizations, so we're going to have to use a sort of surrogate, and that is plausible estimates of world populations. As the agrarian civilizations of Afro-Eurasia incorporated probably an increasing proportion of world populations, this may give us some very rough idea of how the spread of agriculture continued to sustain population growth—and how the spread of agrarian civilizations parallels growth in populations.

So, here are some figures for world populations. Again, of course, they're very rough estimates. They're probably the best we can do at the moment, but this is the story they tell. Ten thousand years ago, world populations are estimated to have been about 5 million or 6 million.

By 5,000 years ago, by 3000 B.C.E., there were probably about 50 million people on Earth. Now, what this means is that in the early Agrarian era, human populations had multiplied by about 10 times. Then by 1,000 years ago, at the end of the later Agrarian era, there may have been about 250 million people on Earth. So, let's just think about those figures for a moment. What that means is that populations had multiplied by 5 times in 4,000 years. They multiplied by 10 times in 5,000 years, in the early Agrarian era. What's this telling us? Well, I suppose we can say these rates of growth are roughly comparable. If anything, they suggest that rates of population growth may have been slightly slower in the later Agrarian era, and that's slightly surprising. It suggests that population growth was not more rapid in this era than in the early Agrarian era. It's curious, and it's a fact that we're going to pick up later on, because it may be telling us some quite important things about the nature of agrarian civilizations.

Okay. Taagepera's figures also remind us of the limits of agrarian civilizations. They remind us that until quite recently many, many people in Afro-Eurasia still lived outside agrarian civilizations—in small communities of pastoralists, foragers, or independent peasants. We must not let ourselves get so dazzled by them that we lose sight of these many communities.

But, what they do do is chart a fundamental transformation in human society. Five thousand years ago, most humans in Afro-Eurasia lived outside of agrarian civilizations. Three thousand years later, it's probable that most humans lived within them. This is at the time of the Roman and Han empires. And by 2,000 years ago, agrarian civilizations had become the normal type of community for human beings in Afro-Eurasia and probably throughout the world. The role and significance of agrarian civilizations in human history had been transformed in this 3,000- to 4,000-year period. From a new but rare and atypical type of community, they had become—by 1,000 years ago—the most important, powerful, and numerous of all human communities. And most humans on Earth almost certainly lived within the borders of one of them.

Now I want to look at the second major change in the later Agrarian era, and that is the increasing power of states. States lie at the hub of agrarian civilizations. They are the crucial organizing structures of agrarian civilizations. The area under agrarian civilizations expanded, at least in part—one of the factors was because tributary rulers learned to control larger areas. So, what I want to look at now is, as it were, this evolution in statecraft as tributary states became, on a long trend, more efficient at doing what they did best, which was control large areas and exact tributes.

In 3000 B.C.E., tributary states were new phenomena; they were novelties, and their rulers were still unsure of the best ways of managing such vast and complex communities. But over the next 4,000 years, a lot of political, military, and economic skills accumulate, and—as a result—the reach and power of tributary states expanded.

The basic challenge was to maximize the resources rulers extracted from populations that consisted mainly of small-holding peasants. And we've seen that we call resources that are extracted in this way, always with the threat of coercion in the background, though often through claims that states have the right to exact them, we call them "tributes." And we do that to contrast them with two other ways of moving resources. One is "gifts." That is a situation in which someone freely and willingly gives resources to someone else. And the second is "profits." Profits are transfers of wealth that are generated through exchanges on competitive markets—and profits are going to become a very important form of wealth generation in the Modern era.

Tributes could be exacted through the crudest of coercive methods, but we'll see that states, like disease parasites, in general found that they could actually extract resources more efficiently and for much longer periods if they used subtler methods where possible. And these methods included claims to legitimacy—the blessing of the gods, for example—and claims to provide services, such as protection from foreign invaders. One reason why rulers so often portray themselves on monumental architecture as killing the soldiers of foreign armies is presumably to inspire confidence that they can do this, that they can protect you. It's a way of encouraging people to join their team, rather than the other one, in return for tributes. Now, the trick of being a successful tributary ruler is to maximize resource exaction without exhausting the capacity of peasants to keep paying. That's the general trick.

Now, Rein Taagepera has tried to estimate, roughly, changes in the areas controlled by particular states. Now, we're no longer looking at agrarian civilizations as a whole, we're looking at the areas controlled by particular states. So, let's look at his calculations. His calculations highlight four main eras in the expansion of state power.

The first city-states cover tiny areas. Uruk covered about 2.5 square kilometers. That's a tiny fraction of a square megameter, though its rulers also controlled nearby villages. The first Mesopotamian state to include several city-states—that of Sargon of Akkad—may have controlled 0.6 square megameters. So, these are rather small states. The Sargon state is significantly bigger than that of, say, Uruk. It includes several city-states.

In the 2nd millennium B.C.E., the very largest states, those of Egypt at its height and Shang China, probably controlled a maximum of about 1 square megameter of territory. That, let me remind you, is about the size of modern Egypt—and most states controlled much less. So, 1 square megameter seems to have been a sort of upper limit for empires formed before about 1000 B.C.E.

Then we get a huge leap forward, and it seems to be associated with the Achaemenid Empire, which was founded by Cyrus II in Persia, 2,500 years after the appearance of the first states. It was founded in 560 B.C.E., and it was then overthrown by Alexander the Great in 330 B.C.E. The Achaemenid Empire covered, at its height, about 5.5 square megameters. For the next 1,500 years, the largest states that appeared would range from about 4 square megameters (that was probably the size of the Roman Empire) up to about 10 square megameters (the size of some of the earliest Islamic empires).

In the last 1,500 years, much bigger empires have appeared, starting with the Mongol Empire, which briefly controlled about 24 square megameters. Now, again, this is a sketch—these are very large trends. And what these figures hide is eras of collapse and decline, such as the decline of Mesopotamian states early in the 2nd millennium, which we've talked about already. And we need to remind ourselves that contemporaries almost certainly did not experience history as a prolonged expansion of agrarian civilizations. They were much more likely to be aware of the slow rise and fall of dynasties and empires. And that's a phenomenon that we'll look at in Lecture Thirty-Five, when we look at factors that checked growth in the era of agrarian civilizations. Nevertheless, with the benefit of hindsight and Taagepera's calculations, the long trend toward increasing state power seems unmistakable.

Now, what was going on? What was it that states did that increased their reach and power?

Clearly there was a slow learning process going on, as each ruler learned new techniques of rule and as these techniques slowly diffused between different states. Let me just look at some of what seem to have been the critical changes here.

One is simply improved military techniques. These are states that do rely to a considerable degree on coercion. They seem to have been engaged in warfare of some kind almost continuously. So, military improvements may be part of this. Rulers learned to recruit and equip larger armies. They learned to use auxiliaries, such as pastoral nomads from the Eurasian steppes. They introduced increasingly sophisticated weapons, such as chariots and siege weapons.

Some of the more important innovations in this area actually came from the Inner Asian steppes, a region dominated by pastoral nomads, where mobile cavalry warfare was practiced with great efficiency by nomads, such as the Scythians. Chariots with solid wheels drawn by oxen are depicted in Mesopotamia as early as 3000 B.C.E., but the first evidence of light, rapid, and highly mobile war chariots drawn by horses and with spoked wheels appears in tombs of the steppes of modern Kazakhstan about 2000 B.C.E. And that technology spread rapidly both east and west. It spread to China, and it spread to Mesopotamia and to the Indian subcontinent. In the Indian Rig-veda, we learned that chariots were used either for the hurling of spears or in ritual races. They become both symbolically and in real terms crucial to warfare.

Improved communications are also part of it. The most powerful and the most successful rulers often spent a lot of effort road building, in establishing large roads along which armies and messengers could be sent. And they also established courier systems or post-horse systems that allowed probably the most rapid transmission information of anywhere in the world. Let me briefly describe one of the most famous of these roads. It's known as the Persian "Royal Road," and we have a wonderful description of it from the Greek writer Herodotus.

It was built between 550 and 486 B.C.E. by Cyrus II and his successor Darius I, and it was about 1,500 miles long. It ran from Susa in southern Persia through Babylon and Nineveh to Izmir and Ephesus on the Aegean coast of modern Turkey. It probably followed the path of an earlier road, which was really a track that may have existed as early as 3500 B.C.E. In 475 B.C.E., Herodotus said that it normally took about 90 days to travel the entire route. The royal-post riders could travel it in as little as 20 days. It was guarded along its entire length. And Herodotus writes in Book 5 of his *Histories* that: "Royal stations exist along its whole length, and excellent caravanserais," stations where you could stay overnight; restaurants, hotels, motels, we'd call them today, "and throughout," he continues, "it traverses an inhabited tract, and is free from danger."

In Chapter 8:98 of his *Histories*, he describes how the system of roads and post houses was used to transmit royal messages. And let me quote this passage. "Nothing," he writes:

> Nothing mortal travels so fast as these Persian messengers. The entire plan is a Persian invention; and this is the method of it. Along the whole line of road there are men ... stationed with horses, in number equal to the number of days which the journey takes, allowing a man and horse to each day; and these men will not be hindered from accomplishing at their best speed the distance which they have to go, either by snow or rain, or heat, or by the darkness of night. The first rider delivers his dispatch to the second, and the second passes it to the third; and so it is borne from hand to hand along the whole line, like the light in the torch-race, which the Greeks celebrate to Vulcan.

A wonderful description, and it shows that the most intelligent and far-sighted rulers could do a lot of work on what today we might call "infrastructure."

There are also improved systems for collecting tributes. In all agrarian civilizations, tributes seem to have been collected through chains of intermediaries, with local power brokers extracting local taxes and then passing them on to regional governors, regional authorities, governors, or "satraps" they were called in Achaemenid Persia, who passed them on to the central ruler. Once again, from Achaemenid Persia, we have a wonderful literary and visual description of the system by which tributes were exacted under the rule of Darius. In 518, Darius created 20 distinct provinces, each headed by a governor, a satrap, and a separate military commander. And Herodotus in his *Histories* lists the amount of tributes paid by each province. For example, Babylon and Syria—two of the core provinces in the empire, both in Mesopotamia and probably the richest of the provinces—each paid 1,000 talents, the equivalent of about 30 tons of silver. And the trading provinces of Phoenicia, Palestine, and Cyprus paid about 350. Some of this wealth was turned into coins, which were the first to circulate in Central Asia. And the empire as a whole was run from a central bureaucracy in Susa.

Subtler methods of skimming off taxes also developed. As their reach increased, states created large zones of relative stability within which peasants and merchants flourished, so that both populations and available resources increased. And in such times, the interests of rulers, peasants, and merchants probably came closer together than ever before. And the most skillful rulers recognized the fact that if they looked after their people it might eventually benefit them, like the most intelligent disease parasites. Here's a nice quote from an 11th-century Persian prince writing to his son. He says:

> Make it your constant endeavor to improve cultivation and to govern well; for understand this truth; the kingdom can be held by the army, and the army by gold; and gold is acquired through agricultural development and agricultural development through justice and equity. Therefore be just and equitable.

Now, finally, rulers often use their wealth to enhance their power in other ways. Today, we might call this "propaganda." They bound ruling elites together through distributing wealth; they overawed their subjects by displays of religious monuments or other monuments. In an age before newspapers, these were powerful forms of propaganda. And once again, there's a wonderful example from the Achaemenid Empire; it's the Behistun Inscription carved by the Achaemenid Emperor Darius in 515 B.C.E. on a cliff face in Kermanshah Province in Iran. Darius proclaims on these inscriptions high up on a cliff: "I am Darius, the great king, king of kings, the king of Persia, the king of countries, the son of Hystaspes, the grandson of Arsames, the Achaemenid."

And accompanying the inscriptions are wonderful, vivid bas-relief depictions of 10 captured subordinate rulers wearing the appropriate dress—they're tied, they're clearly captives—they wear the appropriate dress of peoples from different regions. These inscriptions, incidentally, were the key eventually to deciphering ancient Persian, ancient Elamite, and ancient Babylonian.

Okay. We've seen, therefore, a lot of ways in which agrarian civilizations expanded and spread, and we've seen also how tributary states became more powerful and better at their job over a period of 4,000 years.

Now, the next lecture is going to ask a slightly different question. Is this growth that we're looking at—to what extent is it dependent on innovation? Did agrarian civilizations encourage or discourage the capacity for innovation that is such a distinctive feature of our species? That's our next question.

Thank you.

Long Trends—Rates of Innovation
Lecture 34

One more example [of micro-innovations] may be the slow spread of windmills. We first get evidence of them in Persia late in the 1ˢᵗ millennium C.E. And then they start to spread quite widely throughout the Mediterranean, eventually in Europe.

By modern standards, change was slow in the era of Agrarian civilizations. So it is all too easy to think of this as an era of stagnation. Yet we have also seen that there was considerable long-term growth in this period, and that suggests that there must have been a continuous trickle of innovations. What factors encouraged innovation in the era of Agrarian civilizations? Earlier lectures argued that collective learning—the ability to share and accumulate learned information—is what makes our species different. Ultimately, collective learning is the source of all innovation in human history. Indeed, collective learning can generate cycles of positive feedback, as innovations allow population growth, which increases the number of people contributing to innovation. But specific features in each era and region can also accelerate or slow the pace of innovation. This lecture discusses four features of Agrarian civilizations that could stimulate innovation.

- Population growth.

- Expanding networks of exchange.

- Increasing market activity.

- The role of states.

Danish economist Ester Boserup (1910–1999) argued famously that population growth can stimulate innovation, as those at the edges of society are forced to seek new ways of feeding and supporting themselves. During the 4,000 years of the later Agrarian era, human populations multiplied by about five times, growing from about 50 million to about 250 million people.

Feeding these growing populations depended on a constant trickle of mini-innovations, some of which were almost certainly driven by population pressure. Peasants or their masters sought out new lands to farm and encouraged settlement in new regions. That meant adapting to new soils, climates, and neighbors and adopting new farming techniques and crops. Examples include new crops such as the strains of rye that allowed farmers migrating from eastern Europe to begin settling the lands of modern Russia some 1,500 years ago, or the slow spread of windmills, which are first recorded in Persia late in the 1st millennium C.E.

Despite their hostility to commerce, tribute-taking rulers could also stimulate innovation and growth.

The increasing size and variety of exchange networks could also stimulate the spread of innovations. Roughly speaking, the larger and more diverse the networks of exchange, the larger the pool of ideas they contained, and the greater the chances for the spread of significant innovations. In the later Agrarian era, the most important large exchange networks were the "silk roads," which crossed most of the Afro-Eurasian world zone.

As early as 4,000 years ago, innovations such as horse-riding and the use of chariots may have diffused from the steppelands to the Mediterranean region and also to China, while Indo-European languages, which probably originated in modern Russia, were spreading toward China, India, and Mesopotamia. Two thousand years ago, trans-Eurasian exchanges became more common. Chinese governments traded with Central Asia, Chinese silks entered Mediterranean markets, and Buddhism traveled from India to China. The travels of Chinese envoy Chang Ch'ien to Central Asia in the reign of Han Emperor Wu-ti (141–87 B.C.E.), or the astonishing military campaigns of Alexander the Great (365–323 B.C.E.), provide vivid illustrations of how Agrarian civilizations from different ends of the Eurasian landmass came into closer contact with each other. Sea trade also increased between the Mediterranean, India, Southeast Asia, and China, as mariners learned to exploit the monsoon winds of the Indian Ocean. By 2,000 years ago, and perhaps earlier, most of Afro-Eurasia belonged to a single "world system." (The term "world system" is derived from the work of Immanuel Wallerstein and refers to a large region linked within a single network of exchanges.) This meant that goods, ideas, religions, and technologies were now being exchanged across the largest of all the world zones.

The expansion of commerce and trade was also a crucial source of innovation. Since Adam Smith (1723–1790), economists have understood that competitive markets encourage innovation. Unlike tributary rulers, merchants lacked the power to generate wealth by force; instead, they had to use finesse. They had to produce and sell goods as efficiently and cheaply as possible. That required a constant openness to innovation. This is "Smithian" growth. Tributary rulers normally despised commerce, but they also needed goods such as rare stones or silks, or horses that only merchants could supply, so they often protected commerce. But merchants flourished best in the cracks between Agrarian empires, such as in small city-states that traded with wealthy neighbors. Venice and Genoa in Renaissance Italy and ancient Phoenicia are good examples of such highly commercial city-states. Urbanization stimulated commerce because cities sucked in goods, techniques, and people from large hinterlands. In 3000 B.C.E., few cities had more than 30,000 inhabitants, and most were in Mesopotamia or Egypt. By 100 C.E., there may have been over 70 large cities spread throughout Afro-Eurasia, some with populations of several hundred thousand (Christian, *Maps of Time*, p. 326).

Despite their hostility to commerce, tribute-taking rulers could also stimulate innovation and growth. Generally, tribute-takers had less incentive to innovate than merchants, because they could extract resources coercively. Indeed, in an era when growth was painfully slow by modern standards, it often made more sense to capture wealth through war, than to produce wealth through investments that could take generations to mature. That is why most rulers in the later Agrarian era thought of themselves primarily as warriors rather than producers. They admired warfare, found fulfillment in it, and spent much time preparing for it. Nevertheless, to succeed as tributary rulers, they sometimes had to encourage innovation. Heavy taxation encouraged innovation, as peasants were forced to raise production in order to feed themselves and pay taxes. The most farsighted rulers understood that they could increase tributes by stimulating production and maintaining infrastructure. That meant protecting peasants, building and maintaining irrigation systems, and avoiding excessive taxation. Military and strategic factors encouraged rulers to undertake large projects that often encouraged trade and commerce. In the Roman Empire, military needs stimulated innovation in road building, bridge building, the construction of aqueducts, and the building of elaborate military catapults and siege engines. Such innovations had significant "trickle-down" effects. Joel Mokyr writes, "The Rome of 100 A.D. had better paved streets, sewage disposal, water supply, and fire protection than the capitals of civilized Europe in 1800" (Christian, *Maps of Time*, p. 321). The building of monuments such as the pyramids could also provide employment and encourage innovation in areas such as architecture, engineering, and mathematics.

We have seen that there were several features of Agrarian civilizations that tended to encourage innovation and growth. Yet we also know that in this era, innovation was much slower than in the Modern era. Why? There must have been other factors that retarded innovation and growth, and indeed there were. We will describe some of them in the next lecture. ∎

Essential Reading

Bentley and Ziegler, *Traditions and Encounters*, chap. 12.

Christian, *Maps of Time*, chap. 10.

Fernandez-Armesto, *The World*, chaps. 7, 8.

Supplementary Reading

Brown, *Big History*, chaps. 7, 8.

Chase-Dunn and Hall, *Rise and Demise*.

Mokyr, *The Lever of Riches*, Introduction, chap. 1.

1. What evidence is there that significant innovation occurred during the era of Agrarian civilizations?

2. What were the main forces that stimulated innovation in the era of Agrarian civilizations?

Long Trends—Rates of Innovation
Lecture 34—Transcript

Growth and constant innovation are often thought to be quite distinctive features of the modern world. And in consequence, all earlier ages of human history are all too easily thought of as eras of stagnation. This is a phenomenon we've encountered several times before. In comparison with today, this is certainly true. Growth and innovation both occurred extremely slowly in all earlier eras of human history. Yet we've seen that even in the Paleolithic and the early Agrarian eras, plenty happened—and there was, indeed, plenty of change, and plenty of that change took forms that we can describe as growth, either as spreading of humans into new areas or an increase in human populations.

Indeed, we've also seen that growth in some sense, the capacity to get more resources, which allows population growth, is intrinsic to our species. It's built into the very idea of "collective learning." And that's why change—and in some sense we can call it "growth"—was always more rapid in human history than it is in the animal world. Nevertheless, it is also true that rates of growth and innovation have varied significantly in different eras of human history. And the most spectacular example is, of course, modern society. Today growth and innovation are much, much faster than ever before. And this, we'll see, is one of the defining features of modern society.

So, now I'd like to ask: What's the difference? To understand these differences we need to ask the sort of questions economists ask. We need to ask: What are the drivers of growth? I've argued in very general terms that collective learning is a sort of general driver of growth throughout human history. But in different epochs, collective learning may take different forms. So we need to ask: What specific drivers shaped innovation and growth in particular periods? And here we look at the later Agrarian era.

We ask: Did agrarian civilizations accelerate the pace of change? Did they tend to stifle change? Is there anything in their structures that had a tendency to increase or retard patterns of growth and innovation? And we'll, in fact, find both. But in this lecture I'm going to focus on structural features of agrarian civilizations that tended to stimulate growth. And we'll see there were quite a few of them.

So, the previous lecture described the long-term expansion of agrarian civilizations and states. And what we're doing here is we're trying to look at some of the drivers that lay behind that long-term process of expansion. So, we'll see that several structural features of agrarian civilizations did clearly encourage growth and innovation. This is not an era of stagnation at all. What were they?

This lecture discusses four features of agrarian civilizations that could stimulate innovation. This is not, of course, a complete list. One could imagine many other factors that might have stimulated innovation, including, for example, the extent and scale of educational systems, which are generally very limited in agrarian civilizations, or government investment in innovation, also extremely rare—with some remarkable exceptions such as the famous Library of Alexandria, which was founded about 300 B.C. with the support of a Roman Egyptian ruler, Ptolemy II.

But with these exceptions, the factors I'm going to describe probably count as some of the main structural features of agrarian civilizations that tended to encourage innovation. Let's look at them. The first is population growth. Could population growth itself drive innovation? The second is expanding networks of exchange, an increase in the area over which humans and different societies exchanged information. The third is increasing market activity. And the fourth is the role of states. So, let's look at each of these possible drivers in turn.

First, population growth as a source of innovation. In previous lectures, we've taken population growth as a sort of indicator of growth. But it's also possible to treat it as a possible driver of growth. This idea is associated often with the work of a Danish economist, Ester Boserup, whose dates are 1910 to 1999. She argued famously that population growth, particularly in agrarian societies, can itself stimulate innovation, as those at the edges of society are forced to seek new ways of feeding and supporting themselves. Now, this is a mechanism we've already touched on in looking at the early Agrarian era.

During the 4,000 years of the later Agrarian era, human populations multiplied a lot, by about five times, we've seen—from about 50 million to about 250 million people. Clearly, this meant a growing need to feed larger and larger numbers of people. And that implies that there had to be innovations to do it. Now, to what extent did population growth itself drive these innovations? It almost certainly drove at least some innovation. We know that throughout this era, peasants or their masters were seeking out new lands to farm. There's plenty of evidence in the spread of agriculture, of farmers, peasants, sometimes with the help of overlords, incorporating new land into their farms, settling new regions, and so on.

That meant, always, tiny bits of innovation. It meant adapting to new soils. It meant getting used to new rainfall regimes. It meant dealing with new types of pests, new types of predators. So, always, settling new areas meant innovation of some kind. We can imagine villages where populations grew so that younger people wanting to set up a household no longer could do so in the village. They had to spread to a neighboring region. And that, too, might involve tiny modifications of traditional techniques. This is micro-innovation, but it's going on over a huge area, and millions of people are involved in the process. And it may have been one of the key dynamics of agrarian civilizations. A lot of their expansion may have been driven by this steady, constant trickle of micro-innovation similar to, but much more rapid than, the micro-innovations that sustained migrations in the Paleolithic era.

Now, if this is true, if this idea is right, it suggests that in this era a lot of innovation was coming from peasant farmers. Occasionally, of course, their overlords may have helped them with projects such as the building of dams or helping them to migrate to new regions. Examples of such innovations might include new strains of crops. For example, we know that the regions between the Urals and eastern Europe that are now parts of Russia and Ukraine weren't farmed extensively, didn't have large populations of farmers, until about 1,500 years ago. And then, relatively suddenly, we get migrations from eastern Europe into this region. And we're still not absolutely sure what causes this. But almost certainly, once again, it's a series of micro-innovations. Now, one of them might have been the development of new strains of rye. Rye is crucial for this migration that laid the foundations for the first medieval state of Russia. And that may have allowed farmers to begin settling these lands 1,500 years ago.

Another example is the new types of horse yokes that appear in medieval Europe. Earlier horse yokes in medieval Europe sort of were fixed around the necks of horses. And the result is if the horse pulled too hard, it tended to choke. New yokes evolved that actually were attached to the shoulders of the horse. And this meant that the horse could exert its full force without choking. And that, of course, meant that you could plow deeper, you've got more draft power available, and that can allow you to plow lands you couldn't plow before, and so on. So, a lot of these micro-innovations could make a lot of difference.

One more example may be the slow spread of windmills. We first get evidence of them in Persia late in the 1st millennium C.E. And then they start to spread quite widely throughout the Mediterranean, eventually in Europe. So, that's the first factor. Population growth itself may have driven lots of micro-innovations as peasants (particularly at the margins of society) sought out new lands and new techniques to enable them to survive in a world of expanding populations.

The second is expanding networks of exchange as sources of innovation. The idea of collective learning implies, of course, that the foundation of innovation in human history is exchanges of ideas between different individuals and different populations. So, here we're building on that idea.

If it's true that exchanges of ideas between different populations are an important source of the accumulation of new technologies, then it should also follow that as people exchange ideas, goods, technologies, and migrants over larger areas, this expansion in exchange networks should itself generate a new synergy in collective learning. So, it makes sense to assume that increasing exchange networks themselves drives innovation. So, we're saying that, roughly speaking, we assume that the larger and more diverse the networks of exchange, the larger the pool of ideas they contain, and the greater the chances for the spread of significant innovations.

So, the question is: Can we sort of track an expansion in exchange networks? And, indeed, we can throughout the later Agrarian era. And essentially, what we can show is that though agrarian civilization appeared first in a series of distinct regions—slowly, over 4,000 years, those regions become more integrated internally, and then eventually more contacts develop between them. Perhaps the best known example of this, or illustration of this, is the famous "silk roads," which crossed most of the Afro-Eurasian world zone leading from the Mediterranean right across Eurasia to China, and there are also north-south branches that led into northern India.

Pastoral nomads play a crucial role in the evolution of the silk roads. Pastoral nomadism is itself a product of the secondary products revolution, and it begins to spread in the Inner Asian steppes, certainly from about 3000 B.C.E. And by about 2000 B.C.E.—that's to say about 4,000 years ago—pastoral nomads occupy much of the Inner Asian steppe. So, here you have a zone of immense mobility, so that ideas and technologies can move through this zone much more easily than in more sedentary regions. And there's very good reason to think that a number of technologies, such as horse-riding and many of the technologies that go with it, and also the use of chariots, diffused from regions of pastoral nomadism in Inner Asia through to the Mediterranean in the West and to China in the East. The first clear evidence of chariots is actually found in Kazakhstan in about 2000 B.C.E.

And pastoral nomads may also play a crucial role in the spread of languages, another form of exchange of populations and ideas. Indo-European languages quite probably—this is not yet certain—developed somewhere on the border between modern Russia and Kazakhstan among populations that would eventually become pastoral nomads. And as pastoral nomadism spread, it seems that it carried with it early forms of Indo-European languages.

So, pastoral nomadism itself did a lot to connect different regions, different agrarian civilizations of Afro-Eurasia. By about 2,000 years ago, these connections are becoming tighter and having a much greater impact. Trans-Eurasian exchanges begin to become much more common. We'll see that the Chinese government is beginning to trade with Central Asia in the last century of the 1st millennium B.C.E. Chinese silks start entering Mediterranean markets. Roman coins begin to be carried in the opposite direction—Mediterranean glassware as well. And Buddhism begins to travel, to make its epic journey from India to China. So ideas, religion, technologies, and goods begin to be transmitted between all the great regions of agrarian civilization in Afro-Eurasia, certainly from about 2,000 years ago—and this is when the silk roads really begin to flourish.

Now, let me try and illustrate this process a bit less abstractly. This talk of exchange networks all sounds very abstract, but if you associate it with, say, the travels of a Marco Polo in the 13th century or the campaigns of an Alexander the Great, it's much more vivid. So, I'd like to give one wonderful example of what processes lay behind this gradual integration of Afro-Eurasian agrarian civilizations into a larger network of exchange.

This comes from the Han era of Chinese history from the 2nd and 1st centuries B.C.E. And I'm going to describe an immensely important episode in Chinese history that is described by the imperial historian Ssu-ma Ch'ien, whose dates are 145 to 85 B.C.E. In 139 B.C.E., the great Han emperor, Wu-ti, whose dates are 141 to 87 B.C.E., was engaged in a prolonged campaign against a pastoral nomadic empire known as the Xiongnu, who are precursors of the Mongols—and they were based, like the Mongols, in Mongolia. He decided to try to outflank them by finding if he could find allies to the west. But the Chinese government at this time knew very little about what lay off to the west. So what he did was he sent an envoy, an official called Chang Ch'ien, to contact another group of nomads, the Yüeh-chih, who had migrated westwards after being defeated by the Xiongnu. So, Wu-ti sends Chang Ch'ien westwards to try and find allies against the Xiongnu.

Now, this was an extremely dangerous mission. The Xiongnu still controlled the Kansu corridor. The Gobi Desert runs through a lot of it, and it reaches from western China over to Central Asia. The Xiongnu still controlled much of this area through which Chang Ch'ien would have to travel. Now, he sets out in 139 B.C.E. with a Xiongnu slave and interpreter, Kan Fu, and an embassy of 100 men. But he's captured pretty soon in the Kansu corridor, and he's captured by the Xiongnu, and he's held by them for 10 years. But eventually, with Kan Fu and a Xiongnu bride, he escapes, and he travels on through modern Sinkiang to the kingdom of Ta-Yüan, which is modern Fergana in modern Uzbekistan in Central Asia. With help from the ruler of

Ta-Yüan, he travels on to the kingdom of the Yüeh-chih, who are now settled in the north of modern Afghanistan and in southern Uzbekistan. And he finds that they're not at all interested in an alliance. They've escaped from the Xiongnu, and they're happy in southern Uzbekistan. And so he returns, but he returns with a lot of new information.

He returns through the Tarim Basin, this amazing circle of trading cities that Marco Polo would travel through more than a millennium later. And he's captured once more by the Xiongnu on his way back. He escapes again after another year of captivity. And then, in 125 B.C.E., 13 years after he had left, he finally returns to China with only his wife and his slave.

Chang Ch'ien's trip was an event of great significance in the history of Han China (and even, in a sense, of Eurasia as a whole), for it marks the beginning of the first successful attempts by China and Chinese governments to establish official diplomatic, political, and commercial links with Central Asia. In his report to Emperor Wu-ti, Chang Ch'ien described the walled cities of Fergana, the region's famous wines, and its heavenly horses that seemed to sweat blood. And he also passed on indirect descriptions of other lands about which the Chinese knew almost nothing, including India, Parthia, and Mesopotamia. This, remember, is just over 2,000 years ago. And the fact that they knew nothing is a reminder of how limited contacts were between different regions of Afro-Eurasia. So, his expedition vastly expanded Chinese knowledge of other regions of Afro-Eurasia.

Knowledge of the wealthy lands of Central Asia encouraged Wu-ti to attempt to establish Chinese alliances with them and maybe suzerainty over them. In 117 B.C.E., Chang Ch'ien, though now in disgrace for his failures in a campaign against the Xiongnu, is given a chance to redeem himself by leading a second expedition westwards. He establishes regular diplomatic relations with nomadic communities on the route to Central Asia, potential allies against the Xiongnu. And eventually, a later expedition—a massive expedition sent from China under a Korean commander—finally manages to conquer some of the kingdoms of Central Asia.

Now, we can imagine many such episodes in different parts of Eurasia, each of which has the result of slowly, slowly integrating the agrarian civilizations of the entire landmass and massively increasing the information that is exchanged between different regions.

Early in the 1st millennium C.E., sea routes also began to flourish around the south of Eurasia. Sea trade increased rapidly between the Mediterranean, India, Southeast Asia, and China at the same time as land contacts were multiplying along the silk roads. And this was partly because mariners from the Mediterranean region finally learned to exploit the monsoon winds of the Indian Ocean.

Now, the result of all of this was that by about 2,000 years ago, as the late Andre Gunder Frank has argued, most of Afro-Eurasia belonged to a single "world system." The term "world system" is derived from the work of sociologist Immanuel Wallerstein, and it refers to a large region in which several different agrarian civilizations are linked within a single network of commercial and intellectual and political exchanges. So, what this means is that goods, ideas, religions, and technologies are now being exchanged across the largest of all the world zones. So, I hope you get a sense of the sort of power of this integrative process. It's an early stage of what today we call "globalization," and it has a similar stimulating effect on innovation.

Now, here's a third factor: commerce and trade as sources of innovation. The expansion of commerce and trade was undoubtedly a very powerful source of innovation throughout this era. Since the time of Adam Smith, whose dates are 1723 to 1790, economists have understood perfectly well (and this is really Econ 101) that competitive markets encourage innovation. And the essential reason is this: Tributary rulers have the power to exact resources by force in the form of tributes. Merchants, by and large, lacked the power to generate wealth by force. Instead, they had to generate wealth by finesse, and this normally meant that they had to produce and sell goods as efficiently and cheaply as possible. They had to produce them more efficiently, they could distribute them more efficiently, they could find new markets—but however they did it, most methods of making a profit required an openness to innovation. This is what we can call "Smithian" growth—innovation driven by commerce on competitive markets.

We need to be very clear about the logic of this. Tributary rulers, we'll see, normally despised commerce. But they also needed goods (such as rare stones or silks) or horses (such as the blood-sweating horses of Fergana that Emperor Wu-ti was so keen to get hold of). And if these goods lay beyond their frontiers, you could only really get them through merchants. So, very often we find governments, tributary rulers, supporting the activities of merchants because it's the only way of getting certain goods.

However, merchants—though sometimes they found sponsors among tributary rulers—tended to flourish best in the cracks between agrarian empires, such as in small city-states that traded with or between agrarian civilizations. Venice and Genoa in the last millennium are a spectacular example of such systems. Earlier on, Phoenicia in modern Lebanon was a very good example of highly developed, small commercial city-states that flourished in between great and wealthy tributary empires.

Urbanization also stimulated commerce in this period because cities sucked in goods, techniques, and people from large hinterlands. So, urbanization undoubtedly stimulated commerce, too. In 3000 B.C.E., few cities had more than 30,000 inhabitants. Most were in Mesopotamia or Egypt. By about 1200 B.C.E., it's been estimated large cities had also appeared in India and China. And by about 100 C.E., there may have been over 70 large cities in Afro-Eurasia. So, we can sort of track the spread in the number and size of cities in Afro-Eurasia. And this undoubtedly stimulated commerce, and as we've seen, it's a very good presumption that as commerce spread, it encouraged innovation.

Now, a fourth driver of innovation in this period is tribute-taking states themselves. Tribute-taking states were immensely powerful organizers, so we really need to look carefully at them and their impact on innovation. Could they stimulate innovation or not? Well, here we're going to see the story's a bit ambiguous.

By and large, tribute-taking elites tended to be quite hostile to commerce. They tended to despise commerce. They didn't need to negotiate for wealth; they took it. Nevertheless, there were various ways in which they could stimulate innovation. One we've seen already is by encouraging commerce in areas where they needed to get strategic foreign goods. But generally, tribute-taking states and the elites that ran them had less incentive to innovate than merchants. And there's a very simple reason for this. They could extract resources coercively. They could take resources by force. And this is a very powerful general rule.

In an era when growth was painfully slow by modern standards, it often made more sense to *capture* wealth through war, if you had the ability to do so, than to *produce* wealth through investments that might take generations to mature. Now that, I think, is a fundamental reason why most rulers in the later Agrarian era thought of themselves primarily as warriors rather than producers, as takers of wealth rather than generators of wealth. They admired warfare, and they found fulfillment in it. And that's an attitude that is not that easy to appreciate in a world committed, formally at least, to the virtues of peace. Let me just quote a very short passage that conveys this kind of exuberant, unashamed delight in warfare and slaughter, the bloodiest parts of warfare. It comes from a 12th-century French writer who's describing, we have to call it "the joy of battle," and this is what he says:

> I tell you that I never eat or sleep or drink so well as when I hear the cry, "Up and at 'em!" from both sides, and when I hear the neighing of riderless horses in the brush and hear shouts of "Help! Help!" and see men fall and the dead pierced in the side by gaily-pennoned spears.

Now, it's a literary example, but I think it conveys an entire world in which warfare was seen as fulfillment, as self-expression, and as what rulers did.

There's a lovely quote also from Machiavelli. In *The Prince* he's very clear about this. And he writes that if you're a prince, what you need to think about all the time is war. War is the key to success. "A Prince, therefore," he writes, "should have no other object or thought, nor acquire skill in anything, except war, its organization, and its discipline. The art of war is all that is expected of a ruler."

Now, I have to say that Machiavelli is writing at a time and in a place where these rules are changing. So, he's really describing those kinds of archetypes of the tribute-taking world. "The first way to lose your state," he writes, "is to neglect the art of war; the first way to win a state is to be skilled in the art of war." And this fact, that taking wealth is the key to success in a world of tributary states and tribute-taking states, has lots of consequences for elite culture. Machiavelli describes them well:

> The Prince [he writes] should never let his thoughts stray from military exercises, which he should pursue more vigorously in peace than in war. These exercises can be both physical and mental. As for the first, besides keeping his men well organized and trained, he should always be out hunting.

This, I think, suggests why hunting has always been such an admired skill among the elites of tribute-taking states. By hunting he is accustoming his body to hardships and also learning some practical geography—how the mountains slope, how the valleys open, how the plains spread out.

So, the basic skill of being a tributary ruler is military: It's knowing how to handle warfare. Nevertheless, having said all of this, sometimes to succeed, tributary rulers had to encourage innovation. For example, in some situations, heavy taxation could encourage innovation by forcing peasants to raise production in order to feed themselves and pay taxes. We've seen that some rulers knew perfectly well that they could increase tributes by stimulating production and maintaining infrastructure. That meant protecting peasants, building and maintaining irrigation systems, and avoiding excessive taxation.

And finally, military and strategic factors encouraged rulers to undertake large projects that often encouraged trade and commerce. In the Roman Empire, military needs stimulated innovation in road building, bridge building, the construction of aqueducts, and the building of elaborate military catapults and siege engines. And such innovations could have a significant "trickle-down" effect, to use modern jargon. Joel Mokyr writes in *A History of Technology*: "The Rome of A.D. 100 [100 C.E. in our terminology] had better paved streets, sewage disposal, water supply, and fire protection than the capitals of civilized Europe in 1800."

Finally, the building of monumental architecture (the building of pyramids, for example) could provide employment and encourage innovation in areas such as architecture, engineering, and mathematics.

So, there were several areas in which the activities of tribute-taking states encouraged innovation, particularly areas of direct interest themselves—such as architecture, building, and warfare. So, in all of these ways, agrarian civilizations could drive growth. These are some of the specific mechanisms of growth in agrarian civilizations. And yet, we know growth was nothing like as fast as today. Why not? We'll ask that question in the next lecture.

Thank you.

Long Trends—Disease and Malthusian Cycles
Lecture 35

Tribute-taking states, we've seen, could encourage growth in several ways, but they could also discourage it. So, their overall impact on growth was rather contradictory. They stifled growth in many subtle and not-so-subtle ways.

The previous lecture described some of the ways in which Agrarian civilizations could stimulate innovation. Yet if this is true, why were rates of innovation so much slower than in the modern world? Why were there such regular famines, and why did entire civilizations seem periodically to collapse? We will see that sometimes the same features that stimulated growth and innovation could also act as checks to growth. These factors help explain why ancient society did not show the productive dynamism of the most productive of modern societies. Exploring these features will eventually help us to better appreciate some of the distinctive features of the Modern era.

Because we have been focusing on long-term trends, we have focused on growth. But at smaller scales, and to thoughtful contemporaries, what stood out more sharply was a pattern of rise and fall that made history seem cyclical rather than directional. Peasants, too, were more aware of the cycles of the seasons and of years of feast and famine than of the long-term trend toward growth. Why did growth in this era always seem to be followed by collapse? Two main types of collapse stand out: political collapse (such as the decline of the Roman Empire) and demographic collapse (such as the Black Death), and often the two went hand in hand.

Shelley's poem *Ozymandias,* written in 1817, provides a powerful symbol of political decline. As it happens, we know more or less who "Ozymandias" was. Shelley wrote his poem after hearing of the imminent arrival in the British Museum of a bust of Pharaoh Ramses II, "The Great," who ruled Egypt for much of the 13th century B.C.E. What factors tended to undermine the power of rulers such as Ramses?

There is also a demographic oddity about this era. We have seen that, despite improved forms of agriculture and irrigation, populations grew no faster in the later Agrarian era than in the early Agrarian era. Indeed, in the 1st millennium C.E. there appears to have been hardly any growth at all in Afro-Eurasia. What factors checked population growth?

There was plenty of innovation in this era, but it was never rapid enough to keep pace with population growth.

One of the curiosities of the later Agrarian era is that the same factors that stimulated innovation could also check growth. The political structures of tribute-taking states could certainly encourage growth in some areas, but they also stifled growth in many subtle and not-so-subtle ways. Normally, tribute-taking rulers were more interested in capturing wealth than in producing it. A successful war could generate wealth much more quickly than investment in infrastructure. Seeing themselves as capturers rather than producers of wealth, tribute-taking elites generally despised producers and merchants and took limited interest in how goods were produced and traded. Such activities discouraged policies that actively supported production and commerce. The structures of tributary power also stifled growth in subtler ways. As Marx pointed out, tribute-taking states had to ensure that peasants had access to land. However, this limited wage-earning employment. It also deprived peasants of any incentive to raise productivity, as they knew that any surpluses would be skimmed by their overlords. In summary, those who produced society's wealth generally lacked the education, the capital, and the incentive to innovate; while the elites, who had the education and the wealth, generally despised productive or commercial activities and preferred to take wealth rather than to generate it. Outside the specialist domains of warfare and administration, tribute-taking rulers took little interest in improved efficiency or innovation.

Patterns of disease frequently checked population growth. Two factors stand out, both closely linked to factors that, in other ways, could stimulate growth. While cities could stimulate growth by encouraging commerce, they could also stifle demographic growth (itself a key driver of growth, as we have seen) by creating lethal disease environments, so urban populations had to be constantly replenished by immigration from rural areas. Diseases spread rapidly in filthy city streets; human and animal wastes accumulated in public places and waterways; rivers were treated as sewers and dumps; and city air was often polluted by fires and manufacturing processes such as smelting or tanning. The expansion of exchange networks, another important driver of growth in this era, also encouraged the spread of disease. As William McNeill showed in his classic study *Plagues and Peoples*, diseases spread along trade routes, along with goods and ideas. As exchange networks expanded, they spread diseases to new regions. Indeed, he argues that both the Roman and Han empires may have declined, in part, because of the spread of devastating plagues along Eurasia's expanding trade routes.

While humans are very good at finding new ways of exploiting their environments, they are not as good at identifying the limits of ecological exploitation. Time and again, Agrarian civilizations grew so rapidly that they began to overuse their forests, their rivers, and their crop lands to the point where entire civilizations collapsed. Estimates of populations in Mesopotamia over 7,000 years show two periods of sudden decline. The sudden collapse early in the 2nd millennium B.C.E. was almost certainly caused by over-irrigation leading to salination and declining harvests. According to one estimate, Mesopotamian populations fell from over 600,000 in 1900 B.C.E. to about 270,000 by 1600 B.C.E., not to rise again for at least a millennium. A similar pattern of growth and decline would be repeated again early in the second millennium C.E.

These and other factors meant that, alongside the positive feedback cycles that drove innovation and growth, there were also negative feedback cycles that inhibited growth. This balance shaped the fundamental rhythms of historical change throughout the later Agrarian era. A typical cycle began with innovations that stimulated population growth, which in turn stimulated growth in other sectors. Eventually, though, populations began to press against ecological constraints. Shortages appeared, as did growing evidence of malnutrition, which encouraged disease. States increasingly began to fight over scarce resources; and finally, through warfare, disease, or famine, populations crashed. These rhythms are very clear on a graph of Eurasian populations over the last 2,000 years.

We will call these rhythms, which dominate the history of the later Agrarian era, "Malthusian cycles." Thomas Malthus was one of the pioneers of modern demography. He argued that in all species, populations tend to grow geometrically while resources tend to grow arithmetically. Eventually, this means that population growth is bound to outstrip the available resources, leading to disease, famine, and demographic collapse. Economic historian Robert Lopez describes these cycles as "an alternation of crest, trough and crest ... [that] can be observed not only in the economic field, but in almost every aspect of life" (Christian, *Maps of Time*, p. 309). As French historian Le Roy Ladurie puts it, these cycles were like the "respiration," the in-breaths and out-breaths, of an entire social structure (Christian, *Maps of Time*, p. 309). Explaining these cycles takes us to the heart of the issue of innovation in Agrarian civilizations. There was plenty of innovation in this era, but it

was never rapid enough to keep pace with population growth. This fundamental fact explains the persistence of Malthusian cycles over several millennia despite a long term tendency toward growth throughout the later Agrarian era.

Corel Stock Photo Library.

Rameses, Egyptian ruler for much of the 13th century, built this tomb, Ramesseum, for himself outside of Thebes.

We have seen that in the later Agrarian era many of the factors that stimulated growth in some ways could also inhibit or help to stifle growth and innovation. This balance of forces that encouraged and stifled growth explains why, eventually, each phase of expansion ended in collapse. In the last three lectures we have concentrated on Afro-Eurasia. But how typical was the history of the Afro-Eurasian zone of humanity as a whole? To answer that question we shift our focus to the Australasian, Pacific, and American world zones and ask what was happening there. ∎

Essential Reading

Christian, *Maps of Time*, chap. 10.

Fernandez-Armesto, *The World*, chaps. 4, 8, 14.

Supplementary Reading

Mann, *1491*.

McNeill, *Plagues and Peoples*.

Questions to Consider

1. What forces inhibited innovation in the era of Agrarian civilizations?

2. Why did Malthusian cycles play such a dominant role in the history of all Agrarian civilizations?

Long Trends—Disease and Malthusian Cycles
Lecture 35—Transcript

In the previous lecture, we saw that there was actually significant growth in the era of agrarian civilizations, and significant innovation. And that lecture showed that there were several structural features of agrarian civilizations that encouraged innovation and growth. Now, if that's true, though, there's a problem that a modern economist or economic historian will naturally stumble over. If there was so much growth and innovation going on in the later Agrarian era, why didn't ancient societies innovate at the same rate as modern societies? Why didn't they generate the astonishing material wealth of the most productive of modern societies? What was wrong with them, frankly? Why were there such regular famines? And why did civilization seem to periodically collapse?

What we'll see in this lecture is that there were also important features of agrarian civilizations—and often they were the same features operating in slightly different ways—that tended to retard growth. And it's these factors that help explain why no ancient society showed anything like the productive dynamism of the most productive of modern societies.

So, considering this question about the era of agrarian civilizations, why growth wasn't faster, will eventually help us understand better what is so distinctive about the Modern era. Because one of the things we'll see is that eventually, in the last few centuries, it's as if the brakes were taken off. So, why was growth so slow in the era of agrarian civilizations by modern standards? And why was it so often followed by catastrophic crashes?

Now, it may seem as if in the last few lectures I've been offering a story of progress, an ever onward and upward story of unending progress, as collective learning leads to constant increases in productivity. And we need to remind ourselves that the very large view of big history is capable of hiding things as well as the small view. And what we've been focusing on are such large chunks of time that we've missed the middle range trends that are so familiar to what we can call the "rise and fall school of historiography."

Many traditional historians saw history fundamentally as cyclical. And this is because what they were aware of was the periods of decline as well as the periods of growth. And we, too, need to take those periods seriously. A cyclical view of history probably represented quite well the experience of contemporaries—most of whom were peasants, remember, for whom the cycles of the seasons or the eras of feast and famine were by far the most striking rhythms of life.

What the large view of big history brings out more clearly is that despite these cycles there were long-term increases in scale and productivity. But this long trend was not necessarily apparent in smaller scales. In many eras and for many individuals, decline must have been more apparent than growth. So why? What factors tended to slow innovation and growth, and why did civilizations periodically break down?

In this lecture we look at some of these factors that tended to break down, to nibble away at the complexity of the agrarian world. We're looking, in effect, at the workings of the social equivalent of entropy. So, what we're going to look at now are these large cyclical trends. And in particular, what we're going to look at are the causes for the decline: for the decline and fall of Rome, of the rise and fall of Chinese dynasties. Why these cycles?

Now, let's begin with Shelley's poem *Ozymandias*. It captures poetically this sense of decline, of periodic decline, of nothing being durable in this era. Let me just quote Shelley's poem. Here's how it goes:

> I met a traveler from an antique land
> Who said: Two vast and trunkless legs of stone
> Stand in the desert. ... Near them, on the sand,
> Half sunk, a shattered visage lies, whose frown,
> And wrinkled lip, and sneer of cold command,
> Tell that its sculptor well those passions read
> Which yet survive, stamped on these lifeless things,
> The hand that mocked them, and the heart that fed:
> And on the pedestal these words appear:
> "My name is Ozymandias, king of kings:
> Look on my works, ye Mighty, and despair!"

Nothing beside remains. Round the decay
Of that colossal wreck, boundless and bare
The lone and level sands stretch far away.

It's a wonderful evocation of the decline of the greatest tributary rulers and the civilizations they built. Now, as it happens, we know more or less who "Ozymandias" was. Shelley wrote the poem in 1817 after hearing of the imminent arrival in the British Museum of a bust of Pharaoh Rameses II, Rameses "The Great." *Ozymandias* is probably a Greek rendition of his Egyptian throne name. Rameses "The Great" ruled Egypt for much of the 13th century B.C.E. The figure had been taken from the tomb known as the Ramesseum, the temple that Rameses built for himself outside of Thebes, which is modern Luxor. And you can still see the Ramesseum.

Now, how can we explain these periodic crashes? What was it that consigned the glory of so many different Ozymandiases to dust?

Apart from the periodic crashes of entire civilizations, there's also a demographic oddity about this era that needs to be explained. We saw in an earlier lecture that our very, very rough estimates of world population suggest that in the 4,000 years of the era of agrarian civilizations, world population grew at about the same pace as in the early Agrarian era, or possibly even more slowly. It grew from about 50 million to about 250 million. This means that it multiplied by about 5 times in 4,000 years, in comparison with the multiplication of about 10 times in 5,000 years during the early Agrarian era. Indeed, the available evidence suggests there was hardly any growth at all in the 1st millennium C.E.—that's the era after the decline of the Roman and Han Chinese empires.

Now, if these figures are conveying the right impression—and they're so rough that they could well be deceiving us—but if they're conveying the right impression, we have to ask why, despite the innovation that undoubtedly occurred in the later Agrarian era—and it included, I remind you, such things as the spread of the secondary products revolution, plow agriculture, and the spread of irrigation—why didn't population grow any faster?

Okay. Let's look now at some of the factors that slowed growth. There were doubtless many more factors than the ones I mention. But what we're going to see is that one of the curiosities of this era is that some of the factors that encouraged growth in this era were also responsible in different forms for checking growth. Now, let's begin by looking at the nature of tribute-taking states and the political structures associated with tribute-taking states. Incidentally, I'll be using the terms "tribute-taking states" and "tributary states" more or less interchangeably.

Tribute-taking states, we've seen, could encourage growth in several ways, but they could also discourage it. So, their overall impact on growth was rather contradictory. They stifled growth in many subtle and not-so-subtle ways. And here's the first. Normally, tributary rulers, tribute-taking rulers, the kings and emperors of this world, were more interested in capturing wealth than in producing it. A successful war could generate wealth much more quickly and much more effectively than investment in infrastructure. And there's a very basic and simple reason for this. This is an era in which rates of growth are so slow that if you invest in growth you may have to wait several generations before you gain something from it. So, the slowness of growth itself encouraged rulers to think of wealth as something to be seized rather than to be generated or invested in.

Now, seeing themselves as capturers rather than producers of wealth, tribute-taking elites, as we've seen, generally despised those who produced wealth—the peasants and the merchants of their societies. And they took very limited interest in how goods were produced and traded. This is why we get so little work on economics from this period. The literate elites weren't terribly interested in such activities.

So, these attitudes discouraged policies that might have actively stimulated production and commerce. The following quotation illustrates these attitudes very, very nicely indeed. It comes from just over 1,000 years ago, from a state at the very beginning of its career, and that's the state of Kievan Rus, the first great state of Russia. It's a chronicle account of a conversation that was overheard by Grand Prince Vladimir, whose dates are 958 to 1015. He was the prince who converted the early Rus to Christianity. And here's how it goes: "On one occasion … after the guests were drunk"—I have to remind you that the early rulers of Rus came from Viking ancestors, and you can still see some of the traditions of a Viking lord with his retinue in this account. So:

> On one occasion … after the guests were drunk, [his retinue] began to grumble against the prince, complaining that they were mistreated because he allowed them to eat with wooden spoons, instead of silver ones. When Vladimir heard of this complaint, he ordered that silver spoons should be moulded for his retinue to eat with, remarking that with silver and gold he could not secure a retinue but that with a retinue he was in a position to win these treasures, even as his grandfather and his father had sought riches with their followers.

So, I hope you see the logic of this very, very clearly. The point of the quote is that for Vladimir, as indeed for most rulers throughout the era of agrarian civilizations, for most tributary rulers, force was the essential means of getting wealth. That's the reverse, incidentally, of today's world, in which wealth is the means of buying force. So, the first priority of governments today is to encourage growth. Innovation in the Agrarian era wasn't crucial in an environment where rulers saw wealth as something to be captured by military power rather than through the deliberate stimulation of economic growth.

Now, there's another aspect to this stifling of growth by the structures of tributary societies. And this concerns not the people at the top of tribute-taking states but the people at the bottom, the peasants who were the foundation of all tribute-taking states. As Marx pointed out in his analysis of pre-capitalist states, tribute-taking states had to ensure that peasants had access to land. This was where all the wealth came from, so they needed peasants to be farming the land. But what this did was to limit wage-earning employment. It severely limited wage earning. And it did one more thing. It deprived peasants of any incentive to raise productivity. And the reason was: They knew that any surpluses would be skimmed by their overlords.

So, imagine you're a peasant in one of the great agrarian civilizations. You have another child on the way, last year's crop was small, you suddenly have this feeling that you really need to build up your economy, and you've heard of a new crop. You introduce it, you work very hard, and you increase your crops. What's going to happen? Well, it's perfectly clear what's going to happen is your overlords, they may be the state, they may be a private landlord, are simply going to say: "Wonderful, the peasants are producing more. Let's skim more off them." This is a world, remember, in which the taking of wealth is much more arbitrary than it is in our world today, where it's fenced about with far more legal controls.

So in summary, those who produce society's wealth generally lacked the education, the capital, and the incentive to innovate. While the elites, who had the education and the wealth, generally despised productive or commercial activities and preferred to take wealth rather than generate it. Outside the specialist domains of warfare and administration, this means tribute-taking rulers took little interest in improved efficiency or innovation. So, in both these ways, the structures of tribute-taking states could stifle innovation and growth.

Now let's look at the second major factor that could stifle innovation and growth, and that's disease—leading to periodic, sharp population declines. Patterns of disease frequently checked the population growth that itself could be a major driver of growth in the later Agrarian era. There are two interesting ways in which this could happen. First, cities are one cause of population decline through disease. Now, we've seen that cities could stimulate growth. They were huge centers for commerce, they drew in commerce, and they attracted commerce. In this way they could encourage innovation and growth. But they, like tributary-states, could also dampen growth. And they did so by checking population growth. And the reason is this: All towns in pre-modern societies, in all agrarian civilizations, were lethal places. Death rates were much higher in most pre-modern cities than in the countryside. And this means that their populations had to be constantly replenished by immigrants from rural areas.

Now, why was this so? We've already seen some hints of this. We think of the environment of a typical pre-modern city. Diseases spread very rapidly in filthy, crowded city streets. Human and animal wastes accumulated in public places and waterways. There's no sewage system, so where do these wastes go? You tip chamber pots into the street, or you tip them into the nearest river. Rivers were treated as sewers and dumps, but they were also sources of drinking water, and they were where people washed. And city air was often polluted by fires and manufacturing processes such as smelting or tanning. And remember, this is a world in which people didn't understand how diseases were communicated. So, systems of quarantine were very rudimentary. And this means that the mere existence of cities could dampen population growth.

Now, here's a second mechanism that could dampen population growth through the spread of disease, and that also is a mechanism that earlier we saw as a mechanism that could stimulate growth, and that's the expansion of exchange networks. We saw that as exchange networks developed, for example through the silk roads, they could encourage the exchange of technologies, ideas, innovations of various kinds—but they could also stimulate the spread of disease, and this could take catastrophic forms. So here, too, we have a structural feature of agrarian civilizations that had a contradictory impact on growth rates.

Here's how it worked. William McNeill explored this aspect of Eurasian history in his wonderful study, *Plagues and Peoples*. He showed that as exchange networks expanded, there would come a point where regions that had previously had very little contact would have enough contact that they would start swapping disease vectors. Now, once this happens, if diseases move into areas where people have no immunities, the results can be catastrophic. The disease that is not terribly dangerous among populations used to it can be like a plague in another region.

So, what he showed is that as Eurasia began to get more integrated, you get more and more of these exchanges of diseases. Indeed, he argues that one component in the demographic and political decline of both the Roman and Han empires about 1,500 years ago may have been precisely the exchange of diseases between these two regions as contacts between them became more common. As he points out, the Mediterranean region and China, being at the edges of Eurasia, were more likely to have populations that lacked immunities to diseases from other parts of Eurasia. So, this may be why when smallpox, for example, arrives in the Byzantine Empire, it can be so catastrophic in its effects.

So by 2,000 years ago there is increasing evidence of diseases such as smallpox and eventually the bubonic plague spreading across Eurasia as the silk roads flourished, and eventually the "Black Death" may have spread in a similar way from the Far East to the western end of Eurasia in the 14th century.

So, that's a second mechanism. Both the disease environment of cities and the exchanges of diseases through exchange networks could dampen population growth by causing periodic—or in the case of cities, quite regular—decimations of populations.

Now here's the third mechanism, and I'll call it "ecological overreach" or "over-exploitation." We see that humans are brilliant at finding new ways of exploiting their environments. What we are not so good at is making sure that, in applying these new methods, we don't undermine the environments on which we depend. Time and again agrarian civilizations overreach, they over-exploited their natural resources to the point where entire civilizations collapsed. One of the most spectacular examples comes from the population history of Mesopotamia.

Estimates of population in Mesopotamia over 7,000 years show two periods of sudden decline. We've already mentioned the sudden collapse at the end of the 3rd millennium, early in the 2nd millennium B.C.E., which was almost certainly caused by over-irrigation, which led to salination and declining harvests. Sumerian civilization collapsed, and the region's center of gravity shifted permanently to the north. According to one estimate, Mesopotamian populations fell from about 630,000 in 1900 B.C.E. to about 270,000 by 1600 B.C.E. That's more than 50%. And they wouldn't rise again for at least a millennium.

Then the same patterns repeated again. New forms of irrigation are developed, including new devices for lifting water. They allow populations to build up again, and then in the early centuries of Islamic civilization, while populations are built up, then a few centuries later, early in the 2nd millennium C.E., once more you have a collapse. So, ecological overreach is a third crucial way in which agrarian civilizations could dampen growth.

Now, I want to ask: What is the impact of these checks to growth? And we'll see that it's profound, and it explains one of the most striking and common structural features of agrarian civilizations. And I'm going to call that feature "Malthusian cycles," a very distinctive pattern of evolutionary change. Let me explain what I mean. These and other factors that checked growth functioned alongside the positive feedback cycles that drove growth. So, you have "positive feedback cycles" that encourage growth, but you also have what we can call "negative feedback cycles." And it's this balance between the two that shapes the fundamental rhythms of historical change throughout the later Agrarian era.

Let me remind you what a negative feedback cycle is. A positive feedback cycle is a cycle of causation in which one cause encourages another, which encourages a third, and around the circle. So, positive feedback cycles lead to runaway change, very rapid change. A negative feedback cycle is the opposite. The classical model is a thermostat in a heating system. The heating system works, the thermostat eventually is triggered, it switches off the heating system, the temperature cools down again, it reaches a point where the heating system is switched on again, and so on. So, negative feedback cycles tend to dampen down growth—they limit change, they lead to stability.

A typical negative feedback cycle in agrarian civilizations would begin with innovations that stimulated population growth. These, in turn, would stimulate growth in other sectors. They might stimulate commerce, urbanization, and as more and more people became wealthy, they might start funding the arts, new buildings, and so on. So you see growth in many sectors of society.

Eventually though, populations begin to press against ecological constraints. Shortages appear, and there's growing evidence of malnutrition as more and more peasants don't have quite enough to feed themselves. This encourages disease. You very often find that states begin to fight increasingly, or warlords, over scarce resources. And finally, through warfare, disease, or famine, populations crash. Now, if you graph the populations of major regions of Eurasia, so Europe, China, and India, over 2,000 years, you can see these rhythms very, very clearly. They are rhythms of rise and fall, but they're on a long-term trend that is rising.

Now, this rhythm, the Malthusian cycle, dominates the history of the later Agrarian era. Do you remember Malthus, by the way? We last met him as one of the inspirers of Darwin's idea of natural selection. He was also, as we saw then, one of the pioneers of the science of demography, that's the study of the evolution of populations. And one of Malthus's central ideas was that the capacity of societies to reproduce—and he's thinking here of both human and animal societies—would always be greater than their capacity to innovate or to find new resources. Eventually, he argued, population growth would always overtake growth in resources, and there would be a crash. Now, this is a pretty good description of the characteristic rhythms of agrarian civilizations. That's why it's fitting to describe these typical cycles of agrarian civilizations as Malthusian.

The economic historian Robert Lopez has described these cycles as an "alternation of crest, trough and crest [that] can be observed not only in the economic field, but in almost every aspect of life: literature and art, philosophy and thought, [he writes] politics and law were also affected, though not all to the same extent."

And the great French historian Le Roy Ladurie, one of the great historians of the Annales School, who wrote a wonderful account of population rises and falls in the south of France over many centuries, writes of these cycles that they were like the "respiration," the in-breaths and out-breaths, of an entire social structure.

So, Malthus's mechanism, what Malthus actually said, by the way, was that populations increased geometrically by multiplication whereas resources increased arithmetically by addition. This is why population would always outstrip resources. So, this is the key mechanism. Now, what's the explanation for it? Why, over and over again in agrarian civilizations, do we see these same Malthusian cycles? The explanation, in fact, is very simple indeed. And it takes us right to the heart of the issue, the nature and rate of innovation in agrarian civilizations.

The fact that there was innovation in this era, but never quite enough to keep pace with population growth, is what explains the persistence of this depressing rhythm over several millennia. In other words, the Malthusian cycle must be explained fundamentally by the fact that innovation existed in the Agrarian era, but it was never quite fast enough to keep up with population growth. And that's why we get these periodic crashes. So, that's the explanation for Malthusian cycles that dominate the history of the later Agrarian era and that create this sense of long-term cycles of rise and fall, even beyond the rise and fall of particular rulers, such as Ozymandias.

So, what we've seen is that some of the same factors that stimulated growth in agrarian civilizations—including the functioning of tribute-taking states, the role of cities, and the expansion of exchange networks—could also stifle innovation and growth, or they could cut population growth. And in combination, this balance of forces between factors encouraging growth and factors limiting growth explains why, eventually, each phase of expansion ended in collapse.

Now, in the last three lectures, we've concentrated on Afro-Eurasia, on how agrarian civilizations worked in Afro-Eurasia. Now we need to ask: How typical was the history of the Afro-Eurasia zone of humanity as a whole? How typical of the rest of the world? And to answer that question, we're going to shift our focus to the other three world zones—the Australasian, Pacific, and American world zones—and find out what was happening there.

Thank you.

Comparing the World Zones
Lecture 36

The ice age continent of Sahul included modern Australia, Papua New Guinea, and Tasmania. It was unified because lower sea levels at the height of the last ice age filled the bridges between these areas—so, it was a single landmass.

How typical was Afro-Eurasia of the sort of historical changes that occurred in other parts of the world? To answer this question, the next two lectures survey developments in the American, Australasian, and Pacific world zones. At first sight, what stand out are the huge differences between these different worlds. But as we look more carefully, we will also begin to see some surprising and important similarities.

Comparisons between world zones are important for two main reasons. First, the differences mattered. They shaped the diverse histories of each region; but they also shaped the history of the world as a whole in the last 500 years, since the coming together of the world zones. Second, if we find important similarities between the zones despite the lack of significant contact between them, this may hint at some deep patterns in human history as a whole.

Here, I will summarize information on the early history of the various world zones. During the ice ages, modern Australia, Papua New Guinea, and Tasmania were united within the continent of Sahul. The Australasian zone was smaller in area than the Afro-Eurasian or American zones, and less diverse, with relatively arid climates and flat landscapes (except in modern Papua New Guinea). Its soils were old and relatively infertile. Sahul inherited the marsupial fauna of the supercontinent of Gondwanaland, of which it was a fragment, but it had separated from Gondwanaland almost 100 million years ago, so its plant life and animal life were quite distinctive. The human history of Sahul began 40,000 to 50,000 years ago, during the last ice, when it still formed a single continent. To reach Sahul from Outer Eurasia, humans had to cross at least 60 kilometers of open sea and adapt to entirely new flora and fauna. No other large mammal made this crossing, so it provides clear evidence of our ancestors' unique ecological adaptability. Megafaunal extinctions and the widespread use of firestick farming demonstrate that even where agriculture did not appear, humans could have a significant impact on their environments.

The American world zone formed just 3 million years ago, when a large fragment of the supercontinent of Laurasia (North America) touched a large fragment of Gondwanaland (South America) at the isthmus of Panama. As a result, this zone (uniquely) stretches from the Antarctic to the Arctic and spans all major ecological and climatic zones. As Jared Diamond has pointed out, this north-south orientation means that when humans arrived they found that most migrations led them into new and unfamiliar environments, in contrast to Afro-Eurasia, where it was possible to migrate huge distances east or west while remaining in regions of roughly similar climate and ecology. Did the north-south orientation of the Americas slow the pace of change here? Humans entered the Americas from East Siberia, certainly by 13,000 years ago and maybe several millennia earlier. As in Sahul, the sudden entry of humans into unfamiliar territory may help explain the massive megafaunal extinctions. The removal of so many large species of mammal may have had a significant impact on American history because it meant that there could be no American equivalent of the "secondary products revolution."

Estimates of the population of the Americas 500 years ago range widely from about 40 million to as high as about 100 million.

The Pacific world zone formed a huge island archipelago whose communities were separated by hundreds or thousands of miles of open sea. Each island had distinctive features and therefore a distinctive history. But all (except New Zealand) were small. (As Jared Diamond has pointed out, the diverse ecologies of different Pacific islands set up a wonderful series of natural experiments in the impact of environment on human history.) The Pacific world zone was not occupied until the later Agrarian era. It was settled by migrants who brought knowledge of farming and superb navigational skills. It used to be assumed (for example, by Norwegian scholar and adventurer Thor Heyerdahl) that the Polynesians came from the Americas. However, the similarity of their Austronesian languages, and the spread of a distinctive type of pottery (Lapita ware), has shown that the Pacific islands were settled by people whose ancestors probably came from the mainland of Southeast Asia. The islands of Melanesia (to the east of Papua New Guinea, reaching as far as Fiji and Tonga) were settled over tens of thousands of years by migrants traveling in huge, oceangoing double-hulled canoes, carrying taro, yam, breadfruit, coconuts, and sugarcane as well as chickens, dogs, and pigs. The remoter islands of eastern Polynesia were mostly settled during the 1st millennium C.E. New Zealand, one of the last regions to be settled, was probably colonized between 1000 and 1200 C.E.

How did the agricultural revolution play out in each of these zones? In the Australasian zone, agriculture appeared early, but only in modern Papua New Guinea. In Papua New Guinea, agriculture was based on root crops such as taro that did not store well, which may be why no Agrarian civilizations emerged here. However, there did emerge flourishing and highly competitive "early Agrarian" village communities, which have survived to the present day. Agriculture flourished because Papua New Guinea was at the leading edge of the Australian tectonic plate as it plowed north so that, unlike other parts of Australia, its landscapes were warped to form a great variety of different soils and terrains. In Australia and Tasmania, landscapes were older and flatter, and soils were poorer. Foraging technologies survived to modern times. However, even in Australia there was significant change within recent millennia. Indeed, in some regions there appeared semi-sedentary communities that are reminiscent of the affluent Natufian foragers of the Fertile Crescent 12,000 years ago. By 500 years ago, when the world zones would at last be joined, the population of Sahul cannot have been more than about 2 million.

In the American zone, agriculture evolved later than in the Afro-Eurasian zone, and in different ways. Though maize and squashes may have been cultivated earlier, the earliest dated samples of domesticated maize were grown about 3500 B.C.E., in the Tehuacán valley southeast of Mexico City. In South America, guinea pigs, llamas, and alpacas were domesticated by 2000 B.C.E. The relatively late development of cultivation in the Americas may reflect the absence of "easy" domesticates. Crops such as maize had to undergo significant changes before they could support large populations, and many large mammals had been driven to extinction. Estimates of the population of the Americas 500 years ago range widely from about 40 million to as high as about 100 million. In the Pacific zone, migrants brought agricultural technologies with them. However, on some of the smaller islands, including Easter Island, agriculture eventually failed, leading to a return to modified forms of foraging. The total population of the zone is unlikely to have exceeded 1–2 million.

We have seen some striking differences in the historical trajectories of the different world zones, including a very significant demographic imbalance. Five hundred years ago, populations ranged from about 400–500 million in Afro-Eurasia to 50–100 million in the Americas, to just 1 or 2 million in the Australasian and Pacific zones. Nevertheless, there are also important similarities. In each zone, human numbers increased as innovations allowed humans to extract more resources from a given area. Even in Australia, populations increased significantly in recent millennia. So differences in the histories of each region were at least in part a matter of timing rather than of substance. Many of the differences reflect differences in natural endowment, in the size of local populations, and therefore in the "synergy of collective learning" in each region. Differences in the pace and timing of change would matter profoundly when the four zones were finally joined in the last 500 years.

We have seen that, despite important differences, there were also striking parallels in the histories of the four world zones. The most important was a universal long-term trend toward "intensification": innovation characterized by the possibility of larger populations per given area and increasing complexity. ∎

Essential Reading

Bentley and Ziegler, *Traditions and Encounters*, chaps. 6, 21.

Christian, *Maps of Time*, chap. 10.

Diamond, *Collapse*

———, *Guns, Germs, and Steel*.

Supplementary Reading

Bellwood, *The Polynesians*.

Flood, *Archaeology of the Dreamtime.*

Mann, *1491*.

Questions to Consider

1. What were the most important geographical differences between the four major world zones?

2. How did geographical differences shape the histories of the four major world zones?

Comparing the World Zones
Lecture 36—Transcript

We often take the geography of our Earth for granted. But in this course we've seen that the Earth's geography, too, has a history like the Universe, like the planet, like life on Earth, like human beings. And we saw that about 200 million years ago, most of the Earth's continents were joined together in a huge supercontinent, Pangaea, that ran from north to south. That's the supercontinent that Wegener proposed must have existed at some time.

Now, it's worth asking the question: How different would human history have been if all humans had lived throughout their history on the single continent of Pangaea? And one difference is surely that once humans had started constructing large and powerful agrarian civilizations, however long it took and wherever it happened on Pangaea, all those civilizations would eventually have contacted each other, as there were no seas to separate them. Many of the processes of global history would have been similar to some of the processes we've seen in the history of Afro-Eurasia. Human history would have taken place on a single stage.

But our world is very different. We happen to live in an era in which continents are separated by huge seas, so that as a matter of fact, human history took place on a number of quite separate stages, which I've called the "world zones."

So, we've spent several lectures looking at what happened in Afro-Eurasia from our combination space ship/time capsule orbiting the Earth. Now we need to ask questions about the Earth as a whole. With similar changes occurring elsewhere, how typical was Afro-Eurasia? Did agrarian civilization expand elsewhere as well? Did states become more powerful? Did exchange networks expand, linking different regions into large world systems? Is there evidence of innovation or of Malthusian cycles? If there were differences between the zones, then to what extent and in what ways were those differences shaped by the different geographies of each world zone?

So, what we do now is we try to look at the other world zones and get some feeling for how different the trajectories of human history were in each zone and some of the reasons why they might have been different. The comparison between these regions, between the various world zones, is important for two main reasons. The first is that the differences really mattered. We'll see that they mattered most and most obviously during the last 500 years, when at last the world zones were joined. The history of each of the world zones since that time has been very much shaped by the trajectory of history in that zone before the unification of the world. So, these differences really mattered.

But secondly, there's the theoretical point that we've touched on already. If we find important similarities between the zones despite the lack of significant contacts between them, then these may hint at some deep patterns in human history as a whole. If we find just random variation, if we find that the stories of each world zone are completely different, then we shouldn't be looking for any large directional trajectories for human history. So, that's the crucial question behind all of this.

As Jared Diamond has suggested, the (contingent) fact that we evolved in an era when the world's continental plates were scattered across the Earth's surface has set up a series of revealing "natural experiments," as he calls them, for it suggests how human history could evolve from different starting points. Let me quote Jared Diamond on this. And this is from his bestseller, *Guns, Germs, and Steel*. He writes:

> While neither astronomers studying galaxy formation nor human historians can manipulate their systems in controlled laboratory experiments, they both can take advantage of natural experiments, by comparing systems different in the presence or absence (or in the strong or weak effect) of some putative causative factor. For example, ... cultural anthropologists, unable to provide human groups experimentally with varying resource abundances.

What he's saying here is you can't simply take human groups, put them in a lab, give them certain conditions like rats, and then see what happens. That's impossible. The fact that you can't do this means we can "still study long-term effects of resource abundance on human societies by comparing [for example] recent Polynesian populations living on islands differing naturally in resource abundance."

So, we can't deal with human history experimentally. What we can do is look for natural experiments set up by the fact that human history has taken place in a number of different environments, and we can see what happens. So, if we find no significant similarities as we've seen, we might conclude that human history is an entirely contingent process—it's driven by accidents of geography and the unpredictable choices of millions of individuals. But if we find significant similarities, we may have to conclude that some powerful general forces have steered human history down certain tracks despite the play of contingency.

Let's look at each of these zones and try and tease out some of the large general features that shaped its history and its geography. Let's begin with how history began in each zone. And we'll see that human history seems to begin in rather different ways in each of these zones. Now, for some of this I'm going to be collecting information—some of which we've already encountered in earlier lectures—on the early history of the various world zones, but I want to put it all together so we can see the contrasts quite clearly between them.

Okay, first the Afro-Eurasian zone. And just in summary, the Afro-Eurasian zone was the oldest, it was the largest in terms of landmass, and it was the most varied of the world zones—and it played a dominant role in world history. It was here that human history began some 200,000 years ago, because our species evolved in Africa. And we've looked at the Afro-Eurasian zone.

Now, let's go on to a second zone, the "Australasian" zone, as I've called it; that was the second to be settled by human beings. The ice age continent of "Sahul" included modern Australia, Papua New Guinea, and Tasmania. It was unified because lower sea levels at the height of the last ice age filled the bridges between these areas—so, it was a single landmass. It was smaller in area—much smaller than Afro-Eurasia, and smaller than the Americas. And it was also—for the most part—less diverse, with relatively arid climates and flat, old, ancient landscapes, with the exception of the northern rim that eventually would form modern Papua New Guinea. Its soils, for the most part, were old and relatively infertile. Sahul had once been part of the supercontinent of Gondwanaland. You'll remember that when Pangaea broke up, it broke first into two huge supercontinents: Laurasia and Gondwanaland—and

Gondwanaland was in the south. Sahul had been part of Gondwanaland, and it inherited the marsupial fauna of Gondwanaland. But it had separated from Gondwanaland almost 100 million years ago, so its plant life and animal life by this time were really quite distinctive. It had a very unique flora and fauna.

The human history of Sahul began 40,000 to 50,000 years ago, during the last ice age, when it was still a single continent. We saw that to reach Sahul from Outer Eurasia, humans had to cross at least 50 to 60 kilometers of open sea, even at the height of the last ice age. We now have some idea of where these humans came from. Excavations at Jerimalai cave in East Timor by Susan O'Connor have shown that humans probably lived here about 40,000 years ago. The remains of tuna at these sites suggest that they were fishing, and they were fishing quite well away from the shores—and that's a powerful hint that they had quite significant seagoing skills and sea craft that could go some way offshore.

We saw that no other large mammal made the crossing to Sahul, so it provides very clear evidence of our ancestors' unique ecological adaptability. And once they arrived, they had to keep adapting, because they had to adapt to Sahul's almost entirely novel flora and fauna.

The encounter between newly arrived humans and indigenous species that had no experience of humans and no understanding of how dangerous they could be may help explain the massive extent of the die-off of large mammals in Sahul in the millennia after the arrival of humans. Megafaunal extinctions and the widespread use of firestick farming suggest that even in Australia, where agriculture did not appear before modern times, humans nevertheless had a significant impact on their environment. And this is one of the reasons for thinking that this very general trajectory that I've talked about, driven by collective learning, of a capacity to spread into new environments, is something that we can see very clearly—certainly in the Australasian world zone, even if it doesn't take quite the same forms as elsewhere.

Now let's look at the Americas and the beginnings of history in the Americas. The American world zone formed, actually, quite recently. It formed about 3 million years ago, when a large fragment of Laurasia, that fragment we now refer to as North America, touched a large fragment of Gondwanaland that we now refer to as South America, and they joined at the Isthmus of Panama, creating a single, united world zone. As a result, this zone, uniquely, stretches from Gondwanaland to Laurasia, from the Antarctic to the Arctic, and it spans all major ecological and climatic zones.

Jared Diamond has pointed out that this north-south orientation means that when humans arrived, they found that most long-distance migrations would lead them into new and unfamiliar climatic zones. Now his point is that this is very different from Afro-Eurasia. Afro-Eurasia, certainly the Eurasian part of it, is sort of oriented east-west. The Americas are oriented north-south. And the significance for early humans is this: If you're migrating over long distances in Afro-Eurasia, a lot of those migrations can be done within a single climate zone, and that tends to minimize the amount of change you need to introduce. Climates, at least, don't change too much, even if topologies may. So, his point is that it was by and large easier to migrate over large distances in Afro-Eurasia. In the Americas, in contrast, the major migrations north and south were constantly taking you into new climatic zones. So, the amount of adaptation that had to be done to migrate through the Americas was significantly greater than in Afro-Eurasia. And he's argued that this difference in geographical orientation may have played a fundamental role in the history of the Americas. Here's how he puts it:

> Axis orientations affected the rate of spread of crops and livestock, and possibly also of writing, wheels, and other inventions. This basic feature of geography thereby contributed heavily to the very different experiences of Native Americans, Africans, and Eurasians in the last 500 years.

It's at least an intriguing idea, and it's possible that this played a role in perhaps slowing down American migrations through the Americas; though I have to say there's also counter-evidence suggesting that despite these difficulties, Americans traveled through—the early inhabitants of America traveled from north to south quite quickly.

We've seen that humans enter the Americas from East Siberia. They entered either across the Bering Straits land bridge, which was exposed during the last ice age, or perhaps by short sea voyages around the coastline, around the coastline from eastern Siberia, around the Bering Straits, past Alaska, and down to the northwest coast of North America.

Humans had certainly arrived by 13,000 years ago, and genetic evidence hints that—or at least to put it more precisely, there are those who've argued that there are genetic hints that—humans may have arrived as early as 30,000 years ago. Genetic evidence from some communities in Central America has been used to claim that these communities or their ancestors left Siberia at least 20,000 and possibly 40,000 years ago. But as we've seen, the consensus at the moment is that humans had certainly arrived by 13,000 years ago, and there's no hard evidence yet of earlier arrivals.

Now here, as in Sahul, the entry of humans into unfamiliar territory, unfamiliar terrain—facing new flora, new fauna—and the fact that local animals had no understanding of our species may help explain the massive megafaunal extinctions that occurred here, too, roughly at the time that humans first arrived. If humans did indeed contribute to these extinctions, we must conclude that they had a substantial impact on their environment even before the appearance of agriculture. Jared Diamond has also pointed out that the removal of these species—and in the Americas they included, for example, the horse, a species that evolved in the Americas and was then driven to extinction; they also included many species of large camelids—and he argues that this may have had a very significant impact on the history of the Americas. Above all, what it meant was that here in the Americas, there could be no real equivalent of the "secondary products revolution" that had such an impact on communications, on the spread of plow agriculture, on the emergence of pastoral nomadism in Afro-Eurasia. So, that's a sketch of the very early history of the American zone.

Now, the Pacific zone: The Pacific world zone actually was the largest of all the world zones: It covers most of the Pacific Ocean, the largest mass of water on Earth. Nevertheless, its actual land area was the smallest, because it formed a huge island archipelago. So, the communities were separated by hundreds or thousands of miles of open sea. Each island had distinctive features and therefore a distinctive history. So, here you get a wonderful natural experiment of the kind that Jared Diamond described earlier. And it's an experiment that he analyzes very, very carefully in his book *Collapse*, which is about how natural conditions may make it easier or harder for human societies to live sustainably in a particular environment. As he's shown, the size, fertility, and remoteness of each island could have a very powerful impact on its history, affecting its populations, population densities, and the stability of the societies that were created. Some islands—for example, Easter Island (or Rapa Nui), which we will discuss later in this course—were so small that they required very delicate handling, and any ecological overreach, any failure to maintain local resources, could easily prove catastrophic.

The Pacific world zone—and this is one of the most striking distinctive features of this zone, apart from the fact that it was an archipelago—was not occupied until the later Agrarian era, and it was settled by migrants who brought knowledge of farming and superb navigational skills. In other words, this world zone bypassed the Paleolithic era entirely, and it began its history with its own equivalent of the "early Agrarian" era. The migrations that settled first Melanesia, the islands of the eastern Papua New Guinea, and then Polynesia, the islands further to the west in the Pacific Ocean, count as a wonderful counterpart of the migrations of the Paleolithic era. They're a sign of the astonishing capacity of humans to seek out and explore new environments and find distinctive ways of exploiting them.

So, where did the migrants come from? For a long time it was assumed that the Pacific Islands had largely been settled from the Americas. This was the basic assumption that underlay Thor Heyerdahl's famous expedition on the *Kon-Tiki* in 1947. You may remember that he built a raft modeled on types of raft you could find in the Pacific, and he sailed it with a crew from Peru to the Tuamotu Islands. But since he did that—and what he did, of course, was to prove that it was possible—but since that time, a large body of evidence has shown that the migrations actually took place in the opposite direction, from Asia and the West. Some of the crucial evidence includes the similarity of the Austronesian languages of Melanesia and Polynesia to languages of Southeast Asia and the spread of a distinctive type of pottery known as "Lapita ware" as a result of these migrations. Now, this evidence has shown that the Pacific Islands were settled, in fact, by people whose ancestors probably came ultimately from the mainland of Southeast Asia.

The islands of Melanesia, to the east of Papua New Guinea reaching as far as Fiji and Tonga, were settled over quite a large period of time. The Solomon Islands may have been settled by as early as 35,000 B.C.E., but remoter regions, remoter islands in Melanesia, were settled as late as 1000 B.C.E., 3,000 years ago. And the migrants who arrived there traveled in huge oceangoing double-hulled canoes, and they carried with them crops that included taro, yam, breadfruit, coconuts, and sugarcane. And they also carried domesticated animals with them—in particular chickens, dogs, and pigs. And it's very likely that rats traveled with them as hitchhikers.

The remoter islands of eastern Polynesia were mostly settled during the 1st millennium C.E. New Zealand, one of the last regions to be settled, was probably colonized between 1000 and 1200 C.E.

We now know quite a lot about how these migrations were conducted, and we know this—a lot of this comes from experimental archaeology, which has involved recreating and sailing Polynesian ships and recovering some of the skills of their navigators through interviews with surviving navigators and their families. And what this evidence has shown is that these astonishing migrations were the result of systematic, well-prepared journeys of exploration in ships that could carry sometimes as many as 200 people, along with samples of their crops, and chicken, and pigs. And they were guided by navigators who sometimes memorized maps of the stars or used special reed maps of Polynesia, and they could tell from signs, such as subtle shifts in currents or the presence of seabirds, where to expect landfall. One of the most remarkable aspects of this is that when clouds obscured the skies, navigators claimed to be able to hunker down within the ships, close their eyes, and feel from the subtler movements of the ship and the wind where there might be land.

Okay. That's a sketch of the early history of these zones. Now, let's talk briefly about how the "agricultural revolution" played out in each of these zones. Let's begin with the Australasian zone. And it may seem at first as if there's not that much to be said about the Australasian zone. But I think, in fact, there may be quite a lot to be said. Agriculture appeared early in Sahul, remember, but only in the far north, in modern Papua New Guinea. In Papua New Guinea, agriculture was based on root crops, such as taro, that did not store well. And as we've seen, that may be why no agrarian civilizations emerged here. However, there did emerge flourishing and highly competitive early Agrarian village communities, some of which have survived to the present day. And they flourished throughout the best part of 10,000 years without ever developing a fully grown agrarian civilization.

In Australia and Tasmania, foraging technologies survived to modern times. Now, why the difference between these two parts of Sahul? One reason may be geological. Papua New Guinea provided a sort of snowplow as the plate on which Sahul rested drove north from Gondwanaland. And that sort of snowplow drove into the smaller plates of the complex tectonics system of Southeast Asia, driving up mountains within Papua New Guinea. So, Papua New Guinea has accumulated a much more varied ecology and topology than the rest of Sahul. It has areas of rich soils and a great variety of different ecological zones, whereas most of Australia is older, flatter, less varied, and has thin and far less productive soils. So, it could be just that agriculture was intrinsically much more difficult in the mainland of Australia rather than in the northern regions that became Papua New Guinea.

However, we shouldn't exaggerate these differences. During the last 5,000 years, there's plenty of evidence in the archaeology of Australia of various processes of "intensification" and of slow increases in population and even, in some regions, the appearance of sedentary affluent foragers a bit reminiscent of the Natufians. Now, I say this just so that we don't fall into the trap of thinking that somehow history stopped in regions like Australia. We find evidence in the last 5,000 years of more finely made and more varied stone tools. We find evidence of population growth. The dingo, a semi-domesticated dog, appeared about 4,000 years ago, probably across the Indian Ocean, because it seems to be genetically closely related to Indian species of dogs. And in some areas, people began to become more sedentary. This happened along some of the coasts and regions where they depended on fishing.

One of the most spectacular examples comes from the state of Victoria, where people built elaborate eel traps, some incorporating canals up to 300 meters long as sort of holding tanks for eels. These could be harvested using special eel pots made from strips of bark or plaited rushes. And once caught, the eels were killed—I love this bit—they were killed by biting them on the back of the head. No, thank you. So many eels could be stored in this way that people began to construct relatively permanent settlements around them—and in one case, as many as 146 low stone huts were found at a single site. These were, in fact, villages. And I hope you'll see the similarities with the Natufians. So, this is clearly evidence of a tendency towards forms of intensification, even if the threshold to fully developed agriculture is never quite crossed.

We can see other examples elsewhere in Central Australia; for example, 19th-century European travelers observed communities harvesting wild millet with stone sickles and storing it in large hayricks. Given more time, it's hard to think that Australia, too, would not have launched its own indigenous agricultural revolution.

Now, how significant was the Australasian zone demographically? By 500 years ago, when the world zones would at last be joined, the population of Sahul cannot have been more than about 2 million. It was tiny demographically.

In the American zone, agriculture evolved later than the Afro-Eurasian zone and in different ways. Now, I'm going to come back to the American zone later, so I'll just summarize the evidence very briefly. Crops such as maize and squashes may have been cultivated early, but the earliest dated samples of domesticated maize were grown about 3500 B.C.E., in the Tehuacán valley southeast of Mexico City.

In South America, guinea pigs, llamas, and alpacas were domesticated by 2000 B.C.E. Think, incidentally, how different the region's history might have been if they could also have domesticated horses and large camelids—species that had flourished just a few thousand years earlier.

The relatively late development of cultivation in the Americas may reflect the absence of "easy" domesticates. Crops such as maize had to undergo significant changes before they could support large populations. Besides, as we've seen, many potential domesticates were no longer available.

Now, as to the population of this zone, estimates of the population of the Americas 500 years ago vary quite widely, from about 40 million to as high as about 100 million. This is a lot larger demographically than Australasia but still nothing like as large as Afro-Eurasia.

In the Pacific zone, migrants, as we've seen, brought agricultural technologies with them. There was no Paleolithic era here. Though on some smaller islands, including eventually Easter Island, agriculture eventually failed and populations began to revert to modified forms of foraging. So, here we have an example of the possibility of human societies actually becoming simpler, particularly in regions with extremely limited resources.

And the population of this zone—it's extremely unlikely that 500 years ago the Pacific zone had more than 1 to 2 million. For the sake of comparison, it's worth reminding you that the population of Afro-Eurasia 500 years ago was probably about 400 to 500 million. So, this gives us a powerful idea of the demographic imbalance between the different zones.

Now, in summary, we've seen that there were some striking differences in the historical trajectories of these different zones. These are very, very different stories. Those differences include a striking demographic imbalance with populations ranging from 400 to 500 million for Afro-Eurasia, to 50 to 100 million for the Americas, and to a mere 1 or 2 million for the Australasian and Pacific zones.

So, it's easy to assume that these are completely different histories. But I think that may be deceptive. There are also, beneath these differences, some striking parallels, and above all we find intensification of some kind in all four world zones. In each zone, human numbers tended for the most part to increase over large time scales. And they did so as a result of innovations that allowed humans to extract more resources from a given area. And we've seen this is true even in Australia, where there's plenty of evidence pointing towards intensification and movements in the direction of a sort of agricultural revolution. Here, too, humans occupied an increasing range of different environments, from lush coastal regions to the arid interior, and they begin processes of intensification.

So, these comparisons suggest that the differences between the world zones and their histories may have been more a matter of timing than of substance.

In each region, we see evidence of innovations that allowed the settlement of new areas and prepared the way for forms of intensification. Here we may be seeing similarities that imply that everywhere, collective learning led to technological change of some kind. And they suggested that the differences between the histories of these regions reflect differences in their natural endowment, their geography, and sometimes the size of their populations—and therefore, in what I called the "synergy of collective learning."

Now, I want to explore these comparisons slightly more carefully by looking at the second largest of the world zones, the Americas.

Thank you.

The Americas in the Later Agrarian Era
Lecture 37

> Market relations and warfare seem to have linked all these areas of evolving Agrarian civilization into a large network of exchanges and warfare. So, it may be appropriate to talk of an evolving Mesoamerican "world system."

How similar was the evolution of Agrarian civilizations in the American and Afro-Eurasian world zones? And what were the crucial differences? In the Americas, Agrarian civilizations evolved in Mesoamerica and the Andes. In both regions, evidence of embryonic Agrarian civilizations began to appear from the 2nd millennium B.C.E. In Mesoamerica, incipient Agrarian civilizations appeared in the middle of the 2nd millennium B.C.E. They appear among the Olmec of Southeast Mexico, near modern Veracruz, on the Gulf of Mexico. Improved varieties of maize, beans, and squash allowed rapid population growth in regions of heavy rainfall, where drainage was more important than irrigation. Towns such as Lorenzo (with a population of about 2,500 people) and La Venta appeared. They had large ceremonial centers, with pyramid-like tombs up to 33 meters high. The Olmec made huge and distinctive basalt stone heads. With no large domestic animals, these had to be transported by humans, presumably under compulsion. The small size of these towns suggests that they represented polities perhaps at the level of chiefdoms. The presence of obsidian and other precious goods at Olmec sites shows the existence of extensive exchange networks. La Venta was destroyed violently in about 400 B.C.E., clear evidence of the importance of warfare. An inscribed stone found in 2006 in Veracruz suggests that the Olmec had already developed a writing system, though it has not yet been deciphered.

After 1000 B.C.E., larger communities evolved in the Oaxaca valley of South Mexico, with evidence of craft specialization, canal building, markets, and writing. By 500 B.C.E., there existed a cluster of city-states, reminiscent of 3rd-millennium Sumer. By 500 C.E., the region's largest settlement, Monte Alban, may have had 20,000 or more inhabitants; it is often thought of as the first large city of the Americas. Carved stone engravings found nearby depict enemies slaughtered in war. Olmec and Oaxacan civilizations created many durable features of Mesoamerican civilizations. By the 1st century C.E., towns, cities, and states could be found near modern Mexico City. Teotihuacán (25 miles northeast of modern Mexico City) had massive pyramids and a population of 100,000 people from many different parts of Mesoamerica. Market relations and warfare linked much of Mesoamerica into a large network of exchanges: a Mesoamerican "world system." In 378, for example, an army from distant Teotihuacán conquered Tikal, in modern Guatemala, and probably killed its king.

Distinctive features of Mesoamerican civilizations include religious beliefs requiring the letting of blood, and extremely accurate calendrical systems that were of great religious and political significance.

The Maya are particularly interesting and, now, since the decipherment of their writing system, they are better known than any other American civilization from before 1500.

The Maya are particularly interesting and, now, since the decipherment of their writing system, they are better known than any other American civilization from before 1500. Mayan civilization emerged as early as 1000 B.C.E., in the lowland rainforests of the Yucatan peninsula in South Mexico, Belize, and Guatemala. Villagers initially practiced swidden agriculture, but by the end of the 1st millennium B.C.E. large temple complexes appeared, with pyramids, causeways, and public squares. In the "classical period," in the middle of the 1st millennium C.E., the Maya were organized in competing city-states that formed complex and shifting alliance systems reminiscent of Sumer in the 3rd millennium B.C.E. The Maya developed remarkably accurate calendars, with a sacred year of 260 days and a secular year of 365 days. As in China, calendars had great political significance, as rulers were expected to identify auspicious dates for political acts such as wars, coronations, or religious celebrations. In conjunction with the calendar, the Maya developed a hieroglyphic script that was used to record political and religious events and royal genealogies. Mayan hieroglyphic, like Sumerian cuneiform, developed into a highly expressive medium by using the "rebus" principle. Mayan civilization declined in the 8th and 9th centuries C.E. in a classic Malthusian collapse.

The causes included increasing warfare triggered by overpopulation (the heartland, near Tikal, may have been more densely settled in 800 C.E. than today), deforestation, erosion, and declining soil fertility. But Mesoamerican civilizations would revive. By 1492, there existed in Central Mexico a huge imperial civilization based on Tenochtitlán (now Mexico City). The Aztec rulers of Tenochtitlán exacted tributes from neighboring regions and cities. Tenochtitlán was one of the most magnificent cities in the world; with nearby towns, it may have had a population of 2 million people. We have a wonderful description of it in the writings of Cortés's lieutenant, Bernal Díaz.

In the Andes region, Agrarian civilizations evolved in modern Ecuador, Peru, and Chile. The main crops were maize, potatoes, and quinoa, and the main animal domesticates were llama, alpaca, and guinea pig. Along the coast, substantial communities emerged in the 2nd millennium B.C.E. They built irrigation systems and ceremonial pyramids.

Incipient Agrarian civilizations emerged in the 1st millennium B.C.E. They exploited different ecological zones extending from the coast, with its arid climates and rich fisheries, to the mountain highlands, with their crops of peanuts, potatoes, cotton, and beans. Towns flourished with populations of more than 10,000 and large public buildings. In the 1st millennium C.E., the Moche state, near the coast of northern Peru, integrated highland and lowland regions, organizing irrigation and managing exchanges between regions using humans, llama, and alpaca. Images show evidence of class hierarchies, warfare (once again we find pictures of rulers inspecting captives), and organized labor. The Moche state collapsed sometime in the 7th century C.E., after a series of spectacular natural disasters ruined irrigation systems and El Niño–driven climate changes ruined the rich anchovy fisheries. No writing is known from these early states. However, by 1500 C.E. the Inka had developed a system based on knotted strings, or "quipu." This worked well for accounting, but probably less well for recording history or literature.

Were the two major American zones of Agrarian civilization as integrated as those of Afro-Eurasia? Maize diffused to South America from Mesoamerica by about 2000 B.C.E. and, when the Spanish arrived, their diseases reached Peru before any of their soldiers did, so there were clearly contacts of some kind. Nevertheless, contacts were much less intense than those linking different regions of Afro-Eurasia through the silk roads. One reason was that, with few animal domesticates, transportation systems were less developed in the Americas. Here, humans were the primary beasts of burden.

How similar are the histories of Agrarian civilizations in Afro-Eurasia and the Americas? The timing of major thresholds is clearly different. In the Americas similar phenomena appeared, but with a time lag of approximately 3,000 years. For example, we have seen that the city of Monte Alban emerged late in the 1st millennium B.C.E., almost 3,000 years after the first large cities had appeared in Afro-Eurasia. By 1500 C.E., large imperial structures had appeared that may be comparable with the political systems of Afro-Eurasia in the 2nd millennium B.C.E., though they were never as large as the Achaemenid Empire at its height. Nevertheless, the general trajectory of change is similar.

In both zones, agriculture appeared independently in several regions and led to population growth; increasing exchanges; and the evolution of cities, states, and empires. As a result, within just two to three millennia of their appearance, Agrarian civilizations incorporated most of the people living in these two world zones. Agrarian civilizations in both zones shared the same emergent properties: cities, militarized states, writing systems, monumental architecture (pyramids seemed to crop up everywhere!), tribute-taking systems, and extensive networks of exchange. American civilizations also displayed a Malthusian pattern of rise and fall. As in Afro-Eurasia, there was plenty of innovation in the Americas, but never enough to avoid eventual demographic collapses. These similarities suggest that similar drivers operated in both zones. Collective learning drove innovation, leading to population increase, which generated a common set of problems and opportunities that yielded parallel solutions and outcomes. There is indeed a shape to human history, and the comparison between these regions illustrates that fundamental truth about human history.

We have seen that, despite many important differences, there were striking similarities in the histories of the different world zones. These suggest that in all zones similar forces were at work. Now we start to explore how these forces shaped the Modern era of human history. ∎

Questions to Consider

1. What are the most striking similarities in the histories of the American and Afro-Eurasian world zones?

2. What were the most striking differences in the histories of these two zones, and why did they matter?

The Americas in the Later Agrarian Era
Lecture 37—Transcript

In the last lecture, we compared the early histories of the four world zones, and we saw that there were some striking differences between them, but also some very interesting parallels. And we saw that this business of comparing the world zones can help us tease out some quite deep issues about the driving forces of human history.

Now what I want to do is look more closely at the Americas. And that's the only other world zone apart from Afro-Eurasia in which agrarian civilizations flourished. So, this gives us a chance to look more carefully at the different trajectories according to which agrarian civilizations evolved in different environments. And remember, once again, these were areas without any significant contact between them. So this is the sort of natural experiment that Jared Diamond talked about. So, how similar was the evolution of agrarian civilizations in these two zones, and what were the crucial differences? And what can they tell us?

In the Americas, agrarian civilizations evolved in two main regions: in Mesoamerica, in the south of Mexico, Guatemala, Belize—Central America; and also in the Andes region—Peru, Bolivia, northern Chile, parts of Ecuador. In both these regions, evidence of embryonic agrarian civilizations and the buildup towards agrarian civilizations begins to appear from about the 2nd millennium B.C.E. Now, there's a third area in the Americas where we see the beginnings of this process, but it never quite reaches the point of developing a flourishing full-blown agrarian civilization—and that's in parts of the U.S., along the Mississippi Valley. About 1,000 years ago, at sites such as Cahokia in Illinois—which, with a population of 10,000 to 20,000 may have been the largest pre-Columbian city of North America—you find all the signs of powerful chiefdoms, of societies just on the verge of building up fully developed agrarian civilizations. The inhabitants of the region not only had quite large small towns, they also built huge artificial mounds. But by 1400 C.E., this civilization, the so-called Mississippian culture, had largely broken down. However, given another millennium it's quite probable, it's a reasonable guess that a full-blown agrarian civilization might have also evolved along the Mississippi.

Now what we'll do is survey the evolution of agrarian civilizations in the two main regions of the Americas in which they developed and flourished. And let's begin with Mesoamerica.

In Mesoamerica, what we can call "incipient" civilizations first appeared after about 2000 B.C.E., in the 2nd millennium B.C.E. The earliest hints of something pointing towards agrarian civilization appear among the Olmec of Southeast Mexico, near modern Veracruz, on the Gulf of Mexico, and they appear in the middle of the 2nd millennium B.C.E.

Here, in this region, improved varieties of maize, beans, and squash allowed rapid population growth in regions of heavy rainfall, where drainage was probably more important than irrigation. But like irrigation regions, this was a region where farming would flourish, but only if there was substantial investment of effort on the part of whole communities. Eventually towns appeared, based on the farming of these rich forest soils—towns such as Lorenzo (which probably had a population of about 2,500 people, so these are not huge towns), and La Venta. But what these towns did have were large ceremonial centers with pyramid-like tombs that could be up to 33 meters high, and they were apparently designed as royal tombs.

The other thing about the Olmec is that they made huge and distinctive basalt stone heads. Most of us have seen pictures of these wonderful, very beautiful objects. With no large domestic animals, these had to be transported by humans, presumably under compulsion. So, as in Afro-Eurasia, monumental construction of this type implies that already there exist quite significant hierarchies of power and wealth. There probably exist regional rulers or chiefs who can exercise at least some degree of coercion. Yet the relatively small size of these towns suggests that they represented polities not quite at the level of a full-blown tributary state.

Yet the presence of obsidian—remember, obsidian is this volcanic glass that can be used to produce very sharp edges; it's very important in all societies of the Neolithic era—the presence of obsidian and other precious goods at Olmec sites shows the existence of quite extensive exchange networks.

We see in the Olmec region some signs of a sort of collapse. La Venta, for example, is destroyed violently in about 400 B.C.E., and this is an indicator of one other component of agrarian civilizations, moderately large-scale warfare.

Finally, an inscribed stone found in 2006 in Veracruz suggests that the Olmec had already developed a writing system, though it's not yet been deciphered. If this is true, then this is probably the first writing system to be developed in the Americas. In short, by 500 B.C.E. and probably earlier, the Olmec, despite the smallness of their polities, show many of the features we expect to find in incipient or embryonic agrarian civilizations, though on a reasonably small scale.

Then, after about 1000 B.C.E., during the 1st millennium B.C.E., large communities evolved in the Oaxaca valley of South Mexico. And here we start to find evidence of significant craft specialization and extensive division of labor. We see signs of canal building, of markets, and also writing systems emerge. And by 500 B.C.E., we have in the Oaxaca region a cluster of city-states that certainly echo the early city-states of Sumer.

By 500 C.E., a thousand years later, Oaxacan civilization is flourishing, and the largest city, Monte Alban, may have had almost 20,000 inhabitants. Indeed, it may have been the first large city to flourish in the Americas. Carved stone engravings found near Monte Alban depict slaughtered enemies, and they show that warfare was on a significant scale. Here we certainly have a flourishing agrarian civilization with large populations, cities, warfare, writing, trade, and monumental architecture on a large scale. I hope by now you're getting very familiar with this sort of checklist of the things that we expect to pop up once we get agrarian civilizations.

Olmec and Oaxacan civilizations created many durable features of Mesoamerican civilizations. By the 1st century C.E. (the 1st century of the Modern era), towns, cities, and states could be found also to the north, near modern Mexico City. Here the largest city, Teotihuacán, which is about 25 miles northeast of modern Mexico City, may have had a population of at least 100,000 people. Now, this is getting huge. This is a huge city. They lived among colossal pyramids, which still survive today. And archaeology has shown that Teotihuacán also included migrants who came from many other parts of Mesoamerica, and you can show this by the distinctive styles of their buildings in different suburbs. To the east, in the Yucatan Peninsula, the Mayan civilization flourished as well.

Market relations and warfare seem to have linked all these areas of evolving agrarian civilization into a large network of exchanges and warfare. So, it may be appropriate to talk of an evolving Mesoamerican "world system." You'll remember the label "world system" refers to large areas of agrarian civilization linked through trade and other exchanges into a large exchange network. Here's one just tiny illustration of the sort of links between them. In 378, we know, an army from Teotihuacán conquered Tikal in modern Guatemala, one of the major cities of the Maya, and probably killed its king and installed a new dynasty.

Distinctive features of Mesoamerican civilizations include religious beliefs that required the letting of blood, and calendrical systems that were of great religious and political significance and were probably more accurate than any that were developed in Afro-Eurasia.

Now, I'd liked to spend a little time talking about the Maya. And the reason is that the Maya are particularly interesting—and particularly now, since it's been possible to decipher their writing system. And the result is that the Maya are now probably better known than any other American civilization before 1500.

Mayan civilization emerged as early as about 1000 B.C.E., or it began to emerge that early, in the lowland rainforests of the Yucatan Peninsula in the region on the border between South Mexico, Belize, and Guatemala. Here villages initially practiced forms of swidden agriculture. But by the end of the 1st millennium, you find large temple complexes appearing in the region, with pyramids, large causeways, and public squares. These are getting quite grand.

In the so-called classical period of Mayan civilization, in the middle of the 1st millennium C.E., the Maya seemed to have been organized in a large number of competing city-states, which may have linked with each other in complex and shifting alliance systems. Here we have very strong echoes of Sumer, perhaps in the time of Gilgamesh.

Eventually, the Maya developed remarkably accurate calendars. Their calendar had several different cycles. One was a sacred year of 260 days that may have been linked to the movements of Venus. And there's also a secular year of 365 days, and in addition to that, a long historical count—so, in effect, three overlapping calendars. And as in China, the calendars seem to have had great political significance, as it seems that power figures in this region were extremely concerned that things happen on auspicious dates. So, the calendars were extremely important political tools.

The Maya also developed a hieroglyphic script that appears to have evolved in conjunction with the development of the calendar, and it was used from the start to record political and religious events and to keep records of royal lineages. So as this gets deciphered we can begin to construct in considerable detail the political history of the Maya in the classical era.

Note that here, writing doesn't appear to evolve from the sort of accounting systems that we saw in Sumer. Nevertheless, the process seems to have been quite similar in several ways. It did evolve from the task of keeping track of something. In this case what was being kept track of was dates that had ritual significance. And there's another striking similarity with Sumerian cuneiform, and that's the use of the rebus principle. We've already encountered this in looking at Sumerian cuneiform. You'll remember the principle. Just as in English, for example, I could use a picture of an eye to represent the personal pronoun, "I," so in Mayan, the symbol of a torch—the word for torch sounded like "*tah*"—sounded the same as and could be used to represent the preposition "at," which was also "*tah*" in Mayan. So, you can use the picture of the torch to represent something much more abstract, a preposition, "at." So here, we see some quite striking similarities in the evolution of written language, though as always we also see interesting differences.

The decline of Mayan civilization is quite striking. Mayan civilization declined rapidly in the 8th and 9th centuries C.E. The causes are still hotly debated, but it seems almost certain that ecological collapse played a very significant role. And all the various theories about collapse suggest to me very powerfully that what we're looking at is a typical Malthusian collapse in which ecological factors, increasing military competition, overpopulation, perhaps breakdowns of political order, all play a similar role.

So here we have the classic pattern of societies under stress: overpopulation. Larger Mayan cities may have had populations, in some cases, of as many as 120,000 people. And these are based on forest soils, which aren't that fertile unless you farmed them very, very carefully using elaborate techniques such as terracing. Many more lived in the surrounding settlements. So, population densities were very, very high in the Mayan heartland, around the city of Tikal. In this region it's been estimated that population densities may have been greater in 800 C.E. than they are today.

Now, this sort of overpopulation, particularly if agriculture is not quite fertile enough to support populations, could very easily lead to conflicts over land, to sustained warfare between neighboring city-states, and eventually it can lead to a breakdown of agricultural systems—particularly if you need to maintain irrigation structures, or in this case, probably terraced agriculture on hillsides or the building of reservoirs—and eventual collapse. So, this whole complex in some ways looks very familiar indeed, bringing together climatic problems, ecological overreach, political overreach, overpopulation, and growing political crisis.

Here's a quotation from a scholar of this region that captures this well. Coe writes:

> The Classic Maya population of the southern lowlands had probably increased beyond the carrying capacity of the land, no matter what system of agriculture was in use. There is mounting evidence for massive deforestation and erosion throughout the Central Area, only alleviated in a few favorable zones by dry slope terracing. In short, over-population and environmental degradation had advanced to a degree only matched by what is happening in many of the poorest tropical countries today. The Maya apocalypse, [he writes] for such it surely was, surely had ecological roots.

But this was not the end. This was a Malthusian collapse followed by a subsequent Malthusian revival. Mesoamerican civilizations would revive. By 1492, when Columbus reached the Caribbean, there existed in Central Mexico a huge imperial civilization based on the capital city of Tenochtitlán, now Mexico City, which was built on Lake Texcoco. The Aztec rulers of Tenochtitlán exacted tributes from neighboring regions and cities using pretty coercive methods. They had a very powerful army. And by this time, Tenochtitlán was probably one of the most magnificent cities in the world. With nearby towns, it may have had a population of 2 million people. Now, as it happens, we have a wonderful description of it in the writings of Cortés's lieutenant, Bernal Díaz, who first saw it in 1519. So, I'd love to quote from Bernal Díaz's description of first seeing Tenochtitlán.

> Next morning, we came to a broad causeway and continued our march towards Iztapalapa. [Tenochtitlán was built on Lake Texcoco—so it was built out on the lake, and this is the meaning of the causeways.] And when we saw all those cities and villages built in the water, and other great towns on dry land, and that straight and level causeway leading to Mexico [Tenochtitlán], we were astounded. These great towns and ... buildings rising from the water, all made of stone, seemed like an enchanted vision from the tale of Amadis. Indeed, some of our soldiers asked whether it was not all a dream. ... It was all so wonderful that I do not know how to describe this first glimpse of things never heard of, seen or dreamed of before.

It's a lovely description of some of the astonishment felt when the different world zones came together and people learned of the existence of civilizations, whole populations, they've never known of before.

Okay, now let's move on to the Andes region. In the Andes region, agrarian civilizations evolved in modern Ecuador, Peru, and Chile, and also parts of modern Bolivia. The main crops here were maize, potatoes, and quinoa, a plant grown mainly for its edible seeds. And the main animal domesticates were llama, alpaca, and guinea pig. Along the Pacific coast, substantial communities emerged in the 2nd millennium B.C.E. So here, as in Mesoamerica, the critical period in which agrarian civilizations are being built up seems to be the 2nd millennium B.C.E. Here populations built irrigation systems and ceremonial pyramids. By now you'll be alert to the fact that this ought to be telling us that we're beginning to see the appearance of, at the very least, quite powerful chiefdoms—even if we're not yet talking about agrarian civilizations.

The first, I'll say incipient agrarian civilizations, and that's really a way of ducking the question of whether they exactly are or not, emerged in the 1st millennium B.C.E. The crucial basis for agrarian civilizations in this area, according to a fairly broad consensus among anthropologists, is the ability of emerging states to exploit different ecological zones that extended from the coast (with its arid climates and its rich fishing) to the mountain highlands, with their crops of peanuts, potatoes, cotton, and beans. Towns began to appear, some of them with populations of more than 10,000 each and large public buildings. So, this is looking a bit like Olmec civilization or Olmec chiefdoms.

A millennium later, the Moche state (centered near the coast of northern Peru) integrated highland and lowland regions of northern Peru. It organized irrigation. It managed exchanges between the coast and the highland regions using human porters, llama, and alpaca. Carved images show evidence of class hierarchies and of warfare once again. As we've seen over and over again, once again we find these ubiquitous pictures of rulers inspecting prisoners and apparently executing at least some of them. And we also see lots of evidence of organized labor.

The Moche state collapsed sometime in the 7th century C.E.—this is at about the same time as the Maya—after a series of spectacular natural disasters ruined irrigation systems, while El Niño systems ruined the rich anchovy fisheries of the shore. And once again, it's very tempting to think that what we're dealing with here is a regulation Malthusian crisis.

No writing is known from these early states. However, by 1500 C.E., a later imperial power, the Inka, had developed a system of communication or accounting based on knotted strings or "quipu." The quipu system is slowly being deciphered. And what's very clear is you can use it to convey quite a lot of information of an accounting type, but also political information about instructions to officials, for example. So, this worked pretty well for politics and accounting. We have no evidence that it was rich enough to work well for the recording of history or literature. But clearly, it's evolving in that direction.

Now, were these two major American zones of agrarian civilization linked? We've seen that in Afro-Eurasia by the time of Marco Polo there are quite substantial exchanges of people, of trade, of religions, even of diseases right across the Eurasian landmass from China to the Mediterranean. So, what's the evidence in the Americas?

Well, there is certainly some evidence of diffusion and contact between these two zones. Maize appears to have diffused to South America from Mesoamerica by about 2000 B.C.E. And there's one more sign that there were exchanges going on, though they're below the radar of the historians. When the Spanish arrived, some of the diseases they brought with them appeared to have reached Peru before any of their soldiers did. So, there were clearly contacts of some kind.

Nevertheless, these contacts were much less intense than those that linked different regions of Afro-Eurasia through the silk roads. So here, we have an area of agrarian civilization or two areas of agrarian civilization that cover less territory and include less population than those of Afro-Eurasia, but they're also less interlinked than those of Afro-Eurasia. And one of the crucial reasons may be that with few animal domesticates, transportation systems were less developed in the Americas. Here, humans were the primary beasts of burden. This is a reminder incidentally, once again, of how important the secondary products revolution was in Eurasia.

Now let's try and summarize some of this discussion and try and get a feeling for some of the similarities and differences between the histories of agrarian civilizations in Afro-Eurasia and the Americas.

The timing of major subordinate thresholds is clearly different. In the Americas, similar phenomena appeared, but with a considerable time lag. And roughly speaking, we can even get a feeling for what that time lag was. Judging by what we know of the political evolution of the Americas, it was about 3,000 years.

Now, I don't want to make too much of this. This is again a very, very rough date. But here's the reason for saying that. We've have seen that the city of Monte Alban, perhaps the first real city-state in the Americas, emerged late in the 1st millennium B.C.E. You'll remember that this is some 3,000 years after the first state structures had appeared in Afro-Eurasia in Sumer. Similarly, by 1500 C.E., much larger imperial structures had appeared, such as those of the Inka or the Aztec.

These may be comparable, perhaps, with the political systems of Afro-Eurasia in the 2nd millennium B.C.E. Here's one reason for saying that. You remember Rein Taagepera's estimates of the areas incorporated within major states. Well, he estimates that the Inka and the Aztec controlled empires extending over about 2 megameters. And you'll remember that a megameter is about the size of modern Egypt. This is considerably less than the size of the Achaemenid Empire of the 1st millennium B.C.E., but it's larger than the largest empires of the 2nd millennium B.C.E. in Afro-Eurasia, about 3,000 years earlier. So again, there is a rough correspondence between the Aztec and the Inka and the larger empires of the 2nd millennium B.C.E. in Afro-Eurasia.

There are also many other minor differences between them. There are cultural differences, differences in ritual practice, differences in the way calendars are used, and so on. Yet there are also many striking similarities. In both zones, agriculture appeared independently in several regions, and when it appeared it led to population growth, increasing exchanges, and the evolution of towns, cities, states, and empires. As these large communities evolved and got denser and denser and denser, new problems had to be faced, and in all these regions, they seemed to have led to similar solutions.

So the result was, in both world zones, within about two millennia of the first appearance of agrarian civilizations, in about 1500 C.E. in the case of the Americas, it is likely that agrarian civilizations had come to include most of the populations in their respective world zones. Within about two millennia of appearing, agrarian civilizations include most people in the world zones in which they've appeared.

Furthermore, in both zones, agrarian civilizations shared the same basic emergent properties. And we've seen this list before. They include cities, militarized states, writing systems, and monumental architecture. In fact, one of the most striking of these emergent properties is the fact that pyramids appear in the Americas as early as the Olmec period. There are also tribute-taking systems and extensive networks of exchange.

There's also evidence, as we've seen—particularly spectacular from the Maya collapse, or the collapse of the Moche civilization may represent the same phenomenon—of long-term patterns of rise and fall reminiscent of the Malthusian cycles of Afro-Eurasia. So, there's good reason to think that the Malthusian cycle is a pattern we find in both these world zones. And that suggests that in the Americas, as in Afro-Eurasia, though there was clearly innovation on a long trend, nevertheless it was too slow to avoid eventual periodic demographic, ecological, and political collapses.

So, what do these similarities suggest? They suggest that similar drivers are operating in both zones. Collective learning drove innovation, leading to population increase, which generated a common set of problems and opportunities and eventually yielded parallel solutions and outcomes. If this is true, there is indeed a long-term shape to human history, and the comparison between these regions illustrates that fundamental truth about human history.

So we've seen that, despite many important differences, there were striking similarities in the histories of these different world zones in which agrarian civilizations evolved. And this suggests that in all zones similar forces were at work, even if the pace of historical change was significantly different. Now we start to explore how these forces shaped what I'll call the Modern era of human history.

Thank you.

Threshold 8—The Modern Revolution
Lecture 38

> Then, things seemed to suddenly go very strange. From 1500 onwards, the pace of change accelerates. Suddenly, the isolation of the different world zones is broken in the first phase of what today we call "globalization." The world suddenly comes together. It's interlinked for the first time in human history. Then, from about 1700, changes appear that within 300 years will have transformed the entire world. Population numbers go crazy.

In the last millennium, the pace of change accelerated sharply and decisively. The isolation of the world zones was breached in the 16th century. Then, from 1700 the pace of innovation began to accelerate so rapidly that, within just three centuries, the entire world had been transformed. Global population rose from 250 million in 1000 C.E. to about 700 million in 1700 C.E. and more than 6 billion in 2000 C.E. As Lynn Margulis and Dorion Sagan put it, humans had become a sort of "mammalian weed." Yet productivity rose even faster, so (so far!) there has not yet been a global Malthusian collapse. These transformations mark the eighth threshold of increasing complexity in this course. They lead us into the "Modern era" of human history.

The Modern era is the third major era of human history. So far, it has lasted just a few hundred years. Though all periodizations are somewhat arbitrary, here is the periodization we will use. We will date the beginning of the Modern era to about 1700 C.E., because that is when we first begin to see, in some regions of the world, a transition to radically different types of society capable of extraordinary rates of innovation and change. However, the roots of change lay in the previous millennium, so our explanations of the Modern era will begin more than 1,000 years earlier, in the 1st millennium C.E. I will divide the period after 1700 into two main periods. Between 1700 and 1900, parts of the world—particularly in the Atlantic region—were transformed, acquiring unprecedented wealth and power in the process. During the second period, beginning in about 1900, the Modern Revolution transformed the rest of the world.

What are the most distinctive features of the Modern era? Above all, modern human societies are much more complex than those of all previous eras.

First, they have more structure: For example, the variety of roles available to individuals is vastly greater than it was in the Agrarian world, where most people were peasants. Second, modern societies mobilize energy flows many times greater than those typical of earlier eras of human history. Total human energy use today is almost 250 times what it was just 1,000 years ago (mainly due to the use of fossil fuels). Third, associated with the Modern Revolution is a spectacular range of new, emergent properties—from the ability to communicate instantly across the globe, to the existence of cities of 20 million people, to weaponry capable of obliterating these same cities in a few minutes.

However, identifying the most critical changes is extremely difficult. This is partly because there have been so many different types of change, partly because the changes are still continuing today, and partly because, as yet, there exists little scholarly consensus about the nature of modernity. The discussion that follows represents an attempt to pick out the crucial features of the Modern Revolution, as seen through the wide lens of big history. We try to see this threshold as one in a sequence that reaches back to the very origins of our Universe. Our discussion builds on a long tradition of debate about modernity that includes major thinkers from Adam Smith to Karl Marx and Max Weber. So we have plenty of ideas! But the big history perspective has certain consequences for our view of modernity. The first is that some familiar landmarks (e.g., the French Revolution or the Renaissance or the Enlightenment) may vanish entirely at these scales. A second consequence of the big history perspective is that we will try to see the Modern Revolution as a global phenomenon, generated by global exchanges of ideas, technologies, goods, and people. Though many of the crucial changes first became apparent in the Atlantic region, they were the product of global forces.

Four features of the Modern Revolution explain why in this course we treat it as a new threshold of complexity. Rates of innovation accelerated sharply. Accelerating innovation increased the pace of historical change. It took 200,000 years for foraging lifeways to spread around the world, about 10,000 years for agriculture to do so, and just 200 to 300 years for the Modern Revolution to transform the entire world. Innovation increased human control over the energy and resources of the biosphere. Modern forms of education and science have created formal structures that encourage and sustain innovation.

Rapid innovation drove many other changes. It increased available resources, allowing humans to multiply—creating larger, denser, and more complex societies than those of the Agrarian era. Human numbers rose from about 250 million in 1000 C.E., to about 950 million in 1800 C.E., to about 6 billion in 2000 C.E. Larger and denser communities meant new lifeways and new power structures. Wage-earning replaced peasant farming as the normal way of earning a living. Governments became larger, more powerful, and more intrusive, but also more responsive to the needs and capacities of their subjects. Human history became global. Since the 16th century, human societies have exchanged goods, ideas, diseases, and people within a single global network, and rapid improvements in communications and transportation have steadily tightened these links.

The dominant groups are not tribute-takers but entrepreneurs, who make their wealth by trading efficiently on competitive markets.

Our species has begun to transform the biosphere. By some estimates, humans now control 25% to 40% of all the energy that enters the biosphere through photosynthesis (Christian, *Maps of Time*, p. 140). Modern weaponry is so powerful that humans could, if they chose, destroy much of the biosphere within a few hours. Increasing human control of biospheric resources has affected other species through loss of habitat and increasing extinctions, and it is beginning to transform the global climate system. John McNeill writes, "For most of Earth's history, microbes played the leading role of all life in shaping the atmosphere. In the twentieth century, humankind stumbled blindly into this role" (McNeill, *Something New Under the Sun*, p. 51).

How can we explain these vast transformations? I will focus on accelerating innovation, because this is the key to most other aspects of the Modern Revolution. So why did innovation accelerate so sharply? Economists and historians have discussed the main drivers of innovation at least since the publication in 1776 of *The Wealth of Nations*, by Adam Smith (1723–1790). Though historians have identified many possible drivers of change in the Modern era, we will concentrate on three drivers of growth that played only a limited role in the era of Agrarian civilizations: (1) commercialization and the spread of competitive markets, (2) the spread of capitalism, and (3) the expansion of global exchange networks.

Driver 1 is commerce. Adam Smith argued that specialization raises productivity, and specialization depends on the extent of market competition. Smith's idea that the spread of competitive markets drives innovation remains fundamental in modern economic thought.

Driver 2 is the spread of capitalist social structures. Karl Marx (1818–1883), though determined to overthrow capitalism, also admired it because he believed it encouraged innovation. His ideas expand in important ways on those of Smith. Marx offered a "social structure" theory of growth, arguing that different social structures affect innovation differently. We have seen how social structures of the Agrarian era limited innovation because neither peasants nor tribute-taking elites had a sustained interest in generating innovation. Capitalism is different. The dominant groups are not tribute-takers but entrepreneurs, who make their wealth by trading efficiently on competitive markets. The majority class consists not of self-sufficient peasants but of wage earners who have to work hard and efficiently to "market" their labor. Capitalism forces both major social groups to concern themselves with productivity so the spread of capitalist social structures should encourage innovation.

Driver 3 is a sudden expansion in the size and reach of exchange networks. The coming together of the four world zones from the 16th century stimulated commerce and capitalism by expanding the scale and intensity of both entrepreneurial activity and information exchanges. This sudden rearrangement of global networks of exchange also shifted the center of wealth and power in the world away from its traditional centers (in the Afro-Eurasian world) toward a region that had previously been somewhat marginal—the Atlantic seaboard! That would prove one of the most radical of all the changes associated with the Modern Revolution.

This lecture has described some major features of the Modern Revolution and described the strategy we will use in the next three lectures to explain this remarkable transition. ■

Essential Reading

Christian, *Maps of Time*, chap. 11.

Supplementary Reading

Cipolla, *The Economic History of World Population*.

McNeill, *Something New Under the Sun*, Introduction.

Mokyr, *The Lever of Riches*, chaps. 1, 2.

Questions to Consider

1. What features distinguish the "Modern era" most decisively from the "era of Agrarian civilizations"?

2. Is it possible to find a better label than "Modern Revolution" to summarize the major transformations of the Modern era?

Threshold 8—The Modern Revolution
Lecture 38—Transcript

Let's clamber back on board our combined space and time machine orbiting the Earth. We used it to survey the 4,000 years of the later Agrarian era. And what we saw from the machine was the slow expansion of agrarian civilizations, and we also saw their characteristic rhythm of rise and fall, this pattern of Malthusian cycles. And we noted one other crucial thing. We noted the strange parallels between the histories of different world zones, as well as some of the significant differences in the pace of change.

Now what we're going to do is to take a quick look at the next thousand years. For a few centuries it's pretty much plain sailing. It all looks fairly familiar. Though in several regions, both in Afro-Eurasia and the Americas, we can see population expanding quite rapidly and some large and powerful empires appearing. Particularly striking are the Mongol Empire, which reached, in the mid-13th century, from Korea to eastern Europe, and in the Americas, the Aztec and Inka empires.

Then, things seemed to suddenly go very strange. From 1500 onwards the pace of change accelerates. Suddenly, the isolation of the different world zones is broken in the first phase of what today we call "globalization." The world suddenly comes together. It's interlinked for the first time in human history. Then, from about 1700, changes appear that within 300 years will have transformed the entire world. Population numbers go crazy.

Now, it's tempting to think that if the appearance of the first cities and states parallel star formation, the "Modern Revolution" is like a supernova. It's breaking down existing structures, and it's scattering new elements into space. But even this image doesn't really capture the creative aspects of the Modern Revolution.

Here are some of the more astonishing things we'll see, some of the more astonishing changes that we'll see from our time-and-space capsule. One of the most astonishing is changes in the number of human beings on planet Earth. In 1000 C.E., there are 250 million humans on Earth; by 1700, there are almost 700 million; by 1900, there are 1.6 billion; and by 2000, there are 6 billion of us. In my own lifetime, human population has increased by 3.5 billion. And remember, just a thousand years ago, the total population on Earth was just 250 million. As Lynn Margulis and Dorion Sagan put it, humans had become a sort of "mammalian weed." And Carlo Cipolla comments that, "a biologist, looking at the diagram showing the recent growth of world population in a long-range perspective," is almost bound to say, faced with this graph, that what they're seeing is the "curve of a microbe population in a body suddenly struck by some infectious disease." And Cipolla ends by commenting: "The 'bacillus' man is taking over the world."

We see huge cities begin to light up around the world, and by some estimates, total global output of goods and services may have increased by 100 times in just 250 years. That helps explain why, despite rapid population growth, somehow most of those people are still being clothed, fed, and housed—and though many live in dire poverty, considerable numbers live at higher material living standards than ever before. This is the world we live in today.

Now, what is it about this new world that allows it to support such staggering numbers of human beings? Clearly by now we're no longer in the agrarian world. We've crossed a new threshold. We've crossed the eighth and final threshold of this course. And I will call this threshold the "Modern Revolution." What this lecture does is introduce the idea of the Modern Revolution and try to suggest how we might begin trying to both understand it, to grasp its essence, and to explain how it happened.

So, what is the Modern Revolution? A simple answer is that the Modern Revolution is the series of explosive changes we saw from our time-and-space machine. But can we get a slightly more precise grip on this astonishing phenomenon?

Well, let's begin with chronology. Let's clarify chronology first. The "Modern era" is the third of our three great eras—the first two being the Paleolithic era, which lasted about 200,000 years, and the Agrarian era, which lasted about 10,000 years. The Modern era has lasted, so far—remember, it's still continuing—just a few hundred years. Of course, all periodizations are somewhat arbitrary. But, for the sake of clarity, let me set out the periodization that I'm going to use in the lectures that follow.

I'll suggest that we define the Modern era as having started about 300 years ago, in 1700. Now that's, of course, a slightly symbolic date. But I picked 1700 because that is when we first begin to see, in some regions of the world, a transition to radically different types of society that are capable of extraordinarily rapid rates of innovation and change.

However, the roots of change lay in the previous millennium or so—so our explanations of the appearance of the Modern era will begin almost 1,000 years earlier, sometime in the 1st millennium C.E. As for the period after 1700, I'm going to divide it into two main sections. The first extends approximately from 1700 to 1900. In this period, parts of the world, particularly in Europe and the Atlantic region, were transformed. And as a result of that transformation, they acquired unprecedented wealth and power.

The second period begins in about 1900, and it embraces the 20th century and the early years of the 21st century. In it, modernity began to transform the rest of the world as well. So, what we've seen is that within just 300 years the entire world has been transformed. The speed and comprehensiveness of this change is itself one of the most striking features of the Modern Revolution. Remember, it took 200,000 years for Paleolithic populations to spread around the world. It took 10,000 years for agrarian civilizations to transform much of the world. The impact of the Modern Revolution has been felt within just three centuries.

Okay. Definitions. Now, let's try and zero in on what we mean by this phrase the "Modern Revolution." Let's begin with the reality that today's world is simply radically different from the world of 1,000 years ago. Now, I could pick a million examples. Let me just pick one random but spectacular— and I think rather important—example of what I mean. We've seen that our unique ability to adapt and change as humans depends on what I've called "collective learning." This is the ability to swap information with great efficiency. And I've argued that this is fundamental to our ability to adapt and change. Eight hundred years ago, the fastest way of transporting information from community A to community B, of transporting information over a large area, was along the courier systems established throughout the Mongol Empire. Marco Polo gives a wonderful description of these. They were one of the major political projects of the Mongol Empire, and the rulers of the Mongol Empire regarded this post-horse system as extremely important.

Marco Polo estimated that couriers could travel, if necessary, as fast as 250 miles a day, changing horses perhaps every 25 miles. But frankly this was really no faster than the post-horse systems of the Achaemenid Empire, which we heard Herodotus describing. The thought that just a few centuries after Marco Polo, an ordinary citizen might be able to communicate instantaneously with another citizen anywhere in the world, or even, if they really wanted to, that they might be able to fly to the other side of the world in less than 24 hours, would have seemed the purest fantasy—yet that's the world we live in today. It's a world in which exchanges on a global scale of information, collective learning in fact, can take place instantaneously around the entire globe.

I've called the Modern Revolution one of our eight main thresholds, and this is because it does, indeed, count as a revolution in complexity. And we've seen already, Eric Chaisson's calculations of energy density flows carry the implication, if they're accurate, that modern human societies may be one of the most complex things we know. So, in describing the Modern Revolution, we're watching the creation of this astonishingly complex phenomenon.

In what ways does this count as more complex? Well, first, modern society has more structure than any earlier types of human communities. Just one illustration is the huge variety of roles that are available to individuals in this world. It's much greater than it was in the agrarian world, where the majority of people were peasants.

And the structures of the modern world now are not just modern or regional, they're global—they extend across the entire world. Think of the astonishing organizational and technological challenge of keeping a modern city going like New York, or Beijing, or Mumbai. It's staggering. There's nothing like it in the Agrarian era. So first, there's simply more structure. The modern world involves more complex components, more components, and they're linked together in more complex ways.

Second, modern societies mobilize and use energy flows many times greater than those typical of earlier eras of human history. Now, here's just one calculation that tries to give some feeling to this: Ian Simmons estimates that humans today may be using, on average—per capita, that is to say—about 230 kilocalories a day. That's almost 10 times as much energy as his calculation for humans who lived 1,000 years ago. Yet, in the same period, human populations have risen by about 24 times, from about 250 million to about 6 billion. And what that suggests is that total energy use today, if these figures are right, is about 10 times 24, or about 240 times what it was just 1,000 years ago. And, of course, the key to this is the use of fossil fuels.

Third—we've seen there's more structure, we've seen there are far greater energy flows—third, associated with the Modern Revolution is a spectacular range of new emergent properties. This is where the analogy with the supernovae works quite nicely. Supernovae, we saw, spilled new chemical ingredients into the Universe. These properties—we could spend a long time listing them—they include the ability to fly, to communicate instantly across the globe, they include the existence of cities of 20 million people, they include also weaponry capable of obliterating these same cities in a few minutes. So, we can also say there are new emergent properties.

And what about stability, the fourth element in complexity? How stable are they? Now that's an interesting question that we're going to have to leave hanging in the air, because all of this change is so rapid that as yet we don't really know the answer to that question.

Okay. Can we pin down these changes? Can we define their essence? Now, the trouble is there have been so many of them, they're so various, they've transformed human life in so many areas, that it's extremely difficult to pin down the essential nature of these changes. Here, with the Modern Revolution, more than ever before in this course, the challenge is to see the whole elephant and not just the wrinkles on its skin. Now, the result of this blur of information and changes is that describing what we mean by modernity or the Modern Revolution is extremely difficult. We have to try somehow, though, to grasp the essence of modernity from a big history perspective. What does it look like from our time-and-space capsule?

There are other difficulties. One is that the changes continue today, which makes it very difficult to grasp the overall shape of change in the Modern era. The changes are continuing. We can't see the overall shape of this era. In fact, that's why I've labeled it the "Modern era." And I'm using the adjective "Modern" deliberately in a fairly empty sense, to simply mean the era closest to us, because it's very hard to pin down its essence. With agriculture you could say agriculture was the essence of those changes. In modernity, it's not absolutely clear yet what is the essence of change.

The result of all these difficulties is profound disagreement about what we mean by modernity. Some will say it meant new ways of thinking, new attitudes—that these began, perhaps, during the European Enlightenment. Some will stress economics. Some will even claim that modernity is over, that we now live in a post-Modern era.

The result of all these disagreements is that I'm going to have to take some decisions about what we focus on. And the discussion that follows represents an attempt to pick out the crucial features of the Modern Revolution, as seen through the wide lens of big history—and that's a lens that tries to see this threshold as one in a long sequence of thresholds that reaches back to the very origins of our Universe.

The approach I'll adopt builds, however, on a long tradition of debate about modernity that includes major thinkers—from Adam Smith, to Karl Marx and Max Weber, and up to many contemporary thinkers. So, we have plenty of ideas. Once again, though, the problem is so many ideas, it's hard to decide which are the most crucial ones. Now, one more thing, the big history perspective has certain consequences for how we look at modernity. The first is going to be (and this is the sort of product warning) that some familiar landmarks—such as the French Revolution, or the Renaissance, or the Enlightenment—may seem to vanish entirely at these scales. For example, the Renaissance is going to zoom past so quickly it'll be a bit of a blur, a bit like a passing train in the night. What we're looking for are the very large patterns of change.

A second consequence of the big history perspective is that we'll try to see the Modern Revolution as a global phenomenon, unlike many traditional accounts that have seen it largely as a product of changes in Europe or the West. Recent scholarship in world history has shown very, very clearly that the transformations were indeed global, and they had global roots. Modernity is not just a European or Western phenomenon. The Americas, for example, played a crucial role early on as suppliers of new crops and also as suppliers of vast amounts of silver to the world economy. And today, of course, the Americas are the home of the most powerful and richest nation on Earth.

Okay. With those preliminaries out of the way, I'm going to stick my neck out and suggest four defining features of the Modern Revolution. This is the first, and I'll argue later it's probably the most fundamental: Rates of innovation accelerated sharply. Now, let me remind you the word "innovation" is a modern economist's term, but it sort of overlaps with the biologist's term "adaptation." So, we're talking about adaptation. This is absolutely fundamental. It represents a sort of gearshift in the "synergy of collective learning."

This acceleration in innovation or adaptation had several consequences. It increased the pace of historical change. We've seen it took 200,000 years for foraging lifeways to spread around the world, about 10,000 years for agriculture to do so, and just 200 to 300 years for the Modern Revolution. And that's a direct consequence of this increase in the speed of innovation and change.

Innovation also increased human control over the energy and resources of the biosphere, because this is what innovation always does. It always means finding new ways of extracting resources from the biosphere. But there are further aspects to this. What's happened is that innovation has become institutionalized in the Modern era, in modern institutions of education and science that have constructed formal structures to encourage and sustain innovation. So, we're now deliberately innovating in a way that has no parallel in earlier epochs.

Now, here's the second crucial defining feature of the Modern era: It is that innovations drove many other changes. They increased available resources. This allowed humans to multiply—creating larger, denser, and more complex societies than those of the Agrarian era. The general pattern is one we've seen before. Innovations lead to intensification, to increasing population density, creating greater social complexity.

We've seen the numbers already. Human numbers rise from 250 million 1,000 years ago, to about 950 million in 1800 C.E., to about 6 billion in 2000 C.E. What we're seeing is a 30-fold increase in human population in 1,000 years.

As in the Agrarian era, larger communities meant new lifeways, new types of power structure. Wage earning replaced peasant farming as the normal way of earning a living. And this is probably one of those things that is less obvious, but it's one of the changes that affected probably the largest number of people. In some European societies, peasants became less than 50% of the population as early as the 18th century. Globally, this threshold had probably been reached by the end of the 20th century. The great British historian Eric Hobsbawm puts this almost at the center of his account of the 20th century. He writes: "The most dramatic and far-reaching social change of the second half of [the 20th century], and the one which cuts us off forever from the world of the past, is the death of the peasantry."

As a part of this buildup of resources, governments became larger, more powerful, and more intrusive. They had the capacity to interfere in daily life on a vastly greater scale than the rather clumsy tributary governments of the Agrarian era. But they also became more responsive to the needs and capacities of their subjects. And we'll see that this was necessary simply to handle the complexity of modern societies.

And human society became global. Since the 16th century, this is the third great feature of modernity. Human society becomes global. It's globalization, an early stage in globalization. Since the 16th century, human societies have exchanged goods, ideas, diseases, and people within a single global network. For the first time, humans meet each other not within the limits of these world zones, but globally. Improved technologies of communications and transportation have steadily tightened these links over the last few hundred years. That's the third feature: globalization.

And the fourth is that our species has begun to transform the biosphere. By some estimates, humans may now be controlling or managing the disposal of 25% to 40% of all the energy that enters the biosphere through photosynthesis. This is staggering ecological power for a single species.

And there are other ways of measuring this—and these are just illustrative. Modern weaponry is now so powerful that humans could, if they chose, destroy much of the biosphere within a few hours. The bomb dropped on Hiroshima on August 6, 1945, was simply a horrifying demonstration of this power.

The diversion of biospheric resources to human use has also had a profound effect on other species, on other parts of the biosphere, through loss of habitat and increasing extinctions. And as we now know, it's beginning to transform the global climate system, mainly through "global warming." And here's a quote from two scholars—Revelle and Suess—that captures this very nicely. They wrote this:

> [As early as 1957], human beings are now carrying out a large-scale geophysical experiment of a kind that could not have happened in the past nor be reproduced in the future. Within a few centuries we are returning to the atmosphere and oceans the concentrated organic carbon stored in sedimentary rocks over hundreds of millions of years.

The environmental historian John McNeill writes: "For most of Earth's history, microbes played the leading role of all life in shaping the atmosphere. In the 20th century," he writes, "humankind stumbled blindly into this role."

So, here are our four defining features: a sharp increase in innovation; innovation had a large number of consequences in other areas; the globalization of human history; and finally, a sharp increase in human impacts on the biosphere.

Now let's start talking about the even more difficult problem of explaining this. Defining the Modern Revolution is tough enough; can we explain it? What I want to do is describe the strategy I'm going to adopt for explaining the Modern Revolution. I'm going to begin by focusing on one of these four features, and that is the first, accelerating innovation, because this is really the key to most other aspects of the Modern Revolution. Only a very sharp increase in innovation or adaptation can possibly explain how within this period humans have found it possible to support so many other humans. Now, if we focus on this accelerating innovation, this simplifies our task a bit. It means we can focus on just trying to explain one of our four features. So now the challenge is—can we explain why innovation accelerated so sharply in the last few hundred years?

Economists and historians have discussed the main drivers of innovation at least since the publication in 1776 of *The Wealth of Nations* by Adam Smith. And in discussing the Agrarian era, we already started looking at these discussions and considering possible drivers of innovation and growth. A short list of familiar drivers of innovation that appear in the literature might include some of the following.

First, the power of states, something we looked at in discussing the Agrarian era. We've seen that tributary states could generate innovation, but we've also seen that they could stifle it. So, this looks like an unpromising candidate for explaining the Modern Revolution.

Here's a second we've looked at: population growth. We saw that Ester Boserup argued that population growth itself encouraged innovation. Yet we've also seen that throughout the later Agrarian era there were these Malthusian crises. Now, if population is encouraging growth, they oughtn't to appear. The fact that they did shows that population growth does not always encourage growth—so let's drop that one.

A third idea: changing ideas. This has played a very important role in a lot of debates about modernity. The German sociologist Max Weber argued that Protestantism encouraged the spread of capitalism. The trouble is, if he's right, how in turn can we explain the rise of Protestantism? Quite apart from the fact that many scholars have shown that many aspects of Catholicism, or Buddhism, for that matter, or Confucianism could also be compatible with capitalism.

So, though these drivers have been discussed a lot, I'm not going to treat them as the keys to explaining modernity. Instead, I'm going to focus on three other drivers, which we've already met in slightly different guises. The first is commercialization and the spread of competitive markets. The second is the spread of capitalism. And the third is the expansion of global exchange networks. And let me describe each of these briefly.

Driver one: increasing commerce. Adam Smith argued that specialization raises productivity; people, if they're highly specialized, can do their work more efficiently than if they're generalists. And specialization, he said, depends on the extent of market competition. Here's how he put it:

> The greatest improvement in the productive power of labour, and the greater part of the skill, dexterity, and judgment with which it is anywhere directed, or applied, seem to have been the effects of the division of labour.

That's chapter 1 of *The Wealth of Nations*. In chapter 2 he writes:

> This division of labour, from which so many advantages are derived, is not originally the effect of any human wisdom, which foresees and intends that general opulence to which it gives occasion. It is the necessary, though very slow and gradual, consequence of a certain propensity in human nature which has in view no such extensive utility; [and that propensity is] the propensity to truck, barter, and exchange one thing for another.

What he's saying, essentially, is as market relations spread, as people are allowed to truck and barter more, that will increase the division of labor, specialization, and productivity. So, here's Smith's key idea, and this is what we've called "Smithian" growth.

Now, here's driver two: capitalism. It sort of overlaps with the first driver. Karl Marx, whose dates are 1818 to 1883, spent most of his life trying to overthrow capitalism. But he was also a greater admirer of capitalism because he saw how powerfully capitalism could raise productivity. His ideas expand in important ways on those of Smith. He offered a social structure theory of growth, which implies that different social structures have different impacts on innovation. And we've already seen this in the Agrarian era. We've seen that neither peasants nor tribute-taking elites really have a sustained interest in innovation, though both groups can occasionally innovate.

Capitalism, Marx argued, is different. The dominant groups are not tribute-takers, but entrepreneurs—and entrepreneurs make their wealth by trading efficiently on competitive markets. They have to spend all their life thinking about innovation. And the majority class in a capitalist society consists not of self-sufficient peasants but of wage earners who have to work hard and efficiently to market their labor. So they, too, have to think about productivity. So, here we have a social structure in capitalism, in which both elites and the majority of the population have to concern themselves with productivity all the time. So, the spread of capitalism ought to encourage innovation.

Driver three is the sudden expansion in the size of exchange networks—and, therefore, of collective learning. The coming together of the four world zones from the 16th century stimulated commerce and capitalism by simply expanding the scale, and intensity, and variety of entrepreneurial activity and information exchanges throughout the world. And we'll see that this sudden rearrangement of global networks of exchange also shifted the centers of wealth and power in the world away from their traditional centers in Afro-Eurasia—in the Mediterranean, Mesopotamian, Persian, Indian, and Chinese zones—to a region that had previously been completely marginal: the Atlantic seaboard. That would prove to be one of the most radical of all the changes associated with the Modern Revolution.

So, now let's take these crucial drivers of innovation and see if we can use them to explain the slow buildup to the critical moment at which modernity really took off, in 1700.

Thank you.

The Medieval Malthusian Cycle, 500–1350
Lecture 39

As in all Malthusian cycles, growth began with innovations that stimulated population growth. New technologies included improved strains of rice in China and improved plows and yokes in Europe.

When did the Modern Revolution really begin? The next two lectures tackle this question using the ideas sketched out in the previous lecture. They will survey world history over the last 1,500 years through two "Malthusian cycles" to see if we can detect elements of modernity falling into place. This lecture describes the medieval Malthusian cycle, which lasted from about 500 C.E. to about 1350 C.E.— from the decline of the Roman and Han empires to the time of the Black Death. We will focus on Afro-Eurasia, the largest and most significant of the four world zones and the region that drove change in the early stages of the Modern Revolution.

We will focus on the central problem of accelerating innovation. Consequently, we will keep our eyes on three crucial drivers of innovation: commercialization, the spread of capitalism, and a rapid expansion in the extent of exchange networks. Can we detect any evidence of an increase in the importance of these drivers of innovation? Did commercialization raise productivity by encouraging specialization and innovation? Did entrepreneurial activity and wage earning (two key features of capitalism) become more important, and if so, did they accelerate innovation? Did exchange networks expand, and if so, did they stimulate commercial activity and information exchanges?

Second, we will look for signs of a shift in wealth and power to a new hub region, around the Atlantic. Can we detect the beginnings of this shift? Third, we must note one more crucial factor: "accumulation." During the 4,000 years of the later Agrarian era, despite many fluctuations, populations increased, markets expanded, and new technologies emerged in much of the world. Without this slow accumulation of skills and resources, the Modern Revolution could not possibly have occurred.

The medieval Malthusian cycle ran from about 500 C.E. to 1350 C.E. Population graphs show the overall shape of the cycle, as populations slowly rose throughout Eurasia from the middle of the millennium before crashing in the middle of the 14th century. Commerce developed so quickly during this cycle that historian Robert Lopez claimed there was a "commercial revolution" in the later Middle Ages.

Populations grew fastest in regions such as South China or eastern Europe that had previously been underpopulated frontier regions. Population growth stimulated commerce, urbanization, and cultural efflorescence. The number and size of cities increased throughout Eurasia. Baghdad and Cairo were among the largest cities in the Muslim lands that dominated the Eurasian heartland; but by the end of the cycle, China was probably the most urbanized region in the world. Hangzhou, the capital of the Southern Song dynasty in China, may have been the world's largest city, with at least a million inhabitants.

Commerce developed so quickly during this cycle that historian Robert Lopez claimed there was a "commercial revolution" in the later Middle Ages.

Trade networks reached further than ever before. Muslims dominated the silk roads, but Europeans were increasingly active. By 1300, the Vikings had reached Iceland, Greenland, and North America (where they established a short-lived colony in Newfoundland in 1000 C.E.), while Venetian traders such as Marco Polo had reached China.

Capitalism flourished as wage earning and entrepreneurial activity expanded. Everywhere, peasants made up most of the population. Yet in many regions, peasants were sucked into capitalist networks. Government demands to pay taxes in cash, land shortages, indebtedness, and the need to buy goods on markets, all forced peasants to earn cash. They earned money by selling surplus produce, by selling goods such as textiles manufactured in the household, or by seeking wagework as laborers or in nearby towns. In such an environment, entrepreneurs flourished. Their power was particularly striking at the edges of the great empires, in Southeast Asia, or the Mediterranean, where powerful small trading states flourished. Some, such as Venice, were ruled by merchants.

The history of Song China (960–1279) illustrates the transformative power of these changes. Since it was first unified in 221 B.C.E., China had been the very epitome of a traditional Agrarian era tribute-taking empire. Its rulers controlled huge revenues produced mostly from the land, and like most Agrarian elites, they despised commerce even though markets were vital to the Chinese economy.

In the 10th century, northern China was conquered by dynasties originating in Manchuria and Tibet. Suddenly, China was divided into three large warring states. Confined to the south, rulers from the Song dynasty faced huge defensive problems and shrinking revenues, so they had to seek revenues from new sources, including commerce. In just 200 years, the share of revenues from foreign trade rose from 2% to 20%. Not surprisingly, the Song began to back traders and encourage trade.

As our model predicts, in such a highly commercialized environment, innovation accelerated. In a now-classic study, Marc Elvin described the remarkable acceleration of innovation in this era. There were innovations in agriculture (including the introduction of new strains of rice from Vietnam, with active government support), in manufacturing (government factories produced 32,000 suits of armor each year in the late 11th century), and in weaponry (this was when gunpowder first began to be used in war). Was China perhaps on the verge of an early industrial revolution? Particularly striking were advances in naval technology in this period. These would make possible an astonishing series of state-sponsored voyages to India, Arabia, and Africa in the early 15th century, under the command of the Muslim admiral and eunuch Zheng He. In 1279, a Mongol dynasty, the Yuan, reunited China under a ruler named Kublai Khan, and in 1368 the Yuan were overthrown by a new Chinese dynasty, the Ming. With fewer rivals and a much larger tax base, government practice slowly reverted to the anticommercial, tribute-taking methods of earlier times, and governments stopped backing commerce and trade. The Ming even tried to ban foreign trade.

Innovation slowed partly because reunited Chinese governments had less need to support commerce, and partly because the world was, as yet, too disconnected for innovations to spread rapidly (though some, such as gunpowder and the compass, did diffuse slowly across Eurasia).

In the mid-14th century, the medieval Malthusian cycle ended in a crash that affected most of Eurasia. Overpopulation and malnutrition were widespread before the plague spread from China, through Central Asia, to the Mediterranean world. In many regions, it killed off a third of the population. The crash suggests that rates of innovation, though impressive in some regions, were not yet rapid enough to match population growth, so the Malthusian pattern would continue. In 1350, the main structures of Agrarian civilizations, including tribute-taking elites and peasant farmers, remained firmly in place, and Eurasia was still dominated by the traditional hub regions.

Though commerce, capitalism, and international exchanges flourished during the medieval Malthusian cycle, they could not yet overcome the technological inertia of Agrarian civilizations. The next lecture surveys changes during the "early Modern Malthusian cycle," which lasted from about 1350 to 1700 C.E. ∎

Essential Reading

Bentley and Ziegler, *Traditions and Encounters*, chaps. 15, 17, 18, 20.

Christian, *Maps of Time*, chap. 12.

Fernandez-Armesto, *The World*, chaps. 10, 12, 13, 14.

Supplementary Reading

Abu-Lughod, *Before European Hegemony.*

Elvin, *The Pattern of the Chinese Past.*

McNeill, *Plagues and Peoples.*

1. What were the most important changes during the medieval Malthusian cycle?

2. What reasons are there for concluding that the world in 1500 had not yet crossed the threshold into modernity?

The Medieval Malthusian Cycle, 500–1350
Lecture 39—Transcript

So, when did the Modern Revolution begin? When and how was the explosion of the Modern Revolution ignited? What are the signs we should look for? This is a question very similar to the one we've asked about earlier thresholds, such as the threshold leading to the appearance of human beings or agriculture. In the next two lectures I try to answer these questions, to define and identify the moment when the threshold was crossed, and I'll do so using ideas sketched out in the previous lecture.

What I'm going to do is to survey world history over roughly the last 1,500 years through two Malthusian cycles to see if we can detect elements of modernity falling into place. Remember what we mean by "Malthusian cycles." These are cycles in which population growth may initially stimulate growth in other sectors of society—economy, even culture or the expansion of political systems—but eventually population growth outstrips growth in resources. And that leads to an eventual collapse of populations of states and sometimes entire civilizations. And that's why we call it a "cycle."

This lecture describes what I'll call the "medieval Malthusian cycle." It begins roughly in the middle of the 1st millennium, about 500 C.E.—this is not long after the decline of the Roman and Han empires—and it continues to about 1350, the time of the Black Death. The second cycle we'll look at in the next lecture, and I'll call it the "early modern Malthusian cycle." That begins at the time of the Black Death, about 1350, and lasts until about 1700. In this first lecture, as we follow the medieval Malthusian cycle, we'll focus almost entirely on Afro-Eurasia, which was the largest and most significant of the four world zones, but it was also the region that probably drove most of the change in the early stages of the Modern Revolution.

So, here's our strategy. We're going to focus on one key aspect of modernity—accelerating innovation—because, as I argued in the last lecture, this seems to be the key to understanding all other, or at least most other, aspects of modernity. Consequently, we're going to try and keep our eyes on three crucial drivers of innovation, three factors that might have led to an acceleration in rates of innovation. And let me remind you, these three are commercialism—that is to say the spread of competitive markets and of entrepreneurial activity associated with markets; secondly, the spread of capitalism; and thirdly, a rapid expansion in the extent of exchange networks.

So we'll ask: Can we detect any evidence of an increase in the importance of these drivers of innovation that might help explain an increase in rates of innovation? And we'll also try and find if we can see in this period any evidence that rates of innovation are beginning to rise. So we'll be asking: Did commercialization raise productivity by encouraging specialization? This is "Smithian" growth. We'll ask: Did entrepreneurial activity and wage earning (the two key features of capitalism) become more important, and if so, did they tend to accelerate innovation? And third, we'll ask: Did exchange networks expand, and if so, did they stimulate commercial activity and information exchanges?

The other thing we're going to look for is signs of a shift in wealth and power to a new hub region around the Atlantic. Remember, the great powers—that is to say, the major centers of wealth, of urbanization, of high culture, and of political power during most of the later Agrarian era—could be found around the Mediterranean, in the north of the Indian subcontinent, and in China. The great powers of the Modern Revolution, so far—and I have to say this because this could change within a generation or two—have been located in the Atlantic region, and that was a region completely marginal to world history before the last millennium.

So, can we detect the beginnings of this shift in wealth and power from the traditional centers of Eurasia to the Atlantic region, a region that was completely marginal before? Northwest Europe, remember, was an area of barbarians, even in the time of the Roman Empire. The eastern seaboard of the U.S. had even less connection with major centers of agrarian civilization.

And finally, there's one more thing we must keep an eye out for or at least remember during this discussion, and that is the idea of "accumulation." During the 4,000 years of the later Agrarian era, despite Malthusian fluctuations, we saw that on a long trend, populations increased, markets expanded, and new technologies emerged in much of the world. Without this slow accumulation of skills, and resources, and technologies, and experience, the Modern Revolution could not possibly have occurred. So, this was the foundation for it all: the slow accumulation of wealth, populations, technologies, and organizational skills during the later Agrarian era. That was the foundation.

Okay. Let's look at the medieval Malthusian cycle, which ran, I'll remind you, from about 500 C.E.—that's a largely symbolic date: I mean somewhere in the middle of the 1st millennium—to about 1350 C.E., the time of the Black Death. Let's begin with population figures, because Malthusian cycles are most easily seen as patterns of rise and fall in population.

Now, I'm going to have to ask you to upload into your imagination a sort of graph-drawing machine. I'm going to give you the figures and see if you can mentally draw the graph. It's not that hard, and it's a fairly simple graph. You'll need, first, to place dates along the vertical axis. So, let me give you the crucial dates. Here are the dates.

The first is 600 C.E. Now, that's two centuries after the fall of the Roman Empire. The second date is 1000 C.E., that's when the Vikings set up a colony in Newfoundland; that didn't last long. That is the first contact that we know of between the Eurasian zone and the Americas in recent millennia. That's the second date, 1000 C.E. The third is 1300 C.E. Marco Polo has just been released from a Genoese jail where, with a fellow convict, a writer of romances from Pisa called Rustichello, he has just completed an account of his travels to China. That's 1300 C.E. And the fourth date is 1400 C.E. In Mesoamerica, the Mexica, from their city in what is now Mexico City, Tenochtitlán, were beginning to build the Aztec empire.

So, here are the data you need to add to the graph. And remember our four dates are 600, 1000, 1300, and 1400.

European population rose from about 22 million in 600 C.E., to about 30 million in 1000 C.E., to about 70 million in 1300 C.E., and then it dropped to about 52 million in 1400 C.E. There's the Malthusian downturn. But if you look at this sequence of figures as a whole, you'll also see something else, and that is that the long trend is still a rise. Even after the collapse, population in Europe is larger than it was at the beginning of the cycle. So, that's why I argue that Malthusian cycles, for the most part, seem to have been cycles on a rising trend.

Now, here are the figures for China: 49 million in 600 C.E.; 56 million in 1000 C.E.; 83 million in 1300 C.E.; and 70 million in 1400 C.E. You can see the same pattern. You can see the Malthusian downturn, and you can also see the general trend, which is towards increasing population.

And finally, the figures for the Indian subcontinent—and once again, we're going to see the same thing. Here are the figures: 37 million in 600 C.E.; 40 in 1000 C.E.; 100 in 1300 C.E.; and 74 in 1400 C.E. So, that is a kind of graphic sketch of this medieval Malthusian cycle.

Now, let's look at some of the things that happened during this cycle. Well, commerce develops very rapidly—in fact, so fast during this cycle that the historian Robert Lopez claimed that there was a "commercial revolution" in Europe in the later Middle Ages. And Robert Lopez and many historians of his generation have often been inclined to think that this is the key to understanding modernity. But since he wrote, several decades of work by world historians have shown a slightly different picture. And that picture is that the commercial revolution was not just a European phenomenon; it affected all of Eurasia.

As in all Malthusian cycles, growth began with innovations that stimulated population growth. New technologies included improved strains of rice in China and improved plows and yokes in Europe. We've already met these improved yokes. They allowed you to harness a horse without choking it when it pulled too hard, because they were attached more to its shoulders than to its neck. Populations grew fastest in regions such as South China or eastern Europe that had previously been underpopulated frontier regions.

Population growth, in turn, stimulated growth in other sectors of society. They stimulated commerce; as villages and towns expanded, there's more exchange between them. They stimulated urbanization—the appearance of new towns, of new villages, of new major cities. And they also stimulated cultural efflorescence: Where there's a lot of money about, you find patrons and you find governments with spare cash, and they may invest it in things like Gothic cathedrals.

So, the number and size of cities and the richness of the culture they can support increased throughout Eurasia—and populations became very dense in this period. According to Asa Briggs, by the late 13th century, and I quote: "A bigger area was cultivated [in England] than at any period before the wars of the twentieth century." Baghdad and Cairo were among the largest cities in the Muslim lands that dominated the Eurasian heartland. But by the end of the cycle, it may have been that China was the most urbanized region in the world.

By the 12th century, China may already have been extremely highly urbanized, with well over 10% of its people in the towns. Hangzhou, Marco Polo's "Kinsai"—that's what Marco Polo called the city—was the capital of the Southern Song dynasty. And it may have been the world's largest city, with at least a million inhabitants. It contained many different suburbs. It contained working-class suburbs with crowded, multi-story houses. It contained foreign quarters with sections for Christians, Jews, and Turks. It had a large Muslim quarter with many foreign traders—and it also had a wealthy southern region that was dominated by government officials and rich merchants.

And we have some idea of the astonishing variety of trades conducted in the town. Jacques Gernet's list of the guilds of Hangzhou include jewelers; gilders; glue makers; art and antique dealers; sellers of crabs, olives, honey, or ginger; doctors; soothsayers; scavengers; boot makers; bath keepers; and money changers.

So in this period, the largest cities in the world could probably be found mainly in China. Let me remind you, that wonderful list of different professions is what Smith is talking about when he's talking about the division of labor—people becoming more and more specialized in very highly specialized professions or activities as the size of the market expands and it can support more and more highly specialized professions.

Now let's look at trade networks. We've looked at some of the phenomena of expansion in this period, and now let's look at trade networks. Trade networks—or networks of exchanges, another phrase I've used—reached further in this era than they ever had before. Muslims dominated the silk roads—which were, I suppose, the sort of backbone of exchanges in Eurasia. They extended, as we've seen, from China through to the Mediterranean and down into India.

But Europeans were increasingly active. So Europe, which had been a marginal zone in the time of the Roman Empire, is becoming increasingly significant in international exchanges. By 1300 C.E., Vikings had reached Iceland, Greenland, and even North America (where they established the short-lived colony of Newfoundland in 1000 C.E.), while Venetian traders—such as Marco Polo—had reached China. Indeed, this occurred in Marco Polo's time, in about 1300 C.E., just after publishers began issuing regular travel guides to travelers heading for China. These are sort of medieval versions of the sort of travel guides we use today, except they're aimed primarily at merchants—so they tell you about prices, where you find translators, what sort of money to take with you, what sort of goods to take with you, where you're going to make your best sales, and so on.

As exchange networks increased commercial activity and other exchanges between different regions, capitalism flourished. And as capitalism flourished, wage earning and entrepreneurial activity expanded. Let's begin with wage earning. Wage earning is a crucial part of the story. We saw that in agrarian civilizations, peasants—as a rule of thumb—probably made up 90% of the population. They are not very specialized, and for the most part, they have limited incentives to innovate. So, as the number of wage earners expands in society, this itself may be a very powerful index of commercialization and of the emergence of more capitalistic types of societies.

What very often happened is that peasants in many regions found themselves sucked into capitalist networks. Government demands to pay taxes in cash could force them to try and find cash. If governments would no longer accept payment in kind—in animals, or in eggs, or in wheat—you have to find cash, and you have to look beyond your peasant farm for it.

Land shortage could also drive them to seek cash—if they don't have enough land to support their household—as can indebtedness. They run into debt, and then they're going to have to pay their debtors in cash—or the need to buy goods in markets. All of these forces could drive peasants to earn cash, and that meant drive them onto markets in various ways.

They could earn money by selling surplus produce, but generally that was available to the wealthier peasants. Or they could earn money, perhaps, by selling goods, such as textiles manufactured in the households. Now this, of course, means they're functioning not just as pure peasants supporting themselves from the land, they're also functioning as petty artisans. They might be making silk or they might be making textiles, but they're half in the peasant world, and they're half in the wage-earning world.

Or, finally, if things get really tough, peasants might send one or two members of a household to seek wagework as laborers in nearby towns or on nearby farms. So, in all these ways peasants could slowly find themselves getting sucked into networks of commerce and wage earning. And these are some of the very subtle ways in which peasantries slowly began to turn into classes of wage earners.

In this sort of environment, entrepreneurs also flourished. Their power was particularly striking at the edges of the great empires—in Southeast Asia, or the Mediterranean, where powerful small trading states flourished, such as Venice or Genoa. In fact, in those cases, we are talking about states where mercantile activity is so important that merchants actually rule them.

Now, to illustrate the power of some of these changes to stimulate innovation, I want to focus in on China between 960 and 1279 C.E., in the era of the Song dynasty, because the history of China in this era illustrates very well the transformative power of these changes. First, let's go back in time. Since China was first unified in 221 B.C.E. by the first unified emperor, Shi Huangdi, China had been the very epitome of a traditional Agrarian era tribute-taking empire. Its rulers controlled huge revenues exacted mostly in the form of tributes from a vast peasantry, and most of those tributes came from the land. And like most agrarian elite groups, they tended to despise commerce, even though markets flourished in China and played a pretty significant role in its economy. So, here we have a very conventional tributary state.

But then in the 10ᵗʰ century, things start to change. Now, this is a pattern that had occurred before, as central government broke down and was then revived. But the striking thing about China is for how much of the last 2,000 years it was ruled by unified governments. And we'll see Europe's very different.

In the 10ᵗʰ century, North China was conquered by dynasties originating in Manchuria and in Tibet. Suddenly China, instead of being a unified empire, is divided into three large warring states, and the Song dynasty is now confined to the south. Its rulers find themselves facing very serious military challenges from their rivals to the north. And they also have a shrinking tax base because they ruled a smaller area. And this poses very severe problems. You have very severe military problems, and you've got less revenue to deal with it.

So, what happens is the Song rulers suddenly find that despite their distaste for mercantile activity, they're forced to start exacting revenue from commercial activity, and that means they're forced to start working with entrepreneurs, with merchants—and in fact, behaving a bit like the entrepreneurial rulers of commercial city-states such as Venice or Genoa. Here's one piece of evidence of this. In just 200 years, the share of Chinese government revenues from foreign trade rose from just 2% initially (a tiny share) to 20% (a quite substantial share). Not surprisingly, the Song government began to back traders and to encourage trade, including foreign trade.

Now, our model of drivers of innovation predicts that if commercial activity becomes more and more important, if governments start supporting it actively, we should expect innovation to accelerate. Does it?

In a now-classic study, Mark Elvin—the study's called *The Pattern of the Chinese Past*—describes the remarkable acceleration of innovation in this era. Here are just some illustrations of it. There were innovations in agriculture. New strains of rice from Vietnam led to rapid population growth in the south. And it's striking that the use of these new strains was actively encouraged by government propaganda, using wood-block printing so that they could distribute leaflets to provincial officials—telling them how to use these strains, how to encourage their use, and so on.

In manufacturing, government factories produced 32,000 suits of armor each year in the 11th century. In this period, iron was produced in amounts that would not be matched again until the Industrial Revolution in 18th-century Europe. And copper production rose so fast that ice cores taken from Greenland glaciers today show a sudden increase in atmospheric copper pollution in this era. In weaponry, this was the era when gunpowder first began to be used in war. So, there's an astonishing range of innovations. It really looks as if innovation is beginning to take off. So we have to ask: Was Song China perhaps on the verge of an early industrial revolution, as society and governments became more commercialized and more capitalistic?

Well, foreign trade's a wonderful illustration of this. Particularly striking in this period are advances in naval technology. Between 1405 and 1433, a Muslim admiral and eunuch, Zheng He, led seven huge Chinese fleets with up to 60 ships and 40,000 soldiers in voyages to India, Southwest Asia, and East Africa. On the coast of East Africa, you can still find the remains of Ming vases left by these expeditions. And we know that at least one giraffe was brought back by these fleets to China. There's no good evidence, incidentally, that his ships reached the Americas, though they might have had the ability to do so in theory. Zheng He's largest ships were at least five times the length of Columbus's ships. They had watertight internal compartments. They used compasses to navigate. All in all, this is fantastically sophisticated navigation. And it shows that Song China is not merely highly commercialized, highly innovative, but it's also beginning to reach out to other parts of the world.

Then what happens? In 1279, a Mongol dynasty, which took the Chinese name of the Yuan, reunited China under a ruler named Kublai Khan. He was the grandson of Genghis Khan. And in 1368, the Yuan themselves were overthrown by a new Chinese dynasty: the Ming. So now what you have is a reunited China. Many of the pressures on governments to engage more seriously in commercial activities of various kinds are now off. The pressure diminishes, and they can revert to the behavior of much more conventional agrarian tribute-taking states. And they can fall back on the norms of

Confucianism and traditional cultural attitudes, which despised commerce. Slowly, government practice reverted to the anticommercial, tribute-taking methods of earlier times. The amount of revenue from trade diminishes. Governments stop backing commerce and trade—and the Ming even tried to ban foreign trade. It was in this period that the voyages of Zheng He are ended.

So, innovation slowed. It slowed partly because reunited Chinese governments had less need to support commerce. So, the entire commercial activity of China, instead of being backed by states, is now being stifled by state activity. But the other reason why this did not lead to a sort of takeoff was because the world as a whole was, as yet, too disconnected for innovations to spread rapidly. So, what was happening in China didn't turn out to be the starting point for a global industrial revolution. Some of the changes, some of the innovations (such as gunpowder and the use of the compass), did indeed diffuse slowly across Eurasia, but it took a long time.

In the mid-14th century, then, the medieval Malthusian cycle ended— and it ended in a crash that affected most of Eurasia. We find signs of ecological overreach in many parts of Eurasia. It's been particularly well studied in Europe. You find overpopulation, and you find increasing numbers of famines, and you find weakened populations more subject to disease. Overpopulation and malnutrition become more common. And then eventually, in the middle of the 14th century, the plague spreads from China, through Central Asia, to the Mediterranean world. In many regions, it killed off a third of the population.

What this crash suggests is that rates of innovation, though impressive in some regions, were still not yet rapid enough to match population growth— so the Malthusian pattern would continue. In 1350, the main structures of agrarian civilizations—including tribute-taking elites and peasant farmers— remained firmly in place, and Eurasia was still dominated by the traditional hub regions. So, the structures of the later Agrarian era still seemed to dominate change in the history of the whole of Eurasia.

Though commerce, capitalism, and international exchanges flourished during the medieval Malthusian cycle—and remember we called it a "cycle" precisely because it doesn't lead to sustained growth—they could not yet overcome the technological inertia that was characteristic, as we've seen, of most agrarian civilizations. And this is why the medieval Malthusian cycle, for all its innovation, for all the growth that occurred during it, should not count as a significant turning point on the road to modernity.

The next lecture is going to survey changes during the "early modern Malthusian cycle," which lasted from 1350 to 1700, and we'll ask the same questions. Is there any evidence *here* that we're on the verge of a breakthrough?

Thank you.

The Early Modern Cycle, 1350–1700
Lecture 40

The first and most spectacular change probably of all in this period was in exchange networks. And this has to count as one of the most spectacular changes in all of human history. What happens after the voyages of Columbus is that the four world zones are linked, over the next 200 years, for the first time in human history.

The "early Modern" Malthusian cycle lasted from about 1350 to about 1700. By 1500, most areas of Afro-Eurasia had recovered from the Black Death and continued to rise. In the 17th century, populations stagnated or declined slightly in some areas, but there was no population crash similar to that of the 14th century. Is this a hint that rates of innovation were beginning to accelerate? How rapidly did commerce and capitalism expand in this period? The evidence is contradictory.

The most spectacular change in this period was the unification of all four world zones into a single global network of exchange. This change stimulated commerce and capitalism throughout the world as goods, crops, ideas, and people began to circulate on a larger scale than ever before.

The linking of the four world zones was the work of European mariners, using highly maneuverable ships equipped with cannons and backed by aggressive, commercially minded governments. The first captain known to have circumnavigated the globe was Juan Sebastian del Cano, a commander in Ferdinand Magellan's fleet who returned to Spain in 1522. The sudden expansion of world markets stimulated commerce and capitalism so decisively that Karl Marx described this as one of the great turning points in human history.

American crops such as maize, potatoes, manioc, and tomatoes stimulated population growth in China, Europe, and Africa, where they could be grown in regions unsuitable for local staples. Between 1400 and 1700, the populations of China, India, and Europe all doubled. Increasing trade stimulated commerce and capitalism. As China's population and economy expanded, it sucked in silver for coinage. This benefited European middlemen who used brutal methods to extract silver by force from American mines such as Potosi in modern Bolivia. Increasing commercialization began to transform the lives of China's peasants.

The emergence of a global network of exchanges transformed the global geography of wealth and power. For most of the Agrarian era, the Atlantic region was marginal to world history. In Afro-Eurasia, the major centers of economic and political power were in the eastern Mediterranean, North India, and China; in the American world zone, they lay in Mesoamerica and the Andes. Suddenly, Europe found itself at the center of the first global world system. European merchants not only pioneered the first transoceanic exchange networks but also maintained control of them for several centuries.

Between 1400 and 1700, the populations of China, India, and Europe all doubled.

A durable pattern of small- or medium-sized states, engaged in constant competition, forced European rulers to seek commercial sources of revenue. So European states were generally more supportive of commerce than the great empires of the Muslim world or China.

With supportive governments and a central position in global commercial networks, European societies became increasingly capitalistic, and their governments became more supportive of entrepreneurial activity. In Britain, these changes are evident from the remarkable statistics assembled by Gregory King (1648–1712), one of the pioneers of modern statistics.

According to King, in 1688, 43% of the British population consisted of "cottagers and paupers" or of "laboring people and out servants." In other words, almost half of Britain's population had no land and had to survive entirely from wage labor. Modern studies suggest that in the late 17th century, more than half of British national income came from commercial activities (Christian, *Maps of Time*, p. 413). By the early 18th century, most of the revenues of the British government came from commercial sources, which ensured that the government would aggressively back commerce. The importance of commerce was evident from the many merchants in the British Parliament.

Yet, despite these changes, there was no sharp acceleration in global rates of innovation. There were significant improvements in shipping and military technology, and in mining and instrument building. But in general, global rates of innovation remained sluggish. Populations grew less because of significant innovations than because of changes such as the introduction of American crops or government backing for the settlement of new lands, from Siberia to South America. The European Scientific Revolution may have been a product, in part, of the torrent of new information that flowed through European societies as Europe found itself at the center of the first global network of information. But as yet, science had little impact on technological innovation.

In the smaller world zones, the initial results of global unification were catastrophic. Globalization exposed the smaller world zones to colonization and brutal exploitation by European invaders. In the silver mines of Potosi, in modern Bolivia, miners (many of them children) were routinely worked to death, or their health was destroyed by the handling of mercury, all to ensure the flows of American silver that drove global commerce.

Europeans brought diseases such as smallpox that decimated indigenous populations. In Afro-Eurasia, the widespread use of domesticated animals allowed diseases to cross species, creating a rich palette of diseases and toughening immune systems. The other world zones had smaller populations, few or no domesticated animals, smaller exchange networks, and a less rich disease environment. As a result, the introduction of Afro-Eurasian diseases such as smallpox was catastrophic, mimicking the impact of Eurasian plagues but on a far larger scale. In the more densely settled regions of Mesoamerica and Peru, populations may have fallen 50%–70% in the course of the 16th century. For Americans, this was an apocalyptic calamity.

How much had the world changed by 1700? Globalization stimulated commerce and capitalism, and it transformed some regions, particularly in Europe and (more destructively) the Americas. Yet most states were still dominated by traditional tribute-taking elites with traditional aristocratic values. Peasants, though increasingly enmeshed in market exchanges, remained the vast majority of the population in most countries. The survival of traditional social structures may help explain why, on a global scale, innovation remained sluggish.

In the early Modern Malthusian cycle, as in the medieval cycle, there was much change, yet the basic structures of the Agrarian era remained in place, and that may explain why rates of innovation remained low. When, where, and why did the breakthrough to modernity occur? ∎

Essential Reading

Bentley and Ziegler, *Traditions and Encounters*, chaps. 23–26.

Christian, *Maps of Time*, chap. 12.

Supplementary Reading

Crosby, *The Columbian Exchange*.

McNeill, *The Pursuit of Power*.

Questions to Consider

1. What were the most important changes during the early Modern Malthusian cycle?

2. What were the most important consequences of the first wave of "globalization" between 1500 and 1700?

The Early Modern Cycle, 1350–1700
Lecture 40—Transcript

So when did change become so rapid that we can no longer say we're still in the Agrarian era? We ask this question of the medieval Malthusian cycle that ran from 500 to 1350 C.E. And all we saw was that though we can see an increase in the significance of our three main drivers of growth—which are commerce, capitalism, and the expansion of exchange networks—the population crash at the end of the cycle confirms the impression that we've not yet left the agrarian age.

Now we ask similar questions of the next large Malthusian cycle, which extends from about 1350, the year of the Black Death, to about 1700. And this I'll call the "early Modern Malthusian cycle."

Let me first give you the population figures so you get a sense of the general shape of this Malthusian cycle. Once more you might want to mentally upload a graph—and it's got the following dates: The first date is 1400. Remember that's when the Aztecs are building their empire in Central Mexico and much of Eurasia is recovering from the Black Death. The next date is 1500, just eight years after Columbus's return from his first trip to the Americas. The next date is 1600. This is a very easy sequence; we're going century by century. The year 1600 is when figures such as Galileo are beginning to transform European science, while the Americas are beginning to recover from a demographic catastrophe far more severe than the Black Death. And the last date is 1700, which we take as a symbolic starting date for the Modern era.

So let me give you some population figures. Let's begin with Europe. European population in 1400 was about 52 million. In 1500, it was 67 million. In 1600, it was 89 million. And in 1700, it was 95 million. Now, you'll note we're not seeing a crash here. At most we're seeing a sort of slowdown in growth in the late 17th century. And there is indeed evidence of a sort of minor dip in the 17th century—in fact throughout much of Eurasia. There's no real crash.

Here are the equivalent figures for China: 70, 84, 110, and 150 million. And the figures for India are 74, 95, 145, and finally 175 million. Now, in the case of China, too, you can find evidence for slowdowns certainly in the 17th century, but here we find no evidence of a crash at the end of this cycle. And this provides the first hint that global rates of productivity may have been beginning to keep pace with population growth better than ever before. So that's already an interesting sign that we may be on the verge of modernity.

So did this cycle bring the world closer to modernity? Did rates of innovation begin to accelerate sharply? How rapidly did commerce and capitalism expand? Did the world become more interconnected? And we'll see that the answers to these questions are slightly contradictory.

First, the first and most spectacular change probably of all in this period was in exchange networks. And this has to count as one of the most spectacular changes in all of human history. What happens after the voyages of Columbus is that the four world zones are linked, over the next 200 years, for the first time in human history. And the creation of this first global exchange network stimulated commerce and capitalism. The linking of the four world zones counts, as I've said, as one of the great events of human history. Suddenly it was a bit as if Pangaea had been re-created—as ideas, goods, crops, people, and also diseases began to circulate rapidly across the entire globe as they never had before. We've seen before, history seemed to take place in four completely isolated domains. Now, for the first time—this is the first step toward what we call "globalization" today—human history is taking place on a single, integrated stage—much larger, and more varied, and more diverse than any of the stages on which it had taken place before.

This weaving together of the four world zones was the work of European mariners using highly maneuverable ships equipped with cannon, and they were backed by aggressive commercially minded governments. Christopher Columbus crossed the Atlantic and headed back in 1492. The first captain known to have circumnavigated the globe was Juan Sebastian del Cano. He was a commander in the fleet of Ferdinand Magellan, and he returned to Spain with the remnants of the fleet in 1522.

Magellan's fleet traveled around South America, around Cape Horn, and then across the Pacific to the Philippines. And it was here in the Philippines that its commander, Ferdinand Magellan, was killed on the island of Cebu in battle with the local chief called Lapu-Lapu. Now, after these voyages, for the first time in history, the world is united.

This sudden expansion of world markets stimulated commerce and capitalism very, very significantly. Even Karl Marx regarded this as a fundamental turning point in the history of capitalism. And that's why he writes: "World trade and the world market date from the 16th century, and from then on the modern history of Capital starts to unfold."

A lot of things happened. These exchanges were significant almost immediately in the 16th century. They took the form, or at least one form of these exchanges was what the historian Alfred Crosby has called the "Columbian exchange"—a massive exchange of goods, and people, and diseases between the Americas and the Afro-Eurasian zone.

Here are some of the things that exchanged: American crops—such as maize, potatoes, manioc, and tomatoes—were quite soon being grown in many parts of Eurasia, including China, Europe, and Africa. And here they soon stimulated population growth, because they could often be grown in regions that were unsuitable for local staples. So the effect of introducing these crops was to widen the area that could be farmed and to increase total output of food and other projects.

Between 1400 and 1700, the populations of China, India, and Europe all doubled. Increasing trade stimulated commerce and capitalism in most of the old hub regions of Eurasia: the eastern Mediterranean, the Muslim world, northern India, and in China. As China's population and economy expanded, it began to suck in silver for coinage. In the 16th century, Chinese governments began to demand that taxes be paid in silver, and this had a huge impact on the world economy. That, incidentally, is a measure of how huge the Chinese economy was and what a significant driver it was of world economic change. But this also benefited European middlemen, who extracted the silver by force from American mines.

Where did the silver come from? Well, much of it came from a single place: Potosi, in modern Bolivia. The city was created when Spanish colonists discovered that the region around Potosi included a virtual mountain of silver, and they discovered this in 1545. Within 30 years, Potosi had a population of 120,000—and it was certainly one of the largest cities in the world by then. In 1650, its population may have been 160,000. But after that, it began to decline with the decline in silver output.

At its height, Potosi was a brutal and violent place, and Potosi illustrates very well some of the brutal sides of what I've called the "Columbian exchange." This was not a peaceful process. Indians were forced to labor in the mines and died in huge numbers from overwork, exposure, and brutal treatment—particularly children—but they also died from mercury poisoning. The silver ore extracted from Potosi was crushed, and then it was mixed with mercury, after which workers were forced to tread it into a compound with mercury. The mixture of mercury and silver ore was then heated to drive off the mercury, leaving pure silver and deadly fumes. As locals died in huge numbers, they were often replaced with African slaves. This is not a pretty story.

Increasing commercialization began to transform the lives of peasants in many areas. Now here's just an illustration from China. And I've gone back to Mark Elvin's book, *The Pattern of the Chinese Past*, for this quotation—and here's Elvin's account of how Chinese peasants were increasingly sucked into markets. And let me remind you that what's going on here is that people who had been peasants are slowly, slowly being transformed into wage earners. And that's a process that will continue and is continuing today in the early 21st century.

> Increased contact with the market made the Chinese peasantry into a class of adaptable, rational, profit-oriented, petty entrepreneurs. A wide range of new occupations opened up in the countryside. In the hills, timber was grown for the booming boat-building industry and for the construction of houses in the expanding cities. Vegetables and fruit were produced for urban consumption. All sorts of oils were pressed for cooking, lighting, waterproofing, and [even] to go in hair creams and medicines. Sugar was refined, crystallized, and used as a preservative. Fish were raised in ponds and reservoirs to

the point where the rearing of newly-hatched young fish for stock became a major business ... Growing mulberry leaves [for silk-making] became a major business.

Now once again, I hope that what that passage does is illustrate the huge number of different ways in which peasants could find themselves slowly sucked into market activities and on the slippery slope of becoming, eventually, wage earners.

The emergence of a single global network of exchanges began to transform the global geography of wealth and power. And this is one of the major changes of this period. For most of the Agrarian era, we've seen the Atlantic region was marginal to world history. In Afro-Eurasia, the major centers were in the eastern Mediterranean, north India, and China. In the American zone, they lay in Mesoamerica and the Andes. Suddenly, Europe now finds itself at the center of the first global world system. And this is largely because of the role that European merchants and European mariners have played in weaving the four world zones together. European merchants not only pioneered the first transoceanic exchange networks, but they also managed to maintain control of them for several centuries.

Europe itself is becoming more distinctive in this period. It's an odd world. A durable pattern emerges in Europe very different from that in China, at the other end of Eurasia. Not of large unified empires that encourage the patterns of tribute-taking of traditional tributary states, but something really rather different. In Europe what you get is a durable pattern of small or medium-sized states that seem to be engaged in constant competition.

This world ought to remind you slightly of the world of the Song dynasty that I described in the last lectures. European rulers are ruling medium states. They don't have colossal resources available if they try to survive merely by exacting tributes from peasants. And yet, they face constant warfare—a very, very competitive international political situation. So they have to seek commercial sources of revenue. And the result is that European rulers find themselves generally more supportive of commerce than the great empires of the Muslim world or China. Somewhere like Venice or Genoa is an archetype of a mercantile state, but many of the cities of Europe are sort of somewhere between the two. We have rulers whose attitudes very much look like those of traditional tributary rulers, but in fact they're becoming increasingly dependent on commercial revenues and increasingly supportive of commercial activity.

With supportive governments and a central position in global commercial networks, European societies become increasingly capitalistic. And the governments become increasingly supportive of entrepreneurial activity, above all on the international stage of which Europe now finds itself at the center.

In Britain, the slow transformations of society that go on as a result of this increasing commercial pressure are evident from the remarkable statistics assembled by Gregory King, who lived in the late 17th century—his dates are 1648 to 1712. Gregory King is a fascinating figure, and he's one of the pioneers of modern statistical studies. We're surrounded by statistics today. We often forget how recent this barrage of statistics is, and Gregory King is one of the crucial figures. He worked for many years in the College of Arms. It still exists. It was founded in the Middle Ages, and what it does is it keeps records of the coats of arms of British families. And it may have been this position that gave him access to a lot of important government information at the end of the 17th century.

In 1696, King compiled a manuscript called "Natural and Political Observations upon the State and Condition of England." In it, he estimated the population and wealth of England and Wales. He also offered statistics on demographic facts such as the numbers of those in different classes, the numbers of people of different ages, the percentage of those who are married, and so on. As an aside, he also attempted to calculate the amount of beer drunk each year. King's statistics are a wonderful treasure trove for modern historians of 17th- and 18th-century Britain. And here are some of the things that come out of these statistics. According to King, in 1688, 43% of the British population consisted of, and I quote: "cottagers and paupers" or of "laboring people and out servants." Now, it may not be immediately obvious why this is so striking. But what King is really saying here is that almost half of Britain's population had no land and had to survive entirely from wage labor. Cottagers and paupers, laboring people and out servants, these are not fully viable peasants who are supporting themselves from the land. These are people who might look like peasants, but they're really at the margins, and most of their income has to come from wage labor of some kind. Now, that's very striking.

If you remember our rule of thumb, that roughly speaking 9 out of every 10 people in agrarian civilizations were probably peasants, here we have a society in which 40% to 50% seem to be wage earners of some type. And modern studies, many of them using some of King's statistics, suggest that in the late 17th century more than half of British national income came from commercial activities of various kinds.

By the early 18th century, most of the revenues of the British government came from commercial sources. And this ensured that the British government would aggressively back commerce. And the importance of commerce was evident also from the many merchants in the British Parliament of the 18th century. So here we have a society which in many ways still looked like a traditional tributary society, but if you start looking more closely at flows of wealth, sources of revenue, and so on, you find a society that is becoming increasingly commercialized, increasingly capitalistic.

So at least in some areas of the world, we find capitalist social structures are becoming more dominant. Commercial activity is spreading widely, and in the world as a whole we've seen global networks have stimulated exchange and commerce on a huge scale.

Now, if indeed these drivers—capitalism, commerce, and expansion of exchange networks—are flourishing, are more and more visible in this era, shouldn't this be stimulating innovation? Shouldn't there be a sharp acceleration in global rates of innovation? Is there?

Well, here the evidence really is ambiguous. There were significant improvements in shipping in this period and in military technology. This is after all the era of the gunpowder revolution. Also, there were significant improvements in mining and in instrument building of various kinds. And you could list a number of other fields. But, in general, global rates of innovation appear to have remained fairly sluggish. Populations grew less because of significant innovations than because of other changes, such as, for example, the introduction of American crops or government backing for the settlement of new lands—from Siberia to South America.

In the early Modern period, there's a mass of government activity designed to support migration to new areas. The Russians are supporting emigration to Siberia, the Chinese are supporting emigration to underpopulated regions of China, and the Europeans are supporting emigration to the Americas.

It may seem that the European Scientific Revolution is an exception. So we need to consider this. The European Scientific Revolution itself may well have been a product in part of the torrent of new information that flowed through European societies as Europe found itself at the center of the first global network of information.

After all, think of the implications of this. Suddenly Europe finds itself a sort of clearinghouse for information from around the world. No society in previous human history has actually had access to information from around the world—information about new cultures, different technologies, different religious beliefs, different types of people, and different types of societies. And this is what's happening in Europe in the 16th and 17th centuries. Suddenly there's this torrent of new information, much of it completely unexpected. It's almost as if new planets have been discovered.

What's the impact of this bound to be? Well, the main impact seems to have been to encourage European thinkers, philosophers, natural scientists, even theologians to start questioning authority. So many of the things that traditional knowledge had said about the world have turned out to be wrong that increasingly, European natural philosophers find themselves saying: Well, where's the evidence? And this is what Bacon says loud and clear: "Where's the evidence?"

So this is the start of what we've seen throughout this course, this commitment to knowledge based not on authority, but evidence. So this is an immensely important transformation. Yet, the crucial thing is that as yet, and probably not until the 19th century, science had very little impact on technological innovation. Only in the 19th century for the first time do you start getting factories, for example, setting up labs to research innovation. So for a surprisingly long period, science had a rather limited impact on technological innovation.

Now let's look at the other world zones outside Afro-Eurasia. What was the impact of this global unification on them? And the short answer is: It was catastrophic. We've seen that there are ways in which the Afro-Eurasian zone flourished as a result of this unification of the world. In other regions, the results were quite catastrophic. Why? Globalization exposed the other world zones to colonization and to brutal exploitation by European invaders. We've already had a look at the silver mines of Potosi in modern Bolivia as an example of this sort of exploitation—all of this designed to ensure flows of silver that eventually reached China and profited Europeans.

But there's another crucial factor here, and that is disease. This is a pattern we've seen before in the era of agrarian civilizations. As exchange networks expand, disease vectors also start moving into new regions. And if diseases move into regions where there's no immunity, the results can be catastrophic. And this is what happened in the 16th century as a result of the coming together of the world zones.

Europeans brought with them, to the Americas and eventually to the Australasian zone in the Pacific, diseases for which indigenous populations had no immunity at all. Smallpox was perhaps the most lethal of all of these, and smallpox appears in Central America within 15, 20 years of the arrival of Columbus.

Why was this coming together so catastrophic in disease terms? Well, we've seen already in Afro-Eurasia, there were several reasons why immune systems over Afro-Eurasia should have been becoming increasingly hardened. The widespread use of domesticated animals allowed diseases to cross species, creating a rich palette of diseases. Furthermore, we've seen trans-Eurasian exchange networks created multiple immunities in the major population zones of Afro-Eurasia. So by 1500, Afro-Eurasia as a whole, particularly its cities, is a zone in which people have immunities to a wide range of diseases. The other world zones had smaller populations, few or no domesticated animals, and much smaller exchange networks. And the result was a less rich disease environment and much more limited immunities.

So, when Afro-Eurasian diseases such as smallpox are introduced, the results are catastrophic. And what they do is they mimic the impact of Eurasian plagues, but sometimes on a far larger scale. In the more densely settled regions of Mesoamerica and Peru, it has been estimated that populations may have fallen from 50% to 70%. This is a highly controversial area, but what there's no doubt about is that the population decline is very severe in the course of the 16th century. For indigenous Americans, this was an apocalyptic calamity.

Here, just to illustrate this, is an account of what happened and what this meant, from sources in the Yucatan Peninsula. This is just one description of what this may have meant to indigenous Americans in the Yucatan, in the Mayan area. Before the Europeans arrived, says this account:

> there was then no sickness; they had no aching bones; they had then no high fever; they had then no smallpox; they had then no burning chest; they had then no abdominal pain; they had then no consumption; they had then no headache. At that time the course of humanity was orderly. The foreigners made it otherwise when they arrived here.

And that's cited from Alfred Crosby's book on the Columbian exchange.

Here's another description of what happened, and it's from the other side of this disease holocaust, written by Thomas Harriot, who was the surveyor from the English colony on Roanoke Island:

> within a few dayes after our departure from everies such townes … people began to die very fast, and many in short space; in some townes about twenties, in some fourtie, in some sixtie, and in one six score, which in truth was very manie in respect to their numbers … The diseases also was so strange that they neither knew what it was, nor how to cure it; the like by report of the oldest men in the countrey never happened before, time out of mind.

Okay. Now, can we summarize? How much had the world changed by 1700? There's no doubt that globalization had stimulated commerce and capitalism, particularly in the Afro-Eurasian zone, but also in many areas of the Americas, and eventually would do so in the other world zones of Australasia and the Pacific. But the process had been particularly destructive, of course, in the Americas. So, our drivers of growth are clearly flourishing in this era. Yet, in much of the world, states were still dominated by traditional tribute-taking elites with traditional aristocratic values—and that means attitudes that were fundamentally anticommerce, opposed to the development of capitalistic activities. Peasants, though increasingly enmeshed in market exchanges, remained the vast majority of the population in most countries.

So these traditional social structures, which still dominate much of the world, may explain why, on a global scale, innovation remained sluggish. We certainly don't yet see the spectacular rates of innovation characteristic of modernity. So in the early Modern Malthusian cycle, though there are some areas (such as parts of Europe) where changes are beginning to look very decisive indeed, and though we've seen the downturn was nothing like as severe as in the medieval cycle—nevertheless, the basic structures of the Agrarian era remained in place. And that may explain why rates of innovation remained low. So when did the breakthrough to modernity finally occur?

Thank you.

Breakthrough—The Industrial Revolution
Lecture 41

> Now, something also happens to the nature of land ownership. Increasingly, the land vacated by peasants was taken over by large landowners who farmed it for profit. In Britain, this transfer of land from small pockets of peasant farming to much larger areas, farmed more commercially, was dominated by the idea of enclosures.

By 1700 many elements of modernity seemed to be in place, yet global rates of innovation remained slow. This lecture describes the breakthrough to modernity after 1700. It focuses on one country, Britain, where the transformation has been studied most intensively. To understand these changes we need statistics. First, we discuss estimates of changes in total global production from 1500–1998. What do these estimates show? First, they show an astonishing increase in total production: Between 1500 and 2000, global production increased by 135 times. Second, the increases really became evident in the 19th century and were most striking in the 20th century. Increasing production allowed population to multiply by almost 14 times in the same period. Once again, this is an accelerating process. Particularly striking is the fact that production rose faster than population. In other words, more goods and services were being produced *per person*. Production per person increased by about 10 times between 1500 and 1998. Once more, this is an accelerating trend. These figures show that in the Modern era, rates of innovation have begun to outstrip rates of population growth, promising to make Malthusian crises a thing of the past.

A second set of figures illustrates how these changes transformed the global geography of wealth and power. Here we compare the combined production of Britain and the U.S. (two major powers of the emerging Atlantic hub zone) with the combined production of India and China (the ancient economic heartlands of the pre-modern world). In 1750, India and China accounted for almost 60% of global production, while Britain and the U.S. accounted for just 2% of global production (Christian, *Maps of Time*, p. 366). In 1830, India and China still accounted for just under 50%, while the U.S. and Britain accounted for 13%. The relationship changes drastically in the mid-19th century. By 1860, each region produced about 28% of global gross domestic product. Then India and China started to fall behind rapidly. By 1900 the U.S. and UK produced about 42% of global output, and India and China produced merely 8%. By 1950, the U.S. and UK produced 53%, and India and China a mere 4%. Of course, that's not the end of the story. From the mid-20th century, the tide has started to turn once more.

The breakthrough to modernity can be seen most easily in Britain. Many historians argue that Britain was the first country to experience the sustained growth rates typical of the Modern Revolution. Patrick O'Brien writes, "Between 1750 and 1850, the long-term rate of growth of the British economy became historically unique and internationally remarkable" (Christian, *Maps of Time*, p. 411). In 18th-century Britain we can see three interrelated revolutions: a transformation in social structures that created a more capitalistic society, a revolution in the agricultural sector, and a revolution in manufacturing.

By 1700 Britain was probably the most capitalistic and highly commercialized country in the world. It was also one of the best connected, being at the center of global exchange networks. Our model suggests that in such an environment rates of innovation ought to have accelerated as entrepreneurs competed to raise output and as markets expanded, with increasing numbers of wage earners who had to purchase both basic food and clothing with cash. That is exactly what we observe. Agriculture was the fundamental economic sector in all Agrarian societies. Productivity first began to rise in this sector from the 17th century. By 1700 many British peasants had become wage earners. This rapidly growing class provided a source of cheap labor and also a rising source of demand for basic consumer goods. Much of the land vacated by peasants was taken over by large landowners who farmed for profit. Often, they were helped by Parliament, which passed "Enclosure Acts," granting them full possession of land that had once been available for communal use. On these large, consolidated plots of land, the new owners could introduce commercial farming methods, producing goods for sale rather than subsistence. Agriculture became a business.

Farming for profit meant competing with other producers, and that meant increasing efficiency. British farmers raised productivity by introducing techniques that had been known for many centuries. What was new was not the techniques but the increasing incentives to apply them on a large scale. Farmers raised soil fertility by planting legumes; they improved irrigation, bred better-quality animals, and used improved methods of planting and preparing their land.

Between 1700 and 1850, British agricultural output increased 3.5 times, while the numbers employed in agriculture fell from 61% to 29% of the population. For the first time in human history, a minority of the population was feeding a majority. Expanding internal and foreign markets, a supportive government, and a stable financial system that could provide cheap capital (the Bank of England had been incorporated in 1694) encouraged investment in manufacturing as well as in agriculture.

In most Agrarian societies, textile production was the largest sector after agriculture.

In most Agrarian societies, textile production was the largest sector after agriculture. Innovations in cotton spinning reduced the time taken to spin 100 pounds of cotton from 50,000 hours to 300 hours in the late 18th century and stimulated the mechanization of weaving. A shortage of wood encouraged greater use of coal. That meant improving the technologies used to pump water out of coal mines. In the 1760s, James Watt (1736–1819) improved the efficiency of the steam engines traditionally used to pump out mines. More efficient steam engines made it economical for the first time to use coal to drive machines even well away from the coal fields. This encouraged the creation of large factories driven by steam power.

Putting steam engines on wheels early in the 19th century revolutionized land transportation and slashed transportation costs. The first steam engine designed for passengers as well as for freight was the "Rocket," designed by George Stephenson. We have a wonderful description from the actress Fanny Kemble (1809–1893), who traveled on one of Stephenson's trains in 1830.

Putting steam power on wheels in the early 19th century revolutionized land transportation and slashed transportation costs.

By the early 19th century, innovation was raising productivity in many sectors of manufacturing, including textiles, coal, and metals; building; and consumer goods. Between 1770 and 1830, the value of cotton production in Britain rose over 40 times, that of coal production almost 9 times, that of iron production about 5 times, and that of building by more than 11 times.

The English Industrial Revolution provides a good illustration of the model of innovation proposed in Lecture Thirty-One. It suggests that once societies emerged that were highly commercialized, capitalistic in their social structures, and well-connected to global markets, new incentives would stimulate innovation. But the innovations themselves were also important, above all the discovery of a massive new energy source: fossil fuels. The steam engine, followed by technologies that exploited oil and natural gas, allowed humans to tap into the vast reserves of fossilized energy that had been laid down over several hundred million years. Before the steam engine, the most powerful prime mover available was probably a windmill, which could deliver about 9 horsepower. Watt's steam engine delivered 134 horsepower.

269

By the early 19th century, contemporaries began to notice these changes. In 1837, French Revolutionary Blanqui described the changes in Britain as an "Industrial Revolution," his way of saying that they were at least as important as the French revolution, the most momentous event in recent European history.

We have seen how, in Britain, a high level of commercialization, a highly capitalistic social structure, and multiple connections to global markets encouraged soaring innovation. The next lecture asks: How, why, and when did these innovations spread to other parts of the world? ■

Essential Reading

Christian, *Maps of Time*, chap. 13.

Supplementary Reading

Maddison, *The World Economy*.

Stearns, *The Industrial Revolution in World History*.

Wrigley, *Continuity, Chance, and Change*.

Questions to Consider

1. What evidence justifies Blanqui's claim that an "Industrial Revolution" had occurred in Britain by the early 19th century?

2. What factors did most to stimulate innovation in Britain during the Industrial Revolution?

Breakthrough—The Industrial Revolution
Lecture 41—Transcript

If we look down on the world from our imaginary space-time capsule in 1700, and then we move forward rapidly 100 years, then 200 years, we'll start to see a lot of lights turning on. This is the beginning of the Modern Revolution.

We saw in the last lecture that by 1700, many of the elements of modernity seemed to be in place. We saw that there were areas in which our capitalist social structures were well developed. We saw that commerce was widely developed in many parts of the world, flourishing in many parts of the world, and we also saw that the world was now globally integrated in a way it never was before.

Yet despite all of this, we saw that global rates of innovation didn't yet seem particularly spectacular. And I remind you, what we're looking for when we're looking for the breakthrough to modernity is precisely a breakthrough in rates of innovation. So when do the crucial breakthroughs occur, and how?

In this lecture I want to describe the breakthrough to modernity after 1700. And for a lot of this lecture, I'm going to focus on one country, Britain, where the transformation has been studied most intensively. Now, to understand these changes, we're going to need statistics. One of the wonderful things about the modern world is that suddenly we have a mass of statistics. We've seen that in dealing with early eras of human history, we're generally scrabbling around for the least crumb of data. Now, suddenly, we're drowning in data. And particularly, we have a huge amount of statistical data. Most of that data refers only to the last century or two, but some scholars have attempted the difficult task of trying to reconstruct statistical series on matters such as production, population, productivity, that extend back several centuries. This is a tricky and delicate business, but I'll be relying on some of these estimates in what follows.

We do need to remember how much guesswork is involved in these reconstructions. Indeed, we need to remember that the very idea of gross domestic product—which is one of the concepts that they project back into the past—is, in it's modern sense, a 20th-century concept. But the good news is that these reconstructions are so rough-and-ready that they encourage us to look at the very large picture they convey. That is more likely to convey a realistic impression than the details or the figures they reconstruct. So we shouldn't get too caught up in the details, which are much more likely to mislead us.

Now, those of you with "statisticophobia" can contemplate the idea that a table of statistics or a set of figures, if studied carefully, can provide a beautiful snapshot of large economic changes, and that's why economic historians in particular love them. The trick is to spend time with them. If you do, then what they can do is to provide a pretty good alternative to the imaginary time-space machine that we've used in recent lectures.

So, here are some figures. The first set of figures shows increasing output. It attempts to recalculate the idea of gross domestic product over several centuries. The first set of figures estimates total global production from 1500 to 1998. Gross domestic product, which is the term they use, is an estimate of the value of total output of goods and services.

So, what do these estimates suggest? Well first, the first thing they show is an astonishing increase in total production. Between 1500 and 2000, global production on these estimates multiplied by something like 135 times in 500 years. Now, the second thing we see from these figures is that the increases become really evident in the 19th century. This is an accelerating trend, and they become most striking in the 20th century. In the four centuries up to 1913, production had increased by about 11 times. In the next century alone, up to 1998, it would increase another 12 times. So, this is an accelerating trend. It's getting faster and faster.

So, what's the first thing we see? Massive increase in total production of goods and services. And once again, even if these figures are very, very rough estimates, they seem to be telling us something very important.

Now, here's our second set of figures, and they're on population. These suggest that increasing production of energy and of resources and foodstuffs and textiles and so on allowed populations to multiply by almost 14 times in the same period, that's over 500 years. Now, once again, if we look more closely at these figures, they're clearly an accelerating trend. Population growth accelerated from the late 18th century, but much faster in the 19th, and particularly in the 20th century.

And here's just one figure that captures that. In the four centuries up to 1913, global populations increased a bit more than 4 times, that's in 400 years. In the next 100 years, up to 1998, they would increase by another 3 times. So, once again, we have an accelerating trend.

Now, you may have noticed that there is something very striking about comparing these two sets of figures—and this is the fact that production rose much faster than population. Remember, total production has risen by 130 times in 500 years on these figures, and population by 14 times. So what this means is that more goods and services are being produced at the end of this period *per person*, despite extraordinary rates of population growth.

This trend is demonstrated by a third set of figures, on per capita production. Production per person, that is to say total production divided by population, production per person multiplied by about 10 times between 1500 and 1998. And once more, this is an accelerating trend. In the four centuries up to 1913, production per person increased a little more than 2.5 times. In the next century alone, it increased by almost 4 times. Here, in this figure for increasing productivity and in the comparison between the two earlier sets of figures, is the first indicator that one of the results of the Modern Revolution may be that production effectively, for the first time in human history, begins to match or even outstrip population growth.

Now, remember, the lag of production behind population growth was the key to the Malthusian cycles that were the dominant pattern of rise and fall in the later Agrarian era. So far in the Modern era, and I have to say I'm touching wood at this point, but so far in the Modern era, the world has avoided a global Malthusian crisis—that is to say, a global crisis caused by not producing enough stuff.

Now I want to move on to a second data set. And this is a series of figures that illustrates how these changes transformed the global geography of wealth and power and how, as a result of these changes, new power centers emerged and old power centers, some of which had been significant centers of power for several thousand years, began to decline—and to decline very rapidly.

Here's what I'm going to do. I'm going to take figures for production by Britain and the U.S., two of the major powers of the new Atlantic hub zone, and compare them with figures for the combined production of India and China. So we have two groups—one is Britain and the U.S., and the other is India and China. In each case, the figures I'm going to give, give you how much of global GNP is produced by each of those blocs. Now, India and China, remember, were the ancient economic heartlands of the pre-modern world. Britain and the U.S. will be the heartlands of the emerging Atlantic world, the new hub zone of the Modern era.

Okay, here are some figures. Let's go back to 1750. In 1750, India and China accounted for almost 60% of global production. Now again, I have to remind you how rough these figures are. It's the orders of magnitude that concern us here. Adam Smith, incidentally, who wrote *The Wealth of Nations* in 1776, understood this very, very well. He said: "China is a much richer country than any part of Europe." At the same time, in 1750, Britain and the British Atlantic colonies accounted for just 2% of global production. It's a tiny share of global production. Now, let's move forward 80 years. In 1830, India and China, the old hub region, still accounted for just under 50% of global production, as late as 1830. At the same date, the U.S. and Britain accounted for about 13%.

Now, if these figures are giving the right impression, they suggest two things. First, the Atlantic region still, even in 1830, lagged some way behind the old producing zones. But it also suggests something else: They are catching up very rapidly indeed.

And now, the relationship will change very rapidly in the middle of the 19th century. By 1860, these two regions, the new Atlantic region and the old hub zone of China and India, are neck and neck—each producing about 28% of global GDP. Then, at that point, India and China start to fall behind very rapidly. By 1900, the U.S. and UK are producing about 42% of global output, and India and China are producing nearly 8%. And by 1950, the U.S. and

UK are producing about 53%, more than half, and India and China a mere 4%. Of course, by 1950, most of that figure of production for the Atlantic is now coming from the U.S. Of course, I need to add that that's not by any means the end of the story. After 1950, the tide will begin to turn again, and by the middle of the 21st century, India and China will almost certainly have reestablished themselves as major economic powers—but that's a story for the future.

Okay. That's a sort of statistical picture of some of the very large changes that we see between 1700 and 1900. Now I want to focus on one particular area so we can look at the moment of breakthrough more carefully, and that area is Britain. This is where we can see the breakthrough to modernity most clearly. So, just as we concentrated on Mesopotamia when discussing the appearance of agriculture, and again when we discussed the appearance of the first tribute-taking state, now we're going to focus on Britain.

Many historians have argued that Britain was the first country to experience the sustained growth rates that are typical of the Modern Revolution. Patrick O'Brien, for example, writes, and I quote: "Between 1750 and 1850, the long-term rate of growth of the British economy became historically unique and internationally remarkable." Now, I should add that eventually other economies would exceed these rates of growth—but in the middle of the 19th century, no other country throughout human history had matched these rates of growth.

Now, to understand what form the breakthrough took, it may help to think of three related revolutions that, in combination, transformed Britain in the 18th and early 19th centuries. The first of these revolutions was a revolution in social structure, and what it did was to create a society that was more highly commercialized and, in the language we've used earlier, more capitalistic. Entrepreneurs played a more important role, and wage earning played a more important role in that society. So that's the first change, a change in social structure.

The second was a revolutionary transformation of British agriculture. And agriculture, let me remind you, is the largest sector of the economy of all Agrarian era economies. So here we're talking about a transformation of the largest, most fundamental sector of the British economy in the 17th and 18th centuries. And the third change we'll look at is a transformation in industrial production.

So let's begin with changes in social structure. We've seen that by 1700, Britain was, by many measures, one of the most capitalistic societies on Earth. About half of its population, according to the figures of Gregory King, was dependent mainly on wages. So instead of being a society where most of the population were small farmers, small peasants, here we have a society in which at least half of the population is dependent on wages, and we've seen that its elite groups, too, are very highly dependent on commerce of various kinds. It was also one of the best-connected regions in the world, being at the center of global exchange networks. And it was in control of a modest but rapidly growing overseas empire. And it had a government that valued these assets and supported commerce.

Now, the model I proposed in an earlier lecture suggests that in such an environment—with a capitalistic social structure, flourishing commerce, contacts with the global world system, and supportive governments—innovation ought to have accelerated. And it ought to have accelerated as entrepreneurs began to compete to raise output, as markets expanded with increasing numbers of wage earners who had to purchase their food, clothing, and other needs with cash.

Now, does this work? Does this sort of social structure really generate innovation? Well, in Britain, in the 18th century, it certainly does. And let's begin with the transformation of the agricultural sector. So that's the change in social structure that we've seen already. Now, how does it affect agriculture?

Agriculture was the fundamental economic sector in all agrarian societies. Productivity first began to rise in this sector from the 17th century. Now, we've seen that by 1700, many English peasants had become, in effect, wage earners. That change itself had momentous implications for economic development. As this rapidly growing class of impoverished peasants competed for employment, what they provided was a large supply of cheap labor. So as Britain's peasantry is slowly destroyed, what employers get is an increasing amount of cheap labor.

Secondly, this growing class of wage earners, who from their own perspective might have thought of themselves as failed peasants, from an employer's perspective or an entrepreneur's perspective provide a rapidly growing market for basic consumer goods, such as food and textiles. Traditional peasants, remember, are growing food for themselves. They are sometimes even making their own textiles. They're not so dependent on the market. But wage earners have to buy most of what they use on the market. So here's a rapidly growing market for basic consumer goods.

Now, something also happens to the nature of land ownership. Increasingly, the land vacated by peasants was taken over by large landowners who farmed it for profit. In Britain, this transfer of land from small pockets of peasant farming to much larger areas, farmed more commercially, was dominated by the idea of enclosures. Actually from as early as the 16th century, acts of Parliament in area after area, town by town, would allow local landlords to buy up consolidated plots of land and annul traditional rights of use on that land. So what they allowed was the emergence of full private property over large consolidated blocks of land. And landowners took over traditional plots of land that once had been divided into small peasant plots increasingly rapidly in the 18th century, during the enclosure movement. They frequently planted hedges around these newly consolidated blocks of land to mark them out clearly, and that created much of the distinctive English landscape we see today.

Meanwhile, on these large blocks of land, they're now free to introduce new techniques that could benefit from economies of scale that were unavailable to small peasant farmers. If you think about it, agriculture or farming on large blocks of land is almost bound to be a very different thing from farming on small blocks of land, as in the traditional peasant way. This marks a crucial difference between two very different types of agriculture. If you farm a small plot as a peasant, a lot of your farming is for subsistence, and that means you need to grow a variety of plots—and if you have a small area of land, it's hard to introduce more advanced techniques. If you grow on a large plot of land, you're clearly not growing for subsistence, and this means you can grow, you can focus on particular crops, you can introduce modern techniques, and you can benefit from economies of scale. If you're growing on large plots of land, almost inevitably you are a commercial farmer. You're growing for profit, not for subsistence.

So, this change in land ownership marks a fundamental transformation in agriculture. It marks the commercialization of agriculture and the appearance of an agriculture dominated by the profit motive, an entrepreneurial agriculture.

The process has been studied extremely well in British economic history. And here's just one illustration. An English historian, W. G. Hoskins, studied what the process meant in one village—Wigston Magna in Leicestershire. And he found, in the 18th century, absolute transformation in the life of peasants. Peasants whose forefathers had rarely needed to handle cash, they really weren't involved in the cash economy, suddenly become wage earners. They have to think about cash, they have to count every cent, and they have to think very hard about the value of their labor. And he writes: "For Wigston Magna, the Enclosure Act of 1765 was a cataclysm." Small owner-occupiers disappeared as a group within about 60 years, and they became, instead, rural laborers working for other people, or framework knitters weaving in their own homes, or paupers—people right at the edges of society.

Now let's look at the farmers who took over the land. Farming for profit meant competing with other producers, and that meant increasing efficiency. Here's the mechanism Adam Smith saw: the drive of competitive markets. Increasing efficiency meant that English farmers began to improve their farming, usually with techniques that had been known for many centuries. There's nothing much that's new about the actual techniques that were introduced. Rather, as in the early Agrarian revolution 10,000 years ago, where the techniques weren't new, what was new was the way they were introduced and the scale on which they were introduced and implemented. So now there are increasing incentives for large farmers, commercial farmers, to apply them on a large scale.

And farmers begin raising soil fertility by planting legumes, for example, rather than just by leaving land fallow. This means you can keep land in continuous cultivation much longer without destroying its fertility. They improved irrigation. They bred better-quality animals. Incidentally, improvements in animal breeding are part of the background to the growing interest in evolution of figures such as Darwin's grandfather, Erasmus Darwin. They also used improved methods of planting and preparing the land. One of the most famous of the improvers, Lord Townsend, advocated the planting of turnips, for which he became known as "Turnip Townsend."

Now, the results of all of this were striking. Between 1700 and 1850, British agricultural output increased about three and a half times. Yet at the same time, the numbers employed in agriculture fell from about 61% to 29% of the population. Now, here's an entirely new phenomenon in human history. For the first time in human history, you have a medium-sized country in which a minority of the population is feeding a majority.

Now, those are the transformations in the agricultural sector. Now let's look at industry. Expanding internal and foreign markets—internal markets expanded, remember, as more and more peasants became wage earners and consumers, and external markets expanded with the growth of empire and international trade—as well as a supportive government, most of whose revenues now came from commercial sources; and a stable financial system, which made cheap capital available (remember, the Bank of England had been incorporated in 1694): All of these features encouraged investment in manufacturing, as well as in agriculture. So they drew investment into manufacturing. In most agrarian societies, textile production was by far the largest economic sector, after agriculture. Innovations in cotton spinning in this period reduced the time taken to spin 100 pounds of cotton from 50,000 hours to 300 hours in the late 18th century, and this stimulated the mechanization of weaving. And remember, this is stimulated partly by the fact that the market for textiles is growing very rapidly.

Another crucial area of innovation, which will turn out to be absolutely critical later, is coal. A shortage of wood in Britain encouraged greater use of coal. That meant improving the technologies used to pump water out of coal mines so that you could mine deeper, and that meant pumps. A French inventor, Denis Papin, had first demonstrated the potential of steam engines as early as 1691. His engine used steam pressure to raise a cylinder, after which the source of heat was removed, allowing atmospheric pressure to push the cylinder down again. Thomas Newcomen introduced an improved version in

1712. What this one did was spray cold water into the cylinder at the top of the cycle to initiate the downstroke. Now, in both these machines, most of the thrust came from atmospheric pressure. The cylinders were then attached to a beam that worked a pump.

One of the problems was that the rapid heating and cooling of the cylinder was extremely inefficient and required lots of fuel. So these pumps were only cost-effective in mines close to abundant coal, and that's why their use didn't spread widely into other sectors of industry. Then in the 1760s, James Watt improved the efficiency of the steam engines that were traditionally used to pump out mines. What did he do? Watt did two main things. First, he separated the condenser so that the cylinder could remain permanently at a high temperature. And secondly, more precise engineering of the cylinder allowed him to use the force of expanding steam to drive the engine, rather than simply the force of atmospheric pressure.

Now, these changes greatly increased the efficiency and fuel economy of the machine, and they help explain its rapid adoption in different sectors of industry. Improved steam engines made it economical, for the first time, to use coal to drive machines well away from the coal fields, and this encouraged the creation of large factories driven by steam power.

The next transformative use of steam power was to put it on wheels early in the 19th century, and what this would do is to revolutionize land transportation and slash transportation costs. The first steam engine began operation on September 27, 1825, in the county of Durham, and the first design for passengers, as well as freight, was the "Rocket," designed by George Stephenson.

We have a wonderful description of it by the actress Fanny Kemble, who described traveling on one of the first railways in 1830 with George Stephenson—who, incidentally, had acquired his engineering skills operating Newcomen's steam engines at a colliery in Newcastle. Now, here's Fanny Kemble's wonderful description. She prides herself in not understanding the technology that's involved, so it's a delightful description.

We were introduced to the little engine which was to drag us along the rails. She (for they make these curious little fire-horses all mares) consisted of a boiler, a stove, a small platform, a bench, and behind the bench a barrel containing enough water to prevent her being thirsty for fifteen miles—the whole machine was not bigger than a common fire-engine. She goes upon … wheels, which are her feet, and are moved by bright steel legs called pistons; these are propelled by steam, and in proportion as more steam is applied to the upper extremities (the hip-joints, I suppose) of these pistons, the faster they move the wheels. … The coals, which are its oats, were under the bench, and there was a small glass tube affixed to the boiler, with water in it, which indicates by its fullness or emptiness when the creature wants water, which is immediately conveyed to it from its reservoirs.

And then what she does is she describes the journey, and this gives a wonderful sense of how new the experience was, a bit like one of us being invited to fly in the space shuttle, I suspect.

This snorting little animal, which I felt rather inclined to pat, was then harnessed to our carriage, and, Mr. Stephenson having taken me on the bench of the engine with him, we started at about ten miles an hour. … [later] the engine having received its supply of water, the carriage was placed behind it, for it cannot turn, and was set off at its utmost speed, [which was] thirty-five miles an hour, swifter than a bird flies (for they tried the experiment with a snipe).

And I think this conveys very well how utterly new this phenomenon was.

By the early 19th century, innovation was raising productivity in many sectors of manufacturing, including textiles, coal and metals, building, and consumer goods. Between 1770 and 1830, the value of cotton production rose over 40 times, that of coal almost 9 times, that of iron about 5 times, and that of the building industry by more than 11 times.

Now, the English Industrial Revolution provides a very good illustration of the model of innovation proposed in Lecture Thirty-One. It suggests that once societies emerged that were highly commercialized, capitalistic in their social structures, and well-connected to global markets, new incentives would begin to stimulate an acceleration in innovation—and that, we've seen, is the key to the Modern Revolution.

But the innovations themselves mattered—above all, the discovery of a massive new energy source, fossil fuels. The steam engine, followed by technologies that exploited oil and natural gas, allowed humans to tap into the vast reserves of fossilized energy that had been laid down in the previous several hundred million years. This is what we mean by the "fossil fuels revolution." It was a wholly unprecedented energy bonanza for our species.

Before the steam engine, the most powerful prime mover available was probably a windmill, which could deliver about 9 horsepower. Watt's steam engine delivered 134 horsepower, which was a very, very significant increase—and just the beginning. A modern Boeing 747, for example, can deliver about 80,000.

So by the early 19th century, the changes were so striking in Britain that some contemporaries began to notice them. And in 1837, the French revolutionary Blanqui described the changes in Britain as an "Industrial Revolution." Now the question is: How far and how fast would the British Industrial Revolution spread elsewhere?

Thank you.

Spread of the Industrial Revolution to 1900
Lecture 42

What made the Modern Revolution so different is that instead of dying away like this, the process of innovation continued and spread around the entire world—and it's still continuing today, more than two centuries later.

Within just two centuries industrialization had transformed the entire world. No earlier transformation in human history had been so rapid or so far-reaching. This lecture describes the impact of industrialization before 1900. There were four main waves of change before 1900. The first wave began in the late 18th century. It mainly affected Britain and the western edge of Europe. New technologies included a more productive Agrarian sector, improved steam engines, the mechanization of textile production, and increased production of coal and iron.

The second wave took place early in the 19th century. Innovation accelerated in many parts of western Europe, and also along the eastern seaboard of the newly independent U.S. Technological changes included the increased use of steam engines in manufacturing and the spread of railways and steamships. Steam transportation sped up commercial exchanges and cut transportation costs, which stimulated commerce and manufacturing, particularly in large countries such as the U.S. or Canada, where cheaper land transport had a revolutionary impact on commerce in general.

The third wave dominated the middle decades of the 19th century. Industrialization accelerated within Europe, particularly within Germany (now united economically within a common custom zone, the *Zollverein*) and in the eastern U.S. Technological innovations included the industrial production of chemicals (such as dyes and artificial fertilizers), steel-making (with the introduction of the Bessemer process), and the industrial use of electricity. Domestic lighting revolutionized patterns of work and leisure by lighting up the night. Railways, and new and more powerful weapons such as machine guns, revolutionized warfare. The American Civil War was the first major war of the industrial era. The telegraph (first introduced in 1837) and telephone (invented in 1876) revolutionized communications. In 1901, Guglielmo Marconi sent the first wireless signal across the Atlantic.

A fourth wave of innovation dominated the late 19th and early 20th centuries. Industrialization took off in Russia and Japan, and spread westward within the United States. The oil age launched a second phase of the fossil fuels revolution, with the invention of the internal combustion engine. The Wright brothers flew the first powered heavier-than-air plane in 1903. In 1913, Henry Ford produced the first Model T Ford in 1913, pioneering mass production for a new mass consumer market.

Library of Congress, Prints and Photographs Division, LC-USZ62-77563.

Increasing productivity transformed the role and power of governments. Governments acquired new forms of power but also faced new and more complex challenges.

War was a major driver of change. With increasing production, states had to become more effective at mobilizing national resources of both manpower and materials. The armies of revolutionary France pioneered in the challenge of

Marchese Guglielmo Marconi sent the first wireless transmission across the Atlantic in 1901.

raising large citizen armies using the appeal of nationalism. But nationalism meant giving citizens a greater sense of ownership of society: a change achieved, in part, through democratic processes such as elections. To mobilize support from populations that were becoming more mobile, more urbanized, and better educated, governments had to provide new services such as policing, health services, and mass education, which few Agrarian-era states had offered. The power of modern governments depended more and more on economic growth, so they increasingly became economic managers, concerned with creating environments in which commerce could flourish.

The role and scope of government inevitably increased in societies in which most people were wage earners. This is because whereas peasants were largely self-sufficient, wage earners depend on the maintenance of markets, on education, and on the maintenance of law and order within rapidly growing towns. Inevitably, this meant that governments became more involved in the day-to-day lives of most of their citizens.

In short, the rules of political success had changed. Larger, more mobile, and better-educated societies had to be managed rather than simply coerced. In the Atlantic hub zone, the beginnings of these changes were already evident in the "democratic revolutions" of the late 18th and early 19th centuries.

Increasing productivity transformed the role and power of governments.

While modern states have become more democratic, their power to coerce has also increased. Industrialization magnified the military power of states by enabling them to transport soldiers and weapons larger distances, and by increasing the destructiveness of weaponry. Their increased military power was apparent in the astonishing speed with which, in the late 19th century, governments from the new Atlantic hub region conquered much of Africa, Asia, and the Americas.

Cultural life and popular lifeways were transformed. Everywhere, peasants slowly turned into wage earners as they were squeezed off the land by more efficient commercial farmers. Because of the variety of activities for which they had to be prepared, wage earners needed education—so, beginning in France and Germany early in the 19th century, governments began to introduce systems of mass education.

Elite culture was transformed, particularly by science. The first industrial science laboratories were created in Germany in the middle of the 19th century. As the economic, technological, and military importance of science rose, it challenged the traditional role of ancient religious traditions in education and culture by offering new materialistic accounts of the Universe that offered little room for traditional deities.

Growth in industrializing regions was accompanied by sometimes catastrophic decline elsewhere. As productivity rose in the new hub regions, regional differentials in wealth and power widened. The once awesome power of ancient tribute-taking empires evaporated. China's share of global production fell from 33% in 1800 to 6% in 1900, and in the 1840s, British gunboats forced China to trade in opium with the remarkably hypocritical argument that they were defending free trade. China was then forced to accept humiliating controls on its foreign trade. By 1900, states from the new hub regions dominated much of the world, directly or indirectly.

This sudden transformation depended in part on new industrial weaponry. The first successful machine gun, the Gatling gun, was used in the later stages of the American Civil War. It could fire 1,000 rounds a minute. The Maxim gun, the first machine gun to use a belt feed, was invented in 1884 and used by British troops in the Matabele war in 1893–1894. Hilaire Belloc wrote, with vicious irony:

> Whatever happens
> We have got
> The Maxim gun
> And they have not.

> —(Belloc, *The Modern Traveler*)

The vast regional differences in wealth and power that are familiar today first appeared in the late 19th century. Mike Davis has shown that it was in the late 19th century, for the first time, that differences in living standards between different parts of the world began to widen sharply. This was when the "third world" was born (Christian, *Maps of Time*, pp. 435–36).

This lecture has traced how the Modern Revolution spread around the world, transforming governments and cultures as well as economies. It also showed how industrialization created new regional disparities in wealth and power. Would these changes continue? Yes, and they would even accelerate in the 20th century. ■

Essential Reading

Christian, *Maps of Time*, chap. 13.

Supplementary Reading

Bayly, *The Birth of the Modern World*.

Davis, *Late Victorian Holocausts*.

Headrick, "Technological Change."

Questions to Consider

1. What were the main achievements of the first four "waves" of global industrialization?

2. Why was global industrialization so damaging to many societies outside the new Atlantic hub zone?

Spread of the Industrial Revolution to 1900
Lecture 42—Transcript

Do you remember the "near industrial revolution" of Song China in the 11th and 12th centuries C.E.? We saw how in an environment that was subtly more commercialized, more competitive than in the past, innovation suddenly increased, and a huge amount of innovation occurred in agriculture, in industry, in economic organization, and so on. But then what happened was that it all fell away again from the end of the 13th and 14th centuries.

What made the Modern Revolution so different is that instead of dying away like this, the process of innovation continued and spread around the entire world—and it's still continuing today, more than two centuries later. Now, why the difference between the outcomes of these two periods of very rapid, almost explosive, growth? Partly, the difference is that the world of the 19th century was so much more integrated and interconnected than the world of the 12th century. Remember, the world of the 12th century, the world of Song China, was still a world divided into four main world zones, and even connections between the different parts of Eurasia—between, say, China and the Mediterranean—were slow. It took several centuries for Chinese innovations to diffuse through Eurasia.

Now we look at this later Industrial Revolution. How rapidly did the changes we have observed during the British Industrial Revolution spread to other parts of the world, and how great was their impact?

Well, the short answer is that within just two centuries, industrialization had transformed the entire world, for better or worse. No earlier transformation in human history had ever been so rapid or so far-reaching. Just remember, in the Paleolithic era, the first era of human history, it took humans almost 200,000 years to spread around the entire world. So what I want to do in this lecture is to describe the impact of industrialization up to about 1900.

To get a clear overview of these changes, it might help to think of four main waves of change before 1900. The real processes, of course, were much more intricate, much more complicated. But this idea of four main waves provides a very helpful broad sketch of the main changes. So we'll survey in each of these waves the region it affected, the period it occurred, and the distinctive technologies associated with that wave. So let's begin with the first of these four waves.

Wave one. The first wave begins in the late 18th century, and we described some aspects of it in the previous lecture. It mainly affected Britain. It also touched the western edge of Europe and in some sense touched in the eastern seaboard of the United States. New technologies in this wave included a much more productive agrarian sector, improved steam engines—steam engines that were now efficient enough to be taken up widely in other industries and therefore allowed humans to tap into the immense reserves of energy stored in fossil fuels—the mechanization of cotton textile production, and increased production of coal and iron. And we saw, also, that changes occurred in a large number of other sectors as well; but these are the main sectors, the ones where the changes are most striking.

The cotton gin, incidentally—cotton gin (or "engine")—was a particularly important American contribution to this phase, invented by Eli Whitney in 1793. It was a mechanical device for separating cotton seeds from cotton fibers. Here in this case, we can measure the result in increasing productivity very easily. It now took one person to do what had previously taken 50 people working by hand. Unfortunately, as with many of these innovations, the initial impact of this was simply to increase the scale of sweated labor—or in the case of the United States, of slavery.

Now, wave two. Wave two took place in the early 19th century. Innovation accelerated in many parts of western Europe—including Belgium, France, and Germany—and also along the eastern seaboard of the newly independent United States. Technological changes in the second wave included the increased use of steam engines in manufacturing and the spread of railways and steamships.

Railways spread rapidly in Europe and in the U.S. The first commercial steamship was a paddle ship designed by Robert Fulton, which traveled between New York and Albany, beginning in 1807. It used a Watt steam engine.

The first oceangoing steamship was called the *Great Western*. It was designed by the great British designer Isambard Kingdom Brunel, and it was launched in 1837. It crossed to New York the next year. In 1843, he launched another steamship, known as the *Great Britain*. This was the first large iron ship in the world and the first to use a screw propeller. Its maiden voyage to New York took 14 days. It had an interesting subsequent history. It ended its days as a coal bunker on the Falkland Islands, but then in 1970, it was finally refloated, towed to England, and it's now been renovated as a museum that can be seen in Bristol.

Steam transportation was immensely important. It sped up commercial exchanges, and it cut transportation costs, which stimulated commerce and manufacturing. Now this was particularly true in very large countries, such as the U.S. or Canada, where cheaper land transport had a revolutionary impact on commerce in general. By 1917, there were about 1 million miles of railways throughout the world, and about one-third of them were in North America.

Now, why was the railway so revolutionary? Well, here's one way of looking at it. Throughout the Agrarian era, transportation by land had been slower and more expensive than transportation by sea. That explains, incidentally, why regions such as the Mediterranean, where a lot of exchanges could take place by sea, or those connected by great river systems, such as Egypt and Mesopotamia, flourished economically. It's at least one of the important factors in their economic growth. With the railway, for the first time in human history, transportation by land became as cheap and as rapid as transportation by sea. And this provided a massive stimulus for economic development, particularly in regions such as North America, where most transportation had to be by land. So, that's the second wave, and it's dominated by railways.

The third wave we can assign, roughly speaking, to the middle of the 19th century. It dominates the middle decades of the 19th century. Industrialization accelerates within Europe, particularly within Germany. And Germany, since the '20s, has been united economically within a common custom zone, the *Zollverein*. And by 1871, it would also be united politically. Change is also rapid in the eastern U.S.

Technological innovations in this period include the industrial production of chemicals, such as dyes and artificial fertilizers, which revolutionized agriculture. Fertilizers would be immensely important in supporting and supplying food to the rapidly growing populations of the Modern era. And the ability to produce artificial fertilizers greatly cheapened the use of fertilizers.

Steel-making was made more effective with the introduction of the Bessemer process. And this is the era, also, in which the industrial use of electricity began. Domestic lighting began to revolutionize patterns of work and leisure by lighting up the night. All previous forms of lighting had severe limitations; electricity could provide a sort of brightness that had no parallel elsewhere and, for some purposes, obliterate the distinction between day and night. So the humble light bulb transformed life, and it transformed urban life in particular. Its inventor was, of course, Thomas Edison. Edison is remarkable. He took out patents on more than 1,000 inventions, and these included the light bulb—and also the phonograph and the first motion-picture camera.

Warfare was revolutionized in this period. Railways made it possible to transport large numbers of troops, and equipment, and material. And new and more powerful weapons, such as machine guns, began to greatly increase the killing power of those who were armed with them. So the American Civil War is widely regarded as the first major war of the industrial era.

The telegraph and telephone revolutionized communications. Now, today it's all too easy to take for granted this revolution in communications, but we need to remind ourselves what a strange phenomenon it was. The idea of instantaneous communication over huge distances transformed the possibilities for what we have called in this course "collective learning." The first forms, the telegraph and early telephones, transmitted messages along electric cables. The electrical telegraph was invented in Britain in 1837, and the Morse code at the same time in the United States. Within just 25 years, most of the world was linked by telegraph communication.

The telephone was invented in 1876 by Alexander Bell. But its reach would soon be extended by improvements introduced by the ubiquitous Thomas Edison, who in 1878 made a call from New York to Philadelphia. But it was possible to communicate even without cables. And this was a possibility explored by an Italian, Guglielmo Marconi. By 1895, he had found he could send a message over a few kilometers without wires, and on December 12, 1901, he sent the first wireless transmission across the Atlantic.

Now, while we're on the subject of modern communications, here's an anecdote about the wonder of instantaneous broadcasting around the world. Chronologically, it belongs strictly to a later period, but I can't resist a cricket story, and I promise it's the only one in this course.

International cricket matches are called "test matches," and they began to be broadcast live in the 1920s. Now, you have to understand that broadcasting cricket was a challenge, because a test match can last five days, and for much of that period, particularly if there's bad weather, not much is happening. In the 1940s, test matches began to be broadcast around the world. And Australian commentators began to commentate on test matches going on in Britain. And what they did was they used to receive streams of cables from Britain detailing what happened to each ball. They would sit in their studios, and they would tell the stories as if they were watching the match themselves—complete with vivid, sometimes largely imaginary details about the scene. And they'd also use special sound effects, such as tapping the microphone to simulate the sound of a bat hitting a ball. The Australian audiences, I'm told, were spellbound. Now, that little story, I hope, just is a reminder of how recent these changes are, and how remarkable they are.

Now let's move on to the fourth wave, the late 19th century—strictly, we should probably say the late 19th century and early 20th century. The fourth wave dominated that period, and in this period, industrialization (we can say) spreads. For example, it spreads to Russia and Japan, and it spreads west within the United States and Canada.

In Russia, railway-building—particularly the building of the Trans-Siberian Railroad, which was completed in 1904 and ran from Moscow to the Pacific coast—stimulated iron production and manufacturing. And it made it possible to export grain more cheaply and also stimulated internal trade. Now, this is an example of one of the early phases of state-driven industrialization. The initiative came largely from the state—so did much of the initial financing.

This is the age when a second fossil fuel, oil, begins to be used. The oil age launched a second phase of the fossil fuels revolution with the invention of the internal combustion engine in the late 19th century. The Wright brothers showed how you could use an engine to drive a heavier-than-air plane in 1903. This is, again, an idea that we take for granted, but we need to remind ourselves how remarkable it is. The idea that humans might one day routinely fly around the world would have seemed the purest fantasy just a few centuries earlier. Today, if you go to Kitty Hawk, you can see a modern replica of their plane—which can, in fact, fly. It's a beautiful machine. I've seen it myself.

In 1913, Henry Ford produced the first Model T Ford, which pioneered mass production for a new mass consumer market, making the internal combustion engine and the car not just elite products, but products aimed at a much, much larger market—almost like textiles.

Now, I've described the four main phases. The next thing I want to do is describe how these changes, which I've described mainly in economic terms, began to affect other sectors of life. And the first area I want to look at is government. How did these changes affect government?

The short answer is that they were transformative. We use the same word, "government," for modern governments and those of the Agrarian era, but frankly, these are utterly different beasts. Economic changes and rising productivity transformed the power and the very nature of government in the state during this era. Governments acquired new forms of power, but they also found that they faced new and much more complex challenges than had been faced by the relatively much simpler tribute-taking states of the later Agrarian era.

War was a major driver of change. With increasing production, states from the 18th and early 19th centuries found that they had to become much more effective at mobilizing national resources, both of manpower and materials. In fact, increasingly, success in war meant success in mobilizing all the resources of your economy. The armies of revolutionary France pioneered in the challenge of raising large citizen armies using the appeal of nationalism, and nationalism was becoming immensely important in the Modern era.

It was a way of creating what the sociologist Benedict Anderson called an "imagined community" to which all citizens of a particular state were encouraged to think of themselves as belonging, so that they would commit themselves to the support of that community—and, if necessary, die for it.

But nationalism wouldn't work if states treated their citizens in the fundamentally exploitative way that was characteristic of most tribute-taking governments. If you want your citizens to actually support you as a government, as a state, you have to give them a greater sense of ownership of society. And this was a change that was achieved, in part, through the introduction of more democratic methods of rule, of which perhaps the most important is the use of elections.

Industrializing governments in general found that to mobilize support from below, from a population that was now very different from the peasant populations of the later Agrarian era—it was more mobile, it was more urbanized, it was generally better educated, and it was not self-sufficient—in order to gain support from these populations, they had to provide new services. And these services included policing—and you see the introduction of the first modern police systems in France during the French Revolution. It involved the provision of more health services, and also of mass education. These were services that hardly any Agrarian era states had seriously thought of providing.

There's another feature of this. The power of modern governments depended increasingly on economic growth. So they became increasingly economic managers rather than just takers of wealth. To survive, they had to spend a lot of effort and a lot of time worrying about how to stimulate growth, how to create environments in which commerce could flourish, how to create legal systems that protected entrepreneurship, how to create banking systems that created stable financial systems. This change alone, the fact that governments became managers rather than simply coercers and tribute-takers, was revolutionary. Remember Prince Vladimir of Kiev, who saw military power as the key to acquiring wealth. He saw coercion as the key to getting wealth. In the Modern era, essentially, the roles have been reversed. Increasingly, for modern states, the fundamental rule is wealth gives you power. A wealthy, highly productive economy is the key to military power. So, success for a state in the Modern era means building economic growth.

There's another way in which the role of government was bound to increase in societies in which most people were wage earners. And this is because wage earners, unlike independent peasants who were largely self-sufficient, depend on the provision of basic services such as markets. To survive as a wage earner, you have to find employment. There have to be markets on which you can buy goods and projects. There have to be legal systems that protect the conditions of employment and so on. And inevitably, what this meant was that governments became more involved in the day-to-day life of most of their citizens. To put it very crudely, whereas in the late Agrarian era 80% to 90% of the population could be left most of the time just to get on with it—peasants didn't need the state to interfere—in the Modern era, most of the population needs the services that states provide. So, states had to protect property, they had to maintain law and order, and they had to ensure stable currencies. To do that, they needed increasing information about their populations—about the health, the education, and the incomes of the populations they ruled.

So to summarize some of these political changes, the rules of political success have changed in the Modern era. Larger, more mobile, and better-educated societies had to be managed rather than simply coerced. In the Atlantic hub zone, the beginnings of these changes were already evident in the political revolutions of the late 18th and early 19th centuries. This is the era described famously by the American historian R. R. Palmer as the "Age of the Democratic Revolution." And here is Charles Tilly's pithy summary of the changes that created the modern state. Here is how he puts it:

> Over the last thousand years, European states [but a lot of what he says applies to modern states in general] have undergone a peculiar evolution: from wasps to locomotives. Long they concentrated on war, leaving most activities to other organizations, just so long as those organizations yielded tribute at appropriate intervals. Tribute-taking states remained fierce but light in weight by comparison with their bulky successors; they stung, but they didn't suck dry. As time went on, states—even the capital-intensive varieties—took on activities, powers, and commitments whose very support constrained them. These locomotives ran on the rails of sustenance

from the civilian population and maintenance by a civilian staff. Off the rails, the warlike engines could not run at all.

In short, modern states have to be, in some sense, democratic. They have to work with their populations because of the extreme complexity of the societies they rule.

Industrializations also, on the other hand, magnified the coercive power of states. So here's a paradox. On the one hand, modern states have to be more democratic—they have to work more closely with their citizens, they have to gain support from below. On the other hand, they can also coerce more effectively. They have more ability to support what we called earlier "power from above." And this is largely because modern industry has magnified the military power of states. It's enabled them to transport soldiers and weapons larger distances, and it's increased the destructiveness of weaponry. This increased military power was apparent in the astonishing speed with which, in the late 19th century, governments from the new Atlantic hub region conquered much of Africa, Asia, and the Americas.

Now, I'd like to talk briefly about changes in another area of life: cultural life and lifeways. The changes we've looked at, we've looked primarily at their economic aspects and now the political aspects—but they also transformed cultural life and popular lifeways. And here are some of the transformations.

Everywhere, peasants slowly turned into wage earners as they were squeezed off the land by increasingly efficient commercial farmers. Now, we have to remind ourselves that this, too, is a fundamental change in the lifeways of a majority of people on Earth. As wage earners seeking employment needed education more than peasants, governments began to introduce systems of mass education. For the first time, education, which had been largely a matter for upper classes—as a peasant, you learn on the job, as it were—now became a matter that states began to take seriously, and they began to extend to the population as a whole. So mass education began to spread at least in part because most wage-earning employment required at least a minimum of literacy.

The earliest modern national educational systems were established early in the 19th century, in Napoleonic France and Germany. So, from a world in which only a tiny elite were educated, we moved to a world in which the vast majority of the population has at least the rudiments of literacy—but elite culture was transformed also, and particularly by the rising significance of science.

The first industrial science labs were created in Germany in the middle of the 19th century, and that's probably the point at which science begins to play a direct role in encouraging innovation in modern society. Before that, most innovations had been the work of tinkerers, of mechanics who knew machines well but weren't necessarily thinking primarily as scientists.

As the economic, technological, and military importance of science rose, it began to challenge traditional ways of thinking in many, many areas. It began to challenge the traditional role, for example, of ancient religious traditions in education and culture by offering new and fundamentally materialist accounts of the Universe—which offered, as we've seen throughout this course, very little room for traditional deities. So the intellectual world, both of the mass of the population and of elite groups, was also transformed in the course of the Industrial Revolution.

Now I'd like to look at some of the negative sides. It may seem as if I've been telling a totally positive story, as if everything is going wonderfully. There's a profoundly negative side to all of this, and that is the destruction of traditional societies. Growth in industrializing regions was accompanied by sometimes catastrophic decline elsewhere.

As productivity rose in the new hub regions, regional differences in wealth and power widened. We've seen that the once awesome power of ancient tribute-taking empires evaporated. China's share of global production fell from 33% in 1800 to 6% in 1900—and in the 1840s, British gunboats forced China to trade in opium with a remarkably hypocritical argument that they were defending free trade. And China, one of the great empires of the past, was forced to submit to humiliating controls on its foreign trade imposed by these small nations from the other side of the world. By 1900, states from the new hub regions of the Atlantic zone dominated much of the world, directly or indirectly. This transformation depended, in part, on new industrial weaponry.

The first successful machine gun, the Gatling gun, was used in the later stages of the American Civil War. It could fire 1,000 rounds a minute. The Maxim gun, the first machine gun to use a belt feed, was invented in 1884. It was used by British troops in the Matabele War in 1893 to 1894, in modern Zimbabwe. And it gave British troops a devastating and horrifying advantage over their spear-carrying opponents. Hilaire Belloc wrote at the time: with vicious irony:

> Whatever happens
> We have got
> The Maxim gun
> And they have not.

The vast regional differences in wealth and power that are familiar today first appeared in the late 19th century. In an important book on the origins of the third world, which is called *Late Victorian Holocausts*, Mike Davis argues that in 1800, class differences within societies were generally more important than those between different regions of the world. For example, he argues, differences in living standards between a French worker and an Indian farmer were probably far less striking than those between those groups and those who ruled over them. By 1900, he argues, differences in national living standards between wealthier and poorer countries had become, for the first time in human history, as profound as differences within societies. And he concludes that the gross inequalities between different regions of the world that we take for granted today were, and I quote: "As much modern inventions of the late Victorian world as electric lights and Maxim guns."

In summary, this lecture has traced how the Modern Revolution spread around the world. It transformed economies, it transformed governments, and it transformed cultures. And we've also seen how rapid industrialization in some areas of the world undermined the traditional economies, lifeways, and societies of other parts of the world.

Would these changes continue? In the next lecture we look at what happens in the 20th century.

Thank you.

The 20ᵗʰ Century
Lecture 43

Nineteenth-century military innovations ensured that World War I would be particularly bloody. New weapons included machine guns, tanks, airplanes, and chemical weapons such as mustard gas, which could effectively burn out the internal organs of its victims.

Now, after 13 billion years, we enter the era of our own lifetimes! After 1900, the pace of change accelerated and the Modern Revolution began to transform societies throughout the world. A fourth, fifth, and sixth wave of change shaped the history of the 20ᵗʰ century. The fourth wave began in the late 19ᵗʰ century and continued into the early 20ᵗʰ century. It began to transform regions well beyond the new Atlantic core region. Russia and Japan both underwent revolutionary transformations and became major industrial and military superpowers. Then there was a slowdown for much of the first half of the 20ᵗʰ century as the engine of growth seemed to stall in an era of global wars and global depression. The vast casualties of these wars provided a gruesome demonstration of the increasing "productivity" of modern weapons. This violent era culminated in the Nazi Holocaust and the dropping of the first nuclear weapons.

A fifth wave of innovation began after the Second World War and ran until the last decade of the century. It launched the most sustained era of global economic growth ever known—growth built partly on wartime innovations. Atomic power, rocket technology, and the electronic transistor were developed. Some multinational corporations, such as oil companies, became as powerful as medium-sized states. From the 1920s until 1990, the world was divided into capitalist and communist regions, each of which sought to influence the rest of the world (the "third world"). Communist countries included highly industrialized societies in Eastern Europe, Russia, and (after 1949) China, which preserved many elements of tributary societies. Though their elites actively encouraged industrial growth, they rejected commercial activity and relied largely on the power of the state to engineer growth.

A sixth wave of innovation began at the end of the 20th century. Computerization and the Internet transformed communications, business, and information exchanges. Genetic engineering promised to transform medicine and agriculture. Communist societies, lacking the innovative drive of their capitalist rivals, eventually collapsed or reintroduced market economies, leaving capitalism as the dominant form of society. Accelerating globalization allowed instant global transfers of information and money. It also generated new cultural conflicts as groups with very different values and traditions were forced into closer contact with each other. When those conflicts turned violent, the availability of modern weaponry ensured that even small guerilla armies could wield significant military power. Asian economies revived, challenging the dominance of the Atlantic hub zone.

The pace of change itself accelerated. Between 1900 and 2000, world population quadrupled, rising from 1.6 billion to more than 6 billion. The urban population multiplied by 13 times, and by the end of the century, almost half the world's population lived in communities of more than 5,000 people.

Population increases were made possible by increasing industrial and agricultural production. Global economic output increased by about 14 times, and industrial output by about 40 times. Global grain

The dropping of the atomic bomb in Japan ended World War II.

Courtesy National Archives, photo no. 342-AF-58189.

production rose 5 times, from about 400 million tons to about 2,000 million tons. Agricultural productivity tripled, with increased irrigation, increasing use of artificial fertilizers and pesticides, and the introduction of more productive genetically engineered crops. Because food production outstripped population growth, we have not yet seen a global Malthusian crisis in the Modern era (that is, a crisis caused by *under*production), though there have been many regional famines. Energy use increased by about 16 times, mainly through increased use of the three fossil fuels: coal, oil, and natural gas.

The lethality of weapons increased even faster. World War I artillery shells could kill hundreds; the bomb dropped on Hiroshima on August 6, 1945, killed 70,000 people, and a similar number died from wounds or radiation sickness. In the 1950s, the U.S. and the USSR developed even more powerful bombs that used hydrogen fusion, the energy that drives all stars.

Capitalism emerged as the dominant social and economic system. But it also evolved in new directions. I have argued that capitalism was a fundamental driver of the Modern Revolution. That conclusion looks even more plausible after the collapse of the communist societies that had seemed, briefly, to offer an alternative.

Yet the impact of capitalism was contradictory, for it generated unprecedented wealth as well as new forms of poverty. This is because in capitalist societies, innovation is driven by the gradient in wealth and power between entrepreneurs, who own significant capital resources, and wage earners whose main asset is their own labor. Without inequality, capitalism cannot work.

In the wealthiest societies, capitalism evolved into "consumer capitalism," in one of the most important transformations of the century. Karl Marx had argued that as capitalism developed it would impoverish most wage earners, generating huge revolutionary movements that would eventually bring about its collapse. By the end of the 20th century it was clear that this prediction had proved wrong. Why? Marx had missed something that would be seen clearly by industrialists such as Henry Ford, economists such as John Maynard Keynes, and politicians such as Franklin Roosevelt (1882–1945). As productivity outstripped population growth, producers had to work harder to find markets for the massive numbers of goods they produced. Early-20th-century pioneers such as Henry Ford saw that wage earners themselves provided a huge potential market. But they could only purchase goods if their wages rose. So it was in the interests of capitalists to raise wages and increase consumption. Such arguments were tested in the

American "New Deal" and analyzed in the work of economists such as John Maynard Keynes.

In the most developed capitalist societies, led by the U.S., average consumption levels rose, creating a large, affluent middle class. Affluence deflected the revolution Marx had anticipated, as prosperous wage earners became contented supporters of consumer capitalism. Consumer capitalism also generated a new rhythm of change. For the first time in history, major economic crises (such as the Depression) were more likely to be caused by overproduction than underproduction. We can describe these new cycles of boom and bust as "Keynesian" cycles. Whereas in all earlier societies, slow growth had limited consumption, in the era of developed capitalism, consumption became the main driver of growth.

Affluence deflected the revolution Marx had anticipated, as prosperous wage earners became contented supporters of consumer capitalism. Consumer capitalism also generated a new rhythm of change.

Yet as living standards rose in the developed capitalist societies, global inequalities increased. Between 1913 and 1992, the gap between average income levels in the poorest and wealthiest countries grew from 11:1 to 72:1. Poverty affected health and life expectancies. In 2000, life expectancies in the U.S. were 74 (for men) and 80 (for women); in Burkina Faso in West Africa, they were 45 for men and women. Land shortages forced many peasants off the land, and the number living in extreme poverty increased. Paul Harrison's vivid accounts of life in Burkina Faso show what this meant to individuals. Is the widening gap a warning of new crises? Or will the living standards of the very poor slowly rise as consumer capitalism spreads to regions where, so far, it has been experienced just by elite groups?

We have seen that, far from slowing, the pace of change continued to accelerate in the 20th century, reshaping societies throughout the world in the process. This suggests that, far from the revolution of modernity being over, as some have claimed, it may be just beginning. ∎

Essential Reading

Christian, *Maps of Time*, chap. 14.

Supplementary Reading

Hobsbawm, *The Age of Extremes.*

Maddison, *The World Economy.*

Questions to Consider

1. What evidence is there that change was more rapid in the 20th century than ever before in world history?

2. How and why did capitalism morph into "consumer capitalism" during the 20th century?

The 20th Century
Lecture 43—Transcript

Now, after 13 billion years, we enter the era of our own lifetimes. The previous two lectures described the transformative impact of the Modern Revolution between 1700 and 1900. After 1900, the pace of change accelerated even further, and the Modern Revolution began to transform societies throughout the world. I have to say that trying to describe the 20th century from the perspective of big history is one of the hardest challenges in this course.

But with that warning, here goes. Three great waves of change shaped the 20th century. The first of these is the fourth wave that we looked at in the last lecture. It begins in the late 19th century and continues into the early 20th century. So we've already met this wave. It began to really transform regions well beyond the new Atlantic core region, notably in Russia and Japan. This is the era in which Russia and Japan both begin to industrialize very, very rapidly.

In Russia (as in North America) railways and, above all, the Trans-Siberian Railroad (completed in 1904) played a critical role in integrating societies—in integrating, above all, the economy over a vast region. Remember the Russian Empire was by far the largest united state, unified state on Earth. Both Japan and Russia in this period underwent revolutionary transformations, and they became major industrial and military superpowers. Now that's the fourth wave, and we've already looked at it.

Then something slightly odd happens. There's something of a slowdown that affects global growth for much of the first half of the 20th century. It's as if the engine of growth that seems to have been fired up in the last two centuries suddenly seems to stall in an era of global walls and global depression. Global rates of growth slow. The international trading system, which had been one of the main drivers of growth in the late 19th century, begins to break down as states begin to try to carve out their own economic zones in the era of imperialism.

Exactly why the slowdown occurred is not entirely clear, but here's just one possibility. It is that capitalist rulers had to learn how to manage capitalist states. After all, this is very new. Now, we saw that tributary rulers had to learn the best ways of managing tributary states, and it took them a long, long time. The rulers of capitalist states were on a similar steep learning curve, and in the late 19th century it's as if they were still operating with at least some of the habits of the tributary era. And one of them was the habit of thinking that there was only so much wealth to go around and that they'd better get their share, by military force if necessary.

And that may explain the burst of imperialism in the late 19th century, during which major capitalist states carved up much of the world in a vicious competition for control of new colonies. It illustrates this increasingly coercive or militaristic attitude; it illustrates an attitude that sees force, like the tributary era, as the key to growth, rather than effective economic competition. And we'll see that in the 20th century, capitalist states began to slowly realize that in the modern world, under modern conditions, economic competition could often stimulate growth more effectively than military competition—but that was in the future. Meantime, there's no doubt that globally, growth slowed.

Global wars would dominate the first half of the 20th century, slowing growth rates particularly in the European hub lands. The wars, incidentally, demonstrated the extent to what we can call perhaps the "productivity" of weaponry had also increased as a result of the Modern Revolution. Nineteenth-century military innovations ensured that World War I would be particularly bloody. New weapons included machine guns, tanks, airplanes, and chemical weapons such as mustard gas, which could effectively burn out the internal organs of its victims. And ironically, improved medical systems kept more troops at the front, only to be slaughtered in the thousands by machine guns or artillery in often-futile raids on enemy positions.

However, the Second World War in many ways was even more destructive. About 60 million people may have died in World War II, and what World War II introduced to warfare was the refinement of systematic bombing of civilian targets. Most casualties of World War II were civilians, as the aerial bombing of cities became, for the first time, a recognized weapon of modern warfare. The extreme brutality of the war and the extreme potential for brutality of modern states found the most potent symbol in the systematic murder by Hitler's Nazi Party of almost 6 million Jews, in what has come to be known as the Holocaust. The war ended, of course, with the use of the first atomic weapons in Japan. The first atomic bombs were dropped on the Japanese cities of Hiroshima and Nagasaki in August 1945. Colonel Paul Tibbets, Jr., the pilot of the B-29 bomber that dropped the first atomic bomb, had named the plane *Enola Gay*, after his mother. The bomb itself was named "Little Boy."

So, we have a period of slowdown in much of the first half of the 20th century, and then growth takes off again in what we'll call the "fifth wave of modernity." Roughly speaking, the fifth wave runs from 1945 to 1990, and it begins after World War II. The modern global engine of growth seems to fire up again. And this wave sees the most sustained era of global economic growth ever known, growth built in part on wartime innovations. Some of the crucial innovations included atomic power, rocket technology, and the electric transistor. The organization of commerce also changed. During both wars, states had become extremely good at mobilizing entire economies, mobilizing entire populations, and also mobilizing the skills of their scientists and engineers.

After the Second World War, some private corporations began to operate on a scale almost as large as that of states, and multinational corporations (such as oil companies in particular) began to become as powerful as medium-sized states. So, these new economic juggernauts that we call "multinational corporations" began to play an increasingly important role in economic development.

Another crucial feature of this era was that the world was divided into two large blocs. This is a sort of de-globalization that shaped the history of much of the 20th century. It was divided into a capitalist bloc and a communist region, each of which sought to influence the rest of the world, which came to be known as the "third world." Communist countries included highly industrialized societies in Eastern Europe, such as Soviet Russia—and, after 1949, much of Eastern Europe, which was brought within the Soviet bloc by force at the end of the Second World War—and after 1949, it also included China.

With Russia, China, and much of Eastern Europe within the communist bloc, almost half of the world's population found themselves within communist societies. Now, in terms of the logic of this course, what is striking about the communist world and their command economies is that they preserved many of the elements of tributary societies. One of the most striking of these elements is a fundamental hostility to commerce. So, like traditional agrarian civilizations, the elites of the communist societies rejected entrepreneurial activity. They called it "capitalism," and they actively suppressed commerce and tried to organize economies in which the entire workings of the economy in society were planned from above.

Given the model I set up in an earlier lecture of the link between entrepreneurial activity and innovation, it should come as no surprise to find that the problem that eventually led to the collapse of these societies was the sluggishness of innovation. Nevertheless, unlike traditional tributary states of the later Agrarian era, those of the communist world—the states of the communist world—actively encouraged industrial growth in an environment without markets. And to a remarkable extent they were quite successful; they were able to achieve rapid industrialization. But the fact that most innovation depended on state activity or technologies that had evolved elsewhere, mostly in the capitalist world, limited the pace of change and also limited the possibility that innovations might diffuse throughout society. In societies where commerce was largely suppressed, there was really no incentive for anyone to try and take up and make use of some of the innovations pioneered by state activity. So that's the fifth wave.

The sixth wave began at the end of the 20th century, and we're living through it today. Computerization and the Internet transformed communications, they transformed business, and they transformed information exchanges. Genetic engineering also promised to transform medicine and agriculture, and we may not have seen much more than the beginnings of the impact of both of these technologies. Communist societies collapsed, most of them. Now, China, of course, still flourishes—but it flourishes because most of the distinctive features of the communist era are being slowly abandoned, and China is turning rapidly into a successful capitalist society. With the result that capitalism is now the dominant way of organizing societies economically, socially, and politically in the modern world.

So this change, the collapse of the communist world and its planned economies, counts as a sort of economic reunification of the globe after 70 years of division into distinct economic blocs. Entrepreneurial activity within capitalist social structures now shapes the economies and societies of most of the world.

Accelerating globalization allowed instant global transfers of information and money, but it also generated new cultural conflicts, in which powerful but easily accessible weaponry enhanced the power of small guerrilla armies resisting the power of the great capitalist juggernauts. This is one aspect of military innovation, that the increasing power of modern weaponry and its miniaturization has empowered small groups. This is the technological reality behind what we know as the "war on terrorism."

The other reality is cultural. As more traditional communities attempt to defend traditional values against what they see as the onslaught of Western or modern values and attitudes, and as increasing globalization forces traditional communities and value systems into sort of a closer and more uncomfortable cohabitation with the most successful capitalist societies, many feel obliged to resist.

Another feature of this era has been the revival of Asian economies. We saw that the great Asian economies were the dominant economic powers probably for most of the last 2,000 years of the later Agrarian era. And we saw that their economies were deeply undermined in the 19th and early 20th centuries, until their contribution to global production shrank very, very rapidly indeed. In the late 20th century and the early 21st century, these economies have been reviving and beginning to challenge the dominance of the Atlantic hub zone. Watch this space.

Now let's look at some general features of the 20th century. One is acceleration; the pace of change accelerated. Between 1900 and 2000, here are just some figures that illustrate this. World populations quadrupled, rising from 1.6 billion to more than 6 billion. It has taken 100,000 years to reach 1 billion people; it took just 100 years to add another billion people. The urban population multiplied by 13 times, and by the end of the century almost half the world's population lived in communities of more than 5,000 people. So the pace of change has accelerated to an extraordinary degree.

Population increases were made possible by increasing industrial and agricultural production, indeed by accelerating production. Global economic output increased by about 14 times, and industrial output by about 40 times. How were all these people fed? Well, they were fed because global grain production rose 5 times in the 20th century, from about 400 million tons to about 2,000 million tons. Now, this is one of the great achievements of the Modern Revolution in general and of the 20th century in particular, feeding this rapidly growing population.

Agricultural productivity tripled in this period for various reasons. One was increased irrigation; the irrigated area increased by about 5 times in the 20th century. A second was the increasing use of artificial fertilizers (first produced, as we've seen, in the 19th century) and also of pesticides. And the other crucial innovation was the introduction of more productive genetically engineered crops. Because food production outstripped population growth in the 20th century, we've not yet seen a global Malthusian crisis. Now, the last time I said that, I touched wood, and I'm going to do so again. What we've not seen yet is a crisis caused by *under*production that affected the entire world, though there have been many regional famines during this period.

Energy use in the 20th century increased by about 16 times, mainly through increased use of the three main fossil fuels: coal, oil, and natural gas. In the early 21st century, these account for almost 80% of energy use, and nuclear power counts for about 6%. But in this period, I think we can argue that the lethality of weapons increased even more rapidly than productivity. Here are just some indicators of this. A World War I artillery shell could perhaps kill hundreds of people if it landed in the right place. The bomb dropped on Hiroshima on August 6, 1945, killed 70,000 people, and a similar number would die over the next few decades from wounds or radiation sickness. Now, if you want a measure of increasing productivity of weaponry—that is extraordinarily powerful.

In the 1950s, the U.S. and the U.S.S.R. developed even more powerful bombs that used hydrogen fusion, the energy that drives all stars. The result is that humans now have the power to destroy most of the biosphere within just a few hours, whereas just two centuries ago the most lethal weapon available could have killed—at most—a few hundred people. The first H-bomb, based on fusion power, was tested on November 1, 1952, on an island in the Pacific. For the first time, our species had learned to tap into the power at the heart of the Sun.

One of the great technological ambitions of the 21st century will undoubtedly be to find a way of taming this astonishing source of energy so that it can be put to creative rather than just destructive uses. The challenge is to find a container for fusion reactions; they're simply too hot to be contained by solids, so most current work seeks ways to confine them magnetically within powerful magnetic fields. But the point is that the increased productivity of weaponry may by some measures have increased in the 20th century faster than other measures of productivity.

Another feature of the era, of the 20th century, is that capitalism emerges as the dominant social and economic system. But capitalism also began to evolve in the 20th century in striking new ways, and I want to try to describe these carefully. I've argued that capitalism—that is to say, the particular distinctive type of social structure with entrepreneurial elites and a mass of the population that depends on wage earners linked through market activity—I've argued that this type of social structure was a fundamental driver of the Modern Revolution. That conclusion looks even more plausible after the collapse of the communist societies that had seemed for a time to offer an alternative to capitalism.

Yet the impact of capitalism was contradictory—for while it generated unprecedented material wealth, it also generated new forms of poverty. And there's a very good reason for this—this is because in capitalist societies, innovation is driven by the gradient in wealth and power between entrepreneurs (who own significant capital resources) and wage earners (whose main asset is their own labor). Now, there's a striking parallel here to what we saw when discussing entropy, where we saw that in the natural world change is driven by energy gradients that can do work. On a level playing field, not much can happen. And the same is true, in some sense, of capitalism. Without a significant degree of inequality, without some inequality, capitalism cannot work.

In the wealthiest capitalist societies, 20th-century capitalism evolved into a new form that we can describe as "consumer capitalism." And this constitutes, I think, one of the most important and fascinating transformations of the 20th century. So let me try to describe very clearly what I mean by "consumer capitalism." Let's go back to Karl Marx's analysis of capitalism. He and his disciples had argued, roughly speaking, that as capitalism developed, increasing numbers of people within capitalist societies would be impoverished, and their declining living standards would generate revolutionary movements that would eventually overthrow capitalist societies throughout the world.

And now, writing as he did in the 1840s and '50s and '60s, this was not a completely implausible picture of the world. And his good friend, Friedrich Engels, remember, wrote an astonishingly bleak account of working-class life in Manchester. But from the perspective of the early 21st century, it's clear that his prediction was wrong. Despite the spread of communist societies in the middle decades of the 20th century, his prediction has been proved wrong. Why? What happened? What went wrong with it?

Well, what happened, I think, was this. As 20th-century capitalist societies developed, instead of impoverishing their own working classes, as Marx had expected, the most successful capitalist societies began to raise the living standards of their own populations. And we can think of this as a sort of learning curve for the managers and rulers of capitalist societies. It's as if they were slowly learning the best ways of managing this new type of society.

Consumer capitalism raised the living standards of many in the richer capitalist countries, rather than depressing them. Why? Well, Marx had missed something that eventually would become very clear to industrialists, such as Henry Ford; to economists, such as John Maynard Keynes; and to politicians, such as Franklin Delano Roosevelt. And it was this: As productivity rose, as it began to outstrip population growth, producers found they had to work harder and harder to find markets for all the stuff they were producing. This is like the sorcerer's apprentice; they're producing so much stuff that eventually, for the first time in human history, the problem of marketing that stuff becomes the fundamental problem, rather than the problem of producing enough stuff.

Early 20th-century pioneers, such as Henry Ford, began to perceive that if you're looking for new markets, wage earners themselves provided a huge potential market, but they could only purchase goods if their wages rose. So what this meant was instead of making profits by cutting wages—and that's the model of capitalism that Marx had in mind—perhaps the way to ensure future profits was actually to raise wages, to ensure that wage earners in your society could purchase all the goods you were producing with their labor. And this meant that if this was true, it was in the interest of capitalists to raise wages and increase consumption.

Now, similar arguments were tested in the American "New Deal," which put money into people's pockets through, for example, unemployment pay or huge state projects. These arguments were also developed in the work of the economists, such as John Maynard Keynes, and we can see all of this as part of this sort of learning curve of learning how to manage modern capitalism. In the most developed capitalist societies, led by the U.S., average consumption levels began to rise. In fact, in the U.S. you could see this already in the late 19th century—creating not the impoverished working class that Marx had expected but instead a large affluent class of wage earners and professionals.

And what that affluence did was to deflect the revolutionary zeal that Marx had expected to develop among wage earners. As wage earners became more and more prosperous, they became more contented supporters of a flourishing capitalism. In other words, the high living standards of flourishing capitalist societies, which are made possible by their rapidly increasing productivity, have effectively deflected the revolutionary impulse that Marx believed would bring them down.

So what we're saying is that consumer capitalism means a capitalism in which wage earners are not just a source of profit, they're also an important market—with the result that consumer capitalism generates increasingly high material living standards for a larger and larger percentage of the population in flourishing capitalist societies. But this more mature form of capitalism generated some odd new phenomena. For the first time in history, major economic crises—and the most major economic crisis of all was the Depression of the 1930s—began to be caused not by *under*production, not by not producing enough, but by *over*production.

And this is one of the most distinctive features of consumer capitalism. What this has done is to have created an entirely new rhythm of rise and fall. We saw that crises in the era of agrarian civilizations were caused largely by underproduction, by the failure to produce sufficient resources. That led to famine, to disease, to conflict over scarce resources, and eventually to the sort of crash that you find regularly at the end of a Malthusian cycle.

The major crises in a capitalist heartland are being caused by the opposite phenomenon, by the fact that production was outstripping population. Producers found it harder and harder to market goods, and profits began to fall, leading to widespread bankruptcy—and the whole system threatened to break down. This is commonly known as the "business cycle," but to emphasize the parallel with the Malthusian cycle of the late Agrarian era, we might perhaps christen it the "Keynesian" cycle, after John Maynard Keynes, the economist who analyzed the causes of crises such as the Great Depression and suggested ways of dealing with them by helping consumers to consume more—through, for example, the provision of unemployment payments.

Keynesian cycles, in their turn, generate a whole series of new phenomena, one of which is massive advertising. If the main problem of keeping the economy going is not to produce enough but to sell enough, then advertising clearly has to play a crucial role. In a sense I sometimes feel that the advertiser today plays the role of a medieval preacher, but what the advertiser preaches is: "Consume, because if you don't there'll be a crisis." That, of course, is a message diametrically opposite the messages of thrift that were offered to most people, except members of the ruling elite, throughout most of the Agrarian era. Consumption in the era of consumer capitalism has become a virtue, and that, we will see, may prove to be a problem if we discover that there is, in fact, a limit to how much we can consume.

Yet on a global scale the gap between the rich and poor continued to widen. As some areas of the world became astonishingly rich between 1913 and

1992, the gap between average income levels in the poorest and the wealthiest countries grew from 11:1 to 72:1. The gap began to widen between regions. Here's just one extreme example: In 2000, per capita national income in the U.S. was about $34,000. In Burkina Faso in West Africa, a landlocked country with a largely peasant population, it was about $210—about 1/150 of the U.S. level.

Poverty in third world countries affected health and life expectancies. In 2000, life expectancies in the U.S. were 74 for men and 80 for women. In Burkina Faso, they were 45 for men and women.

Land shortage provides a powerful illustration of the destructive power of capitalism in more traditional agrarian societies. The British journalist Paul Harrison, in the 1980s, met and interviewed a 60-year-old farmer called Moumouni in Burkina Faso. Moumouni had lived through several stages in the growing crisis that has ruined much of the traditional croplands across the southern borders of the Sahara. Here's what Moumouni told Harrison. Populations had grown, but the amount of land available had not. So as populations grew, the amount of land available to each household and each individual had declined very, very sharply.

> Moumouni remembered that, when he was a child, only twelve people lived in his father's compound; now there were thirty-four, with five young men working away from home in the Ivory Coast.

Moumouni eventually took Paul Harrison out to show him his land, and what Harrison saw was that Moumouni and other farmers like him were being forced to cultivate land in ways that even they knew were completely unsustainable, because they had to keep land in crops when it needed to be in fallow. And this is what Harrison saw:

> Even close in to the compound, the soil looked poor enough, stony and dusty, without a trace of humus. And this was the only area they ever fertilized, with the droppings of a donkey and a couple of goats. Outside a circle of about fifty yards' diameter round the houses, the ground was a dark red, baked hard. It had been cultivated the year

before, but had yielded very little. Moumouni said he didn't think anything would grow there this year.

So we've seen that the pace of change continued to accelerate in the 20th century, and many did very, very well with the flourishing of consumer capitalism—but there was another side. This flourishing capitalism could also be profoundly destructive, particularly to those continuing to live in traditional ways.

Is this widening gap between the very rich and the very poor sustainable? That's one of the questions we'll start tackling in the next lecture.

Thank you.

The World That the Modern Revolution Made
Lecture 44

> And in the pace of change, this acceleration in the pace of historical change has also had a profound impact on ways of thinking, and we could even say on ways of experiencing the world.

Now, as we did with the era of Agrarian civilizations, we need to stand back and try to get a general impression of the world created by the Modern Revolution. What are the main distinguishing features of the modern world? Unfortunately, the modern world is so changeable, and we are so enmeshed in it, that it is extraordinarily difficult to see beyond the details. Still, we must try, so here is a provisional attempt.

Rapid innovation has meant a speedup. Constant innovation means constant change, so history itself moves faster. The Modern era has lasted for about a third of a millennium. So much historical scholarship is about the Modern era that it is easy to forget how short a period this is. The Agrarian era lasted 30 times as long, and human history as a whole perhaps 600 times as long. If we collapse the history of the Universe into 13 rather than 13 billion years, the Modern era accounts for no more than 6 seconds. Yet in this instant, human societies have been transformed around the entire Earth, which is why despite its brevity the Modern Revolution counts as one of the eight thresholds of this course.

Accelerating change makes it difficult to pick out stable features of our world. In the Paleolithic and Agrarian eras, we could identify features and structures that endured for thousands of years, such as the rhythms of peasant life or the basic structures of tributary states. In the Modern era, it is hard to identify any features that will certainly be present in, say, 500 years. Fundamental change now occurs on the scale of a single lifetime. This affects our personal sense of time and history. Indeed, the modern vision of a Universe in which everything has a history, including the Universe itself, is itself the product of an era of universal change. The astonishing pace of change means that today's world is extremely unstable.

Within just a few generations, the Modern Revolution has destroyed the lifeways and social structures that dominated the Agrarian and Paleolithic eras of human history. Even a century ago, viable communities of foragers and early Agrarian era villages flourished in many parts of the world. Today, none exist outside of a modern state. Particularly striking is the destruction of peasant lifeways, which had shaped the life experience of most humans for almost 10,000 years. The Modern Revolution has also destroyed traditional tribute-taking states.

In just a few generations, the Modern Revolution has also created entirely new types of community and new power structures. Modern communities are extraordinarily large. The modern world is organized into 194 sovereign states. The most populous, the People's Republic of China, had a population of 1.3 billion in 2007, or more than five times the entire population of the Earth 1,000 years earlier. Sovereign states have divided up the entire landmass of the Earth (with the partial exception of Antarctica). Even 1,000 years ago, states controlled only 13% of the Earth, because vast areas in Australia, the Americas, Africa, and Eurasia were beyond their reach. There are now 20 to 30 cities with populations of more than 5 million (the total population of the world 10,000 years ago), and several have populations of more than 10 million.

Today, more people eat well and live without chronic suffering than in any other era of human history.

Modern communities are integrated globally through exchanges of ideas, goods, diseases, and people. Indeed, today's integrated global community of 6 billion modern humans counts as one of the most striking emergent properties of the modern world. Politically, this global community is integrated loosely through international organizations such as the United Nations. These provide a modern equivalent of the meetings once held between Paleolithic communities of foragers. Collective learning is now a global process. The exchanges of information that have been the main driver of human history now take place more or less instantaneously throughout the world within a diverse and often well-educated population of 6 billion people. The increasing "synergy of collective learning" is magnified by the use of intellectual prosthetics such as computers. Global integration has been painful, as it has forced communities with diverse ethical and social norms into close proximity. Modern weaponry has ensured that such conflicts can take highly destructive forms.

Entirely new types of lifeways have evolved. Most people today are no longer foragers or self-sufficient, rural-dwelling peasants. They are wage earners, integrated into modern market systems and living, increasingly, in large towns and cities. Modern lifeways have transformed life experiences. For example, they are transforming gender relations by freeing increasing numbers of women from the lifetime of childbearing and child rearing that was their lot in peasant societies and allowing them to take on many new roles. Though many forms of gender inequality survive, traditional forms of patriarchy are being undermined. The material wealth generated by modern societies has raised the living standards of billions of people. Today, more people eat well and live without chronic suffering than in any other era of human history. The human life span has increased. As rates of child mortality have declined, average global life expectancies have risen from the Agrarian era norm of about 30 years to 65–70 years in 2000. This momentous change may prove a foretaste of future extensions in the span of a single human life.

A fourth striking feature of modern communities is the changing role of coercion. Within the tribute-taking states of the later Agrarian world, coercion was a widely accepted way of controlling behavior. Slavery, coerced labor, and domestic violence flourished. Today, behavior is steered more effectively by market forces rather than by coercion, and modern states increasingly frown on the private use of violence. Yet when they choose to do so, modern states can wield coercion far more effectively than traditional tribute-taking states. Even the most democratic states maintain significant prison populations (0.8% of the population of the U.S. was incarcerated in June 2006). And modern states maintain levels of military power that threaten the future of human society. Even after the Cold War, several thousand nuclear weapons remain on "hair-trigger" alert, and false alarms have led to several close calls.

Do these diverse changes represent "progress" or "betterment"? With their high productivity, modern societies have the ability, in principle, to provide everyone on Earth with a high material living standard. They have solved the fundamental problem of the Agrarian era: underproduction.

Less clear is the relationship between material consumption and well-being. Research into the preconditions for happiness, which has been conducted for many years, points to two clear conclusions. First, rising material living conditions clearly raise levels of well-being as they lift people out of dire poverty. Second, beyond a certain level, increasing consumption has little impact on the sense of well-being. In the U.S. and Japan in the last 50 years, surveys of "contentment" have shown no increase despite massive increases in consumption levels. Is continued growth necessarily a sign of progress? A second deep question is whether the growth of the Modern era is sustainable. Are there ecological limits to growth? And is it possible that the extraordinary complexity of modern human societies is creating new forms of fragility?

We have seen that the Modern Revolution has solved some of the most fundamental problems of the pre-modern world. But it has created new problems as well. Above all, how sustainable is it? Can it possibly endure as long as the Agrarian civilizations or the Paleolithic communities of earlier periods of human history? ∎

Essential Reading

Brown, *Big History*, chap. 12.

Christian, *Maps of Time*, chap. 14.

Supplementary Reading

Harrison, *Inside the Third World.*

Held and McGrew, *Global Transformations.*

Kennedy, *Preparing for the Twenty-First Century.*

Questions to Consider

1. Why is it so hard to identify durable structural features of the modern world?

2. Should we interpret the extraordinary pace of change today as a sign of progress or unsustainability?

The World That the Modern Revolution Made
Lecture 44—Transcript

Where are we? Where have we gotten to? We've surveyed the rapid and turbulent changes that created the modern world. Now, as we did with the era of the agrarian civilizations, we need to try and stand back and get a sense of the overall shape of the world that was created by the Modern Revolution.

How different is our world from that of 1700? How different was it from the world of the preceding 5,000 years that had been dominated by agrarian civilizations? Before we can seriously tackle the question of how sustainable modern society is, we need to try to get a clear idea about some of its basic structures.

We've described a number of distinct types of human communities in this course. We've described the foraging communities of the Paleolithic—these tiny, nomadic, kin-organized groups of the Paleolithic. We've described the village communities of the early Agrarian era. We've described the nomadic pastoralist communities. And we've described the large communities of the agrarian civilizations. So very broadly, that gives us already four quite distinctive types of human societies.

Now, can we sort of describe modern society in the same way? Can we identify some of the key distinguishing features of today's world? Can we look at this new world, as it was, from a distance and see: What are the key distinguishing features of it? Now in fact, doing so is extraordinarily difficult. It's much more difficult than doing so for earlier communities.

Part of the problem is that we're in the middle of change. We still can't see the overall shape of the Modern Revolution we've seen. So we're in the middle of it. And because of that also, we don't have the detachment that we might have when we look, say, at agrarian civilizations. We're in the center of it. It's very hard to stand outside and pick out its main features. Besides, the modern world has evolved so rapidly that it's very hard in the extreme flux and complexity of this world to pick out those features that are likely to be most durable. So having said that, we still have to try to get a grip on the main features that distinguish modern society from those of earlier human history.

So, here goes. Here's my attempt. Now, the first feature I'm going to focus on is the speed of change. I've argued that at the center of the Modern Revolution is an extraordinary acceleration in rates of innovation, in what I've also referred to as the "synergy of collective learning." And this extraordinary acceleration in innovation has meant a sort of speed-up. It's meant a sharp increase in the pace of history.

Now, let's try and see some aspects of that speed-up. What the speed-up means is that our world—the world created by the Modern Revolution, the world we live in today—is exceptionally changeable, as constant innovation constantly undermines existing structures and creates new structures. So history itself moves much faster in the Modern era.

Now, here's one way of seeing this. We've taken the symbolic date of 1700 for the beginning of the Modern era. And if we accept that date, what it implies is that so far, the Modern era has lasted just over 300 years—that's about a third of a millennium. Now, because so much historical scholarship is about the Modern era, it's all too easy to forget how short a period this is. Now, if you think about it, one-third of a millennium is about 1/30 of the length of the Agrarian era, and it's about 1/600 of human history as a whole.

If we go to the scales of big history, we've seen that if we collapse the history of the Universe into 13—rather than 13 billion—years, the Modern era counts for no more than six seconds, six seconds in 13 years. So it's just an instant. Yet in this instant, human societies are being utterly transformed around the entire Earth. And that's why the Modern Revolution counts as one of the eight great thresholds in this course.

The remarkable pace of change in this era contrasts sharply with the relative stability of most earlier types of human community. And in the pace of change, this acceleration in the pace of historical change has also had a profound impact on ways of thinking, and we could even say on ways of experiencing the world. In looking at the Paleolithic world or the world of agrarian civilizations, it was possible to pick out features that persisted over many thousands of years. In the case of Paleolithic societies we could pick out features (such as the existence of nomadic kinship communities) that may have lasted for 200,000 years. These features in agrarian societies include the rhythms of peasant life, or the basic structures of tributary states, or the Malthusian cycles over the last 5,000 years, or the fundamental ideas of some of the great religions. They lasted for centuries; some of them lasted for millennia.

Now, think of asking the same question about today. Is it possible to identify any feature of today's world that will certainly be present in, say, 500 years' time? Now, there may be features that will be present in 500 years' time, but it's extraordinarily difficult to pick them out with any assurance.

Another aspect of the pace of change is that now—probably for the first time in human history—major changes, radical changes, occur within the limits of a single lifetime, and this changes radically the way they're perceived. What it means is that we can perceive large changes as individuals—not just through collective memory or through distant memory of changes in the past, but as individuals.

In my lifetime, the world's population has grown by 3.5 billion; communism has collapsed; the computer revolution has transformed how we communicate with each other and use information. The world I live in today is a very different world from the world I grew up in. So unlike all earlier communities, we know the future will not be the same as the past, and we've experienced these changes. This changeability affects our *personal* sense of both time and history, and in many ways it's one of the things that's shaped our idea of history, and certainly shaped our sense of big history. We've seen many times in this course that before modern times, most cosmologies—that is to say, most descriptions of how the Universe was—tended to assume that there were many things that were permanent, eternal, and unchanging: the skies perhaps, or the landscape perhaps, or the heavens.

The modern vision of a Universe in which every aspect has a history, *including the Universe itself*, may be one product of the now universal experience of constant change. So, the speed of change affects how we experience the world and how we understand it. It also means something else. It means that today's world is extremely unstable. What some see as progress, others may see as a colossal accident waiting to happen. Things are changing so fast it's extraordinarily difficult to know where they're going. So the pace of change itself raises some deep questions about the sustainability of modern society.

So, that's the first broad feature about modern life: the quite exceptional pace of change, the speed-up in the last 300 years. Now, this speed-up, driven by acceleration and innovation, has meant both destruction and creation.

Let's look at the destructive aspects first. Above all, what it has meant is the root-and-branch destruction of all previous human lifeways. Now, this is not something that had happened before. We saw that during the Agrarian era, foragers survived for the entire era—so did communities of the early Agrarian era. One of the first things the Modern Revolution has done is to destroy all previous lifeways—the lifeways of the Paleolithic era, the lifeways of the Agrarian era, and also the tribute-taking political structures of the Agrarian era.

Even a century ago, viable communities of foragers and early Agrarian villages could be found in Papua New Guinea, in the Amazon, in much of Australia, in South Africa, and in other areas. Today, it's reasonable to say that none exist outside a modern state. And what that means is—even if they maintain some of their traditions, some of their cultures, some of their beliefs—they pay taxes, they engage with modern markets, and they use modern technologies. After all, why shouldn't 21st-century Australian aborigines hunt kangaroo using rifles with telescopic lenses and four-wheel drive vehicles?

But perhaps most striking of all is the destruction of peasant lifeways. Peasant lifeways, we saw, dominated the last 10,000 years. If you were dropped into the Agrarian era randomly, the odds are you would have been a peasant. Roughly speaking, we can assume that 9 out of 10 of all people in that era were peasants—and that meant that peasant lifeways dominated the life experience of most people for the last 10,000 years. What's happened in the last 200 or 300 years is that a combination of factors—once again driven by innovation—has undermined, sapped, and eventually is destroying that peasant world. The factors are a combination of overpopulation, leading to land shortage—as we saw in the case of Moumouni, who lived in Burkina Faso; competition from modern commercial agriculture is another crucial factor.

Now, many peasants, of course, still survive today—but more and more of them are being driven off the land, often to end up in the huge shantytowns that surround many major cities. And in those shantytowns, what do they find? They find cities without sewerage, clean water, electricity, or police—environments as dangerous and probably as disease-ridden as ancient Uruk.

The Modern Revolution has not just destroyed lifeways but a whole traditional way of living. It has also destroyed the political structures of the Agrarian era, the traditional tribute-taking states that dominated that era. And one of the fundamental reasons is that we saw that tribute-taking states, although they didn't rely exclusively on coercion, did rely very heavily on coercive methods of rule. And now, coercion simply no longer works in a highly commercialized world as the fundamental way of managing entire societies. I'll give just one illustration of this that seems to me peculiarly powerful. We also know that if you try to rule today as a traditional dictator, simply using ruling by brute force and skimming resources off the population, you're probably not going to survive long.

But a more powerful example is the collapse of the Soviet command economy. And I've argued already that that can be interpreted in part as a result of the fact that the communist command economy deliberately stifled commerce, entrepreneurial activity—but, by doing so, it unwittingly stifled innovation. In his book *Perestroika* that he wrote in 1987, Mikhail Gorbachev put it vividly. The wheels, he said, seemed to be turning, but nothing much was happening. These are the words he used:

> Something strange was taking place: the huge fly-wheel of a powerful machine was revolving, while either transmission from it to work places were skidding or drive belts were too loose.

So here we see a modern state behaving in many ways like a traditional tributary state, and it's as if it can't quite get a purchase on the modern world, and that's why it collapsed. So that's the second thing, the destructive feature of modernity—its extraordinary capacity to destroy traditional types of society, but rapid change has also been extremely creative. So now I want to look at the creative aspect. And above all, I want to look at the way the Modern Revolution has created new types of community and new power structures.

Now, here's the first striking thing about the communities of the modern world. This is the first thing that I think that someone surveying human history over 200,000 years very fast and looking at the size of communities is going to see. They are going to see that modern communities are extraordinarily large—vastly larger than earlier communities.

Here are just some illustrations of that. Politically, the modern world is organized into 194 sovereign states. The United Nations had 192 members in 2007. Two states were missing. Which? That's a great trivia question, and the answer is the Vatican City and Taiwan. So, 194 distinct polities. Of these, some were tiny. Some—like Liechtenstein—were very, very small indeed, but of these, the most populous was China. And in 2007, China had a population of about 1.3 billion. India's population at the same time was 1.1 billion. So here we have single states ruling more than a billion people. And to put that in perspective, remember that in the year 1000 C.E., the total population of the entire world was about 250 million—that is to say, it was about one-fifth of the population of a single state today, modern China. Granted, it's the most populous state in the world.

These states also cover much more territory than the states of the Agrarian era. In fact, they cover the entire landmass of the Earth, with the exception of Antarctica, though even control over Antarctica is partitioned among a number of different states. Let's go back to the figures of Rein Taagepera, whose calculations we've used before. Even 1,000 years ago, he calculated, states—and we're in the later Agrarian era when we say this—states controlled as little as 13% of all the territory controlled by modern states. And the reason for this is that vast areas—including all of Australia, most of the Americas, Siberia, and much of Africa—were not within the control of tribute-taking states.

Now, if these figures are correct, what they're telling us is that in the last 1,000 years, modern states have taken control of the remaining 87% of the Earth's surface. So the state system now covers the entire world. And the result is that unless they're islands (like Iceland, or Australia, or Britain, or Japan), modern states tend to be contiguous—they're squashed together in a crowd. So unlike most states of the Agrarian era—which had borders that tended to be extremely fuzzy and porous and could change from year to year, even month to month, as a result of varying military successes or failures—modern states have precisely defined and carefully policed and fenced-off borders.

Now, what we've said about modern states also applies to modern cities. Estimates of the size of the world's largest cities vary, depending on varying definitions of city limits—but, roughly speaking, there may be 20 or 30 cities today with populations of more than 5 million. Now that, remember, is the total population of the world 10,000 years ago. So what we're saying is 20 or 30 cities today contain what would've been the entire population of the world 10,000 years ago. And several cities today have populations of more than 10 million. Mumbai, the largest, may be approaching 20 million. And remember that 5,000 years ago cities such as Ur seemed remarkable with their populations of 20,000 to 50,000. So, we're talking about cities almost 1,000 times as large as the first cities in the later Agrarian era. So, size and scale. The scale and size of modern cities, modern communities, is extraordinary—and again, that reflects innovation and the huge resources and populations of the Modern era.

Now, a second striking feature of modern communities is that they are, to a remarkable extent, integrated across the entire world through exchanges of ideas, of goods, of diseases, and people. And what this suggests is that if we want to define the distinctive community of the modern world, one way of putting it might be to say that the modern form of community is in reality a single global community of 6 billion people. That is the modern equivalent of the tiny foraging communities of the Paleolithic era.

That global community is even, to some extent—even though so far in a fairly rudimentary way—organized politically; the United Nations is just one of many political organizations that provide a modern equivalent of the meetings that were held periodically between Paleolithic communities. So even politically, modern societies are, to some extent, organized at the global level. You could mention many other forms of integration—including migration patterns, cultural exchanges, and so on, as well as the use of English as an international diplomatic language.

One of the most striking aspects of this global integration is the fact that collective learning now takes place globally. Modern forms of transportation and communications allow real-time communication, as we've seen, between people at opposite sides of the Earth. And what this means is that in principle the exchanges of information that have been the main driver of human history are now taking place throughout the entire world, within a very diverse and often very well-educated population of 6 billion people. Now, if we add to this the ability of sort of intellectual prosthetics (such as computers) to multiply the power of human thought, the effects are even more spectacular. Furthermore, entirely new institutions have emerged to store, generate, and disseminate innovations. They include universities, the institution of mass education in the 19th century, and technologies (such as the computer).

When earlier we compared humans and their close relatives, the great apes, I argued that the difference between us and them was the difference between a stand-alone computer (which is limited by its own computing power and memory) and a network computer (which, in principle, has access to the computing power and memory of millions of other computers). A modern human with a network computer has instant access to much more information than were contained in the very largest of pre-modern libraries. I remember as a child lusting after the *Encyclopædia Britannica*, but buying a set was a major financial investment, and the thing was so large that it also meant rearranging the house. We never got the *Britannica*. But today, I can access it with a few keystrokes through my university library, and I can access a whole series of other encyclopedias, and I can even summon up and print vast numbers of scholarly articles.

Now of course, it's also true that others can dip into my computer, and that's perhaps the downside of all of this. But what seems to be happening in some way is that humans are now so networked, this process of exchanging information is becoming so powerful, that we're beginning to form a sort of vast global brain. Now, I should add that global integration has also been painful for many, because what it has done is it has forced communities with very different ethical and social attitudes into very close proximity. They've been driven together, and they have to deal with each other in a way they didn't before. And the discomfort felt by many traditional communities— for example, when they encounter Western television for the first time—is matched in the Western world by worries about the world the children can find as they surf the Net.

It's a scary world out there, and where such conflicts are felt to undermine deeply cherished values, they can lead to violent and painful conflicts about issues of symbolic importance, such as the wearing of headscarves by Muslim women in Christian countries. You may remember that in 2004 the French National Assembly banned the wearing of headscarves in public schools. It was a difficult and highly contentious issue, and similar issues are cropping up in many countries of the world. So globalization has also been—for many—painful.

So one way of thinking about the significance of global integration is to say that in the modern world the basic type of human community now is one single community of 6 billion people—and this is one of the most remarkable properties of the modern world.

Now, I want to talk about a third striking property of modern communities— their very different lifeways. We've already mentioned in general terms the significance of the fact that the traditional peasant lifeways are gone. Most people are no longer self-sufficient, rural-dwelling peasants. Most people, including surviving peasants, earn wages and are deeply integrated into market systems—and increasingly, they live in towns and cities.

This transformation has had a rather profound impact on gender relations. We've seen that throughout the Agrarian era, peasants typically saw having as many children as they could as the key to prosperity and protection in old age. For wage-earning families, this is no longer true, particularly in wealthier regions of the world. And the result is that women are not so closely tied to their role as child bearers and child rearers in modern societies. And that, among other things, has allowed women to enter more specialized professions, including politics, in far greater numbers. And these changes have begun to undermine deep traditions of patriarchy, though many inequalities remain. For example, female participation in the paid labor force rose significantly in the late 20th century—but, even in 2006, there were only 67 women in paid employment for every 100 men, and they were normally paid about 90% of what men received for similar work.

The extraordinary material wealth generated by modern societies has led to some remarkable improvements in living standards. Average levels of health have probably changed very little throughout the Agrarian era. Today, at least in the wealthier parts of the world, though levels of health vary greatly within and between societies, more people eat well and live healthily without chronic pain or suffering than at any other time in human history. So here is a clear gain from innovation.

And another clear gain is increasing life expectancy. Lives have gotten longer. Average global life expectancies in 1700—and probably throughout the Agrarian era—were probably about 30 years. By 2000, they had doubled to 65 years. The change represented, above all, a decline in infant mortality, in the number of children who died. And once more, this represents a momentous change in the nature of life itself, and it may prove the foretaste of future extensions in the life of a single human, a sort of stretching of the span of human life.

Now here's a fourth striking feature of modern communities, and that is the very different role of coercion in modern societies. In some ways, the changes have been paradoxical. In the later Agrarian world, we saw that coercion was a fundamental mechanism for controlling behavior, and you can see that by looking at the pervasiveness of slavery, for example. As a teacher in a tribute-taking society, I would have been expected to regularly beat my students.

A striking example of what this meant for daily life can be found in the 16th-century Russian manual of household management known as *Domostroi*, which means "organization of the household." In *Domostroi*, we can read the following: "Have you sons? Discipline them and break them in from their earliest years." That's prompted by Ecclesiastes 7:24. "Do not withhold discipline from a boy; take the stick to him, and save him from death. If you take the stick to him yourself, you will preserve him from the jaws of death."

If a wife does not obey, says *Domostroi*, and if she doesn't manage her household correctly, then, and I quote: "the husband should punish his wife. Beat her when you are alone together; then forgive her and remonstrate with her." Now, I have quoted *Domostroi* because in some ways it represents the norm in this world, a world in which coercion was regarded as a normal way of steering behavior. I should say that this world took a long time to vanish. I went to an English public school, where corporal punishment was still regarded as the norm.

Now, in this respect, the modern world is fundamentally different. Behavior is steered much more by market forces, rather than by coercion—so modern states generally frown on the use of violence. Indeed, the German sociologist Max Weber regarded this sort of monopolization of violence by the state as a key feature of modern states. Here's how Charles Tilly describes this process:

> Disarmament of the civilian population took place in many small steps: general seizures of weapons at the ends of rebellions, prohibitions of duels, controls over the production of weapons, introduction of licensing for private arms, restrictions on public displays of armed force.

So we now live in a world that is increasingly hostile to the use of violence in personal relations. Both slavery and domestic violence still exist, but they are widely regarded as illegitimate, and that is surely a gain.

Yet there's another side to this. It is that modern states, when they choose to do so, can wield coercion far more effectively than most Agrarian era states. Even the most democratic of states maintain large prison populations. In the U.S., for example, according to Department of Justice statistics, more than 2.4 million were incarcerated in prisons and jails at the end of June 2006, which represents an astonishing 0.8% of the population, almost 1%. It also represents one of the highest incarceration rates in the world. Now, it's safe to say that no later Agrarian era state would have had the resources to keep so many people incarcerated.

We also have seen that modern states have levels of military power that seriously threaten the future of human society. Despite the end of the Cold War, the U.S. and Russia may have 4,000 nuclear weapons on "hair-trigger" alert today. They could be launched within 15 minutes. In 2005, a plea signed by 32 Nobel laureates and Parliamentarians around the world asked that these be removed from hair-trigger status, noting that there were still enough of them to destroy civilization.

There have been several instances recently, as this petition pointed out, when individuals seem to have stopped what was looking like a process leading to an exchange of nuclear weapons. Here's just one. In January 25, 1995, Russia prepared to launch retaliatory strikes after identifying the launch of what looked like a U.S. Trident missile. They postponed the launch only when the missile landed in the sea and turned out to be a Norwegian research rocket studying the northern lights. The Russian government had been informed, but the information had not been passed on to the radar crew.

Now, let me end with some very brief comments about how we can assess all of this. Does all of this represent "progress" or "betterment?" It's a question we've raised several times in this course—for example, with the reference to living standards in the Paleolithic era or in the early Agrarian era—and each time the answers were contradictory. Well, here are some possible answers for the modern world.

The modern world has solved what was the fundamental problem of the pre-modern world—that is, how to produce enough stuff to support everyone. And that is a great achievement, and it explains the high living standards of so many people today. That's a remarkable achievement, and it's something entirely new.

Yet, this achievement itself has raised new questions. First, it raises the question of whether material living standards can keep improving the quality of life. By raising material standards over and over again, can we keep raising the quality of life? That's one question. Or, will we have to start looking for other ways of improving the quality of life? And a second question is whether modern society is sustainable. Given its extreme complexity and the breakneck pace of change, can this thing be sustained? That's something we'll tackle in the next two lectures.

Thank you.

Human History and the Biosphere
Lecture 45

In the 20ᵗʰ century it became apparent for the first time that humans were beginning to have a huge and perhaps disruptive impact on many aspects of the biosphere.

In the previous lecture we tried to stand back and survey the major structural changes of the Modern era. However, we deliberately skipped one large group of changes: changes in our relationship with the biosphere. These have a direct bearing on the question of sustainability. To see these changes clearly we must widen the lens further to include all of human history.

In the 20ᵗʰ century, it became apparent that humans were beginning to have a huge and disruptive impact on many aspects of the biosphere. The term "biosphere" was invented by Austrian geologist Eduard Suess (1831–1914) and popularized in the 1920s by Russian biologist V. I. Vernadsky (1863–1945). It refers to the region of Earth, water, air, and living organisms at the Earth's surface that sustains life on this planet.

The major turning points in human history are all associated with humans' increasing control, or new forms of control, over the resources of the biosphere. This is what we generally mean by "growth." But setting human history in the context of the biosphere reminds us that this was really a grab for resources by a single species: our own. By the late 20ᵗʰ century, it was apparent that our increasing ecological power was affecting the biosphere as a whole. John McNeill argues (in *Something New Under the Sun*) that our changing relationship to the environment may have been the most important change in the 20ᵗʰ century. To understand these changes, we must review our relationship with the biosphere over the 250,000 years of human history.

What impact did Paleolithic humans have on their environment? The first distinguishing feature of our species was a greatly enhanced ability to adapt through collective learning. Adaptation itself implies an increased capacity to manipulate our surroundings, so collective learning necessarily implies an increasing impact on the environment.

In the Paleolithic era, the impact of this constant exploration of the environment was limited. As "foragers," Paleolithic humans consumed natural products largely in their natural form. Populations were small and communities were scattered, so their ecological "footprint" was small.

Yet even in the Paleolithic era, the environmental impact of our species was remarkable. Our Paleolithic ancestors learned how to exploit natural environments throughout the world. As they did so, they developed new techniques for dealing with different environments, from the tropics to the tundra. Each new migration was a significant technological achievement. Some of the techniques developed in the Paleolithic era had a significant environmental impact. Foragers throughout the world fired the land regularly to increase plant growth and attract prey species. Over thousands of years, such practices could change the mix of plants and animals over entire continents. As their hunting techniques improved, our ancestors may also have helped drive many large mammal species to extinction, particularly in newly colonized lands such as Australia and the Americas, where local fauna had no experience of dealing with humans. Evidence on the "megafaunal" extinctions remains ambiguous, but the fact that these extinctions appear to coincide roughly with the arrival of humans makes it likely that humans played a significant role.

In the Agrarian era, humans began to transform their environments more systematically. Agriculture requires systematic, large-scale manipulation of the natural environment. Farmers transform environments so as to discourage species they don't need (which they call "weeds" or "pests" or "rodents") and encourage species they do need (which they call "domesticates"). This may mean plowing (removing weeds and exposing fertile sub-soils) or the deliberate elimination of pests such as wolves. It may require more elaborate changes such as diverting entire rivers into artificial channels to water crops in arid regions. Used badly, such methods could ruin the fertility of soils over large areas, as seems to have happened in Sumer 4,000 years ago. Swidden agriculture led to widespread deforestation. Farmers also manipulated species of plants and animals through domestication, turning wild plants and animals into "domesticated" species that were more useful to humans and were therefore encouraged to multiply rapidly. In towns and cities, humans created entirely anthropogenic environments. There was little that was not shaped by the presence of humans in even the oldest cities, such as Ur. Increasing control over environmental resources allowed humans to multiply from about 6 million people 10,000 years ago to more than 250 million people just 1,000 years ago.

The Modern Revolution has vastly increased human impacts on the biosphere. Each of the more than 6 billion humans on Earth today consumes approximately 60 times as much as energy as humans of the Paleolithic era. These figures suggest that the total energy consumption of our species has increased by about 60,000 times in 10,000 years. Most of this astonishing increase arises from population increase and the introduction of fossil fuels during the Modern Revolution. John McNeill estimates that in the 20th century humans became the most important movers of earth, more important even than natural erosion. Mining had the greatest impact on soil movements. As humans consume more resources, fewer are available for other species. So rates of extinction have accelerated sharply in the Modern era. Indeed, current rates of extinction may be similar to those of the five or six most spectacular extinction events in the last 600 million years. In the 20th century, humans engaged in a vicious and prolonged war with the bacterial world after the introduction of antibiotics. The outcome of this conflict remains uncertain as bacteria develop new and more resistant strains.

Finally, massive consumption of fossil fuels is increasing the levels of carbon dioxide in the atmosphere, while other activities, including cattle farming, are raising the levels of other greenhouse gases such as methane. The result is that we are beginning to alter global climate patterns. Though there is debate about many aspects of global warming, there is no doubt that the level of carbon dioxide in the atmosphere has increased significantly since the Industrial Revolution. Will global warming cause changes as drastic as

> **The first distinguishing feature of our species was a greatly enhanced ability to adapt through collective learning.**

those of the last ice age—but in the opposite direction? We may find the answer to such questions within our lifetimes.

In summary, evidence is accumulating that we are now using more resources than the biosphere can provide, with the risk of a serious breakdown. We have seen such breakdowns before, but this time it threatens to be global rather than local. Such conclusions suggest the folly of treating human history as separate from the history of the Earth. Human history has evolved within the complex global film of life that James Lovelock has called "Gaia." Lovelock has argued, controversially, that the entire biosphere constitutes a single feedback system that has maintained the surface of the Earth in a state suitable for life. This is a view of evolution in which cooperation seems more important than competition. Yet Lovelock argues that human activity may now be threatening the stability of the global "Gaian" system.

We have seen that in the course of human history, humans have used more and more resources at an accelerating rate. Is this a story of triumph, or a sign of danger? Where is all this going? In the last three lectures of the course we will try to answer this question by peering into the future. ■

Essential Reading

Christian, *Maps of Time*, chap. 14.

McNeill, *Something New Under the Sun*.

Supplementary Reading

Hughes, *An Environmental History of the World*.

Turner et al., *The Earth as Transformed by Human Action*.

1. Why has our species had such an extraordinary impact on the biosphere?

2. How can we assess when human impacts on the biosphere become dangerous both for the biosphere and for our own species?

Human History and the Biosphere
Lecture 45—Transcript

In the previous lecture we began to widen the lens once more by surveying the major structural changes of the Modern era, as we'd done with previous eras. But we deliberately skipped one very large and important group of changes: changes in the relationship between our species and the biosphere. And these issues have a direct bearing on the question of the sustainability of modern society. So to see these changes clearly, what I want to do is widen the lens further to include all of human history, and I want to survey our changing relationship with the biosphere.

In the 20th century it became apparent for the first time that humans were beginning to have a huge and perhaps disruptive impact on many aspects of the biosphere. Let me begin by defining this term "biosphere" clearly. What is the "biosphere"? The term was invented by the Austrian geologist Eduard Suess, who lived in the 19th century and died in 1914. He used it in 1875 to refer to, and I quote: "The place on earth's surface where life dwells." Incidentally, we've met Suess before in this course, as the inventor of the term "Gondwanaland" and a precursor of some of the ideas of Alfred Wegener.

The term "biosphere" was popularized by the Russian biologist V. I. Vernadsky, whose dates are 1863 to 1945, and he popularized it in a book he published in the Soviet Union in the 1920s. He used it on the analogy of other geological terms (such as atmosphere), the sphere of air, or hydrosphere (the sphere of water), to refer to the spherical layer of earth, water, air, and living organisms at the Earth's surface that sustains life on this planet. So, the biosphere didn't include just living things, it included the context in which they existed—and this is a large, complex system of exchanges of energy and resources: the place of life.

Now, we've seen that the major turning points in human history—and I'm thinking really here of the turning points that introduce what I've called the "great eras of human history," including the initial appearance of our species, the introduction of agriculture, and even the appearance and spread of agrarian civilizations—are all associated with increasing control over (or new ways of controlling) the resources, the energy, the space, the material resources of the natural world.

Each new era seems to begin with a sort of acceleration in human control over the biosphere. Now, we've seen that increasing control of the energy, resources, and space of the biosphere can be tracked in several ways, and one is an expansion of the range and the numbers of our species—and we can track it from the Paleolithic to the present day. Each new era marks an acceleration in growth rates.

Let's take population growth rates to illustrate this point. If you take the best available estimates of human populations throughout the course of human history, and you do some rough calculations on them, you find that in the later Paleolithic era, after about 50,000 years ago, human population seemed to have doubled roughly every 10,000 years. In the Agrarian era, they seem to have doubled about every 1,500 years. This is a very significant increase in rates of population growth. And in the last 300 years, they have doubled about every 75 years.

So each of these gearshifts in human control over resources represents increasing human power—ecological power, if you like—increasing human power over the biosphere. Now this is why—particularly when economic historians talk about these processes—they tend to use a word like "growth." But we need to remember that this is a very anthropocentric, or human-centered, view. It may be growth for us, because it means we have more resources and our populations can grow, but is it growth for the biosphere? Not really. What was really going on in each case was that the same amounts of energy were entering the biosphere from sunlight, but more and more of them were being diverted to the use of one species, our own.

In the 20th century, it became apparent that our increasing ecological power was beginning to have a massive impact on the natural world. Some scholars anticipated this earlier. One of the best-known scholars in the U.S. was George Perkins Marsh, whose dates are 1801 to 1882. He was one of the first to understand clearly the scale of human impact on the biosphere—Vernadsky was another—and this realization is also one of the main drivers of modern environmental movements.

So massive have been these changes in recent history that—and here I want to quote from a wonderful recent environmental history of the 20th century by John McNeill; and I'll come back to this book later on, it's called *Something New Under the Sun*—this is what John McNeill writes:

> The human race, without intending anything of the sort, has undertaken a gigantic uncontrolled experiment on the earth. In time, I think, this will appear as the most important aspect of twentieth-century history, more so than World War II, the communist enterprise, the rise of mass literacy, the spread of democracy, or the growing emancipation of women.

The change in our relationship with the biosphere is indeed astonishing. However, to understand what happened in the 20th century, we really need to see these changes in a larger context—and that's why, in the rest of this lecture, I want to retrace our steps and review our changing relationship with the biosphere over the entire course of human history. Now I should note that this is still, surprisingly, a fairly unusual way of looking at human history. The separation of human history and the other humanities from the natural sciences that took place in the late 19th century—which C. P. Snow, in a famous essay of 1959, described as a separation between two intellectual cultures—has meant that historians, for the most part, have tended to treat human history as if it were entirely separate from the natural world.

As this course in big history has shown, this is not true. Human history is deeply imbedded in the biosphere. So now I want to review the increasing environmental impact of our species over 250,000 years. We'll go over data, some of which we've seen already, and assemble that into a coherent account of the changing human relationship with the biosphere.

So let's begin by going back to the Paleolithic era. How can we best describe the Paleolithic relationship with the biosphere, and what impact did humans have on the biosphere in the Paleolithic era? We've seen in this course that the first distinguishing feature of our species was a greatly enhanced ability to adapt through collective learning—to continually find new ways of relating to the environment—and adaptation, by its very nature, implies finding new ways of manipulating the environment.

Now this meant that humans, to a greater extent than any other species, were constantly trying out new ways of using the biosphere, using their own surroundings—trying out new plants or animal species as potential foods or sources of fibers or skins, or trying out the environments and trying out new ways of dealing with those environments. Our impact in this era was, in fact, very limited by modern standards, and there were several reasons for this.

As "foragers," Paleolithic humans gathered what they needed, consuming natural products largely in their natural form, furthermore numbers were small. In fact, some genetic evidence suggests that human numbers may have shrunk to as few as a few thousand as late as 70,000 years ago.

Communities were also widely scattered, so their ecological "footprint" in general, their impact on a particular environment, was limited. And this has led to the basically false assumption that humans had no significant impact on their environment. This is profoundly incorrect. Even in the Paleolithic era, the environmental impact of our species was exceptional.

The first way in which we impacted the environment of the biosphere was by migrating. In the course of 200,000 years, humans explored and learned how to exploit natural environments throughout the entire world—with the exception of Antarctica and the islands of the Pacific, which they would explore later. As they did so, they developed new techniques for dealing with different environments, from the tropics to the tundra. Now, we can easily take—if you look on a map and you look at human migrations in the Paleolithic, it all looks so simple, so we need to remind ourselves that what's going on is technologically revolutionary.

It was in its way a sort of scientific and industrial revolution, though smeared out over many thousands of years. Now, think of some of the things that had to happen for humans to migrate in the way they did in the Paleolithic. They had to deal with a whole range of new environments. For example, they exploited coastal environments by fishing—learning to fish, or collect shellfish, or using seaweed.

Learning to exploit tropical forests was a particularly delicate trick. Think about it: Tropical forests are among the most diverse environments on Earth, so that to learn to exploit them it was necessary to develop first a vast amount of botanical knowledge about different plants. Many of them were toxic—so to use them you had to either avoid them or find ways of leaching out their poisons. Others had particular medicinal values.

Incidentally, modern pharmaceutical companies have sometimes a better appreciation than some scholars of the range and extent of the botanical knowledge of indigenous people, such as the peoples of the Amazon jungle. They very often send out researchers to try and find out the uses of particular plants from indigenous peoples. In addition, they had to deal with many forest animals—from snakes to piranhas—which are dangerous. So this was no mean feat.

Our Paleolithic foragers also learned to exploit desert environments, and this requires an entirely different suite of technologies and knowledges. You have to have very good geographical knowledge of water holes, and which water holes are available at different times of the year. So you need to know about technologies for conserving water, and you need an intimate knowledge of desert species.

And just one more illustration: Think of what it meant for Paleolithic humans to live in arctic environments at the height of the last ice age. Doing this meant learning to hunt arctic species—such as seal, walrus, and elk. You had to have seagoing craft; you had to be able to navigate through ice floes. You had to be able to build shelters that could protect you through the winter and clothing that could protect you while outside in extremely cold temperatures. So the technological innovation of Paleolithic humans, if we understand it rightly, was in fact extraordinary, and it was that that allowed these migrations that look so easy if you just see them on a map.

Now, some of these techniques that were developed in the course of these migrations had a significant environmental impact. An example that we saw earlier was firestick farming. We saw that many Paleolithic communities developed ways of firing the land regularly in order to increase plant growth and to attract prey species. And over thousands of years, these practices—regular firing of the land, repeated over and over again—could slowly change the mix of plant species. It's probable that the Australian landscapes that the first Europeans found there (such as Captain Cook), which were dominated by eucalypts, were actually not natural environments at all. They were, in their way, as much a human-created environment as the regular, neat gardens of 18th-century Europe.

And another example of these impacts was "megafaunal" extinctions. As human hunting techniques improved—and they must have gotten significantly better in arctic terrain, where hunting animals had to provide the main source of food—as they improved, Paleolithic hunters may well have contributed to the die-out of a majority of large mammal species in the Americas and Australia. In the Americas they probably included horses, which were an American species; large camelids; giant sloth; and a large number of other similar species. In Australia, they included giant kangaroos and wombats. We can re-create these extraordinary beasts—but they're gone. The only area of the world where you find large populations of megafauna is our homeland, Africa, and that's because humans and large megafauna evolved together. They knew how to deal with each other.

The results of overhunting were most drastic in newly colonized environments, such as Sahul and the Americas, where local animals were too inexperienced to fear the new arrivals and humans didn't fully understand the ecology of these animals. But foragers may also have contributed to the extinction of Siberian species, such as mammoth and wooly bison. The evidence on the so-called megafaunal extinctions still remains ambiguous, but the fact that they coincide roughly with the appearance of humans makes it really look as if humans had something to do with it.

Now let's move on to the Agrarian era. In the Agrarian era, human environmental impacts increased very significantly. This really is a gearshift. One reason is because agriculture by its very nature requires systematic and large-scale manipulation of the natural environment. Essentially, we've seen, what is going on when you have agriculture is that farmers are clearing away species of animals and plants they don't need (which they classify as "weeds," or "pests," or "rodents"), and they replace them with species that they do need or want—which they call "domesticates." So this by definition involves rearranging the environment around you.

And there are lots of different ways of doing this. It may mean churning up the soil through plowing or using digging sticks to remove weeds and to expose fertile sub-soils in which your domesticates can grow well. It may involve the elimination of pests, such as wolves. Or it may require more elaborate changes, as we've seen, such as diverting entire rivers into artificial channels to water crops in arid regions.

And used badly, we've seen that such methods could destroy the fertility of soils over large areas. The landscape of southern Sumer by the end of the 3rd millennium B.C.E. was profoundly transformed by irrigation—and transformed in ways that made it an impoverished environment for humans. So that's why civilization moved north.

Agriculture can require even more significant changes, including the deforestation of large areas. There are hints of a significant increase in the presence of carbon dioxide in the atmosphere at about the time that early swidden farmers began entering forested regions and clearing or burning them down for farming. In fact, both the burning of trees and the reduction of tree cover would have contributed to an increase in carbon dioxide in the atmosphere. And there was another spike in the amount of methane, another powerful greenhouse gas, once farmers in Southeast Asia began introducing the paddy farming of rice. So here, agricultural populations are beginning to have a noticeable impact on the environment, an impact that's noticeable several thousand years later.

Domestication provides another example of how agriculture encouraged humans to change their environment. Domestication means manipulating the organisms around you to make them more useful, manipulating them genetically. Over many generations humans began to interfere in the evolution of species that were important to them, and by doing so they turned wild plants and animals into what we call "domesticated" species, which are useful to humans and dependent on humans for their survival. Domestic sheep, we've seen, are vastly more numerous than their wild ancestors, but they're weaker, they're slower, and they're stupider. They flourish because of their close symbiotic relations with humans.

How do you change wild sheep into domestic sheep? It's not that hard. From each birth, each group of lambs, you pick the fattest and most docile individuals. You do this for enough generations, and you'll soon breed out the feistiness that makes wild sheep hard to manage. And sheep are successful because of this, and you can measure that in the "biomass" of sheep—much, much larger than that of wild mammals.

In his wonderful chronology of the Universe, *Timescale*, Nigel Calder posed the following delightful scenario, which is a wonderful little parable about the meaning of domestication. It raises the question of who domesticates who. The question is this: If a Martian ecologist were to study the Earth and ask: "What's the dominant species on this planet?" her answer might well be "lawn grass." And Calder explains: Here is a species that appears to cover a large part of the Earth's surface and to have domesticated a large bipedal species of mammal and trained it to groom the grass, to feed it and water it—and, in short, to keep it in style. And that story is a reminder that domestication is a two-way process. We, in many ways, are as dependent on domesticates as they are on us.

Now finally, in the Agrarian era, in regions of the densest sectors such as towns and cities, humans began to create not just landscapes that they had changed, but entirely anthropogenic environments. There was little that was not shaped by the presence of humans in even the oldest cities, such as Ur. This increasing control over environmental resources—over landscapes, over plants, over animals, over energy—is what allowed humans to multiply from 6 million 10,000 years ago to more than 250 million just 1,000 years ago. So one possible interpretation of these figures is that human impact on the environment must have multiplied by at least 10 times, but in fact, as technologies became more productive, the real impact was certainly much greater than that.

Now, having reviewed the Paleolithic and Agrarian eras, we're in a better position to understand and to put in context modern impacts on the environment. The Modern Revolution has vastly increased our impact on the natural environment. Let me just quote a few quick figures from Paul Kennedy, who writes:

In the 20th century alone the world's population quadrupled ... The global economy expanded 14-fold, energy use increased 16 times, and industrial output expanded by a factor of 40. But carbon dioxide emissions also went up 13-fold and water use rose 9 times.

A powerful demonstration of the fact that what we call "economic growth" is always, always based in some way on increased exploitation of the biosphere.

Now let's look more carefully at some of these phenomena. First, energy use. There are now more than 6 billion humans on Earth. On average, each one consumes about 60 times as much energy as humans of the Paleolithic era. 10,000 years ago there were about 6 million humans. In other words, human population has grown 1,000 times in that period. So, on these figures, total energy use by our species has grown about 60,000 times. That's a staggering increase.

Modern humans have also had a massive impact on landscapes. In his *Environmental History of the Twentieth Century*, which I've mentioned already, John McNeill has estimated that in that century humans became, for the first time, the single most significant movers of earth, with a greater impact on the reshaping of the landscape than all natural forces, including glaciation, mountain building, and natural erosion.

The main factor here was, in fact, mining—it had the largest impact. And here's just one statistic to illustrate the spectacular increase in mining. In the 19th century, coal production increased by about 77 times, and in the 20th century it increased by almost another 7 times, so that in a mere 200 years it had increased by more than 500 times. And coal production means, of course, moving a lot of earth. However, other factors—including the building of roads and spread of cities and their suburbs—have also had a significant impact on landscapes.

We've also had a huge impact on other species. If the megafaunal extinctions of the Paleolithic era have deprived the world of a large number of presumably beautiful, exotic, and interesting organisms, today our impact is vastly greater. As we consume more resources, obviously, less are available for other species. So, rates of extinction have accelerated very rapidly during the last two or three centuries. Here's a description by Lester Brown, and he's describing the situation in 1999. He writes:

> Of the 242,000 plant species surveyed by the World Conservation Union-IUCN in 1997, 14 percent or some 33,000 are threatened with extinction ... Of the 9,600 bird species that populate the Earth, two thirds are now in decline, while 11 percent are threatened with extinction. Of the Earth's 4,400 species of mammals, 11 percent are in danger of extinction ... Of the 24,000 species of fish that occupy the oceans and freshwater lakes and rivers, one third are now threatened with extinction.

Now, it's all too easy to let such figures just wash over you, and that's very understandable. But it's very important just to come away with a sense of how huge our impacts on other species are. Even our closest relatives, the chimps, are perilously close to extinction. One way of getting a sense of this impact is to note that the rates of extinction today are comparable with the rates of extinction during the five or six most spectacular extinction events of the last 600 million years. Paleontologists can see these events in the rocks, in the sudden disappearance of whole groups of fossils. So we do have a benchmark to compare what's going on today.

And human impacts are comparable, for example, to the effects of the asteroid that wiped out most of the dinosaurs 65 million years ago. Our impact, in other words, to put it dramatically, is as significant in its way as that of a massive asteroid colliding with the Earth. We've also had an impact on bacteria. John McNeill points out that our relationship with the bacterial world has been transformed in the 20th century. Indeed, for much of the 20th century humans engaged in a violent war with disease bacteria, in which one of the most important weapons was antibiotics. The war was waged across the planet for many decades, and it's still going on. But as he points out, the outcome is not yet certain, and the reason is that bacteria are fighting back, and they're using the techniques of natural selection and their rapid rates of reproduction to outflank us and develop new disease-resistant strains, such as the strains of golden staph increasingly found to be immune to antibiotics.

347

Now we saw that in the past we had an impact on the atmosphere. Our impact on the atmosphere now has grown by leaps and bounds, above all through the massive use of fossil fuels. Now, there's much debate over the details of this process, but there are some figures that are not in serious doubt, and one concerns changes in the amount of greenhouse gases in the atmosphere. During the last ice age, carbon dioxide accounted for about 200 parts per million of the atmosphere. By 1800, the level had risen to about 280 parts, and currently it stands at about 350 parts per million. In other words, since the beginning of the Modern era, levels of carbon dioxide in the atmosphere have doubled. And if current trends continue, they're likely to double again, to almost 600 parts per million, by 2050.

Now, there's very little disputing this, but some of this dispute is merely about the exact impact of this. Increases in the amounts of greenhouse gases, such as carbon dioxide, tend to raise atmospheric temperatures because they absorb sunlight and retain it, rather than allowing it to be reflected back into space. And it's already been predicted that by the middle of the century, the North Pole may be ice-free throughout the year. It increasingly looks as if global warming is itself a direct consequence of human impacts on the environment.

So in summary, evidence is accumulating rapidly that we are now using more resources than the biosphere can keep supplying, and we're using them in ways that are having a massive impact on the environment. Will this lead to the sort of ecological breakdown that we've seen many times in human history, except on a global rather than local scale? Attempts to estimate our "footprint" (that is to say, the amount of energy we use) suggest that we're now using far more energy and resources than the planet as a whole can sustainably reproduce. This looks very dangerous indeed.

So such conclusions show us starkly that human history is not separate from the history of the Earth, because we are part of the complex global film of life that James Lovelock has called "Gaia." Lovelock's controversial but influential idea is similar to the idea of the biosphere. Lovelock argued in a book—published in 1979 and called *Gaia*—that the entire biosphere can usefully be thought of as if it were a single organism. So, "Gaia" in Lovelock's account is a single organism that covers the entire surface of the

Earth. And what Lovelock argues is that Gaia has the capacity to regulate its environment—and to make that environment life friendly.

For example, he points out that the temperature of the Sun has increased over 4.5 billion years—and yet, the surface of the Earth, the temperature, has remained at about the level necessary for liquid water to exist. So, his argument is that Gaia is more or less preserving the Earth in a form necessary for life to persist. Now, Lovelock's been accused of a sort of mysticism, but his argument is that this is simply natural selection, that what Gaia will do through natural selection is remove those organisms that threaten its future.

So, this is a view of evolution in which Gaia, the biosphere, is a single huge organism that has the power to expel members of the biosphere that threaten its future. This is a view of evolution in which cooperation seems (most of the time) to be more important than competition between species, and that's where the warning comes for our species. If indeed, in our aggressive pursuit of more and more resources, we're inflicting great damage on the great superorganism of Gaia, will Gaia eventually expel us, as the white corpuscles of a healthy organism may be able to expel disease bacteria?

We've seen that, in the course of human history, humans have used more and more resources at an accelerating rate. Is this a story of triumph, or a sign of danger? Where is this all going? In the next two lectures we'll try to answer this question by peering into the future.

The Next 100 Years

Lecture 46

> As I worked on these lectures, I soon realized that historians seem to be more or less the only people who refuse to think seriously about the future.

A fter surveying 13 billion years, can we resist peering into the future? I think not. Indeed, I will argue that it is appropriate and necessary to do so. I was first prompted to do this by students who argued that, after surveying 13 billion years, it seemed odd to stop abruptly in the present moment. As a professional historian, I shared the historian's taboo on considering the future. So I had to think hard about how I should approach such a topic. Why and how should historians study the future? I soon realized that thinking about the future is not such a strange activity! On the contrary, all human societies have tried to predict the future, and many professionals in our own society—from stockbrokers to gamblers—make a good living by doing so.

Furthermore, we must take our thoughts about the future seriously because they may influence what we do today, and that in turn may shape the future. Besides, all organisms constantly try to predict; indeed, they are designed by natural selection to do so. Every time you act, you have to predict the likely outcome of your action, and sometimes (as in crossing a busy road) it's vital to predict wisely.

How should we think about the future? Rule 1 is that the future really is unpredictable. Nineteenth-century physicists often claimed we could predict the future if we knew the motion and position of every particle in the Universe. Quantum physics has shown this is not true. At the very smallest scales there is a certain indeterminacy in the behavior of the Universe. Rule 2 is that those who think carefully about the future get it right more often (and, if they are stockbrokers or gamblers, earn more money) than those who do not. Rule 3 is that we must begin with existing trends—in other words, with history. A horse's "form" is not a perfect guide to performance, but it's better than nothing.

We will divide the future into three distinct periods. The first period, the next century, is close enough to matter—and to be shaped by our actions. Existing trends can guide our predictions. The second period, the next thousand years, is harder to discuss. Possibilities multiply too quickly, and the outcomes are too remote to matter as much. Here, anything we say is highly speculative. The third period includes the rest of time. Oddly, in the remote future our predictions become more confident again, as we return to slower and simpler processes such as the evolution of the Sun, the galaxy, and the Universe! This lecture discusses the next hundred years.

What large patterns or trends can guide our ideas about the next century? In his *A Green History of the World*, Clive Ponting took the history of Rapa Nui (Easter Island) as a warning about the dangers of a future Malthusian crisis. Rapa Nui, a tiny Polynesian island just 16 miles long, is one of the most remote places on Earth. It was settled between 1,000 and 1,500 years ago by 20–30 colonists. They kept chickens and grew sweet potato and fished. The population grew to about 7,000, and village chiefs began building the large stone figures for which the island is famous. About 500 years ago, their society suddenly collapsed in warfare, disease, and famine.

Archaeologists have reconstructed much of the story. The stone figures were carved in the island's single quarry and moved on rollers made from trees. As villages competed to build more statues, more trees were cut down until eventually none were left. That meant no wood for boats, houses, or fuel. Islanders must have seen disaster coming as they felled the last trees, but they felled them nonetheless. Could modern consumption patterns cause a similar crisis but on a global scale?

What can this story tell us? Like the Easter Islanders just before their crash, we face some ominous trends. Populations are rising fast, carbon emissions threaten rapid climatic change, most fisheries are in decline, reserves of fresh water are shrinking, and rates of extinction are higher than for many millions of years. Consumption levels are rising fast and will rise even faster as countries like China and India begin to consume at the levels of today's richer capitalist societies.

Yet blocking rising consumption can only lock in existing inequalities and create new conflicts. And, as the U.S. learned in September 2001, modern weaponry allows even small groups to inflict terrible damage. Can global consumption slow in a capitalist world? Does not the logic of consumer capitalism require endless growth throughout the world?

There are also more hopeful trends. Global population growth is slowing as a result of the "demographic transition." As the proportion of peasants has declined and living standards have risen, fertility rates have fallen throughout the world. By the 1980s, fertility levels had fallen to the "replacement level" of 2.1 children per woman in most developed industrialized countries. But rates of population growth are also falling in poorer countries. In the 1960s, global growth rates were over 2% per annum. By 2005 they had fallen to under 1.2% per annum, according to the U.S. Census Bureau. These trends suggest that by the middle of this century, global population may level out at 8 or 9 billion people, rather than the 12–16 billion many had predicted in the 1980s.

> **The collective brain of modern humanity, magnified by billions of networked computers, is the most powerful problem-solving entity we know of.**

Since the 1960s, ecological awareness has increased. Most governments have agencies concerned with environmental issues, there are many nongovernmental agencies concerned with environmental issues, and there have been two international environmental summits, in Rio in 1992 and in Johannesburg in 2002. There have also been some notable successes, such as the 1988 international agreement to reduce production of CFCs because they damage the ozone layer. Despite the existence of nuclear weapons since 1945, we have avoided a global nuclear war.

Capitalism may turn out to be part of the solution as well as part of the problem. Recent centuries have shown capitalism's astonishing capacity to adapt to change and generate social and technological solutions to new problems. Capitalism is particularly good at reacting to scarcities by shifting investment to alternative sources of supply. Already, investment is shifting toward technologies that may reduce dependence on fossil fuels and reduce consumption through recycling. And of course we should not forget "collective learning." The collective brain of modern humanity, magnified by billions of networked computers, is the most powerful problem-solving entity we know of. If there is a solution to the problems that face us and the biosphere, 6 billion networked humans are surely likely to find it.

Which leaves the political question: If solutions can be found, will they be implemented in time? Many would argue that we already know most of the solutions, and the first solution is to slow the rate at which we consume natural resources. Done with care, such a change might not mean a drastic reduction in material living standards, but it will certainly be painful. Will we show the political will and creativity needed to take these decisions? Perhaps the Easter Islanders saw perfectly what needed to be done (stop building ahus!) But their chiefs wouldn't let them, and anyway they wanted to build just one more ahu that was better than that of the neighboring village ... Will modern humans do any better?

Though there are ominous trends in our relationship with the environment and a real threat of a global Malthusian crisis, there is also growing awareness of the dangers. Will we, unlike the islanders on Rapa Nui, show the insight and the political and moral will needed to act before it is too late? ■

Essential Reading

Christian, *Maps of Time*, chap. 15.

Supplementary Reading

Brown, *Eco-Economy*.

Ponting, *A Green History of the World*.

1. Is it legitimate for historians to consider the future? If so, how should they do it?

2. Are we overdue for a global Malthusian crisis? What steps need to be taken to avoid such an outcome?

The Next 100 Years
Lecture 46—Transcript

After surveying 13 billion years, can we resist peering into the future? I think not. Indeed, I'm going to argue that it's appropriate and necessary to do so in a course on big history. I began attempting lectures on the future in this course, when I first began teaching it, because of comments from some of the students I first taught big history to. Some of the best students I taught told me at the end of the course that they felt that in a course that surveyed 13 billion years, it seemed very odd to refuse to look at the next 50 or 100 years. How could we just stop on a dime in the present moment? After all, they argued, we were looking at such huge trends that surely some of them are going to continue into the future. I mean, this is a bit like an oil tanker turning around; an oil tanker is not going to stop suddenly. So if we look at these trends we ought to be able to say something about the future.

In any case, some of them felt that I'd left humanity hanging by a thread at the edge of a huge—possibly Malthusian—cliff, and they felt I owed them some insights into where the story might be going next. Once I thought about what they'd said, I soon realized that they were absolutely right. Because of its scale, because of the scale on which big history looks at the past, big history cries out for discussion of future scenarios in a way that no other approach to history does.

So, now I had to try and think how I could lecture about the future. As a historian, I had been trained in the idea that historians never think about the future; they think about the past. That's what historians do. And in fact, some famous historians have argued that if you find a historian thinking about the future, you know that something's gone seriously wrong.

So, in order to prepare these lectures on the future I had to wrestle with my conscience as a historian, and I had to try to break some very old habits. And I also had to try to ask some new questions.

Why should we take the future seriously and how should we think about the future? As I worked on these lectures, I soon realized that historians seem to be more or less the only people who refuse to think seriously about the future. Many human societies have taken the future very seriously indeed. Do you remember the Mayan calendars, which were so accurate—partly because a lot of politics depended on predicting exactly the right day to do certain things or perform certain rituals? And even within modern society, there are many professions that take the future very seriously. For example, this is what the futures markets are all about, and some of them even make pots of money by doing so. And after all, money is the key test of seriousness in our society. So one reason for thinking about the future is that it really does matter. All human societies have tried to predict the future, and many professionals in our own society—from stockbrokers to gamblers—make a pretty good living by doing so.

Now, there's another reason why we need to think very clearly about the future—and that, I guess, is political. It's that what we think about the future is going to affect what we collectively do today. Now this means we need to be very clear what our ideas are about the future, where we think the world is going, because the conclusions we reach may affect what we do today, and that could itself shape the future.

Should we be so worried about global warming that we begin slapping huge taxes on fuel consumption? Or should we be much more worried about the possibility that such taxes will stifle growth? These are the sorts of questions that we need to think about, and they all involve predictions. I also realized that, in some sense, thinking about the future is something we do all the time—in fact, all living organisms, or all living organisms with sensory systems and brains, think about the future, and they do so a lot of the time. They have to, and so do we.

Every time you act you have to predict the outcome of your action. So whenever we act we have some idea in our mind about the likely consequences of what we're doing—and sometimes it's very important that we get these predictions right. So natural selection has designed organisms so that they were reasonably good at predicting. Let me just give a trivial everyday example. If I cross a busy road, I move when I predict that no car is moving so fast that it will hit me. If I get it wrong, I'll pay a very serious price for it.

So there's nothing odd about trying to predict the future—it's just that we need to think very clearly about how we go about it. All of these arguments persuaded me that, in fact, it was perfectly legitimate for a historian, particularly in a course on big history, to be thinking about the future.

So now the question was: How? How should we think about the future? Well, I formulated a number of rules, and I think they're very familiar to anyone who is in a position where they do have to think seriously about the future. Here's the first. It is that the future really is unpredictable; there are no sure bets. Now it may seem obvious, but I have to say it because in the 19th century there was a widespread belief among physicists that, in some sense, the Universe was deterministic. If you knew the exact position of every particle in the Universe and its exact movements, from then on you could predict the entire future of the Universe.

We now know that this is wrong, and it's wrong at a very deep level. Twentieth-century quantum physics showed that at the very small levels of subatomic particles and photons of light, the world is not deterministic at all. In fact, at that level there's a fair bit of wriggle room. It's impossible sometimes to determine exactly where a particle is, and it may be that, in some sense, it doesn't have a precisely defined position. So indeterminacy, unpredictability is built into the Universe. So that's why we have to take very seriously the fact that the future really is open ended, and that means any prediction we make is a sort of percentage gain; there are no guarantees.

Rule 2: Rule 2 is a rule that stockbrokers and professional gamblers know very well. Those who think carefully about the future are more likely to get it right more often, and as a result they earn more money than those who don't. So this is something worth thinking about very carefully.

And Rule 3 is related to that. The way to think about the future is very often to begin with existing trends, which is the point my students made to me right at the beginning. If you're betting on the horses, the horse's "form," its track record, what it has done over the last year or two, is not a perfect guide to performance—but it's better than nothing. It's a lot better than nothing. I once had a friend who made a living for many years betting on horse races; this was his profession. He knew this was an insecure way of making a living, but he'd also reply that he knew of many more insecure ways. He made a pretty good living, and he worked extremely hard at what he did. Like a good stockbroker, he put a huge amount of time into studying the form, all the factors that might affect the outcome. In fact, he became so good at this that he had to place his bets just before a horse race so as not to influence the odds too much and change the odds.

Okay, with those preliminaries, what I want to do now is to start peering into the future. And what I'm going to do is I'm going to divide the future itself into three distinct periods, rather as we divided human history into distinct periods. Period one is the next century; that's the first period. It's close enough to matter. One way of putting that is to say we will know people—our grandchildren, our great-grandchildren will live in that period—we will know people who will live through it; it matters. It's also close enough to be shaped by our actions. What we do today may shape the future in the next 100 years. And besides, we have some data. We have form; we have existing trends to help us predict. So for these three reasons, the next 100 years is a very interesting scale to think about, and that's the first scale.

The second scale we'll look at is the next millennium, the next 1,000 years—roughly speaking, the next 1,000 years. That is a very different type of scale, and the reason for saying this is that, particularly given the nature and the volatility of modern society, the possibilities of what might happen in that period multiply so fast that it's hard to make any serious predictions that are not largely speculative. So at this scale, our attempts to predict become less and less scientific, and more and more they begin to look like science fiction. Having said that, I'm going to admit that it's fun to look at this scale, and I'm going to let myself speculate nevertheless.

Then period three: Period three is the rest of time, the whole of the rest of time. In the remote future, billions of years away, the odd thing is that our predictions suddenly become a bit more serious and a bit more scientific—and there's a very good reason for this. If we look to the remote future, we're dealing with very large, slow trends—such as the evolution of stars, of galaxies, and of the Universe itself. And those are things about which modern science is reasonably confident that it can say some reasonably precise things. So when we look at the remote future, we'll see in the next lecture that there are some fairly clear things we can say.

Okay, now the rest of this lecture is going to focus on the first scale, the next century. And the next lecture will discuss the second and third scales, the scale of a millennium and the scale of the rest of the future. So what large patterns or trends can guide our ideas about the next century? If we take the idea of complexity seriously, we have to take seriously also the possibility that the sharp increase in the complexity of modern society may make modern societies more fragile than the agrarian civilizations that preceded them—and frankly, it's not hard to see possible routes to breakdown.

So it's hard to avoid scenarios in which we see some sort of breakdown of modern society. One form of this breakdown is simply that someone manages to use some of the many hundreds of atomic weapons that are still deployed and on hair-trigger alert. That would be a very simple, rapid form of breakdown—and it's a very real possibility. But there are also other, subtler scenarios, and these all suggest, or most of them take the form of what I've called in earlier lectures "ecological overreach" of some kind. Except if this happens, if we overreach, if we overuse the resources of the biosphere, this time the crash is likely to be not regional, but global—it might take the form, in other words, of the mother of all Malthusian crises.

In his *A Green History of the World*, published in the early '90s, Clive Ponting took the history of Rapa Nui (Easter Island) as a warning about the dangers of a future Malthusian crisis. Here's how the story goes.

Rapa Nui is a tiny Polynesian island just 16 miles long, and it's one of the most remote places on Earth. It was settled between 1,000 and 1,500 years ago by a group of Polynesian colonists, perhaps a boatload of 20 to 30 people. They grew sweet potato, they fished, and they kept chickens. Population grew to about 7,000, and village chiefs began building the large, stone figures for which the island is famous. You all have seen pictures of these figures; they are large stone heads, some of them 2 meters tall. And some of them have sort of stone topknots that have been put on top of them.

Then about 500 years ago, the society suddenly collapsed. Now, this is a society of several villages, each with their own heads, their own village chiefs. So we can think of this as a society of the early Agrarian era. Then things collapse. About 500 years ago they collapse in warfare, disease, and famine, and what this is looking like is a classic Malthusian crisis.

What happened? Well, there was writing of some kind that developed on Easter Island, but we can't decipher it—so we have to decipher the history of Easter Island almost entirely from archaeological records. And archaeologists have reconstructed much of the story using the evidence available to them. The stone figures, the ahu, it turns out were carved in the island's single quarry, and then they were moved around the island. How? How do you move such huge stone figures? Well, the answer is almost certainly that they were moved on rollers that were made from trees.

Now over time it seems that villages and their chiefs began to compete to build more statues, and the result was more trees were cut down, until eventually none were left. This was a catastrophe. Islanders themselves must have known what it meant as the crisis approached. With no wood, you couldn't build boats, and that meant you couldn't go out to sea and fish. So there's an entire food resource that you cannot get hold of any longer. You can't build houses, so now you have to live in caves. You can't use wood for fuel. So this is a very serious ecological crisis, and the result was the population collapsed and people started living in much simpler and more impoverished ways than they had before.

Now think your way back into Easter Island, Rapa Nui, about 500 years ago. The islanders must have seen the disaster coming as they felled the last trees, but they felled them nonetheless. Could modern consumption patterns cause a similar crisis, but on a global scale? Is it possible that we'll see this thing coming but do nothing about it? In his recent bestseller, *Collapse*, the biologist and historian Jared Diamond—who's made a huge contribution to our understanding of world history by adding a biologist's perspective on it—has explored many other examples of such collapses. And you see similar patterns over and over again—sometimes leading to large crises, sometimes to less.

Now what does this story have to do with us? So far we've seen that there are no signs of a slowing in the astonishing rates of innovation generated by the Modern Revolution. We're not quite yet at the point where the islanders were at when they saw the last trees being cut down. And that is perhaps why, so far, we've avoided a Malthusian crisis. Innovation seems to keep increasing. Despite regional famines—and some of them have been massive—for three centuries, innovation at a global level seems to have kept ahead of population growth. But could that simply mean that we're preparing the way for a huge and global Malthusian crisis, bigger than any that have preceded it? Are we behaving the way the Easter Islanders did just before the crash?

Now, we've already seen some ominous trends, so let me just list some of the more worrying trends. Population is rising extremely fast. Carbon emissions threaten rapid climatic change. Many fisheries—some would say most fisheries—are in decline. Reserves of fresh water are shrinking rapidly, particularly as irrigation increases throughout the world, and rates of extinction, we've seen, are higher than for many millions of years.

So there are many signs of an impending crisis in our relations with the biosphere. Now, here Lester Brown describes one of these trends; it's overconsumption. His description is very vivid—so let me quote it in some detail. He writes:

> If the western model were to become the global model, and if world population were to reach 10 billion during the next century, as the United Nations projects, the effect would be startling. If, for example, the world has one car for every two people in 2050, as in the United States today, there would be 5 billion cars [on Earth]. [Now, that's about 10 times the number today.] Given the congestion, pollution, and the fuel, material, and land requirements of the current [global] fleet of 501 million cars, a global fleet of 5 billion is difficult to imagine. If petroleum use per person were to reach the current U.S. level, the world would consume 360 million barrels per day, compared with current production of 67 million barrels.

Now, that's just talking about cars. Now he talks about consumption at a more general level, above all consumption of food:

> Consider a world of 10 billion people with everyone following an American diet, centered on the consumption of fat-rich livestock products. Ten billion people would require 9 billion tons of grain. The harvest of more than four planets at Earth's current output levels. With massive irrigation-water cutbacks in prospect as aquifers are depleted and with the dramatic slowdown in the rise of land productivity since 1990, achieving even relatively modest gains is becoming difficult.

Now, this is what I meant by saying in the previous lecture that our ecological footprint is, in some sense, larger than the planet today—or it's certainly heading in that direction.

That's one side of it. If we raise living standards throughout the world to those of the richer capitalist countries today, it's hard to see how the biosphere can deal with the pressure we will put on it. But there's another side. Global inequalities today are such that they guarantee increased conflicts if living standards do not rise in poorer regions. Can we imagine a world in which we'd lock in present global inequalities? Now that is surely a recipe for violent global conflict. As the U.S. learned in September 2001, modern weaponry means that even small groups can, in such conflicts, inflict terrible damage.

So this raises further questions. If we seem to be headed for a level of consumption that is unsustainable, can consumption slow in a capitalist world? How does this relate to capitalism or commerce, the basic drivers of innovation in the modern world? Doesn't capitalism require endless growth? Certainly, significant cuts in consumption appear to be extremely unlikely in the richer (and more powerful) countries, whose economies are driven today by the logic of consumer capitalism.

So those are just some of the worrying trends today, but it's not all bad. There are also positive trends. So let's look at some of the positive or more hopeful trends. First, I said that human populations were growing, and they have indeed grown at a spectacular rate in the 20th century—and growth rates were probably at their fastest just after the middle of the century. But since then, in the last few decades, it's become very apparent that rates of population growth are slowing, and they're slowing as a result of what demographers call the "demographic transition." This is an immensely important phenomenon—so let me try to explain it clearly. It has many causes, one of which may be simply the dying out or the vanishing of traditional peasant lifeways.

We saw that peasants, throughout most of the Agrarian era, seemed to be committed to a demography that meant having as many children as you possibly could. There were many reasons for this—one of which, incidentally, was that so many children died young that if you were to maximize the chances of some of them living to adulthood, you had to have as many children as possible. Now as that peasant world slowly fades away and more and more people live as wage earners in towns—and as in increasing parts of the world new forms of social security of some kind are provided, which means that children aren't the only guarantee of security in old age—more and more families are beginning to reduce the number of children they have.

Today, improved health care and increasing incomes have reduced the sort of pressures to have children that peasants experienced. And smaller families have also, as we've seen, transformed the role of women—by freeing them from the duty of lifelong childbearing and child rearing.

Now this change, this slowing down in population growth, has been quite striking, and here's just one illustration. By the 1980s, fertility levels in most developed, industrialized countries had fallen to the level of 2.1 children on average for every woman—and demographers regard this as the "replacement level." This is the level of reproduction necessary to maintain an existing population, but it's too low for growth. In these countries, therefore, population growth has depended increasingly on immigration rather than increases in fertility.

The phenomenon is particularly noticeable in the wealthier capitalist countries, but it's not confined to them, and that has become increasingly clear in the last decade or so. Rates of population growth are beginning to decline throughout the world, even in poorer countries. In the 1960s, global growth rates were over 2% per annum. By 2005, they had fallen to under 1.2% per annum. Now this, from an ecological point of view, has to be a good trend, in the sense to the extent of the sheer numbers of humans who put pressure on the biosphere—this was very positive because what it suggested was that by the middle of the century, global populations may have leveled out at 8, or 9, or perhaps 10 billion people. You'll find different estimates, but nothing like the estimates of 15, or 16, or 18, or 20 billion people that were being chucked around in the middle of the 20th century.

Now here's another trend, a positive trend. Since the 1960s, ecological awareness has increased significantly. One can be cynical about this, but it's worth noting that in the first half of the 20th century, ecological issues were barely on the agenda of any government or any significant international organization. Now today, most governments have agencies concerned with environmental issues, and there are many nongovernmental agencies concerned with the issue, and there have been two international environmental summits: in Rio in 1992, and in Johannesburg in 2002.

Now, again, one can be cynical about these, but it's striking that these were the largest gatherings of heads of state in recent years. That's a sign of considerable seriousness. There have also been some notable successes. One of the most spectacular was the 1988 international agreement to reduce production of CFCs, which damage the ozone layer that protects the Earth from ultraviolet radiation. CFCs—chlorofluorocarbons—were invented in the 1920s. It was not until the 1970s that it was realized that they were beginning to have a damaging impact on the environment.

This is an issue where the United States took the lead—and one of the reasons was that by the 1980s, alternatives had developed that could replace CFCs. Despite international resistance to reform, in 1988 for the first time, very good scientific evidence came in to show that there was a massive hole in the ozone layer over the Antarctic, and this provided the wake-up call that enabled the international community to act seriously on the banning of CFCs. Their production has declined very drastically, and the best evidence at the moment is that the hole in the ozone layer is at least not growing—and may be even shrinking.

That's a good story, and it's a sign that international cooperation on some issues is possible and can be successful. Now here's another good story. Despite the existence of nuclear weapons since 1945, we have avoided a global nuclear war. This is one of those things that is hard to see because it's a negative factor. It's not something that happened—it's something that didn't happen. But we need to take it very, very seriously indeed. The world may have been close to an all-out nuclear war two or three times—the Cuban Missile Crisis was the clearest example—and we need to congratulate those leaders who avoided that crisis.

Now, what is the relationship between capitalism and all of this? Now here's a positive aspect of capitalism. Capitalism may turn out to be part of the solution as well as part of the problem. Recent centuries have shown capitalism's astonishing capacity to adapt to change, to mature, to take new forms, and to find social and technological solutions to new problems— and capitalism is particularly good at reacting to scarcity. So as resources become scarce, their prices tend to grow, and that tends to shift investment to alternative sources of supply. Already now, we see investment shifting towards technologies that may reduce dependence on fossil fuels (by improving alternative sources of energy, such as wind power). And it's possible, therefore, that there's going to be a sort of economic bonanza in sustainable technologies—and capitalism has the flexibility as a driver to shift resources very quickly in that direction.

It's interesting to watch the behavior of the large oil companies as they increasingly present themselves as green organizations, and some of them apparently quite seriously are beginning to position themselves for the role of energy producers in an era of sustainability. And, of course, we shouldn't forget collective learning. The collective brain of modern humanity—armed with the prosthetic brains we call network computers—counts as the most powerful problem-solving, intelligent entity we know of.

If there's a solution to the problems that face us, and that face Gaia, the exchange of ideas between 6 billion and more humans is surely likely to generate that solution—which leaves the problem of politics: whether or not, when we've seen the solution, we will implement it. Many would argue that we can see the solutions already; we know what needs to be done. But will we actually take the hard decisions needed to implement them, and will we be able to take them on a global level?

So though there are ominous trends in our relationship with the environment, and a real threat of a global Malthusian crisis, yet there's also growing awareness of the dangers and of what needs to be done. So perhaps there are prospects that this is a maze that we can see our way through collectively as a global community, avoiding the fate of the islanders of Rapa Nui.

Thank you.

The Next Millennium and the Remote Future
Lecture 47

Is it possible that the dangerous knowledge that accumulates within a species like ours that's capable of collective learning is bound to eventually outweigh the more creative knowledge that such species generate? Or is it simply that such a species is eventually bound to construct societies of such complexity that they're not sustainable?

Now we return to larger spatial and temporal scales. We consider first the next millennium. Then we consider the rest of time, asking about the future of the Earth, the galaxy, and the Universe as a whole. Oddly, we will see that it is easier to discuss the remote future than the next millennium. On the scale of a millennium or so, we have far more questions than answers! Human societies are so complex that, even if we can identify some trends, we know of none that are certain to continue for more than a few decades. All we can really do is to play with different scenarios.

Some scenarios are disastrous for humans and perhaps for the entire biosphere. In *A Canticle for Leibowitz* (1st published in 1959), Walter M. Miller imagined a future in which nuclear weapons were developed and used, then redeveloped and used again. Is this the fate of all species capable of "collective learning"? Is there a necessary limit to collective learning? Could that be why we have failed to detect other species like ourselves?

Geologists now understand that the Earth's history has been interrupted by periodic asteroid impacts such as those that killed off the dinosaurs. Though astronomers can now keep an eye on potentially dangerous objects, we do not yet have the means to protect ourselves adequately from such impacts.

Some scenarios are more optimistic. Perhaps, after a near brush with disaster (such as the regional nuclear wars described in the future histories written by Wagar as well as Stableford and Langford), we will avoid the fate of Easter Island. We will slow consumption levels and find new ways of living that can be satisfying without putting excessive pressure on the environment. If our ancestors avoid disaster, the "Modern era" may turn out to be the prelude to an entire new epoch of human history. Innovation may generate sustainable technologies that we can barely imagine. They may include new energy sources (such as hydrogen fusion) and biotechnologies that create new food sources, eliminate most forms of ill-health, and prolong human life. New social structures may include mechanisms for reducing violent conflict and generating more sustainable notions of progress and well-being.

In reality, of course, the future will probably fall between these extremes. What new things will we learn? Here are areas where there could be profound scientific and technological breakthroughs in the next millennium. Quite soon, we may find evidence for the existence of planets similar to the Earth. Will we also find evidence for the existence of life elsewhere in the Universe? At present, the speed with which bacterial life appeared on our planet makes it seem likely that life of some kind is widespread.

We are less likely to find evidence for creatures like us, capable of collective learning. On Earth it has taken almost 4 billion years to evolve such a species. And a lot of luck was involved. In a famous study of the Cambrian fossils of the Burgess Shale (in the Canadian Rockies), Stephen Jay Gould argued that biological evolution can take many utterly different pathways. On the other hand, Simon Conway, another specialist on the Burgess Shale fossils, has argued that the number of evolutionary pathways may be limited, which makes the evolution of species like us more probable. If our descendants survive disaster, are there new thresholds of complexity waiting to be crossed? Perhaps, like eukaryotic cells in the Cambrian era, they will become so interdependent that they will turn into a single Earth-spanning organism, capable of managing "Gaia."

Our descendants might start migrating again, leaving this Earth just as our ancestors migrated from Africa and through the Pacific. Many of the technologies already exist for migration to the planets and moons of our solar system. But we have none of the technologies needed to reach other star systems. If our descendants do migrate to distant star systems, will they create a vast archipelago like the colonies of Polynesia? If so, will collective learning occur at stellar scales? Or will the distances be so huge that human communities will become isolated culturally, and even genetically? If so, our species will split by allopatric speciation into numerous closely related successor species, just like the Galapagos finches. Will that mark the end of human history?

At larger scales we return to slower and simpler processes, such as the evolution of the Earth, the Sun, and the Universe. These we can predict with more confidence. Studying the movement of tectonic plates hints at what the Earth will look like in 100 or 200 million years' time. The Atlantic will widen; the Pacific will narrow, bringing Asia and North America together; and eventually a new supercontinent will emerge. Los Angeles will slide north and join Canada.

In the late 1990s, astronomers found that the rate of expansion of the Universe is actually increasing. We do not yet know why.

Our Sun is about halfway through its life. In 4–5 billion years it will run out of hydrogen, collapse, and then expand again to form a "red giant." The Earth will be vaporized. Eventually, the Sun will cool and shrink, becoming a "black dwarf." In its retirement, it will keep cooling for countless billions of years. Our galaxy, the "Milky Way," is on a collision course with its neighbor the Andromeda galaxy. The two will collide as our Sun enters its death throes, gliding through each other gracefully, though gravity will introduce some turbulence as they do so.

How will the Universe evolve? One idea, popular in the late 20th century, was that the gravitational pull of all the matter and energy in the Universe would eventually slow expansion until the Universe began to collapse in on itself. Time would reverse, and the Universe would collapse in a "big crunch," to be followed perhaps by a new "big bang," which would create a new Universe.

In the late 1990s, astronomers found that the rate of expansion of the Universe is actually increasing. We do not yet know why. But this suggests the Universe will keep expanding forever. What will that mean? Eventually, all stars will use up their fuel and die. The Universe will darken, and black holes will graze on what's left for countless billions of years. The space between objects will increase, and temperature differentials will narrow. With smaller energy differentials to drive complexity, the Universe will become simpler and more boring. The second law of thermodynamics will have triumphed over complexity. The Universe will continue to get more uninteresting for as many billions of years as there are sand grains on all the beaches and deserts of the Earth. And so on, forever and ever.

Where does that leave us? What is our place in this huge story? The last lecture will recapitulate the story of big history and touch on these large issues of meaning. ■

Essential Reading

Christian, *Maps of Time*, chap. 15.

Prantzos, *Our Cosmic Future*.

Supplementary Reading

Miller, *A Canticle for Leibowitz*.

Stableford and Langford, *The Third Millennium*.

Stearns, *Millennium III, Century XXI*.

Wager, *A Short History of the Future*.

Questions to Consider

1. Are there any reasonable predictions we can make about the next 1,000 years?

2. What can we reasonably say about the future of the Universe?

The Next Millennium and the Remote Future
Lecture 47—Transcript

Now the lens through which we view history is going to begin to widen, and it's going to begin to widen very, very fast indeed, as fast as you like. In fact, in this lecture, we're going to look at a larger chunk of time and a larger chunk of space than in any other lecture in this course. So the lens is widening very, very fast.

We return now to larger scales, like the ones we considered early in this course. In the first part, I'm going to consider the next millennium. Then in the second part, I'm going to consider the rest of time, and we're going to ask about the future of the Earth, the galaxy, and the Universe as a whole. And we'll find that oddly, when we look at this larger scale, it's possible to speculate scientifically about it in a way that's probably impossible in thinking about the next millennium.

Okay, so first let's look at the next millennium, the next 1,000 years. What can we say about the future at the scale of 1,000 years? Well, the first thing we're going to see is on this scale we have far more questions than answers. We've seen that modern human societies are among the most complex things that we know of, and they're also extremely volatile and changeable. And this means that though we can identify some trends, we know of none that are guaranteed to continue for more than a few decades. So really all we can do in looking at the next 1,000 years is to play with some different scenarios. And that's what I'm going to do. Some are scenarios for disaster for humans and, perhaps, for the entire biosphere—and some are scenarios for a more optimistic future, at least from the perspective of humans, and also perhaps from that of the biosphere.

There's a wonderful novel that was published in 1959 called *A Canticle for Leibowitz*, and it was written by Walter M. Miller. Here is a wonderful disaster scenario. What Miller did was imagine a world—remember, this is not long after World War II—Miller imagined a world in which societies evolved to the point where they developed nuclear weapons, at which point they used them. The novel begins in the Utah desert, in a world that should remind the reader of the European Dark Ages after the fall of the Roman

Empire. This is a post-holocaust world, and the people of that world describe the holocaust as the "Flame Deluge."

A monk, Brother Francis Gerard, discovers what the reader will recognize as a bomb shelter from the 20th century, and inside it he is going to discover some documents, which turn out—although they can't be deciphered at the time—to contain important information about nuclear physics. Later segments of the novel take us forward several centuries to eras in which knowledge is slowly building up again, as it did in the European Middle Ages, and through the Renaissance, and the era of the Scientific Revolution—until eventually we enter an era in which there is sufficient scientific knowledge to once again build nuclear weapons. And they are used again—so what happens is they hurl the world back into a new Dark Ages.

And what's clearly implied by the novel is that this process is going to repeat itself over and over again. Now, it's an intriguing scenario. Is this perhaps the fate of all species capable of "collective learning"? Is there a limit to collective learning, or at least a sort of bottleneck of some kind beyond which it's hard to move? Is it that a species capable of collective learning becomes so clever that eventually they are inevitably going to do something really dumb—like explode nuclear weapons? Now, if that's true, if Miller's science fiction scenario actually has some relationship to what has happened in the Universe, that might explain why we fail to detect other talkative species like ourselves despite many decades of looking for them.

Is it possible that the dangerous knowledge that accumulates within a species like ours that's capable of collective learning is bound to eventually outweigh the more creative knowledge that such species generate? Or is it simply that such a species is eventually bound to construct societies of such complexity that they're not sustainable?

Now here's a second type of disaster scenario, and this is a nonhuman type of disaster. Geologists now understand that the Earth's history has been punctuated by periodic impacts from meteorites or asteroids, such as the asteroid impact that wiped out most species of dinosaurs about 65 million years ago. That this is what happened was established actually quite recently, in the 1980s, and it was established largely through the work of

Walter Alvarez, an American geologist who proved that at least one major extinction event in the Earth's history had been caused by a massive asteroid impact. This went against the grain of current geological thinking, so it was a very significant achievement to establish the truth of this.

We now know that this can happen. We saw that in the planet's early history asteroid impacts were very common, but they then became rarer as various objects moving around the solar system were sort of swept up into planets. Astronomers today are keeping a close eye on any objects that could stray too close to us, as we've seen before, but it's by no means certain that we have the technological capacity yet to deal with such a crisis, despite the 1998 Bruce Willis film *Armageddon*. So there's a natural disaster scenario.

Now, some scenarios are more optimistic, so let's look at some of those. Perhaps—there's a whole cluster of scenarios that go like this—perhaps what will happen is that there'll be a sort of wake-up call. It may take the form of a near brush with disaster; we can imagine perhaps a regional nuclear war that will shock the world into a realization of the dangers it faces. That scenario is described very nicely in two good histories of the future. One is by Warren Wagar, a scholar of the work of H. G. Wells, and it's called *A Short History of the Future*. And the other is a fascinating book by Brian Stableford and David Langford called *The Third Millennium*.

In both these books you have a human community that's deeply divided and then shocked into some sort of unified action on behalf of its future by nuclear war. And what that scenario suggests is that this shock may provide the political will and the insight needed to avoid the fate of Easter Island. Humans will perhaps deliberately start slowing consumption levels; they'll find ways of living that can be satisfying without putting too much pressure on the environment, and they'll learn to live sustainably within the biosphere. They will redefine "the good life" so that increasing material consumption is not an essential part of that dream.

Of course, doing so will require the rapid development not just of the technological knowledge needed to generate energy and resources more sustainably and to limit waste, but even more importantly, it will require the rapid development of mechanisms that can enable humans throughout the world to coordinate what they do. It'll involve turning the embryonic human community of today into a more politically organized community that can act with some sort of unity in dealing with major global issues. Now, if we do indeed evolve in this way, the "Modern era," as we've described it, may turn out to be just the prelude to an entire new epoch of human history.

Innovation may generate sustainable technologies that we can barely imagine. They may include new energy sources (perhaps the taming of hydrogen fusion). They may involve biotechnologies that create new food sources that can eliminate most forms of ill-health and that can prolong human life. That last scenario is worth thinking about, because we've already seen the beginnings of it in the 20th century. What would it mean if each of us knew that we might live for 1,000 years or more, or even indefinitely? Would the possibility of a sort of pseudo-immortality change our attitudes to ethics? Presumably so. Or to issues like suicide?

If we knew that most people alive today will not die in the near future, will it follow that we should stop producing more human beings? Perhaps the having of children will cease to be a normal human experience, and what will that do to our sense of biological family? Clearly a radical extension of life spans will mark a revolution in our understanding of what a good human life means. Now we can imagine also the emergence of new social structures that include improved mechanisms for reducing violent conflict and rely less on increasing consumption—on other, more sustainable notions of progress and well-being, as we've seen.

So these are all optimistic scenarios. Now, if we're trying to be just slightly more realistic, we probably have to agree that it's the in-between scenarios that are most likely to occur, a real future that will fall between these extremes—being, like all of human history, a tale of both triumph and tragedy, of creation and destruction. But exactly what form it will take is anyone's guess.

Now, here's a question we can perhaps pose slightly more seriously, and it's this: What new things will we learn? Now let me attempt to list some areas where it's not unreasonable to think that there could be profound scientific and technological breakthroughs in the next millennium. Quite soon we may find evidence for the existence of planets very similar to the Earth. This could happen very quickly, within a decade or two, within just a few years. Within a century or so, will we have also found evidence for the existence of life elsewhere in the Universe? Will we perhaps find that the Universe is, in fact, crawling with life, that this is not the only corner of the Universe with living organisms?

At present, given what we know of the speed with which life appeared on our Earth, that is not an unlikely scenario. Think of the odds: We have been able to observe life on just a single planet so far, and what we've seen is that on that planet life appeared—life in the form of simple, single-cell organisms—almost as soon as the planet was cool enough to sustain life, about 3.8 billion years ago. Now, what that seems to imply is that whenever promising environments are created for life—and presumably they'll be on planets in the vicinity of stars, but not too close (otherwise they'll be too hot) and not too far away (otherwise they'll be too cold)—as soon as, wherever these conditions have appeared, this suggests life is likely to appear. Life, at least in the simple form of single-celled organisms, may therefore turn out to be quite a robust form of complexity that is spread throughout much of the Universe.

But what about the chances of finding creatures like us, creatures capable of collective learning? Now, perhaps they don't need to look like us, but let's define the crucial feature of humans as this ability, this capacity for collective learning. Though we shouldn't rule it out, the chances of finding such organisms seem a lot less likely, and here are some of the reasons. One reason is that on our Earth, it has taken almost 4 billion years to evolve such a species, and we also know that a lot of luck was involved.

For example, the asteroid that wiped out the dinosaurs. Now imagine that it had been on a trajectory just a few minutes earlier or a few minutes later. It would have missed the Earth; the dinosaurs would have continued to flourish, and mammals—as a group of organisms—would have probably remained in their existing niches as small, burrowing, shrew-like, nighttime organisms. They wouldn't have flourished in the way they did after the removal of dinosaurs, and we are part of that massive adaptive radiation of mammals after the removal of the dinosaurs.

Then, even once our species had appeared, what are the chances of it surviving? There are genetic hints, as we've seen, that our species, that our numbers dwindled to just a few thousand, perhaps as recently as 70,000 years ago. At that time, the survival of our species hung on a thread. Now, if these hints are correct, does that mean that we've come perilously close to extinction?

And of course, we also need to add that, like all evolution events, the appearance of our species depended—to a large degree—on genetic chance, on the appearance of a mutation that happened to spread among a small founder population to create our species. How likely was such an event?

Stephen Jay Gould, who I've mentioned before, wrote a famous book on the Burgess Shale. The Burgess Shale is a rich source of fossils from the Middle Cambrian era that was found in the Canadian Rockies. And in his book, Gould argued that many of the forms found in the Burgess Shale are so strange that they prove that the evolution on Earth could have followed many different pathways. So what he's suggesting is that if you start life on Earth and you just tweak the conditions slightly, you'll find that the path of the evolution runs along completely different lines. The story we told, the evolution of life on Earth, would be very different indeed, and the organisms you'd end up with would be completely different from those we know.

If he's right, the line of evolution that led to us is perhaps vanishingly unlikely to be repeated elsewhere. On the other hand, if so, we're extremely unlikely to encounter species anything like us, and perhaps unlikely to encounter any other species capable of collective learning. Yet, there are evolutionary biologists—and one of them is Simon Conway [Morris], another scholar who has worked on the Burgess Shale—who has taken a very different line. What Conway and others who think like him have argued is this: They've argued that there are a limited number of evolutionary pathways, and what they're talking about is the chemistry of biology. There are a limited number of ways in which organisms can be created, in which they can evolve to multi-cellularity, and so on. So he's argued that evolution is not as random or as open-ended as Gould supposed.

There are a limited number of "ground plans," as it were, on which you can build living organisms. If this is true, then it follows that given a reasonable amount of time and given multiple planets on which life evolves, it's quite likely that on at least some of them, evolution is going to follow fairly similar paths to those on Earth, and in some of them they may eventually stumble upon the idea of a large-brained dexterous organism—such as ourselves—that's capable of collective learning.

If so, we might expect that wherever life gets going on a reasonably long-lived planet—that means a planet orbiting a small to middling star—creatures a bit like us might appear. Perhaps even, Conway has argued, with similar sensory organs including eyes, and perhaps with brains and a capacity to manipulate their environments and share information about it. If Conway is right, then we may not be quite so rare in the Universe. So, if so, what are the chances of actually meeting such creatures? Well, they're not good if Walter Miller is right in *A Canticle for Leibowitz*, and all these creatures always reach a certain limit and then blow themselves up.

Now, here's another scenario. Let's imagine that we've survived the various disaster scenarios that are waiting out there for us. Where will our history as a species take us? Are there, perhaps, new thresholds of complexity out there waiting to be crossed? One intriguing possibility is that, like eukaryotic cells in the Cambrian era, we may become so interdependent that there comes a point where we'll start turning into a single Earth-spanning species linked in complex ways with many other species of the biosphere. We've already seen that we are now so networked that we're beginning to function as if we are parts of a huge global brain. And, of course, if James Lovelock's idea of "Gaia" is correct then, like it or not, the biosphere as a whole is already well on the way to being a single organism—and one that may feel, of course, that our species needs to be removed, like a sort of cancer cell.

Okay, here's another scenario, and this is migration. Humans, we've seen, are travelers and explorers, and if we survive the next millennium, our descendents will surely start migrating beyond the Earth as our ancestors migrated beyond the savanna lands of East Africa, and as ancestral Polynesians migrated throughout the vast archipelagos of the Pacific Ocean. And how likely is this scenario? Well, this is reasonably plausible. Many of the necessary technologies already exist for migration to the planets and moons of our solar system—and, of course, humans have already reached the Moon. And within a decade or two, it's very likely that humans will walk on Mars.

So even today, we have some of the technology needed, say, to mine asteroids, or to colonize the Moon for some period of time, or to build artificial space colonies—in fact, there's one already orbiting our Earth, the International Space Station. There's even been some reasonably serious talk—although this is probably on the borderline between serious science and science fiction—of the possibility of "terraforming" Mars to make it more habitable to humans. That would probably involve a sort of artificial global warming, beginning perhaps with massive nuclear explosions, so as to create on Mars a breathable atmosphere and seas. If this were to happen, it would probably take the best part of 1,000 years or more, but we could think of it as a sort of domestication of an entire planet. But at present we have none of the technologies needed to go further than our solar system, none of the technologies needed to migrate to other star systems. Remember, it takes light more than 4 years to travel to the nearest star, and at present we have no idea how you might propel a spaceship fast enough to even begin to match the speed of light.

So for humans, such journeys would presumably take many generations. If they occur, they will be spectacular re-creations of the journeys that Polynesian migrants made when they settled Rapa Nui or Hawaii. And here's one more thing. If our descendents do migrate to distant star systems, we will create a vast archipelago a bit like the colonies of Polynesia. Collective learning will now start occurring at stellar scales. But the distances between these colonies, rather like those between Polynesian islands, will be so huge that these communities will certainly—or at least some of them—will certainly become isolated culturally and even, eventually, genetically.

Slowly our species will start to split through some form of allopatric speciation, a bit like the Galapagos finches. They'll split into species that are very, very similar, but gradually over time they'll become less and less similar. They'll become distinct species. And will that mark the end of our species— and will that mark, perhaps in some sense, the end of human history?

Okay, now let's confess that most of this has been pure speculation. At larger scales, though, we can return to scientifically solid ground, or at least reasonably scientific speculation. So now let's move forward to the remote future, the rest of time. At scales beyond those of human history we return to slower and simpler processes—such as the evolution of the Earth, the Sun, and the Universe. And these processes we can discuss with a bit more confidence.

So let me go through some of the predictions we can make—first, about the geography of the Earth. Studying the movement of tectonic plates is something that we can now do with great precision. Using satellites we can tell exactly how fast plates are moving and exactly in what direction. So these studies hint at what the Earth may look like in 100 or 200 million years, and there are some things we can say. The Atlantic will widen and the Pacific will narrow, bringing Asia and North America together, and eventually a new supercontinent will emerge.

Remember, we've seen in the last billion years supercontinents were formed at least twice, Rodinia perhaps 600 or 700 million years ago, and Pangaea about 200 to 250 million years ago. So eventually a new supercontinent will emerge. As it does so, Los Angeles will slide north, and it will become part of Canada. This will be a world that will look very different from the world of today.

What of the future of our Earth? Our Sun, we've seen, is about halfway through its life. In 3 to 4 billion years the Sun will run out of hydrogen, and then it'll collapse in on itself. As it does so, it'll generate much higher temperatures in its core, and it will expand again to form a "red giant." It'll be much larger than it is at the present, and it will include Mercury and Venus, and the Earth will be sterilized of life, and the oceans will boil away. There'll be no more life on Earth. We should certainly have gotten out by then.

Eventually, when the Sun has burned up all the helium in its core, it'll collapse again. Temperatures will rise once more, and they'll become much higher than they were even in the helium-burning era, and the Sun will get larger than it was before. This time it'll reach the Earth's outer orbit, and our

Earth will be evaporated. By then we need to have seriously gotten out of the inner solar system, and preferably out of our solar system.

Then what will happen? The Sun will expel its outer layers, and what is left will cool down and shrink. It'll become a "black dwarf." It'll be a retired star, an ex-star. And now, what'll it do? In its retirement it will do nothing but keep cooling for countless billions of years. It won't shine any longer; it won't do anything useful for its surroundings. That's the fate of our Sun.

And the future of our galaxy? Well, we can say something even about the future of the "Milky Way." The Milky Way is on a collision course with its neighbor, the Andromeda galaxy. And at about the time that our Sun enters its death throes, the two galaxies will collide. What will happen? Well, it's not going to be a violent collision; they will glide gracefully through each other—though gravity will introduce some turbulence as they do so, but we won't be around to see the spectacular night skies that that will produce.

And finally, the Universe: What is the fate of the Universe? We've seen the beginning of the story; do we have any idea about the end? Actually, cosmologists have some reasonably clear ideas about what is possible. One idea was very popular in the late 20th century, and it was this: It was that all the matter in the Universe and all the energy in the Universe we've seen exert a gravitational pull. So the idea was that this gravitational pull would eventually be so powerful that it would slow down the expansion of the Universe, and there'd come a time when the expansion would slow, grind to a halt, and eventually the Universe would start shrinking again—rather like a vast solar nebula that includes the entire Universe.

Stephen Hawking—perhaps slightly with tongue in cheek—argued that at that point, time might start reversing, and all sorts of processes will go into reverse. So the Universe will start shrinking—over many billions of years it will shrink until eventually it will shrink away to nothing. This will be the "big crunch," as opposed to the "big bang." What will happen then? Well, now here things do get seriously speculative, but many scientists have seriously speculated that out of the big crunch might come another big bang.

So this is the scenario of bouncing Universes. Universes appear, they expand, then they contract again into nothing, and then they expand again. And perhaps there's a sort of larger "Multiverse" that is full of these expanding Universes.

But since the late 1990s, cosmologists have learned that the rate of expansion of the Universe is actually increasing—it's not slowing. We don't clearly know why. But what this suggests is that the more likely scenario is that the Universe will keep expanding forever and ever. Now, what will that mean?

Well, here are some of the things that will happen. Eventually every star in the Universe will have used up its fuel and died; they'll all be retired. The Universe will darken. Over countless billions of years, black holes will graze on the remaining bits of matter. And when I say "countless billions of years," I'm talking about gazillions of billions of years. I said earlier we can imagine in the Universe that there are as many stars as there are sand grains on all the deserts and beaches of the Earth. Well, now start thinking that many billions of years in the future.

The Universe will keep expanding; the space between remaining objects will increase. Temperature differentials will narrow. With smaller energy differentials—there are no stars, for example—to drive complexity, the Universe will become simpler and more boring. Any complex things will slowly simplify; the Universe as a whole will become simpler.

The second law of thermodynamics will have triumphed over complexity. And this is what was known in the 19th century as the "heat death" of the Universe. And what will happen next? Well, the Universe will continue to get more and more uninteresting for as many billions of years as there are sand grains on all the beaches and deserts of the Earth—and so on, forever and ever.

Where does that leave you and me? What's our place in this huge story? The last lecture in this course will touch on some of these large issues of meaning, and it will also briefly recapitulate the story of big history.

Thank you.

Big History—Humans in the Cosmos
Lecture 48

> Agriculture appeared about 10,000 or 11,000 years ago. Before the
> appearance of agriculture, all human beings were foragers.

I f asked (perhaps around a campfire) to explain how everything got to be
the way it is, how might we respond? Let's begin with human history. We
live in the largest and most complex human community ever created. Six
billion humans, often in conflict with each other, are linked through trade,
travel, and modern forms of communications into a single global community.
This community was created in just a few hundred years. About 300 years
ago, human beings crossed a sort of threshold as human societies became
more interconnected and began to innovate faster than ever before. For 5,000
years before this, most people had lived in the large, powerful communities
we call "Agrarian civilizations." They had cities with magnificent
architecture and powerful rulers sustained by large populations of peasants
who produced most of society's resources. Innovation was slower, so history
moved more slowly, and there were fewer people than today. Two thousand
years ago, there were about 250 million people on Earth.

The first Agrarian civilizations appeared in regions such as Mesopotamia,
Egypt, and China. During the previous 5,000 years, humans had increasingly
lived in small peasant villages governed by local chiefs. Yet many still lived
by foraging, gathering what they needed as they migrated through their
home territories. The appearance of agriculture, just over 10,000 years ago,
counts as a fundamental historical threshold because agriculture increased
the amount of resources humans could extract from a given area. By doing
so, it stimulated population growth and innovation and laid the foundations
for the first Agrarian civilizations.

In the preceding 200,000 to 300,000 years, all humans had lived as foragers,
in nomadic, family-sized communities. Slowly, they spread through Africa
and around the world. For most of this time, humans were only slightly more
numerous than our close relatives, the great apes, are today. Our species,
Homo sapiens, appeared about 200,000 to 300,000 years ago somewhere in

Africa. What made them different from all other animals, and enabled them to explore so many different environments, was their remarkable ability to exchange and store information about their environments. Humans could talk to each other, they could tell stories, and unlike any other animals, they could ask about the meaning of existence! Their appearance counts as a fundamental threshold in our story.

To understand how the first humans appeared, we must survey the history of life on Earth. Like all other species, our ancestors evolved by natural selection. They evolved from intelligent, bipedal, ape-like ancestors known as "hominines" that had appeared about 6 million years earlier. The hominines were descended from primates: tree-dwelling mammals with large brains and dexterous hands that had first appeared about 65 million years ago.

The mammals were furry, warm-blooded animals that had first evolved about 250 million years ago. They were descended from large creatures with backbones, whose ancestors had left the seas to live on the land about 400 million years ago. These were descended from the first multi-celled organisms, which appeared about 600 million years ago in the Cambrian era.

During the preceding 3 billion years, all living organisms on Earth were single-celled. The first living organisms had appeared by about 3.8 billion years ago, just 700 million years after the formation of our Earth. They were the ancestors of all living creatures on today's Earth. The speed with which they appeared suggests that life is likely to appear wherever there are planets bathed in the light and energy of nearby stars but far enough away for liquid water to form. The appearance of life is one of the most important thresholds in the big history story.

Life could evolve only after the crossing of three earlier thresholds: the creation of planets, stars, and chemical elements. Our Earth was formed about 4.5 billion years ago, along with all the other planets, moons, and asteroids and comets of our solar system, from the debris formed as our Sun was created. Solar systems probably formed countless billions of times in the history of the Universe.

Our planet, like the living organisms that inhabit it, is made up of many different chemical elements, so neither could have formed if the chemical elements had not been manufactured in the violent death throes of large stars (in supernovae) or in the last dying days of other stars. The earliest stars may have died within a billion years of the creation of the Universe. Since then, billions upon billions of stars have died and scattered new elements into interstellar space. The first stars were born, like our Sun, from collapsing clouds of gas within about 200 million years of the big bang. Today, there may be more stars than there are grains of sand on all the beaches and deserts of our Earth. And that takes us back to the beginning. Our Universe began as a tiny, hot, expanding ball of something popped out of nothingness like an explosion about 13.7 billion years ago. The explosion has continued ever since, and we are part of the debris it has created.

Trying to imagine the long, drawn-out death of our Universe suggests that we may live in the most exciting era of the Universe's history.

The story told in this course is our best shot at explaining origins of all kinds. Like all origin stories, it is far from perfect and will change in the future. Important details, including the date of the big bang, have been clarified in the last decade or two. Here are some other possible areas in which the story may change. Cosmologists will keep pushing back their understanding of the origins of the Universe. The holy grail will be a theory explaining *why* the Universe popped out of nothing, or perhaps *what* it popped out of. Cosmologists will try to understand "dark matter" and "dark energy." Biologists will acquire a better understanding of the origins of life on Earth (and perhaps elsewhere).

Anthropologists will seek new evidence on the origins of our species. To do this they will have to invest more time and energy in the archaeology of Africa in the Paleolithic period and improve their understanding of the evolution of symbolic language and collective learning. Genetic dating techniques will allow us to track human migrations with much greater precision. We also need an improved interdisciplinary understanding of complexity that can illuminate our understanding both of stars and of modern human societies and can tease out the many links between different types of complexity.

Despite the limitations of any account of big history, the story is one we need to know and tell. Telling it backward is a good way of showing how such stories can help us map ourselves onto the cosmos. We see how the modern world fits into the larger story of human history, how human history fits into the history of life on Earth, and how these stories fit into the largest story of all—that of the Universe as a whole. Like the different parts of a Russian matryoshka doll, each story is nested in and helps explain the stories surrounding it. This sort of "mapping" is closely linked to our sense of meaning. Scientists are usually reluctant to discuss meanings and prefer to concentrate on getting the story right. But as symbolic beings, most of us have to look for meaning in any universal story. So what meanings may be hidden within big history?

The suggestions that follow are personal answers prompted by teaching big history for almost 20 years. Trying to imagine the long, drawn-out death of our Universe suggests that we may live in the most exciting era of the Universe's history: its springtime, when there existed the perfect balance of energy and space to make complex things such as ourselves. We have also seen that the societies we live in today may represent the most complex structures in our part of the galaxy. Can our Universe create more complex structures? Either way, our extraordinary complexity makes us rather interesting!

We are also the only creatures we know of that are capable of seeking meaning and purpose in the Universe. In the scientific view of the Universe, in which there is no deity or conscious creator, that means that we become the Universe's bearers of purpose and meaning. It is, after all, awe-inspiring to think that blind algorithmic processes might have successfully created an organism clever enough to figure out how those blind algorithmic processes created an entire Universe!

And that's where we'll end! I hope you have enjoyed this telling of our modern creation story, and I hope you will want to encourage others to become acquainted with it. If they are young enough, they may be the ones who will help construct a new and perhaps better story in the future. ■

Christian, *Maps of Time*, 497–99 (a brief synopsis of the modern creation story).

Christian, "World History in Context."

1. What do you regard as the most important themes of the modern creation story?

2. Does the modern creation story carry ethical baggage like all earlier creation stories?

Big History—Humans in the Cosmos
Lecture 48—Transcript

Early in this course I said that one way of thinking about big history might be to imagine a community of people, old and young, around a campfire. As I say this, I'm actually thinking of some wonderful holidays that my wife and I spent with our children and friends of ours who also had children. And we spent them at a lake in Australia, north of Sydney. Each evening we would build a fire, and because all children are natural pyromaniacs, we would sit around it till late at night, and they'd poke sticks into it. And eventually we could look up and see a wonderful starlit southern-hemisphere sky. I'm sure you can think of similar occasions. And it's not at all hard to imagine that most people perhaps throughout most of human history have had similar experiences.

Now, we can imagine that the youngest people in the group start asking questions, they start asking questions about the meaning of life and about where things come from. So they say: "Why are there so many people in the world?" for example—or, "How big is the world really?" And imagine that we try to give them the best and most intelligent answers we can. Our answers might take the form of the story we've been following throughout this course, but played in reverse. So here's how it might sound if I told this to an adult audience.

Let's begin with human history. Today's society is the largest and by far the most complex human society that has ever existed. Today there are more than 6 billion humans. And though they live in distinct societies with different states that are often in conflict with each other, all these communities are linked through trade, travel, and modern forms of communication into a single global community.

This modern global community, which is the world we live in today, was created very recently, just during the last 300 years. About 300 or 400 years ago, human beings—initially in some parts of the world and then eventually throughout the world—crossed a sort of threshold. Human societies became more interconnected, and as commerce was becoming more important than ever before, people in some regions began to innovate faster than ever before.

Now, these changes are often described as the "Industrial Revolution." What they did was to lay the foundations for today's vast and rapidly changing societies by suddenly introducing a whole new wave of new ways of dealing with the environment and getting energy.

For several thousand years before this, most people had lived in the large, powerful communities that we describe as "agrarian civilizations." They had cities with magnificent monumental architecture. They had powerful rulers. And these state systems were sustained by large populations of peasants who lived in the countryside and produced most of society's resources. Innovation was much slower than today, and that's why things tended to change much more slowly. The pace of history was slower. And there were far fewer people than today. Two thousand years ago, for example, there were probably only about 250 million people on Earth.

Where did the agrarian civilizations come from? Well, the first agrarian civilizations appeared in regions such as Mesopotamia, Egypt, and China. And they appeared about 5,000 years ago. During the previous 5,000 years, an increasing number of humans lived in small, relatively independent communities of small farmers that were governed by local chiefs. But there also existed many people who lived not by farming, but by foraging—that is to say, by gathering the resources they needed as they migrated through their territories.

Agriculture appeared about 10,000 or 11,000 years ago. Before the appearance of agriculture, all human beings were foragers. They all lived like foragers (or hunter-gatherers). What agriculture did was to greatly increase the amount of resources that human communities could extract from a given area. And the result was it led to rapid population growth, and eventually that led to the creation of the very large human communities that were the first agrarian civilizations. So that's why the appearance of agriculture counts as the most important threshold in history before the appearance of the modern world.

For the 200,000 years or so before agriculture, all humans had lived as foragers. That means they lived in small, family-sized nomadic communities of perhaps less than 50 people for the most part, sometimes with links with their neighbors. For most of this time, there were very few humans on Earth, probably little more than the numbers of great apes in the world today. So that's a period of about 200,000 years.

The first members of our species, *Homo sapiens*, appeared about 200,000 to 300,000 years ago. We don't know exactly when, but we're pretty sure they appeared somewhere in Africa. Their appearance counts as the most important threshold before the appearance of agriculture. What made these first humans different from all other animals and what accounted for their ability to explore so many different environments was their ability to exchange and store information about their environments.

Humans could talk to each other. And they could exchange information with a speed and efficiency that no other animal could match. And that means they could store information. In addition, unlike any other animals, they could ask about the meaning of existence. Humans were probably storytellers from the very beginning of their history.

Now that's a brief history of how human societies developed into the remarkable global community of today. But how were the first human societies created? Humans after all are living organisms. So to explore the origin of humans, of our species, we must describe the history of living organisms. And that's the next stage in this story.

Our species evolved in the same way as all other species, by natural selection: Tiny changes in the average qualities of each community slowly accumulated over many generations, until the nature of each species slowly changes. And this is the process that created the huge variety of species today. Our ancestors evolved from highly intelligent bipedal ape-like ancestors known as hominines. The first hominines appeared about 6 million years before the appearance of *Homo sapiens*, our species.

The hominines, in turn, were descended from the mammals known as primates. They were related most closely of all to the great apes, such as the chimpanzees and gorillas. The primates as a group were tree-dwelling mammals, they had large brains, they had dexterous hands, and they had stereoscopic vision. These are all the things you need to live in trees. And as a group, they had appeared about 65 million years ago.

The primates were mammals. Mammals were a type of animal that had first evolved about 250 million years ago. The mammals, in turn, were descended from large creatures with backbones whose ancestors had learned to live on the land about 400 million years ago. All amphibians and reptiles are also descended from these ancestors.

Large multi-celled organisms—like ourselves—had only been around since about 600 million years ago. That's the first time—during the so-called Cambrian era—that you get very large animals made up of billions of individual cells. Before that, all living organisms on Earth were single-celled. Most would have been invisible to a human eye. The first living organisms on this planet seem to have appeared as early as 3.8 billion years ago. That's just 700 million years after the formation of our Earth. They were the remote ancestors of all living creatures on Earth today, including you and me.

What's remarkable is the speed with which they appeared, just 700 million years after the creation of our planet—and our early planet was not a very hospitable place for life. So the speed with which they appeared suggests that life is likely to appear in our Universe wherever the conditions are right, and that means wherever we find planets that are bathed in the light from nearby stars, but far enough away for liquid water to form—because water in liquid form provides an ideal environment for complex chemical reactions like those that formed living organisms.

The other crucial ingredient, of course, is a rich mixture of chemicals. So it seems that wherever you get a hospitable environment for life in our Universe, it's very probable that life will appear. So the formation of life itself as we move back in time is the next most important threshold before the appearance of our species, though we've also seen lots of minor thresholds as life evolved.

Life, in turn, was only possible where the conditions were right. So to understand the appearance of life, we need to understand the appearance of planets, of stars, and of chemical elements. That takes us to the history of geology and into astronomy.

Our Earth was formed about 4.5 billion years ago. And it was formed along with all the other planets, moons, and asteroids and comets of our solar system. All of them were formed as a byproduct of the processes that created our Sun. What happened was that debris—leftover bits and pieces, if you like—orbiting the Sun smashed together within the Earth's orbit and slowly accumulated into larger and larger lumps until eventually they all aggregated into a single large lump, which was our early planet.

The formation of our planet, therefore, is the next important threshold in our story as we move back in time. Now, how common was this process? Well, solar systems may have formed countless billions of times in the history of the Universe. But this happens to be the only solar system whose origins we know much about at present.

Our planet, like the living organisms that inhabit it, is made up of many different chemical elements. In fact, in our body, you can probably find traces of elements from across the periodic table. So neither our planet, neither our Earth, nor you and me could have been formed if the chemical elements had not been manufactured. They were manufactured in the violent death throes of large stars, in supernovae, or in the dying days of other stars.

We don't know when the first stars died and scattered new elements into space. But it's very probable that it happened within 1 billion years of the creation of the Universe. So this new threshold, the creation of chemical elements, takes us back more than 12 billion years, close to the beginnings of the Universe.

Since then, billions upon billions of stars have died, scattering new elements into interstellar space. Now obviously, stars could not have died if stars had not been born. Stars were born—like our Sun—as clouds of gas, clouds of matter collapsing under the pressure of gravity heated up in their centers until eventually hydrogen began to fuse, and at that point they lit up. They turned into stars. Star formation has continued ever since the first stars appeared—that's why, as I said in an earlier lecture, there are probably more stars in the Universe than there are grains of sand on all the beaches and deserts of our Earth.

The first stars may have been formed more than 13 billion years ago—quite soon, within 200 or 300 million years of the origins of our Universe. So as we move back in time, the creation of stars counts as one more great turning point in the story. So we've looked at human societies, life, the creation of planets and stars. And that takes us back to the beginning.

Obviously nothing could have existed if the Universe itself had not been created. The Universe, we now know, was created about 13.7 billion years ago. Stars were formed from great clouds of hydrogen and helium atoms— which, like the force of gravity itself, were created at the moment of the creation of our Universe. This is the first turning point of all, the first threshold of all—and in many ways it's the most mysterious. Our Universe began as a tiny, hot, expanding ball of *something* that popped out of nothingness like an explosion—and the explosion, which cosmologists call the big bang, has continued ever since. You and I and the planet we live on are simply part of the debris. That's the very beginning of the story. And we can't go further back in time.

So that's a quick summary of the story we've told in this course. The story I've just told is a highly condensed summary of the best modern scientific attempts to understand origins, to understand how everything around us was created. It's our best shot at explaining origins—just as every traditional creation story also represented the best attempt, given the available knowledge, to answer all the fundamental questions about origins.

Now, it needs to be said that the story told in this course, that I've just summarized, is far from perfect. Like all previous creation stories, it will be eventually superseded. Indeed, important details have changed or been clarified just in the decade or two since I began teaching big history. When I started teaching, for example, the best date available for the origins of the Universe was somewhere vaguely between 10 and 20 billion years ago. Now, I have to say as a teacher it's much more satisfying to be able to say to students: 13.7 billion years ago, rather than vaguely between 10 and 20 billion years ago. At that time, no planets had been detected beyond our solar system. We still had no certainty that planets existed anywhere else in the Universe. We now know that they do. And genetic dating techniques were just beginning to revolutionize the study of human evolution. We've seen that those techniques have completely changed our sense of the timing of human evolution.

Especially exciting at the moment is the use of genetic comparisons to track human migrations in recent millennia. Perhaps in 10 years' time, if I'm still teaching this course, we'll be able to describe these migrations in much more detail even for times when we have no written records. Within decades, the story I've told will also undergo pretty significant renovation. Where? Well, here is just a preliminary list of some of the areas in the story where we might expect to see significant changes.

Cosmologists will continue to try to push back their understanding of the origins of the Universe. At the moment, they're within a fraction of a second of the origins of the moment of creation. But they're going to push the story back. The holy grail will be a theory that explains why the Universe popped out of nothing, or perhaps that explains what it popped out of. At the moment, it has to be said, there are lots of theories, lots of ideas, but the main problem is finding evidence that could test them.

Cosmologists will also look for better understanding of the significance of dark matter and dark energy. Now, you may remember when we talked about star formation. Astronomers and cosmologists are pretty confident that we know a lot about the Universe. But they also know—and this is a kind of deep, dark secret of astronomy—that there's a lot of stuff out there that they don't understand anything about. They know it's there, because it's clearly exerting a powerful gravitational pull. And you can detect it by the movements of galaxies and clusters of galaxies. And the pull is powerful enough that this stuff may make up 95% of the stuff, the matter, and the energy in the Universe. But we have no idea what it is. Now, that's extremely odd. And if the problem is solved, say within the next 10 or 20 years, it could revolutionize our understanding of cosmology, and it could end up changing quite a few of the details of the story as I've told it.

Another area where there may be significant breakthroughs is the understanding of the origins of life on Earth. Now, here it's probably as if we're very close, and we're going to just fill in some final pieces of a puzzle. At present it looks as if we have most of the story, most of the jigsaw, and we're just looking for the last pieces. And the last pieces will probably tell us how DNA evolved, and how the very elaborate and precise mechanism of reproduction that's present in all living organisms today itself evolved.

When it comes to human evolution, anthropologists will seek new evidence on the origins of our own species. The early stages of our species' history are still a bit fuzzy, and what we need above all is more data from Africa, more archaeological data above all. So this story may get clearer, particularly if archaeologists do more work in Africa, where our species evolved.

Another area that could add a lot to our understanding of human evolution is a better understanding of how symbolic language evolved. And that will probably come from studies in neuropsychology, understanding the brain, and theory of language—and that would contribute a lot to our understanding of how our species evolved and why language played such a crucial role in our history.

But finally, and this is a problem that appears particularly clearly within a course on big history, we need a better understanding of complexity. Complexity, we've seen, is an issue that crosses all the disciplines touched on in this course. It's something that's approached in different ways within different disciplines; mathematicians approach it in one way, and sociologists approach it another way. But what we really need is an understanding of complexity that crosses all of these disciplines and that can simultaneously illuminate our understanding of stars and of modern human societies, and that can also show the many links between these different types of complexity.

This is one of those fields where the fragmentation of modern knowledge seems to be the main barrier. There are plenty of ideas there, and what we really need to do is bring them together into a coherent transdisciplinary understanding of what complexity means across all these disciplines. And that's an area where big history itself may have a significant contribution to make.

So the story we've told has limitations. Nevertheless, it's a story we really need to know. In fact, telling it backwards, as I've just done, is a pretty good way of showing how such stories can provide meaning. They provide meaning by providing sort of maps of time and space. Telling the story backwards shows how the modern world of humanity fits into the larger story of human history; how human history, in turn, fits into the larger story of the history of life; and how all these stories fit into the largest story of all, that of the Universe as a whole.

Like the different parts of a Russian matryoshka doll—you remember these dolls, you have a tiny doll in the center that is in a slightly larger doll, in a slightly larger doll, and so on—each of these stories is nested in a larger story. And each of the stories can help illuminate the stories both at larger and at smaller scales. So each part of this story can illuminate the other parts of it. And in this way, what these stories can do, these collections of stories, is help each of us identify our place within time and space, our place within the space-time of our Universe. And knowing where we fit in—in other words, mapping ourselves onto space-time—already tells us a lot about who we are.

So this story, even if we think of it simply as a sort of mapping, is full of meaning. Are there other meanings in it? Well, scientists are for the most part reluctant to look for the meanings of the stories they tell. Most scientists just want to get the story right and let other people worry about its meaning.

But of course for ordinary human beings, for you and me, it's impossible not to look for meaning. Indeed, our need for meaning may be closely related to our ability to think symbolically, and to use symbolic language, and to exchange ideas with each other. The very idea of meaning is symbolic—and that means there's very good reason to think that chimps, however clever they may be, don't seek out meaning in their Universe. Chimps just deal with the Universe. We try to seek out meaning.

I've suggested that the map of space and time provided by big history is the first form of meaning that this story offers. But what other forms of meaning can we find? Now here I'm sort of going to go a bit beyond what most scientists would say and offer an answer that has to count as largely personal, and it's based on 20 years of teaching big history and also responding to the questions of my students.

So here's one possible meaning. Think of the story I told in the last lecture, of the eventual death by tedium of our Universe. That story suggests something very interesting about the time in the Universe's history when we're alive. What it suggests is that we live at perhaps the most exciting and interesting period in the Universe's history. We live in a sort of springtime of our Universe. We live in a period when there existed the perfect balance of energy, space, and stuff to make complex things, such as ourselves.

There's lots of energy in the Universe. There's also lots of space. There's not *too* much energy, so you can create complex things. Eventually in the future it'll be impossible. In the very early Universe, everything was too violent to create complex things. So that's one form of meaning. It tells us about the period of the Universe's history that we live in.

Now here's a second possible meaning lurking within the story. We saw in a very early lecture that humans seem tiny on the scales of space and time. But we've also seen since that modern human society may be in some sense the most complex thing we know. Indeed, we've hinted at the possibility that it may be the most complex thing to be found within our galaxy. So how complex is complex?

Are we perhaps the most complex thing in the Milky Way? Strictly, is modern human society the most complex thing in the Milky Way? Now, there's a powerful reason for saying this may be true. And the main reason is that despite searching for signs of extraterrestrial life for several decades through the SETI project, the Search for Extra-Terrestrial Intelligence, no signs have been found. If intelligent life—or to be more precise, life capable of "collective learning"—is fairly common in the Universe, then that is distinctly odd.

If intelligent civilizations that adapt through collective learning are common, there ought to be many—perhaps millions—in our galaxy, and lots of them in our part of the galaxy. And surely many of them are likely to be much more sophisticated than us, with much more powerful means of communication and transmission of signals, for example. Yet our civilization is already pumping episodes of *I Love Lucy* out into the cosmos.

If we're already doing it, we should expect that at least some of the others would be indiscreet enough to have been pumping similar signals out into space for much longer and in much greater quantities. But so far we haven't picked up a thing, zilch. So that may suggest that we are alone. We represent a sort of pinnacle of complexity. So, does modern human society—this astonishing product of just the last few centuries in our corner of the Universe—represent perhaps the most complex thing in our part of the galaxy, or in the galaxy as a whole? Well, if so, it makes us rather interesting.

Now, here's a third possible meaning within the story we've seen. We're not just the most complex things we know of so far. We're also the only creatures we know of that are capable of seeking meaning and purpose in the Universe, of looking for meaning. In the scientific view of the Universe we've seen, there is no deity and no conscious creator—and that means that we become the Universe's bearers of conscious purpose and meaning. Modern science rejects the idea of a creator deity or deities—so it's left with the vision of a Universe constructed by blind natural laws that when repeated over and over again, billions of times, can slowly construct very complex and interesting things. But it's all done without purpose, just because that's the way things are.

Now, this is an astonishing image of the Universe itself. And for many people it's also a quite satisfying one. But there's something even more astonishing about it. Out of these apparently blind algorithmic processes repeated billions of times over billions of years, there has emerged at least once in the Universe a group of beings that do have a sense of purpose and do want a sense of meaning. Indeed, beings that have the astonishing ability to figure out how and when the Universe was created. We can easily take it for granted, but if you think about it, it's an astonishing achievement. These are beings who can construct a history of the entire Universe. So we are, in a sense, the eyes and ears of the Universe—its way of knowing itself.

And that's where we'll end. I hope you've enjoyed this telling of our modern creation story, our modern scientific creation story. And I hope you will want to encourage others to become acquainted with it. If they're young enough, they may be the ones who will eventually help construct a new and perhaps better story in the future.

Thank you.

The Scale of the Cosmos: 13.7 Billion Years

Big Bang
Release of cosmic background radiation
First stars and galaxies
First supernovae create new elements

BILLIONS OF YEARS BEFORE PRESENT

13
12
11
10
9
8
7
6
5 — Sun, Earth, solar system formed
4 — Earliest life on Earth?
— First evidence of photosynthesis
3 — Oxygen in atmosphere begins to increase
2 — First eukaryotic organisms
1 — First multi-cellular organisms
0 — Dinosaurs extinct

Timeline

398

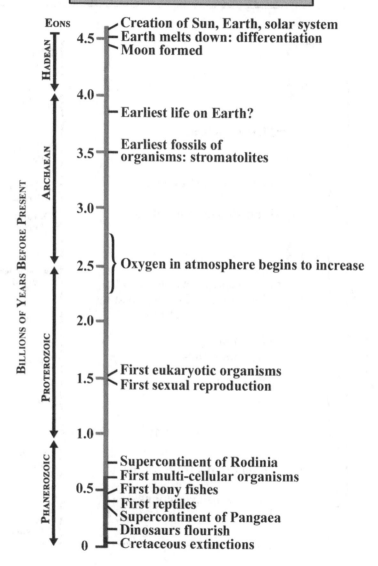

The Scale of the Earth: 4.5 Billion Years

BILLIONS OF YEARS BEFORE PRESENT

EONS

HADEAN
4.5 — Creation of Sun, Earth, solar system
Earth melts down: differentiation
Moon formed

4.0 —

ARCHAEAN
Earliest life on Earth?

3.5 — Earliest fossils of organisms: stromatolites

3.0 —

2.5 — Oxygen in atmosphere begins to increase

2.0 —

PROTEROZOIC

1.5 — First eukaryotic organisms
First sexual reproduction

1.0 —

PHANEROZOIC
Supercontinent of Rodinia
First multi-cellular organisms
0.5 — First bony fishes
First reptiles
Supercontinent of Pangaea
Dinosaurs flourish
0 — Cretaceous extinctions

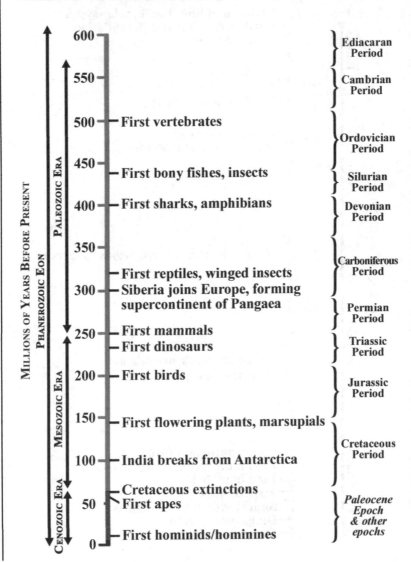

The Scale of Multi-cellular Organisms: 600 Million Years

MILLIONS OF YEARS BEFORE PRESENT

PHANEROZOIC EON

PALEOZOIC ERA

MESOZOIC ERA

CENOZOIC ERA

600		Ediacaran Period
550		Cambrian Period
500	First vertebrates	Ordovician Period
450	First bony fishes, insects	Silurian Period
400	First sharks, amphibians	Devonian Period
350		Carboniferous Period
300	First reptiles, winged insects / Siberia joins Europe, forming supercontinent of Pangaea	Permian Period
250	First mammals / First dinosaurs	Triassic Period
200	First birds	Jurassic Period
150	First flowering plants, marsupials	Cretaceous Period
100	India breaks from Antarctica	
50	Cretaceous extinctions / First apes	Paleocene Epoch & other epochs
0	First hominids/hominines	

Timeline

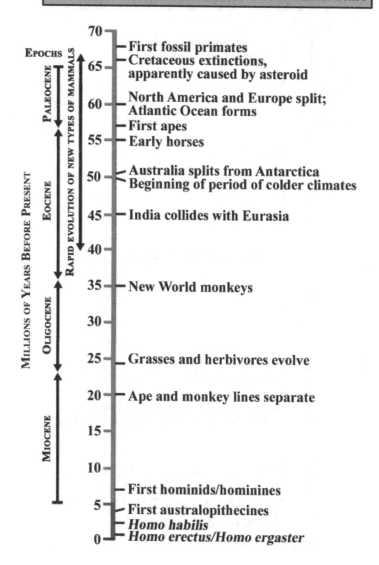

The Scale of Mammalian Evolution: 70 Million Years

EPOCHS

PALEOCENE

EOCENE

OLIGOCENE

MIOCENE

MILLIONS OF YEARS BEFORE PRESENT

RAPID EVOLUTION OF NEW TYPES OF MAMMALS

70 — First fossil primates
65 — Cretaceous extinctions, apparently caused by asteroid
60 — North America and Europe split; Atlantic Ocean forms
— First apes
55 — Early horses
50 — Australia splits from Antarctica
Beginning of period of colder climates
45 — India collides with Eurasia
40
35 — New World monkeys
30
25 — Grasses and herbivores evolve
20 — Ape and monkey lines separate
15
10
— First hominids/hominines
5 — First australopithecines
Homo habilis
0 — *Homo erectus/Homo ergaster*

The Scale of Human Evolution: 7 Million Years

EPOCHS

MILLIONS OF YEARS BEFORE PRESENT

MIOCENE

PLIOCENE

PLEISTOCENE

7 — Earliest remains of bipedal hominine

6 —

5 —

4 — *Ardipithecus ramidus*

First australopithecines

3 —

2 — *Homo habilis*

Homo erectus/Homo ergaster
First hominine migrations to southern Eurasia

1 — Australopithecines and *Homo habilis* extinct

Neanderthals and *Homo sapiens*
Beginning of last ice age

0 — Neanderthals and *Homo erectus* extinct

Timeline

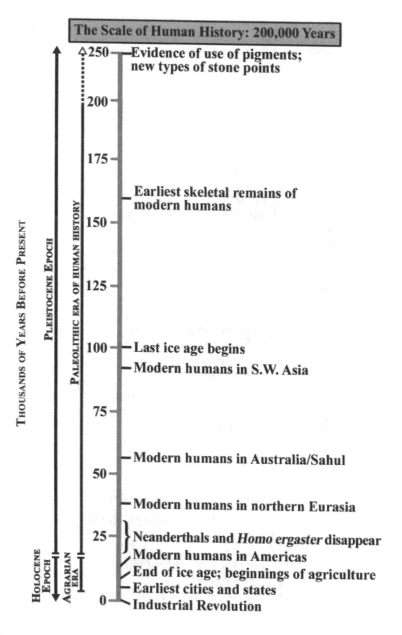

The Scale of Human History: 200,000 Years

THOUSANDS OF YEARS BEFORE PRESENT

PLEISTOCENE EPOCH

PALEOLITHIC ERA OF HUMAN HISTORY

HOLOCENE EPOCH

AGRARIAN ERA

250 — Evidence of use of pigments; new types of stone points

200

175

Earliest skeletal remains of modern humans

150

125

100 — Last ice age begins

— Modern humans in S.W. Asia

75

Modern humans in Australia/Sahul

50

Modern humans in northern Eurasia

25 — } Neanderthals and *Homo ergaster* disappear

Modern humans in Americas

End of ice age; beginnings of agriculture

Earliest cities and states

0 — Industrial Revolution

The Scale of Agrarian Societies: 10,000 Years

THOUSANDS OF YEARS BEFORE PRESENT

- End of ice age
- 11
- Earliest evidence of agriculture in S.W. Asia
- 10
- Earliest evidence of agriculture in S.E. Asia
- 9
- 8
- 7
- Evidence of pastoralism in Russia/Ukraine/Kazakhstan
- 6
- Evidence of agriculture in Americas
- 5 — First cities and city-states
- First empires
- 4
- 3
- First superempire (Persia)
- 2 — Foundation of world religions
- 1 — Largest pastoralist empire (Genghis Khan)
- 0 — Industrial Revolution

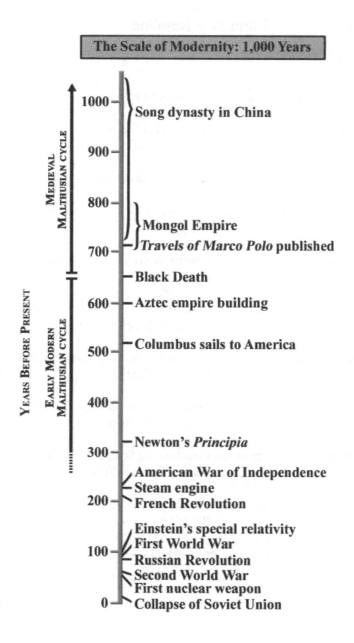

The Scale of Modernity: 1,000 Years

YEARS BEFORE PRESENT

MEDIEVAL MALTHUSIAN CYCLE

EARLY MODERN MALTHUSIAN CYCLE

1000 — Song dynasty in China

900 —

800 —

700 — } Mongol Empire
Travels of Marco Polo published

— Black Death

600 — — Aztec empire building

500 — — Columbus sails to America

400 —

300 — — Newton's *Principia*

— American War of Independence
— Steam engine
200 — — French Revolution

— Einstein's special relativity
— First World War
100 — — Russian Revolution
— Second World War
— First nuclear weapon
0 — — Collapse of Soviet Union

Summary Timeline

13.7 billion years ago .... Origins of Universe.

380,000 years later .... Separation of energy and matter; cosmic background radiation.

200 million years later .... Appearance of first stars.

11–12 billion years ago (bya).......... First supernovae; appearance of new elements.

4.6 bya .... Creation of the Sun, solar system, and Earth.

c. 3.5 bya .... First life forms on Earth; single-celled "prokaryotes"; photosynthesis.

c. 2–3 bya .... Increase of oxygen in atmosphere due to photosynthesis.

c. 1.5 bya .... First complex or "eukaryotic" cells; sexual reproduction?

c. 600 million years ago (mya) .... Cambrian era; first surviving fossils of multi-celled organisms.

c. 500 mya .... First vertebrates; supercontinent of Rodinia breaking up.

c. 475 mya .... First organisms on land.

c. 350 mya .... First reptiles.

c. 250 mya .... First dinosaurs and first mammals; supercontinent of Pangaea.

c. 67 mya .... An asteroid impact destroys many species including dinosaurs.

c. 20 mya .... First apes.

c. 6 mya .... First "hominines" (bipedal apes).

c. 4 mya .... Australopithecines.

c. 2.3 mya .... *Homo habilis.*

c. 1.9 mya .... *Homo erectus* evolves in Africa, but some migrate to Asia.

200,000–300,000 years ago (ya) ..... *Homo sapiens* evolves somewhere in Africa.

100,000 ya .... Beginnings of last ice age.

40,000–50,000 ya .... Humans in Sahul (Australia/Papua New Guinea).

30,000–40,000 ya .... Humans in ice age Siberia.

13,000 ya .... Clear evidence of humans in Americas.

11,500 ya .... End of last ice age; first signs of agriculture.

6,000 ya .... Earliest evidence of pastoralism; domestication in Americas?

5,000 ya	First cities and states in N.W. Africa and S. Mesopotamia.
4,000 ya	First multicity empires; cities and states in India and China.
2,500 ya	First superempire (Achaemenid Persia); first states in Americas?
2,000 ya	Roman, Parthian, Kushan, and Han Empires flourish.
800 ya	Mongol Empire, largest land empire ever created.
650 ya	Black Death.
500 ya	Different world zones linked by sea: Columbian exchange.
300 ya	Scientific Revolution.
200 ya	First industrial revolutions; first "democratic" revolutions.
100–50 ya	Western imperialism; First World War; anticolonial revolutions.
50 ya	First nuclear weapons.
0 ya	Rising consumption levels; serious damage to biosphere.
50 years from now (yfn)	Global populations stabilize?
4 billion yfn	Sun expands, destroying planets, before dying.

Summary Timeline

30 billion yfn.................................... Star formation ceases.

Many billion yfn .... Universe keeps expanding; stars die;
Universe cooler and simpler.

Glossary

Note: Though some of the terms defined below are widely used, some are used in specific senses in this course. All the definitions below refer to the ways that terms are used in this course.

absolute dates: Precise dates on a universal time scale, as opposed to relative dates, which merely give a date relative to the age of some other event.

accretion: The process by which planets were formed, as materials orbiting the young Sun gathered together through collisions or gravitational or electrostatic attraction into larger and larger bodies within each orbit.

acquired characteristics: Characteristics acquired by an organism during its lifetime and therefore not inherited by its offspring.

adaptation: One of the three fundamental features of living organisms; the capacity of living organisms to slowly change from generation to generation so as to maintain their ability to fit into their changing environments (see also *metabolism, reproduction*).

Afro-Eurasia: One of the four major "world zones"; it includes the linked African and Eurasian landmasses.

Agrarian civilizations: Large communities of hundreds of thousands or even millions of people, based on farming, with cities and tribute-taking states.

Agrarian era: One of the three great eras of human history; the era of human history in which most people lived as agriculturalists and most resources were generated through agriculture; roughly from c. 10,000 B.C.E. to c. 1700 C.E.

agriculture: A way of exploiting the environment by increasing the productivity of those plant and animal species most beneficial for human beings. A form of symbiosis, it generally results, over time, in genetic changes in the "domesticated" species. Agriculture is vastly more productive than foraging technologies. Its appearance marks a revolutionary transformation in human history.

allopatric speciation: An evolutionary pattern in which members of a population become separated from other members of their species long enough to diverge genetically, until eventually they can no longer breed with their parent species, and they form a separate species.

amino acids: Basic chemical constituents of all proteins, the basic building blocks of living organisms.

antimatter: Particles of matter with the opposite charge to the dominant forms of matter; thus, positrons are identical to electrons except that they have a positive charge. When particles of matter and antimatter meet, they annihilate each other. It is speculated that during the big bang vast amounts of matter were annihilated in this way, leaving a tiny residue from which our Universe was constructed.

apes: Large, tailless African monkeys, a group that includes humans; members of the primate superfamily of Hominoidea.

australopithecines: A group of hominine species with brains about the size of those of chimpanzees that flourished in Africa between 4 million and 1 million years ago.

axial age: A term first used by the philosopher and historian Karl Jaspers to refer to the era during the first millennium B.C.E. and early in the first millennium C.E. when most of the major "universal" religions emerged in Afro-Eurasia.

B.C.E.: Before the Common Era; the equivalent of "B.C."

big bang cosmology: The modern understanding of the origins of the Universe; first proposed in the 1930s but became the central idea (paradigm) of modern cosmology from the 1960s.

big history: The attempt to construct a unified account of the past at all scales from those of human history to those of cosmology; the modern, scientific equivalent of traditional creation stories; what this course is about!

big men: Anthropological term for powerful leaders in non-state societies, whose power rests mainly on their ability to accumulate and redistribute resources.

biosphere: The network of living organisms found near the surface of the Earth; the region of the Earth in which living organisms can be found (see *Gaia*).

bipedalism: Walking on two legs.

black holes: Regions in space of such high density that their gravitational pull does not even allow light to escape. Black holes can be formed by the collapse of large objects such as supernovae.

BP: Before present.

business cycle: A characteristic rhythm of expansion and contraction in capitalist societies, driven by overproduction and lack of markets.

Cambrian era: From c. 570–510 million years ago, the era in which the first large fossils appear; long thought to be the era in which life first appeared on Earth, though it is now known that single-celled organisms existed for several billion years before this.

capitalism: A type of society characterized by elite groups who generate incomes from entrepreneurial activity; a majority that generates income from wage-earning activity and exchanges on competitive markets; in Marxist thought, capitalism, though exploitative, generated higher rates of innovation than earlier social forms such as tribute-taking societies.

C.E.: Common Era; the equivalent of "A.D."

chemical evolution: Slow change in complex but nonliving chemicals, operating in a similar manner to natural selection and possibly leading to the creation of the first true living organisms.

chiefs: Anthropological term for powerful leaders in non-state societies whose power rests largely on their aristocratic birth, though they may also wield significant coercive power.

coevolution: When two species develop a close symbiotic relationship, evolutionary change in one species must be followed by evolutionary change in the other, so the two species begin to evolve together.

collective learning: The ability, unique to human beings, to share in great detail what each individual learns through symbolic language; collective learning may be the source of the unique technological creativity of our species.

collision margins: Tectonic margins where plates are driven together; either one plate dives beneath the other (as the Pacific plate is diving under South America), or both plates rise to form mountain chains at the borders between them (as in the Himalayas).

Columbian exchange: Term coined by Alfred Crosby for the exchange of diseases, crops, peoples, and goods that followed the linking of the different world zones after 1500 C.E.

complexity: Entities with many precisely linked internal components and novel "emergent" properties, whose survival depends on flows of free energy.

consumer capitalism: The most recent phase in the history of capitalism, in which productivity levels are so high that profits can only be realized by selling goods to the wageworkers who produce them; requires paying workers high enough wages to purchase and encouraging steadily raising average consumption levels. Consumer capitalism originated in the early 20th century and is typical of the wealthiest capitalist countries today.

contingency: The idea that many events (in history or the natural world) are random and unpredictable.

cosmic background radiation: Low energy radiation pervading the entire Universe, released c. 380,000 years after the big bang, when the Universe cooled sufficiently for neutral atoms to form so that energy and matter could separate; its discovery, in 1964, persuaded most cosmologists to accept the big bang theory.

cosmic evolution: A synonym for big history; history on all scales up to those of cosmology.

cosmology: Study of the history and evolution of the Universe.

creation stories: Stories found in all human societies about the origins of all things.

Cretaceous event: The term used to describe the asteroid impact about 67 million years ago that led to the extinction of many species, including the dinosaurs.

cuneiform: A type of writing, common in ancient Mesopotamia, in which symbols are made by pressing wedge-shaped cross sections of reeds into clay.

dark matter/dark energy: Studies of the movements of stars and galaxies have shown that there must exist much more energy and/or matter than we can observe; at present, astronomers have no idea what either dark energy or dark matter consist of; one of the great mysteries of contemporary astronomy.

determinism: The idea, common in the 19th century, that general laws determine the exact course of events so that if we had complete knowledge of reality we could, in theory, predict the future.

differentiation: The process by which, early in the Earth's history, the Earth melted to form a series of different layers, with the heaviest materials (mostly metals) in the core, lighter materials in the mantle, the lightest elements at the surface, and gassy materials in the atmosphere.

diffusion: The spread of ideas or innovations or people from a single center.

dissipative structures: Technical term used by Nobel Prize–winning chemist Ilya Prigogine to describe complex structures (such as stars or living organisms) that exist far from equilibrium and require flows of energy in order to survive; so-called because, by using free energy, they "dissipate" it, thereby increasing entropy.

divergent margins: Geological regions where tectonic plates are driven apart by upwelling magma; a modern example is the center of the Atlantic Ocean.

division of labor: Differentiation in human occupations so that different professions appear and individuals have to exchange goods and services in order to support themselves. There was very little division of labor in the Paleolithic era, but as populations and population densities increased in the Agrarian era the division of labor developed rapidly, generating greater social, economic, and political complexity.

DNA: Deoxyribonucleic acid, the complex, double-stranded molecule that carries genetic information in all living organisms on Earth.

domestication: Genetic modification of species by humans to make them more docile, more productive, and more amenable to human control; a form of symbiosis, in which domesticated species benefit from human protection.

Doppler effect: The stretching out or contraction of wavelengths because of the relative movement of two bodies; the Doppler effect explains why an ambulance siren seems higher when the ambulance is traveling toward you than when it is moving away; it also explains why the light from distant galaxies is displaced toward the red end of the spectrum if they are moving away from us. This is crucial evidence for the idea that our Universe is expanding.

Dreamtime: In indigenous Australian traditions this was the time of beginnings, of origins, and of the law.

early Agrarian era: The early part of the Agrarian era, which lasted, globally, from c. 8000 B.C.E. to c. 3000 B.C.E., though its dates vary in different regions; the 5,000-year-long era of human history during which there were Agrarian societies but no Agrarian civilizations, and the largest human communities were villages.

electromagnetism: One of the four fundamental forces of the physical Universe, responsible for holding positively and negatively charged particles (such as protons and electrons) together; the most important force in many chemical processes.

electrons: Negatively charged subatomic particles that orbit the nuclei of atoms.

elements (chemical): The basic constituents of chemical processes; each atomic element is defined by the number of protons in its nucleus, and elements are listed in the *periodic table*; chemical processes are dominated by the combination of different elements into larger "molecules"; only hydrogen and helium, the simplest elements (with, respectively, one and two protons in their nuclei), were created in the big bang; most other elements were created either in stars or in supernovae.

emergent properties: Properties of a complex entity that are not present within its component parts but emerge only when those parts are linked together in a particular configuration; an automobile has emergent properties that its parts lack when it is dismantled.

Enlightenment: Era of European intellectual history in the 18th century; a period of optimism about the beneficial achievements of science and the necessity of progress.

entrepreneurs: Those who make money primarily by producing, buying, and selling goods or services on competitive markets (distinguished from tribute-takers, who exact resources through the threat of force).

entropy: A measure of disorder; according to the second law of thermodynamics, in any closed system (including the Universe as a whole) the total level of entropy must slowly increase as energy is distributed more and more evenly and is therefore less and less capable of performing work.

eukaryotes: Cells more complex than prokaryotes, in which there are distinct "organelles" (such as *mitochondria*), and in which the genetic material is protected within the nucleus; many single-celled organisms are eukaryotic, and so are *all* multi-celled organisms; Lynn Margulis has shown that the first eukaryotes probably arose through a symbiotic merging of prokaryotic cells.

evolution: Change over time; applied most frequently to the evolution of living organisms according to the principles of natural selection, first discovered by Charles Darwin in the 19th century; does *not* necessarily mean change in the direction of a "higher," more "advanced," or more "progressive" state.

exchange networks: The networks through which humans exchange information, goods, styles, and even diseases.

extensification: An ugly word coined specifically for this course; it describes processes of innovation and growth that lead to more extensive settlement without leading to increase in the size of individual human communities; extensification was the characteristic form of growth in the Paleolithic era; the opposite of *intensification*.

extinctions: There have been several episodes in the Earth's history in which large numbers of species have suddenly become extinct; we are living through such an episode now, and its main cause appears to be increasing human consumption of resources and habitats.

feedback loops (negative): Causal chains in which some factors reduce the impact of other causal factors, potentially leading to stability or equilibrium; a thermostat in a heating system is an example of negative feedback.

feedback loops (positive): Causal chains in which each factor magnifies the impact of other factors; can lead to accelerating or runaway change, as in a nuclear explosion, in which the breakdown of each atom triggers the breakdown of other nearby atoms.

Fertile Crescent: The arc of lands around Mesopotamia, which contain the earliest evidence of agriculture.

firestick farming: *Not* a form of farming, but a foraging strategy; foragers regularly burn the land to prevent wildfires, to encourage new growth, and to attract grazers that can be hunted. Though a form of foraging, it also counts as a way of manipulating the environment in order to increase the productivity of resources useful to humans, so it can be regarded as a step toward farming.

fission: The breaking up of large atoms, such as uranium, releases radioactive energy; when many atoms are close together, the breakup of one atom can release subatomic particles that split other atoms, in a chain reaction; this chain reaction drives nuclear weapons and nuclear reactors.

foraging: Technologies that depend on the use of natural resources more or less in their natural state; hunting and gathering; the dominant type of technology in the Paleolithic era.

fossil fuels: Fuels formed from living organisms fossilized in the remote past, they are the dominant source of energy today; fossil fuels include coal, oil, and natural gas; the "fossil fuels revolution" is the transition to dependence on fossil energy that has occurred since the Industrial Revolution.

free energy: Energy distributed unevenly so that it is capable of doing useful work; a charged battery can do work because negative charges are concentrated at one of its terminals, but as it does work, the balance of negative and positive charges evens out, increasing *entropy* and reducing its capacity to do more work.

free energy rate density: The density of free energy flowing through a complex entity, measured in units of energy passing through a given mass in a given amount of time; Eric Chaisson has argued that the free energy rate density provides a rough measure of levels of complexity.

fusion: Stars are powered for most of their lives by the fusion of hydrogen atoms into helium atoms, as a result of which vast amounts of energy are released; source of the power of hydrogen bombs.

Gaia: The Greek goddess of the Earth; the name was used by James Lovelock to describe the linked actions of all life forms on the surface of the Earth, which for some purposes can be regarded as a single, vast organism that has lived and evolved for almost 4 billion years; as Lovelock has argued, today human activity may be inflicting significant damage on Gaia, though he also argues that Gaia may prove resilient enough to survive and outlast us.

Galapagos Islands: An archipelago of 19 islands in the Pacific Ocean, owned today by Ecuador and visited by Darwin for five weeks in 1835; the many tiny variations he observed between the species on different islands helped crystallize his ideas on natural selection.

galaxies: Large "societies" of stars, held together by their mutual gravitational pull.

global history: Studies of world history since the linking of the world into a single system in the 15th century of the Modern era.

global warming: The observed increase in global average temperatures that is almost certainly due mainly to the rapid increase in the amounts of carbon dioxide in the atmosphere caused by the massive use of fossil fuels in the last two centuries.

globalization: The increasing interlinking of different regions of the world since 1492.

GNP: A standard measure of economic production; a widely calculated measure, for which there are even estimates reaching several centuries into the past. However, because it is based on market prices, it can tell little about nonmarket production or about the ecological costs of production.

Gondwanaland: The large southern supercontinent formed almost 200 million years ago by the breakup of Pangaea; included South America, Antarctica, Australia, Africa, and India; see also *Laurasia*.

grand narrative: Term used in post-modern theory to describe overarching accounts of reality (such as Marxism, or big history); points to the danger that such accounts can mislead or be put to self-interested uses.

grand unified theory: The idea of a single, unified scientific account of all aspects of physical reality; the holy grail of modern physics since the 1960s; remains elusive because of the failure to merge relativity and quantum physics or to explain the nature of dark matter/dark energy.

hafted tools: Tools attached to handles.

half-life: The period during which half of the mass of a given radioactive material decays; the precision with which half-lives can be calculated for different radioactive materials is the basis for most forms of radiometric dating.

helium: The second-simplest atomic element, with two protons and two electrons, produced, like hydrogen, soon after the big bang; helium made up about 24% of the matter in the early Universe but now makes up about 28% as fusion reactions have converted hydrogen atoms into helium.

hominids/hominines: Bipedal apes, ancestors of modern humans; first appeared 6–7 million years ago.

Hominoids/Hominoidea: The superfamily of apes (includes humans).

Homo erectus/ergaster: Hominine species that appeared in Africa almost 2 million years ago; almost as tall as modern humans, their brains were larger than those of *Homo habilis*; some *erectus* migrated into Eurasia, reaching as far as China.

Homo habilis: Hominine species that appeared in Africa between 2 and 3 million years ago; classified by their discoverer, Louis Leakey, within the genus that includes us because they made simple stone tools, they are now thought to have been much closer to australopithecines than to modern humans.

Homo sapiens: Human beings, our own species; probably evolved in Africa between 200,000 and 300,000 years ago; the only species on Earth (or anywhere else as far as we know at the moment) that can adapt by "collective learning."

hub region: A geographical region characterized by an exceptional number of exchanges of people, ideas, and goods taking place; Mesopotamia was an ancient hub region; after 1500, the Atlantic regions became a significant hub region through Europe's control of the major international sea routes.

Hubble constant: The rate of expansion of the Universe; calculating this constant precisely has been extremely difficult; modern estimates range from 55 to 75 km per second per megaparsec, implying that the Universe must be between 10 and 16 billion years old.

hunting and gathering: See _foraging_.

hydrogen: The simplest of all atomic elements, hydrogen was produced soon after the big bang; each hydrogen atom consists of one proton and one electron; deuterium is an isotope (or form) of hydrogen whose nucleus also contains a single neutron; hydrogen made up about 76% of all the matter in the early Universe and still makes up about 71% today.

intensification: The type of growth or innovation characteristic of the Agrarian and Modern eras, in which innovation allows the support of more people from a given area and therefore generates larger and denser human communities; contrast with _extensification_.

isotopes: Atoms of a given element that have varying numbers of neutrons in their nucleus and therefore varying atomic weights; carbon dating techniques depend on measuring changes in the ratio of different isotopes of carbon as carbon 14 (the only radioactive isotope of carbon) breaks down over time.

kin-ordered societies: A term used by Eric Wolf to describe all human societies in which kinship systems are the most important basis for social organization; all societies before the appearance of the first tribute-taking states can be regarded as kin-ordered.

later Agrarian era: From c. 3000 B.C.E. to a few centuries ago; the second part of the Agrarian era, in which there existed Agrarian civilizations; synonym for "era of Agrarian civilizations."

Laurasia: The large northern supercontinent formed almost 200 million years ago by the breakup of Pangaea; included Eurasia and North America; see also *Gondwanaland*.

macrohistory: Study of the past on large scales.

Malthusian cycles: Long cycles of economic, demographic, cultural, and even political expansion, generally followed by periods of crisis; warfare; and demographic, cultural, and political decline. These cycles, generally lasting several centuries, are apparent throughout the Agrarian era and were probably generated by the fact that, though there was innovation (which generated the upward swings), rates of innovation could not keep pace with rates of growth (which explains the eventual crashes).

mantle: Layer of the Earth between the core and the crust; the mantle is semimolten, and convection currents within it drive plate tectonics.

margins, tectonic: Regions where tectonic plates meet; this is where most interesting geological events occur, including mountain building, earthquakes, and volcanic activity.

matter: As Einstein showed, matter and energy are interchangeable (according to the famous formula, e [energy] = m [mass] × c [the speed of light]^2); matter can, therefore be regarded as a form of congealed energy; for much of the first second of the big bang, matter and energy were still interchangeable.

megafaunal extinctions: The extinction of large animal species in the Paleolithic era, probably as a result of overhunting by humans; megafaunal extinctions were particularly severe in lands newly colonized by humans in the Australasian and American world zones, which is why those regions had fewer large mammal species and therefore fewer potential animal domesticates.

metabolism: One of the three fundamental features of living organisms; the ability of all living organisms to take in energy from their surroundings; the methods they use to do so (see also *adaptation, reproduction*).

microhistory: Study of the past on very small scales, often through the biographies of individuals, or through study of particular events.

mitochondria: "Organelles" found within all eukaryotic cells, which specialize in processing the energy of oxygen; they contain their own independent DNA, which suggests, as Lynn Margulis has proposed, that they were once independent organisms incorporated with eukaryotic cells through symbiosis.

Modern era: One of the three great eras of human history, beginning within the last two or three centuries; characterized by sharp increases in innovation and productivity that rapidly transformed human societies throughout the world.

Modern Revolution: A deliberately vague label for the revolutionary transformations that have created the modern world; the "Modern Revolution" ushered in the "Modern era" of human history.

monumental architecture: Large structures, such as pyramids or large statues, that seem to appear wherever powerful leaders emerge; a feature of all Agrarian civilizations.

Natufians: A culture of affluent foragers whose remains are found in much of the Fertile Crescent; from c. 14,000 BP, the Natufians lived in villages but harvested wild grains and hunted gazelle; though they did not farm, their culture suggests some of the transitional stages between affluent foraging and early forms of agriculture.

natural selection: Key idea in the modern understanding of how living organisms change, developed in the 19th century by Charles Darwin; Darwin argued that tiny, random variations in individuals may increase or decrease their chances of survival; those whose chances are enhanced are more likely to pass on their genes to their offspring so that, eventually, more and more individuals will inherit the successful variations; over long periods of time such tiny changes lead to the emergence of new species; the central idea (paradigm) of modern biology.

Neanderthals: A hominine species that appeared within the last million years in Europe, the Middle East, Central Asia and southern Russia; genetic evidence suggests that the human and Neanderthal lines diverged from c. 500,000 years ago; though Neanderthals used more advanced stone technologies than *Homo erectus/ergaster*, it seems unlikely that they were capable of symbolic language; the last Neanderthals lived c. 25,000 years ago in Western Europe.

Neolithic era: "New Stone Age," from about 10,000 years ago; the era in which agriculture first appeared.

neotony: An evolutionary process in which juvenile features of the ancestral species are preserved into adulthood; humans can be regarded as neotenous apes because brain growth continues for much longer than in apes and we preserve into adulthood the flat faces and relative hairlessness of young apes.

net primary productivity (NPP): That portion of energy from sunlight which is used by photosynthesizing organisms and therefore enters the food chain and becomes available to support the biosphere in general; the energy income of the biosphere.

neutrons: Electrically neutral subatomic particles present in the nuclei of most atoms; unlike protons, the number of neutrons in a given element can vary slightly, giving rise to different "isotopes" of each element.

nucleotides: Basic chemical constituents of the genetic material of all living organisms.

obsidian: A hard, glass-like substance formed during volcanic eruptions and widely used in prehistory for the making of sharp and durable blades; widely traded in the Neolithic era.

Olbers' paradox: The observation that if the Universe were infinite in size, there ought to be an infinite amount of light and heat so that the night sky should not be dark.

oxygen: A highly reactive chemical element with eight protons (atomic number 8), normally a gas on Earth; because oxygen is so reactive, the oxygen in the Earth's atmosphere has to be constantly renewed by the activity of photosynthesizing organisms, so free oxygen did not appear in the atmosphere until about halfway through the Earth's history; as James Lovelock pointed out, any planet with free oxygen in its atmosphere must have some chemical mechanism (perhaps associated with living organisms?) that constantly replenishes the supply of oxygen.

ozone layer: Ozone is a molecule consisting of three oxygen atoms, in contrast to the more common form consisting of just two atoms; a thin layer of ozone high in the atmosphere shields the Earth's surface from harmful forms of ultraviolet radiation; in the 1980s it was found that the use of CFCs (chlorofluorocarbons) was breaking up the ozone layer; international treaties have led to the banning of most production and use of CFCs.

Pacific zone: The largest but least populous of the four world zones of human history; created within the last 3,000–4,000 years as migrants from the western edge of the Pacific Ocean slowly settled Pacific islands, bringing with them technologies of farming.

Paleolithic era: One of the three great eras of human history; literally, the "Old Stone Age," as most surviving evidence consists of stone tools; in this course, refers to the era of human history from the origins of our species (perhaps 200,000 years ago) to the appearance of agriculture about 10,000 years ago.

Pangaea: The vast supercontinent formed more than 200 million years ago as plate tectonics joined most of the major continental plates together; it is probable that such supercontinents have formed periodically throughout the Earth's history; the existence of a single huge landmass probably reduced biodiversity.

paradigm: The central organizing idea of a scientific discipline, such as natural selection (in biology), big bang cosmology (in cosmology), or plate tectonics (in geology); as yet, history lacks a paradigmatic idea; the term is associated with the work of philosopher of science T. S. Kuhn.

parallax: The change in the apparent relationship between two fixed objects caused by the movement of the observer; if you hold your finger up and move your head, your finger will appear to move against the background; parallax measurements can be used to measure the distance to the nearest stars.

pastoralism: A life similar to agriculture but based primarily on the exploitation of domesticated animals rather than plants; in order to allow animals to graze over large areas, pastoralists are generally nomadic; pastoralism was made possible as a result of the innovations of the *secondary products revolution* and spread widely in the steppelands of both Eurasia and Africa.

patriarchy: Ideologies and social structures that assume the superiority of males over females.

peasants: Small holding farmers, who generally pay taxes to overlords; the most numerous class in all Agrarian societies.

periodic table: A way of listing chemical elements in groups with common features; first constructed by the great Russian chemist Dmitrii Mendeleev in 1869.

photosynthesis: The use of sunlight by plants or plant-like organisms to store energy; first evidence from c. 3.5 billion years ago; the source of most of the energy that drives life within the biosphere.

planetesimals: Objects formed by accretion during the formation of the solar system; protoplanets.

planets: Chemically complex objects orbiting stars; it is now known planets orbit a majority of stars.

plate tectonics: The central idea (paradigm) of modern Earth sciences since the 1960s; based on the notion that the Earth's crust is broken into separate plates that are in constant motion.

power: Power relations in human societies can usefully be analyzed into two fundamental forms: "power from below" is power granted by followers to a leader to ensure the successful achievement of group tasks (such as the election of captains in sports teams); "power from above" is power that depends, in addition, on the ability of rulers to impose their will by force; in the history of human societies, power from below preceded power from above for the simple reason that to pay for a body of retainers that could impose one's will by force it was necessary already to have the ability to mobilize significant resources.

prestige goods: Goods such as silk or precious metals that combine high value and relatively low bulk or weight; before the Modern era, such goods were more often traded over large distances than goods of greater bulk or lesser value, such as grains.

primary producers: Those groups of people (such as peasants or foragers) who produce resources from the natural environment; elite groups exact resources from primary producers.

primates: An order of mammals that appeared about 70 million years ago, characterized by relatively large brain size, manipulative hands, and stereoscopic vision; all these features may be the result of dwelling in trees; apes (and therefore hominines and humans) belong within this order.

prime movers: Used in these lectures to refer to the most important forces driving innovation and growth in human history; they include commerce, collective learning, and population growth.

prokaryotes: Simple, single-celled organisms in which the genetic material is not bound within a nucleus.

proletarians: The term used within Marxist theory to refer to wage earners, those groups who could bring to markets nothing but their own labor power.

proton: Positively charged subatomic particle present in the nuclei of all atoms.

punctuated evolution: The idea first proposed by Stephen Jay Gould and Niles Eldredge in 1972 that the pace of biological evolution can vary significantly, so that the history of biological species consists of long periods of relative stasis "punctuated" by periods of abrupt change.

quarks: The fundamental constituents of neutrons and protons.

quipu: Knotted strings used by the Inka for accounting and as an embryonic form of writing.

radiometric dating techniques: Techniques for determining the dates of origin of materials by measuring the extent of the breakdown of radioactive materials.

Rapa Nui: A Pacific island (also known as Easter Island) owned by Chile, first settled by Polynesian navigators approximately 1,000 years ago and remarkable for the presence of many large stone figures.

rebus principle: A critical stage in the evolution of writing; if an object that could be easily depicted (say an arrow) sounded similar to a more abstract concept (such as soul), the symbol for the first could be used to refer to the second; this device greatly expanded the ability of written language to mimic spoken language.

reciprocity: Mutual exchanges of gifts; in kinship societies, one of the most powerful ways of holding communities together through the creation of mutual obligations.

red shift: In the 1920s, Edwin Hubble observed that the light from many distant galaxies appeared to be shifted toward the red end of the spectrum; he interpreted this as the result of a Doppler effect, which implied the galaxies emitting such light were moving rapidly away from us; the first piece of evidence that our Universe was expanding.

regimes: Complex structures such as stars or living organisms or entire ecosystems that achieve a certain stability but eventually break down.

relative dates: Dates that can determine the order in which events occurred (such as the order in which different geological epochs occurred) but not the time periods between them (see *absolute dates*).

reproduction: One of the three fundamental features of living organisms; the ability of all living organisms to make almost perfect copies of themselves; the occasional imperfections provide the variety from which natural selection constructs new species (see also *adaptation, metabolism*).

retinues: Armed retainers of political leaders; a critical step toward the creation of states capable of coercive power (*tribute-taking states*), or "power from above."

RNA: Ribonucleic acid; similar to DNA, but it comes in single strands so it can fold like a protein and engage in metabolic activity, yet it can also carry genetic information; RNA, with its ability both to encode genetic information and engage in metabolism, may have played a crucial role in the early evolution of life on Earth.

secondary products revolution: A concept developed by the late Andrew Sherratt to describe a series of technological innovations from about 6,000 years ago that made it possible to exploit domesticated animals more efficiently by using products such as their wool, their milk, and their traction power, all of which could be used without first killing the animals; these innovations revolutionized transportation, made possible plow agriculture, and led to the emergence of pastoralist lifeways.

sedentism: Living in one place for most of the year; sedentism was rare in foraging societies but became widespread with the adoption of agriculture because agriculture made it possible to produce more resources from a given area and encouraged farmers to stay in one place to protect their crops.

sexual reproduction: A form of reproduction that emerged about 1 billion years ago, in which two organisms exchange genetic material before reproduction so that their offspring are not clones of the parents; sexual reproduction increased variations between individuals and thereby sped up the pace of biological evolution.

spectrometer: A prism-like device that can split light into its different wavelengths; fundamental tool in the study of stars.

steady-state theory: An alternative theory to big bang cosmology, holding that the "red shift" was an illusion created by the constant creation of new matter in the Universe; the theory lost credibility after the discovery of the cosmic background radiation, which it could not explain.

supernova: The explosion of a large star at the end of its life; most chemical elements can only be manufactured in supernova explosions.

swidden agriculture: A form of agriculture in which woodlands are burned down, crops are planted in the ashy soil, and then, when the fertility of the newly cleared fields declines, new regions are cleared; because it is seminomadic, swidden agriculture is possible only in regions of low population density, such as the Amazon basin.

symbiosis: Relations of interdependence between different species, such as those between humans and domesticated plants and animals, which offer benefits (of different degrees) to each species; such relations are extremely common in the natural world.

symbolic language: A form of communication unique to human beings, using symbols and grammar; much more powerful and precise than the forms of communication used by all other animals; the basis for "collective learning."

synergy: Processes in which causal factors mutually enhance their combined impact so as to have a greater effect than they might have had on their own.

tectonic margins. See *margins, tectonic.*

tectonic plates: Portions of the Earth's surface or crust that move as a result of movements in the hot, semiliquid magma beneath them.

teosinte: Wild, ancestral form of maize.

thermodynamics, first and second laws of: Two fundamental laws of modern physics; the first law of thermodynamics says that energy is never lost; the second law says that "free energy," i.e., energy distributed in ways that enable it to do work, is slowly dissipated over time as energy differentials tend to even out.

tribute-taking societies: Societies dominated by tribute-taking states, in which the majority of people are small farmers; such societies are characterized by lower rates of innovation than the much more commercialized "capitalist" societies.

tribute-taking states (tribute-takers): States or groups capable of exacting resources from others, if necessary, through the threat of force.

universal Darwinism: Term coined by Richard Dawkins to suggest that change in many different domains, including cosmology and history, is similar to change through natural selection in the biological domain.

universal history: The project of constructing histories at all scales; a project pursued at least since the classical era, sometimes used as a synonym for "big history."

wage labor: Work performed in return for wages rather than under obligation or compulsion.

world history: Historical research and teaching embracing the entire world, generally focusing on the last 10,000 years of human history.

world systems theories: Pioneered by Immanuel Wallerstein, world systems theories explore large networks of interaction through trade or other exchanges.

world zones: Large regions settled by humans, between which there is no significant contact; the main world zones during the era of human history have been Afro-Eurasia, the Americas, Australasia, and the Pacific; similarities and differences in these zones provide powerful evidence of fundamental long-term tendencies in human history.

Bibliography

"Big history" is a new discipline, so there are few books that attempt to tell the whole story, though there are many that recount different parts of the story. H. G. Wells's famous *Outline of History*, first published in 1920 in the aftermath of World War I, was an engaging and immensely successful attempt to write a big history. But Wells wrote before the scientific breakthroughs of the middle of the 20th century allowed us to date events before the appearance of written records. He also wrote before the breakthroughs in cosmology, evolutionary biology, and geology that transformed all these scientific disciplines into *historical* disciplines, disciplines concerned with change over time.

Here, I list some recent attempts to tell the story of big history, or significant parts of it. I have referred most of all to my own book, *Maps of Time*, because that will supplement the arguments presented, in more concise form, in the lectures. For the second half of this course, there are now many fine textbook surveys of world history, some of which are listed in the Reading section below. Fred Spier has compiled a more complete bibliography of works on big history, which is available at: http://www.iis.uva.nl/i2o/object.cfm/objectid=21E38086-9EAF-4BB2-A3327D5C1011F7CC/hoofdstuk=5.

Reading:

Abu-Lughod, Janet. *Before European Hegemony: The World System A.D. 1250–1350*. New York: Oxford University Press, 1989. An influential survey of the "world system" of the 13th century and the many links that bound different parts of the Afro-Eurasian world zone into a single system.

Alvarez, Walter. *T. Rex and the Crater of Doom*. New York: Vintage Books, 1998. A delightful account, written by the geologist at the center of the story, of the science behind the discovery that a meteorite impact probably caused the mass extinctions of 67 million years ago.

Anderson, J. L. *Explaining Long-Term Economic Change*. Basingstoke, England: Macmillan, 1991. A brief and highly accessible survey of theories of long-term economic change.

Bayly, Chris. *The Birth of the Modern World, 1780–1914: Global Connections and Comparisons*. Oxford: Blackwell, 2003. An integrated history of the world during the "long" 19th century, stressing the complexity of cultural, economic, and political interactions between different regions.

Bellwood, Peter. *First Farmers: The Origins of Agricultural Societies*. Oxford: Blackwell, 2005. A thorough, recent discussion of the origins of agriculture.

————. *The Polynesians: Prehistory of an Island People*. rev. ed. London: Thames and Hudson, 1987. A standard history of the colonization of the Pacific.

Bentley, Jerry H., and Herbert F. Ziegler. *Traditions and Encounters: A Global Perspective on the Past*. 3rd ed., Boston: McGraw Hill, 1999. A readable, authoritative, and beautifully produced text on world history.

Brown, Cynthia Stokes. *Big History: From the Big Bang to the Present*. New York: The New Press, 2007. A lucid and engaging new account of the big history story, with an ecological slant.

Brown, Lester R. *Eco-Economy: Building an Economy for the Earth*. New York and London: Norton, 2001. A superb account of current ecological dangers, combined with a blueprint for change, from one of the world's leading environmentalists. Look for updates.

Bryson, Bill. *A Short History of Nearly Everything*. London: Black Swan, 2004. Delightfully written, a fine introduction to the scientists who assembled the different parts of the modern creation story, combined with lucid short introductions to many aspects of the science.

Bulliet, Richard W., Pamela Crossley, and Daniel R. Headrick. *The Earth and its Peoples: A Global History*. 2 vols. Boston: Houghton Mifflin, 2005. One of the best modern texts on world history.

Cairns-Smith, A. G. *Seven Clues to the Origin of Life*. Cambridge: Cambridge University Press, 1985. Cairns-Smith manages to make the details of complex and highly technical debates both clear and fascinating.

Calder, Nigel. *Timescale: An Atlas of the Fourth Dimension*. London: Chatto and Windus, 1983. A remarkable chronology for the whole of time, and a delightful read. Some of the details are now slightly dated.

Chaisson, Eric. *Cosmic Evolution: The Rise of Complexity in Nature*. Cambridge, MA: Harvard University Press, 2001. In this pioneering book, Chaisson argues that increasing complexity provides a promising, unifying theme for any modern attempts at a coherent account of the past.

———. *Epic of Evolution: Seven Ages of the Cosmos*. New York: Columbia University Press, 2006. Eric Chaisson has been teaching an astronomer's version of big history for many decades now, and this book is the result of that experience. [See also Chaisson's website on "Cosmic Evolution": http://www.tufts.edu/as/wright_center/cosmic_evolution/docs/splash.html.]

Charlesworth, Brian and Deborah Charlesworth. *Evolution: A Very Short Introduction*. Oxford: Oxford University Press, 2003. The Oxford "Very Short Introductions" provide brief but expert introductions to important scientific fields.

Chase-Dunn, Christopher, and Thomas D. Hall. *Rise and Demise: Comparing World Systems*. Boulder, CO: Westview Press, 1997. A valuable introduction to "world systems" theory and its relevance for human history on large scales, by two of the pioneers in the field.

Christian, David. "The Case for 'Big History.'" *The Journal of World History* 2, no. 2 (Fall 1991): 223–38. Aimed at historians, this article argued that it was both possible and important for historians to look for the links between their discipline and other historical disciplines, from cosmology to geology and biology, in order to create a unified modern account of the past. It proposed the light-hearted label "big history" for this project. [Available at http://www.fss.uu.nl/wetfil/96-97/big.htm.]

————. *Maps of Time: An Introduction to Big History.* Berkeley: University of California Press. Until the publication of Cynthia Stokes Brown's *Big History*, this was the only available text on big history. I have road-tested this in freshman university courses for 15 years, and its arguments underpin the lectures in this course. Each chapter contains suggestions for further reading. This is a historian's account of big history, so human history looms larger than it does in Eric Chaisson's *Epic of Evolution.*

————. *This Fleeting World: A Short History of Humanity.* Great Barrington, MA: Berkshire Publishing Group, 2007. Originally a series of essays for the *Berkshire Encyclopedia of World History*, this is a *short* history of humanity, designed to be read in one or two sittings so the reader can keep sight of the large patterns.

————. "World History in Context." *Journal of World History* 14, no. 4 (2003): 437–58. Discusses the place of human history in the larger history of the Universe. Available at: http://www.historycooperative.org/journals/jwh/14.4/christian.html.

Cipolla, Carlo M. *The Economic History of World Population.* 6th ed. Harmondsworth, England: Penguin, 1974. A very concise survey of the history of human population, though now slightly dated, particularly on kin-ordered societies.

Coatsworth, John H. "Welfare." *American Historical Review* 101, no. 1 (February 1996): 1–17. Summarizes in very general terms what we know about the major changes in human health and welfare from archaeological evidence.

Cohen, Mark. *Health and the Rise of Civilization.* London and New Haven, CT: Yale University Press, 1989. Argues that in many ways the emergence of agricultural societies meant a decline in general levels of wealth and human welfare.

Coles, Peter. *Cosmology: A Very Short Introduction*. Oxford: Oxford University Press, 2001. The Oxford "Very Short Introductions" provide brief but expert introductions to important scientific fields.

Crosby, Alfred W. *Children of the Sun: A History of Humanity's Unappeasable Appetite for Energy*. New York and London: W. W. Norton, 2006. An overview of human energy use by one of the leading figures in world history.

———. *The Columbian Exchange: Biological and Cultural Consequences of 1492*. Westport, CT: Greenwood Press, 1972. A world history classic, which describes the profound biological and economic impact of the coming together of the Afro-Eurasian and American world zones from the 16th century, and the consequent exchanges of diseases, crops, and goods between the two zones.

Croswell, Ken. *The Alchemy of the Heavens*. Oxford and NY: Oxford University Press, 1996. A fine introduction to the nature and history of stars.

Darwin, Charles. *On the Origin of Species by Means of Natural Selection: A Facsimile of the First Edition*. Cambridge, MA: Harvard University Press, 1975. Darwin's *Origin of Species* was first published in 1859. He was a superb writer and is still very much worth reading today. There are many other editions of *Origin of Species* besides this.

Davies, Paul. *The Fifth Miracle: The Search for the Origin of Life*. Harmondsworth, England: Penguin, 1999. A rich survey of debates about the origins of life, by one of the best contemporary writers on science.

Davis, Mike. *Late Victorian Holocausts: El Niño Famines and the Making of the Third World*. London and New York: Verso, 2001. An idiosyncratic account of the convergence of climatic change and economic change in the formation of the third world late in the 19th century.

Deacon, Terence W. *The Symbolic Species: The Co-evolution of Language and the Brain*. Harmondsworth, England: Penguin, 1997. Not always easy reading, but one of the most interesting recent attempts to explain the origins and significance of human language.

Delsemme, Armand. *Our Cosmic Origins: From the Big Bang to the Emergence of Life and Intelligence.* Cambridge: Cambridge University Press, 1998. A fine scientific introduction to the early parts of the course, up to the evolution of our own species.

Diamond, J. *Collapse: How Societies Choose to Fail or Succeed.* New York: Penguin, 2005. In this important and readable book, Jared Diamond compares the histories of many different societies that have undergone ecological collapse, in order to tease out those factors that may help guide modern societies through the ecological dangers they face today.

————. *Guns, Germs, and Steel: The Fates of Human Societies.* London: Vintage, 1998. A fascinating survey of human history by a biologist who brings a biologist's novel insights to many familiar historical problems.

Dyson, Freeman. *Origins of Life.* 2nd ed. Cambridge: Cambridge University Press, 1999 [1st ed. 1985]. A sometimes technical overview of the complex problem of explaining the origins of life.

Ehrenberg, Margaret. *Women in Prehistory.* Norman: University of Oklahoma Press, 1989. A wide-ranging discussion of gender relations in early human history and a survey of debates about the "origins of patriarchy."

Eldredge, Niles. *Darwin: Discovering the Tree of Life.* New York: Norton, 2005. One of many fine introductions to Darwin's life and thought by one of the major figures on modern biological thinking.

————. "The Sixth Extinction." http://www.actionbioscience.org/newfrontiers/eldredge2.html#Primer A very useful short summary of the major eras of extinction in the last 600 million years by one of the leading biologists of his generation.

Elvin, Mark. *The Pattern of the Chinese Past*. Stanford, CA: Stanford University Press, 1973. An influential analysis of the astonishing burst of growth during the Song era of Chinese history.

Emiliani, Cesare. *The Scientific Companion*. New York: Wiley, 1995. Very useful explanations for nonscientists of some of the basic scientific issues discussed in this course.

Fagan, Brian M. *People of the Earth: An Introduction to World Prehistory*. 11th ed. New York: Prentice Hall, 2003. Extremely thorough in its coverage and probably the most influential contemporary text on human prehistory.

Fernandez-Armesto, Felipe. *The World: A History*. Saddle River, NJ: Prentice Hall, 2007. The most recent and perhaps the most original of a number of very fine and beautifully produced textbook surveys of world history. Fernandez-Armesto has a fine eye for vivid and illuminating detail.

Flannery, Tim. *The Future Eaters: An Ecological History of the Australasian Lands and People*. London: Heinemann, 2001. A delightful, though polemical, account of the ecological impact of Paleolithic humans on one of the world's major world zones, the ice age continent of Sahul.

Flood, Josephine. *Archaeology of the Dreamtime: The Story of Prehistoric Australia and Her People*. Sydney and London: Collins, 1983. A highly accessible account of the archaeology and prehistory of the major continent in one of the world's major world zones.

Fortey, Richard. *Life: An Unauthorised Biography*. London: Flamingo/Harper Collins, 1998. An engaging account of the history of our Earth and of life on Earth.

Gamble, C. *Timewalkers: The Prehistory of Global Colonization*. Harmondsworth, England: Penguin, 1995. A thorough history of the Paleolithic era; focuses on the growing networks of exchange that enabled Paleolithic humans to migrate to an astonishing range of different environments.

Gould, Stephen Jay, ed. *The Book of Life: An Illustrated History of the Evolution of Life on Earth.* New York: W. W. Norton, 2001. A beautifully illustrated collection of essays on the history of life on Earth.

———. *Full House: The Spread of Excellence from Plato to Darwin.* New York: Three Rivers Press, 1997. Anything by the late Stephen Jay Gould is worth reading. This book argues against a central theme of this course: the idea that complexity has increased in the course of biological evolution.

———. *Time's Arrow, Time's Cycle.* London: Penguin, 1988. Gould is always interesting and entertaining to read. Here he discusses some crucial stages in the creation of modern chronologies of the past.

Harris, Marvin. "The Origin of Pristine States." In *Cannibals and Kings.* New York: Vintage Books, 1978, 101–23. Harris writes with verve and passion about anthropology. All the essays in this book are worth reading, but his essay on the origin of state power lays out starkly the revolution that this meant in human lifeways.

Harrison, Paul. *Inside the Third World.* Harmondsworth, England: Penguin, 1982. A vivid and highly readable account of conditions in the third world.

Headrick, Daniel. "Technological Change." In B. L. Turner, W. C. Clark, R. W. Kates, J. F. Richards, J. T. Mathews, W. B. Meyer, eds., *The Earth as Transformed by Human Action: Global and Regional Changes in the Biosphere over the Past 300 Years.* Cambridge: Cambridge University Press, 1990, 55–67. A concise overview of the main waves of industrialization.

Held, David, Anthony McGrew, David Goldblatt, and Jonathan Perraton. *Global Transformations: Politics, Economics and Culture.* Stanford, CA: Stanford University Press, 1999. A fine introduction to the rich literature on globalization, with helpful introductions by the editors.

Hobsbawm, E. J. *The Age of Extremes.* London: Weidenfeld and Nicolson, 1994. A history of the 20th century by one of the greatest modern historians of Europe and the world.

Hoyle, Fred. *The Intelligent Universe*. London: Michael Joseph Limited, 1983. Fred Hoyle's statement of the arguments for "panspermia": the idea that life did not evolve on earth, but elsewhere in the cosmos.

Hughes, J. Donald. *An Environmental History of the World: Humankind's Changing Role in the Community of Life*. London: Routledge, 2001. One of the very few books for the general reader that survey the entire history of human relations with the environment.

Hughes-Warrington, Marnie. "Big History." *Historically Speaking* 20 (November 2002): 16–17. A brief survey of the history of big history by a teacher of big history who is also a historiographer. An expanded version is available in *Social Evolution & History* 4, no. 1 (Spring 2005): 7–21.

Johanson, D. C., and M. Edey. *Lucy: The Beginnings of Humankind*. New York: Simon and Schuster, 1981. A highly readable account of one of the great anthropological discoveries of the 20th century.

Johnson, Allen W., and Timothy Earle. *The Evolution of Human Societies*. 2nd ed. Stanford, CA: Stanford University Press, 2000. An evolutionary account of human history from an anthropological perspective. Particularly interesting on factors that led to increasing social complexity.

Jones, Steve. *Almost Like a Whale: The Origin of Species Updated*. London: Anchor, 2000. A delightful account of what has changed since Darwin's day in our understanding of natural selection and the nature of life.

————, ed. *The Cambridge Encyclopedia of Human Evolution*. Cambridge: Cambridge University Press, 1992. Very full coverage and articles by leading experts.

Kauffman, Stuart. *At Home in the Universe: The Search for the Laws of Self-Organization and Complexity*. New York: Oxford University Press, 1995. Though not always easy reading, this is one of the best introductions to complexity theory for the nonspecialist.

Kelley, Kevin W. *The Home Planet*. Reading, MA: Addison Wesley Publishing Company, 1991. A collection of superb photographs of the Earth from space, accompanied by descriptions by cosmonauts and astronauts of what it meant to them to look down on our Earth from space.

Kennedy, Paul. *Preparing for the Twenty-First Century*. London: Fontana, 1994. Surveys many of the long trends of history in the modern era.

Leakey, Richard, and Roger Lewin. *The Sixth Extinction: Patterns of Life and the Future of Humankind*. New York: Doubleday, 1995. A survey of major extinction events within the last billion years that makes it clear that current rates of extinction, caused largely by human activity, are as rapid as they have ever been during this vast period.

Lewin, Roger. *Human Evolution: An Illustrated Introduction*. 5th ed., Oxford: Blackwell, 2004. A thorough and readable textbook account of human evolution.

Liebes, Sidney, Elisabet Sahtouris, and Brian Swimme. *A Walk Through Time: From Stardust to Us—The Evolution of Life on Earth*. New York: John Wiley, 1998. Big history from a biological and scientific perspective, but with a rich sense of the poetic and mythic overtones of the story.

Lovelock, J. *Gaia: A New Look at Life on Earth*. Oxford: Oxford University Press, 1979, 1987. Lovelock has argued that, at the highest level, all of life constitutes a single, evolving entity that he calls "Gaia." Life, he argues, has played a profound role in maintaining the Earth's surface in a condition that is favorable for the survival of life. An influential argument about the relationship between life and the Earth.

Macdougall, J. D. *A Short History of Planet Earth: Mountains, Mammals, Fire, and Ice*. New York: John Wiley, 1996. A short and accessible history of planet Earth.

Maddison, Angus. *The World Economy: A Millennial Perspective*. Paris: Organisation for Economic Co-operation and Development, 2001. Assembles a variety of statistical series on long-term economic change over the last millennium.

Mann, Charles C. *1491: New Revelations of the Americas Before Columbus.* New York: Alfred A. Knopf, 2005. A highly readable and up to date account of the archaeology of the Americas before 1492.

Margulis, Lynn and Dorion Sagan. *Microcosmos: Four Billion Years of Microbial Evolution.* London: Allen and Unwin, 1987. A rich and highly readable account of the world of micro-organizations, which makes it clear how vital that world is to life in general. Margulis pioneered the idea that eukaryotic cells emerged from a symbiosis between simpler, prokaryotic cells.

Maynard Smith, John, and Eörs Szathmáry. *The Origins of Life: From the Birth of Life to the Origins of Language.* Oxford: Oxford University Press, 2000. Not always easy for the nonspecialist reader, this is a wonderful survey by two distinguished biologists of the increasing complexity in the biological realm, which argues powerfully for the importance of a number of distinct thresholds of increasing complexity in the history of life.

Mayr, Ernst. *One Long Argument: Charles Darwin and the Genesis of Modern Evolutionary Thought.* London: Penguin, 1991. A powerful and readable summary of the logic behind Darwin's thought by one of the foremost late-20th-century Darwinian thinkers.

McBrearty, Sally, and Alison S. Brooks. "The Revolution That Wasn't: A New Interpretation of the Origin of Modern Human Behaviour." *Journal of Human Evolution* 39 (2000): 453–563. A pioneering article that assembles evidence for the claim that our species originated in Africa between 200,000 and 300,000 years ago.

McNeill, John. *Something New Under the Sun: An Environmental History of the Twentieth-Century World.* New York and London: Norton, 2000. A brilliant survey of the revolutionary transformations in the human relationship to the biosphere during the 20th century.

McNeill, J. R., and William H. McNeill. *The Human Web: A Bird's-Eye View of World History*, New York: W. W. Norton, 2003. A synoptic overview of human history by two of the leading figures in world history. It takes as its unifying theme the emergence and evolution of webs of exchange between human communities.

McNeill, William H., ed. *Berkshire Encyclopedia of World History*. 5 vols. Barrington, MA: Berkshire Publishing, 2005. An invaluable reference work for anyone interested in world history, with synoptic essays surveying particular themes over the whole of human history.

———. *Plagues and Peoples*. Oxford: Blackwell, 1977. A pioneering account of the role of diseases and disease exchanges in world history.

———. *The Pursuit of Power: Technology, Armed Force and Society since A.D. 1000*. Oxford: Blackwell, 1982. A world history of the impact of changing military technologies on state power in the early modern period.

———. *The Rise of the West: A History of the Human Community*. Chicago: University of Chicago Press, 1963. Reprinted in 1991 with a retrospective essay, "*The Rise of the West* after Twenty-five Years." McNeill's book became an instant classic on its publication in 1963. Its balance of careful scholarship, clear writing, and a powerful central argument about human history proved the viability of serious scholarship in world history at a time when many historians doubted that serious scholarship was possible on these large scales.

Miller, Walter M. *A Canticle for Leibowitz*. New York: Bantam, 1997. Was first published in 1959. A nightmare vision of the future in which humans destroy their civilizations as soon as they achieve the ability to do so.

Mithen, Steven. *After the Ice: A Global Human History 20,000–5,000 BC*. Cambridge, MA: Harvard University Press, 2004. A vivid portrayal of life in the late Paleolithic and early Neolithic eras based on reconstructions of the lifeways of those who lived in this era, using evidence from some of the major archaeological sites of this period.

Bibliography

Mokyr, Joel. *The Lever of Riches: Technological Creativity and Economic Progress*. New York: Oxford University Press, 1990. A standard history of technological change that contains a fine theoretical discussion of factors driving innovation.

Nissen, H. J. *The Early History of the Ancient Near East*. Chicago: University of Chicago Press, 1988. A classic account of the rise of early states in Mesopotamia.

Pinker, Steven. *The Language Instinct: How the Mind Creates Language*. London: Penguin, 1995. A beautifully written account of the nature of language, which also gives much insight into the many complex arguments that swirl around this fundamental topic.

Pomeranz, Kenneth. *The Great Divergence: China, Europe, and the Making of the Modern World Economy*. Princeton: Princeton University Press, 2000. An important recent discussion of the sources of the modern world economy which argues that significant differences between Atlantic economies and the economies of Asia's major powers emerged only toward the end of the 18th century.

Ponting, C. *A Green History of the World*. Harmondsworth, England: Penguin, 1991. A pioneering (though now slightly dated) overview of the changing relationship of humans to the natural environment over the course of human history. A revised, expanded, and updated edition was published in 2007.

Prantzos, Nikos. *Our Cosmic Future: Humanity's Fate in the Universe*. Cambridge: Cambridge University Press, 2000. A discussion of the possibilities for human migration beyond planet Earth, and of scenarios for the remote future of the Universe.

Redfern, Martin. *The Earth: A Very Short Introduction*. Oxford: Oxford University Press, 2003. The Oxford "Very Short Introductions" provide brief but expert introductions to important scientific fields.

Ristvet, Lauren. *In the Beginning: World History from Human Beginnings to the First States*. New York: McGraw-Hill, 2007. A fine, short introduction to the Paleolithic era of human history by a historian and archaeologist.

Sahlins, Marshall. *Stone Age Economics*. London: Tavistock, 1972. Sahlins's article "The Original Affluent Society" is on pp. 1–39. In it, he argues that Paleolithic lifeways may have been less harsh than is often assumed.

Schrödinger, Erwin. *What is Life?* Cambridge: Cambridge University Press, 2000. First published in 1944. A readable and influential attempt by a great physicist to define what it is that makes life different.

Sherratt, Andrew. "Plough and Pastoralism: Aspects of the Secondary Products Revolution." In *Patterns of the Past*, edited by I. Hodder, G. Isaac, and N. Hammond. Cambridge: Cambridge University Press, 1981, 261–305. A pioneering article that proposed the idea of the "secondary products revolution" as one of the fundamental technological breakthroughs in human history.

Smith, John Maynard. See Maynard Smith, John.

Spier, Fred. *The Structure of Big History: From the Big Bang until Today*, Amsterdam: Amsterdam University Press, 1996. Fred Spier trained as a chemist, an anthropologist, and a historian, and for many years he has taught a course in big history at the University of Amsterdam. By exploring the similarities and differences between the various "regimes" that can be bound at different temporal and spatial scales, Spier's book provides a powerful argument for the project of big history.

Stableford, Brian, and David Langford. *The Third Millennium: A History of the World, AD 2000–3000*. London: Sidgwick and Jackson, 1985. A persuasive and powerful reconstruction of the history of the next millennium. It also reads extremely well.

Stearns, P. N. *The Industrial Revolution in World History*. Boulder, CO: Westview, 1993. A survey of industrialization on a global scale.

————. *Millennium III, Century XXI: A Retrospective on the Future.* Boulder, CO: Westview Press, 1996. An introductory discussion on the perils and the promise of futurology.

Taagepera, R. "Size and Duration of Empires: Systematics of Size." *Social Science Research* 7 (1978):108–27. Rein Taagepera wrote a number of pioneering articles attempting to assemble basic statistical information on large historical processes. His work is not always easy to find.

Tomasello, Michael. *The Cultural Origins of Human Cognition.* Cambridge, MA: Harvard University Press, 1999. Tomasello's idea of "cumulative cultural evolution" is similar to the idea of "collective learning" presented in this course, though he places less emphasis on language in explaining human ecological virtuosity.

Toulmin, Stephen, and June Goodfield. *The Discovery of Time.* Chicago and London: University of Chicago Press, 1965 [reprinted 1977]. Though dated in some of its details, this remains one of the best available histories of the construction of a modern sense of time.

Trigger, B. G. *Early Civilizations: Ancient Egypt in Context.* Cairo: American University in Cairo Press, 1993. A comparative history of the appearance of Agrarian civilizations in different parts of the world.

Turner, B. L., W. C. Clark, R. W. Kates, J. F. Richards, J. T. Mathews, W. B. Meyer, eds. *The Earth as Transformed by Human Action: Global and Regional Changes in the Biosphere over the Past 300 Years.* Cambridge: Cambridge University Press, 1990. A collection of essays on the changing relationship of humans with the biosphere in modern times.

Wagar, Warren. *A Short History of the Future.* 2nd ed. Chicago: University of Chicago Press, 1992. A rich, absorbing, and deeply intelligent "history" of the next few centuries, by a specialist on the work of H. G. Wells.

Watson, J. D. *The Double Helix: A Personal Account of the Discovery of the Structure of DNA.* New York: Touchstone, 2001 [reprint of the 1968 edition].

A vivid and highly personal account of the science and the personal politics behind one of the great scientific breakthroughs of the 20th century.

Wolf, E. R. *Europe and the People Without History*. Berkeley: University of California Press, 1982. A superb, if sometimes difficult, history of the modern world by an anthropologist. It includes a fine survey of the many different types of society that existed on the eve of the Modern Revolution.

Wright, Robert. *Nonzero: The Logic of Human Destiny*. New York: Random House, 2000. A delightfully written argument about the synergetic and cumulative nature of human history.

Wrigley, E. A. *Continuity, Chance, and Change: The Character of the Industrial Revolution in England*. Cambridge: Cambridge University Press, 1988. A highly original discussion of the English Industrial Revolution by a great demographic historian. Wrigley emphasizes the importance of the introduction of fossil fuels.

Useful websites:

Powers of 10. There are several "Powers of 10" websites. They survey the Universe on different scales, changing the scale by 10 times at each step. A superb way of getting a sense of the vast distance we travel as we move from the very large to the very small. For three examples, see: http://micro.magnet. fsu.edu/primer/java/scienceopticsu/powersof10/, http://www.powersof10. com/, and http://www.wordwizz.com/pwrsof10.htm.

Big History. Fred Spier's site includes a bibliography of works on big history: http://www.iis.uva.nl/i2o/object.cfm/objectid=21E38086-9EAF-4BB2-A3327D5C1011F7CC/hoofdstuk=5.

Permissions Acknowledgments

Adapted with permission by the publisher from *Maps of Time: An Introduction to Big History* by David Christian, copyright © 2004 The Regents of the University of California for University of California Press. For ordering information, see the publisher's website (www.ucpress.edu) or Amazon.com.

Eric Chaisson, *Cosmic Evolution* (Cambridge, MA: Harvard University Press, 2001), p. 139.

Global GDP: 1500–1998: Based on Table B-18: World GDP, 20 Countries and Regional Totals, 0–1998 A.D., *The World Economy: Volume 1: A Millennial Perspective and Volume 2: Historical Statistics*, © OECD 2006.

Global GDP per capita 1500–1998: Based on Table B-21: World GDP per Capita, 20 Countries and Regional Averages, 0–1998 A.D., *The World Economy: Volume 1: A Millennial Perspective and Volume 2: Historical Statistics*, © OECD 2006.

Global Population Growth: 1500–1998: Based on Table B-10: World Population, 20 Countries and Regional Totals, 0–1998 A.D., *The World Economy: Volume 1: A Millennial Perspective and Volume 2: Historical Statistics*, © OECD 2006.

Jean-Noël Biraben, "Essai sur le'évolution du nombre des homes," Population (No. 34, 1979), pp.13–25.

Jennifer Isaacs, ed., *Australian Dreaming: 40,000 Years of Aboriginal History* (Sydney: New Holland Publishers, 2005), pp. 49, 51.

Ratio of Wealth in World's Richest Countries and Poorest Countries for years 1913 and 1992 based on data from *Monitoring the World Economy: 1820/1992*, © OECD 1995.

Notes

Notes

Notes

Notes